ABOUT THE AUTHORS

Jegsy Dodd was born before records began and has been a regular at the match since the Shankly era. He contributed the Rome '84 section in the book *Here We Go Gathering Cups in May*. Jegsy has released two albums and a single in recent years 'Wake Up and Smell the Offy', 'Loquacious, Loquacious, Loquacious' and 'Only Football Can Truly Break Your Heart'. He also has far too much to say for himself.

For more info see www.jegsydodd.com and www.redmenbooks.com.

Lifelong Red John Mackin has had a Kop season ticket since 1975. A stalwart of the Liverpool fanzine scene John has contributed to *Through The Wind & Rain* and *Red All Over The Land* as well as editing the *The Rattle*, the Liverpool supporter's website. John has also written about Liverpool FC – and football generally – for Four Four Two, *The Times*, Liverpoolfc.tv, *Ice Magazine* and *Switched On*. In the early 90s John led the campaign to save The Kop from all-seaterdom as well as inaugurating the Kop Flag Days. More recently he was a founder of the RTK (Reclaim The Kop) and the Spirit of Shankly Liverpool Supporters Union, as well as recording 'Yo"ll Never Walk Alone' with Radiohead ... no, okay then, it was Chris De Burgh.

For more info see www.raotl.co.uk and www.redmenbooks.com.

REDMEN

A SEASON ON THE DRINK

Up The Redmen!.

Best wishes

John Mack—

Jegsy Dodd and John Mackin

Edited by
Kevin Sampson

Matador
5 Weir Road
Kibworth Beauchamp
Leicester LE8 0LQ, UK
Tel: (+44) 116 279 2299
Email: books@troubador.co.uk
Web: www.troubador.co.uk/matado

ISBN 978-1848763-074

British Library Cataloguing in Publication Data.
A catalogue record for this book is available from the British Library.

Typeset in 12pt Sabon by Troubador Publishing Ltd, Leicester, UK
Printed and bound in Great Britain by TJ International Ltd, Padstow, Cornwall

Matador is an imprint of Troubador Publishing Ltd

"WINE FOR MY MEN. WE RIDE AT DAWN."

Famous banner by Ritchie Mearns and Paul Stewart.
Original source unknown

ACKNOWLEDGEMENTS

First of all I must say a special thanks to our partners Hema and Ally for putting up with the ridiculous, puerile behaviour of two middle-aged authors who really should know better. Especially the Dark Mysterious One who not only worked tirelessly behind the scenes to get this book into print, but also endured many sleepless nights as I came crashing through the door after midnight singing songs of days gone by. Kevin (Sammo) Sampson must get a huge credit for his edit and Adam Rubin for his snaps of the chaps. Our partners Matador for coming on board ship. A big IS RIGHT to the coach drivers and the skivers and the duckers and divers, the Spanish imports and the Carlsberg exports. Every single one of you. Well in. We couldn't have done it without you. Stand by your beds troops. The Reds are coming up the hill!

INTRODUCTION

Yabba-dabba-doo, dingdangdoo! It's that time of the year again, folks, when all the creatures come out of hibernation and wipe the sleep from their eyes. Yes, the footy is back and me and millions like me are bouncing around the house singing our little hearts out. It's like the night before Christmas when you were five years old. Wives and girlfriends stand open mouthed in awe as their normally emotionless, heartless, grouchy males start moonwalking in their underpants across the kitchen floor, arms outstretched, singing the "Fields of Anfield Rd." How can this be? Normally I wouldn't bat an eyelid if there were lions being tamed in my front room or naked trapeze artists swooping past. Even the odd bomb going off in the front garden would barely register a flicker of interest. But today is different. It's the new season. It's a new dawn and I'm like a butterfly that's just broken free of its chrysalis. The hibernation is over and I'm creaming my kecks with anticipation. In fact this one goes beyond mere anticipation – there's real tension in the air now our envious neighbours down the M62 are closing in on our proudly-polished trophy haul. Twenty years ago we were embarking on the season that'd end in Number 18 for the men in Red. 18 League Championships! Our closest challengers, Newton Heath had bagged a mere 9. If anyone had ventured an opinion way back then, that in twenty years Man United would have 17 while we were still sitting pretty on 18, you'd have had them taken away and shot for their own good. That way, madness lay. Only a rampant nutter like Alex Ferguson could even fantasise about knocking the Liverbird off its unassailable perch but, little by little, year on year, they've been closing in. Whatever 'unassailable' used to mean, we were suddenly in very real danger of getting 'assailed'. In short, this is unthinkable. It must not be allowed to happen.

And we can do it, too. Even standing back and being objective about it (and let's face it, you can't be objective unless you stand back and stroke your chin meaningfully, with a 'shrewd', Columbo-style facial expression as you mull over the evidence) you'd have to say that the spine of our team is the best of any in the Premier (c. Benitez, R). Reina, best keeper. Carragher, Skrtel, Agger, best central defensive trio – perm any two (and Phil Thompson did). Mascherano, Alonso and a certain S.Gerrard have got to be the best midfield, while Torres is far and away the most cunning, the cleverest, the quickest and most lethal striker in all Europe. He's just won the European Championship for Spain fercryinoutloud, and Spain never win nada. So in that central column, Liverpool have got the best that there is. And we've got new signings, too. Riera might be the missing link we've needed for so long – the W word that Liverpool managers have been deaf to for decades, now. Also adding width (and not just to his impressive gut) we now have Dossena, Italy's first choice in the Euro's and a record buy for us at £8 million for a full back. If he does the business though, I'd pay it twice. Which would be £16 million – a lot more expensive. We've also recruited the services of that artful little dodger Robbie Keane. He scored 20-odd last season for Tottenham including a brace against us at Anfield that showed just what a cunning fox he is.

All in all, we Redmen have reasons to be cheerful. We have renewed hope and we have dreams and songs to sing. The journey will be long – nine arduous months of joy and pain. Just like a pregnancy, in fact, with the longed-for delivery of that elusive 19th league title at the end. Yes there will be morning sickness when results don't go our way but today is not a day for such negative thoughts. Today is all about OPTIMISM. It will be a voyage of many ups and downs. The seas will be rough and the sharks will circle but the Promised Land is in sight. Let the madness begin.

JD

Villarreal (a)   0-0

Pre-season friendly   Wed 30ᵗʰ July

"The one sure thing about Sampson," said Jegs drawing on the butt of a rolled-up ciggie that was marginally shorter than the fingernails grasping it, "is that he'll always let you down." I'm discussing with him whether or not he's aboard for the first jaunt of the season ... the trip to Villarreal with me and Sammo.

"He won't be there. I guarantee it," Jegs adds. "The number of times he's seen me onto planes and waved me off at airports ... he's like Humphrey Bogart at the end of Casablanca."

"Well what about you?" I ask. "It's going to be a belter: Spain! great weather, brilliant food and cheap wine!"

"Nah ... count me out ... need to save me pennies ... I'm going to Rangers on the Satdee," he said almost drawing himself up to attention. He looks quite excited. I can see behind the gleam in his eyes that he's already virtually donning the sash. "I'm going on the coach with ... " He then reels of a lengthy list of 40 to 50 year old serial drinkers, ne'er do wells, vagabonds, ex-hooligans and wastrels. I can almost – almost – see his point. It will be a belter. Never one to forego the opportunity of a serious swallee with some of his pals in Glasgow is Jegs, and I realise the utter futility of any argument. I do, however, have to seriously question his priorities. Still, I know his dislike of foreign food (pineapple on a pizza is as exotic as it gets) and the tapas bars and cevezerias of Valencia pale into insignificance next to 48 hrs of chips and lager in Govan. He is from Moreton, after all.

With Jegs definitely out, it leaves Sampson, Joe Corrigan and Nico; all founder members of the Liverpool Gentleman's Dining Club. Just as well the Philistine Dodd isn't coming then, after all. Joe – he of the shock of white hair and the hypnotist's mesmeric stare – works as a London cabbie, which is very

The demon drink

strange as he lives in Holland. He'll be working in London that week taking Arabs on £200 cab rides up and down Bond Street, but he'll fly over to Spain from Stansted and meet us there. Then there is the Belgian, Nico, a.k.a. Chewbacca, or The Hairy Turk. Quite possibly the hairiest man in northern Europe (and I'm allowing for the yet undiscovered Norwegian Yeti), but also a damn fine Red and fellow connoisseur of the grape (I once watched, in astonishment, as he drank red wine all afternoon long in 100 degree heat in Seville whilst I was struggling to neck ice-cold Cruzcampo. I was, though, much less astonished to find him slumped in a corner a couple of hours later). We are all due to arrive within 2 or 3 hours of each other and plan to meet up in the nearest bar to the arrivals gate at Valencia Airport, then get the train into town, lash the bags in the hotel and then go out on a lunchtime tapas crawl. As plans go it's a bloody good one I have to say.

I could quote Robert Burns at this point and say, "The best-laid plans of mice and men, often go awry," but it'd be more succinctly put as "That's when it all went tits up." The evening before we are due to fly I get a call from Sampson.

"I haven't gorra passport! Just went to get it out now and Helen's sent *mine* in with the baby's application form! I'm going to have to go down the Passport Office in town and get it first thing in the morning."

"We're flying at 10:30!"

"I know, I know, if I get to town at 7:30 I could still make it." He doesn't even sounds as though he believes it himself, but I go through the motions and wish him good luck. It was what Jegsy and I have now come to call, the 'Ingrid Bergman moment', and I know I'll be flying solo.

The plans were further torn into tatters by a call very early the following morning from Joe. He's been doing 20 hour shifts in his cab, accruing Abramovich-style riches for the last 3 weeks, and has collapsed into a near-diabetic coma at Stansted. He doesn't sound well at all, in fact he sounds as awful as one of Sampson's excuses. Emergency insulin is administered and he's off back home to Holland.

And then there was one. Well not quite. Onboard the flight I found myself sitting next to Mick Hart from County Rd. and his mate Paul Doran. Now I have a thing about flying – I have to have an aisle seat as close to the back of the plane as possible, and these two had snagged the back row, conveniently leaving the aisle seat free – but it was free for a reason: Paul was completely and totally bladdered. This had put off most passengers from sitting next to him. I mean, I thought twice about it myself. It was barely 10am. What state would he be in in a couple of hours?

Though most of those aboard are couples and families and look like they're heading out to the Costas for some sun and sangria, there are a smattering of blokes aboard who are quite obviously going out for the game: Paul and Shark tops or Lacoste polo shirts, Adidas trainees and hand luggage only. The 'not checking in any bags' rule was invented, it is reputed, by a famous Liverpool fan from the parish of Bootle. His logic being that the 20 minutes spent at the baggage carousel – trying to remember what sodding colour your suitcase was – was time better spent propping up the nearest bar, spilling Guinness all down your top, and asking all and sundry, in an unfeasibly loud voice, where the nearest brass house was.

Paul and Mick were staying on the far side of the city centre from me, so we agree to meet up at the station later that afternoon and travel up to the game together. Paul has also dismissed my protests about Ryanair prices, and insists on buying me a couple of beers for the flight. Well, it would be rude to let him drink alone so I graciously accept so as not to cause offence.

I meet Nico who, ironically, given what is to come, is having a coffee at a bar opposite the arrivals area at Valencia airport. I explain the Ingrid Bergman moment to him and how we now have 3 twin rooms between the two of us. He just shrugs. He doesn't even have a ticket yet, and I know that all he needs is the slightest encouragement, one moment of weakness on my part, to jib the match entirely and find a bodega somewhere for an evening's carousing. Kick-off is about 8 hours away and we still have to work out how to get up the coast some 70 miles to Castillo, the provincial capital and neighbour to sleepy Villarreal. Since our last trip to Valencia to see the European Cup game a few years back (It rained like a monsoon that day I remember), the metro has been extended and now links the airport to the city centre. When we step out of the underground station at Valencia's Del Norte station we are hit by the incredibly bright sunlight and the fierce heat of early afternoon. It was like someone opening the door to a furnace. Having come from the grey skies and showers of an English summer (Global warming, my arse) this is a bit of a shock to the system. I'm aware that I'm beginning to melt and we immediately cross the concourse outside the station to the shaded colonnades of the Plaza Del Toros, the city's handsome brick bullring. We hover there in the cool, dark bowels trying to fathom how far away the hotel is, and would we make it before succumbing to sunstroke and heat exhaustion. A plan is hatched to make our way via a narrow, shaded street instead of the more direct route. It is, however, lined with bars and it takes a steely determination not to suggest stopping for a cana of Cruzcampo even though both our tongues are now hanging out like a tired Labrador's. Stopping now would see stage 1 of a situation known as 'slippage'. Much like 'the best laid plans' going awry, slippage is when the day begins to deviate wildly from the plan thrashed out at an earlier stage:

"Right we check in at 2pm, have some lunch and get the train at 3:20. We should be there by 4, and I've arranged to meet Joe at 4:30 to collect the tickets."

But a beer here, a beer there, "Oh look, they sell San Miguel Selecta!" or "What a charming church, we must stop and check out the frescoes in the nave …," and before you know it the deadline to meet up lies in tatters. In fact, it's now 7pm and you're still only yards away from where you began.

Tickets remain undistributed and phones are ringing every 2 minutes as drunkards try and co-ordinate a ridiculous rendezvous with other drunkards miles away. Ridiculous because for the last hour they've had unbelievable trouble just finding the toilets; making complicated arrangements to meet each other outside football grounds is like asking Shane McGowan to do a shift on air traffic control. Beware, oh reader, of 'slippage'!

After a 20 minute plod in skin-blistering heat we reach the hotel. It's air-conditioned and dark inside the foyer and looks like it has all the luxury we need. We drop the bags at our feet and lean against the cool marble reception desk. Right, so we have 3 twin rooms booked and there's only 2 of us. I ran through the fractured Spanglish in my head "Queremos dos habitaciones para dos noches ... er ... " my mental voice trails away as I notice her name tag; an unintelligible procession of Ks, Ws and Qs. Shit! She's Polish. I raise my hand in salutation and bid her a hearty "Wisla Krakow!" She speaks good English and after I've explained how the Ingrid Bergman moment works she hands over our keys and we go immediately up to our rooms. I throw my bag on the bed, squirt some deodorant all over myself and head straight back downstairs. Nico is already outside, sniffing the air. I'm impressed.

Up behind the Cathedral, in a shadowy side street, is Meson Las Cuevas. And thank God we've found somewhere to shelter from the sun as it must be a million degrees by now. It looks a cracking little bar from the outside and once inside we're not disappointed. A long dark marble bar, tiled walls and floor, and a low beamed ceiling from which hang antique looking lamps. The bar is filled with the smell of grilling fish and seafood, and as we neck our first cold beer of the day we see the barman/waiter/proprietor carrying platters of squid and fish into the dining room at the back. My stomach revolves, but we've no time to eat as we've a train to catch. I remind Nico of the fact. "We better get a move on." He looks at me and orders a couple more beers, which come this time with some tapas: sweet fragrant jamon (cured ham) and crusty bread. It has the dual effect of dulling the immediate hunger pangs whilst making you hungry for more. I can already sense slippage. Panicking, we order more beers, "Dos canas mas, Por favour." We leave after much too short a stay but we promise ourselves and the proprietor we'll be back later that night.

We catch up with Mick and Paul at the station and set about trying to buy train tickets. Tony Barrett – The Liverpool Echo's LFC correspondent – is there with Nick Smith of the Daily Post; they are similarly confused. Now, we're on our holidays and we've a had a few beers, but worryingly for someone who's supposedly here to work Barrett hasn't a clue what he is doing and admits that he managed to buy a train ticket completely by a fluke. After going to and fro several times between ticket windows (mostly on the fro side) we come to realise he wasn't joking. Eventually, after much Spanglish and comedy miming, we come away with single tickets to Villarreal. All the return trains are fully booked and as the Spanish have this outlandish – nay crazy – idea that they shouldn't sell you a ticket if you won't get a seat, we are to be left stranded in a strange town that has no hotel vacancies (we'd already checked before flying out) … Sod it! I pat my pockets; I have all I need to survive several days in the wilderness. Whereas Ray Mears would never venture as far as Greggs the Bakers without a machete, some fishhooks and a hammock, I travel a little lighter. Credit cards, cash, wet wipes and phone: sorted. Believe me, losing your wet wipes on trips like this is only marginally less serious than losing your passport. They are essential to the Salford Sauna. Allow me to elaborate: it's hot and you're grubby and sweaty, you've been travelling all day and need to clean up. First, take your wet wipe and then proceed to wipe your face, neck, underarms, sack and crack (and it has to be in that sequence, though I suspect a true Salford Sauna does it in reverse). I made the mistake of running out of wipes in Athens in November 2000. On the afternoon of the 2-2 UEFA Cup draw with Olympiakos (a game best remembered for the barrage of concrete and bricks we had to endure throughout the match and having to run the gauntlet of the psychotic police at the airport). I went down to the Central Market, an almost medieval bazaar beneath The Acropolis, for some lunch, leaving the infamous Irregulars in the same bar opposite our hotel that we'd been in for the last 24 hours. There was a Kebab café just outside the meat market and I sat down, ordered a beer, and took in the scene: all manner of entrails and offal on slabs, skinned goats hanging by their heels from hooks, eyes bulging in bony sockets and looking for all the world like David Moyes. There were flies everywhere and kidding myself I was an intrepid traveller I took the menu and ordered. It was about an hour later whilst enjoying a few pre-match Mythos lagers back with The Irregulars that I felt the first stomach cramps. During the game I became aware that my bum was leaking and I was afraid to duck to avoid the flying concrete in case I suddenly squirted like a water pistol. On the flight home, after my third or fourth trip to the toilet I looked down to see my underpants doing a fair impression of the Turin shroud. They were stuffed into a sick bag and abandoned. At that moment I would have given a million pounds for a wet wipe. So in the circumstances, probably the last person you'd want to bump was Wilcox. Bobby Wilcox is the definition of the larger-than-life character, a big, fat, irrepressible, infectiously lovable sloth of a man (myself and Sampson once chortled in amazement at the spectacle of Bobby getting stuck in the turnstiles at Bolton). Wilcox is a veteran of almost 50 years following The Reds all over the world, as famous for his generosity of spirit(s) as far his withering sarcasm and, like "Hendrix" and "Floyd" (Pink, as opposed to Keith) has earned the right to be known by one and all simply by his surname. Nevertheless, Wilcox is not the fella you want to bump into after an attack of the wildshites.

"What's the matter John?" his face a picture of concern.

Before I can answer he smells me and jumps back a yard – no mean feat for a man of his abundant corpulence. He put his hand on my shoulder and, in a paternal gesture that I'll always remember and treasure, advised me, "Always look after yer arse, lad. It's your friend." With that he shuffled off.

The train journey north was about an hour's worth of unspectacular scenery. Dry scorched fields punctuated with boulders, pylons and the occasional skeletal olive tree. We pass the time drinking cold cans of Cruzcampo and trying to chat to a group of middle aged housewives about Torres. Every time we mention his name they squeal "El Nino! El Nino!" pretty much like Gary Shaw does. Tony Barrett and the gentlemen of the press are further down the carriage with their laptops open, pretending to work. He looks up and I know he wishes he didn't have to work for the next 8 hours.

I get a text from LouLou, one of the regular Irregulars – a fixture on the infamous Irregulars' coach for many years now – and a mainstay of 306 Block. 306 is towards the back of The Kop, a solid block of lunacy that houses many of Liverpool's old-school, hard-core and most passionate supporters. The Torres Bounce originated here, as do most of the funniest/rudest/most spontaneous songs. LouLou, along with Kayla and Helen (aka Mercy) are among only a handful of women in the block, but they dish it out with the best of them – and bring a whole new dimension to the Bounce. She's out here with Mercy, already gagging for a gargle and wondering where we are.

Villarreal station is very welcome when it appears out of the haze, as there are no toilets on the train. About 30 or so Liverpool fans step down onto the platform and look around for signs of life. We may as well be on Mars. Looking at each other as if to say, "You sure this is the right stop?" we shrug and wander off up the streets looking for refreshments. Everything appears to be covered in a fine layer of sand and the streets are deserted. Its siesta time and

Villarreal has clearly got it's head down. We've no real idea of where we're going – as usual – but eventually find a small café bar, with some familiar faces sitting outside. It's fine but lacks atmosphere and, more importantly as far as Mick is concerned, Jack Daniels. Mick has spent ten minutes trying to explain what it was he wanted, and we all breathed a sigh of relief when the barman finally seemed to understand. Mick's face lit up as the barman gave a young boy some money and ushered him out of the door to buy a bottle of Bourbon . The boy returned 5 minutes later brandishing a bottle of Larios Gin. Mick just looked at it as if he'd brought back an octopus. He then looked at the barman and said, but this time a little louder, "JACK DANIELS!"

The barman smiled and pointed at the octopus. It was time to move on.

We eventually chance upon a bar, painted bright yellow, on a corner of a tree-lined square. It's a simple enough place, one might say 'functional'. What attracts us is the name: 'Cerveceria Club Villarreal'. There's about 3 hours to kick off and only a handful inside and we're the only Liverpool fans in there. The bar's got old black and white photos of the Villarreal team, surprisingly few of the modern side and thankfully none of that hideous ex-Manc Diego Forlan. Behind the bar are some colour photos but we can't recognise any of the players. What Mick does recognise, however, is the square bottle and black label of JD! We order a couple of beers and a huge JD and coke for Mick and start talking to a table of middle-aged guys next to us. Neither group can understand each other much, but we seem to get on well enough. They're drinking from a large jug of beer and we order them a jug when we get the next round in. Nico's ordered me some jamon and red wine as well. He's on a roll now, it's futile to resist and I slip comfortably into his slipstream. The wine arrives just as our Spanish friends are tucking into a bowl of snails. They make a great show of offering us the snails, thinking, I guess, that we'd baulk at the prospect. They do not realise that this is two of the founding members of the Liverpool Gentleman's Dining Club and it'd take more than a few gastropods to put us off our stride. The snails are baked in a tomato sauce and are actually delicious, as Nico tells them, wiping the bowl clean with chunks of bread. They follow this up by giving us plates of a fish, potato and saffron stew, and one of the guys takes great pride in miming that he was the fisherman who caught the fish that morning. I can't think of how we'd reciprocate back in a pub in Liverpool … maybe introduce them to the van driver who delivered the crisps?

Nico's now mumbling on the phone. He has to meet some fellow Reds

John Mackin on the drink

from his neck of the Ardennes who've been here since the weekend and who have our tickets. He may not be British (in fact he may not even be human) but he's a much a Scouser as anyone else I know. His 'Keep Belgium Scouse' badges are far more popular in Liverpool than they are in his home town of Ekeren, on the edge of Antwerp, where I fear the joke is lost. In fact, having met several other Belgium Reds I fear that ANY joke is lost on them. I warn Nico that slippage is imminent and making these ticket transactions more and more impossible, but he assures me that he's got it all sorted.

"I'm going nowhere," he growls, and tells me that the Belgians are coming to him. I'm quite certain that he has no intention of moving from this bar for as long as he can, possibly not until the day it's demolished.

Lou Lou then comes bursting through the door, arms flailing, gabbling fifteen to the dozen and with a sunburnt cleavage like a couple of beef tomatoes.

"Have you got any spares?"

"No mate – we haven't even got ours yet," I tell her. "Nico's mates have the tickets."

"Any spares?" she asks Nico. Nico's head is tilted back as he drains the Rioja, and even then, through the bottom of a wine glass, I can see he's focusing on her cleavage.

"No Lou," he says.

She's come down to Villarreal on a coach from Shankly's Bar in Salou with 50 or so other holidaying Reds. By the looks of her they've not been short of beers. She's determined to get in and looks around the bar for inspiration. There is none.

"I'll bunk it."

"Don't be daft. You're bladdered. You couldn't bunk into a library in that state. Stay here and watch it on the telly."

"No, I'll bunk it," and she wanders off back out of the bar.

Now we've got the tickets from the Belgians we can relax. Nico suggests having another drink but it's getting close to kick-off and we don't know our way around. We have no idea which side of the ground we're in so we set off across the square. There are beer tents surrounding the ground and the thousands of plastic glasses we wade through are evidence that the locals have taken their seats, and that maybe its time we should join them. Nico, however, has decided he wants a pin badge and we head off to the small club shop opposite the main entrance. There are a few shifty looking Liverpool lads in there but, to be frank, there is nothing worth having and they slink out looking rather disappointed. Nico concurs. I hear behind me his incredulous voice.

"20 Euro for a fucking badge? … 20 Euro?" The girl on the till smiles politely and with a "Fuck that!" we beat a retreat next door and into a rapidly emptying bar.

"Just a quick one," Nico assures me.

Once inside Villarreal's smart, though small, new ground we are directed by a steward to two free seats in the centre of the stand, immediately above an exit, up high behind the goal. We're only ten minutes late but the Spaniards – who seem to have all been in here for half an hour at least – are nudging each other, pointing us out, and craning their necks to look at us, I feel like we've stumbled into a funeral playing the trombone. We sit down and I take the scene in. Four individual steep stands – good. There's even a couple of proper floodlight pylons – I like it! There's no away end, as such. I can see the odd red Liverpool top here and there, and spotted a few faces on our hike up to our seats, so I guess we've got less than 200 in the ground, and about another 100 outside mooching about for 'souvenirs' or taking the waters.

I ask Nico, "Is Keane playing or he is on the bench?"

Silence.

"Oh hang on, we're in grey … I thought we were in yellow."

Silence. I turn to Nico. His head has slumped forward and now rests against the railing above the exit. I give him a nudge.

"Nico!"

Nothing. Spaniards around us are looking and smiling. A young girl thinks it's very amusing. I try to explain the situation as best I can, "He's twatted." She nods. It must be the same in Spanish.

"Cerveza?" she asks.

"And Rioja," I add. "Thing is I've got to get him back the zoo before the keepers notice he's gone."

He remains in this position for the rest of the first half. And all during half time. And all of the second half. The game is dull, which is at it should be for a pre-season friendly; after all it's not what we're here for. About 10 minutes from the end, I attempt to rouse the beast. A few nudges, a bit of a shake, and his head slowly rises, blinking against the floodlights. He smiles.

"Where are we?"

"Spain mate … Come 'ed." I grapple him to his feet to genuinely friendly cheers from the Spaniards around us. They've enjoyed having him here, especially the old bloke behind him who rested his sandwiches and bottle of water on his back during the interval. We stumble away swapping 'Adios' with people and back into the bar we visited immediately prior to kick off. The game is still playing on the t.v. and the bar, though far from packed, is busy. I steer Nico through the crowd, prop him up against the bar facing one of the screens, and tell him I'm getting him a coffee. It takes a full ten seconds for these words to register with him.

"I'm not having fucking coffee" he suddenly protests, eating someone's crisps that he's picked up from the bar and spitting crumbs all over me. I hate cruelty to animals so I order us four beers and another packet of crisps.

We head back to the Villarreal Supporters bar about half an hour after the end of the game, to meet up with Mick and Paul and decide what we're going to do about getting back to Valencia. As expected there a few more Reds around. Wilcox is there holding court with several of his regular travelling crew.

"Oh Hello there, er … John … isn't it?" says Bobby, feigning great surprise. "Nice to see you back at the game." He's never forgiven me for missing a pre-season friendly in Switzerland a few years back. I haven't the nerve to tell him (Though I suspect that he knows) that this is my first game of the season, nor am I going to Rangers the day after we get back. The subsequent ritual public humiliation would be unbearable. I know it; he knows it. He lets the moment pass with a knowing glance, his eyes smiling like The Laughing Cavalier. Lou Lou then comes lurching over,

"I got thrown out, I got thrown out!" she wails in indignation.

"What? How?"

The truth is somewhat different; she never actually got in. She'd been passed a used ticket and had been refused at the turnstiles when the barcode showed that the ticket had been previously scanned. Despite much protestation and flashing of breasts, she'd been unable to gain entry and had spent the last 3 hours back in the bar. So much for progress, eh? When a seasoned blagger is defeated, not by the canny-eyed steward or the razorwire-topped fence, but by a computer then you know that the game we knew and loved is fading fast, and that modern football is rubbish.

"You didn't miss much. In fact you probably missed less than Nico did and he got in."

We spend 120 Euros taking a cab back to Valencia around 1am. I sit in the front with the driver and stay awake as I'm carrying the taxi kitty. Mick, Paul and Nico snore like pigs behind me. An hour later we are dropped off at the bull ring and Mick and Paul agree to meet up with us at the beach the next day, or more accurately, later that day. They then head off to their hotel the other side of the city centre. I look at Nico. He's standing with his hands thrust deep into his pockets, head down, chin on his chest. He stares back over the rim of his glasses and grins inanely.

"We going for a bevy then?" I ask him.

He grunts and stumbles off up the road back towards our hotel, mumbling.

"Come on, Spain only comes alive at night pal. Lets got for a swallee." I place my arm around his shoulder and guide him over the road. When we reach the Plaza Ayuntamiento, I suggest we head back up to Meson Las Cuevas for a few night caps.

"Ok. Where is it?" he says.

"The place we went at lunchtime … remember?" He stands upright, eyes narrowing, hopelessly trying to remember the events of just 12 hours ago. He then nods. I take this as meaning "Yes I remember."

"Okay, hang on I need this cashpoint." I turn around to withdraw some cash and when I turn back, barely 90 seconds later, Nico's gone. I look up and down the street. Gone. I walk to the edge of the pavement and check down the grid. Gone. Despite a series of frustrating phone calls during which he assures me he's still there behind me at the cashpoint, I give up and head off to Las Cuevas hoping he's stumbled on ahead of me. Alas, Las Cuevas is shut as are most of the bars in the vicinity. Crowds of young Spaniards sit on the pavements chatting and sharing cans of beer. Fucked if I can see where they've bought them from though. I soon find a takeaway and buy a huge kebab covered in all sorts of melted cheese, sweetcorn, salad dressing and pickles, and a litre bottle of Amstel which I take back to the hotel and eat in bed, whilst flicking channels on Spanish tv desperately searching for 'El Porno'.

The following morning there's no response either from Nico's hotel room nor his phone. He could be dead, lying in a ditch somewhere covered in flies, with a small dog sniffing at him, but sod it, I need some breakfast. I go for a walk and get a cup of coffee. It's only 10am and already getting very warm; it's going to be another scorcher. After visiting a few sights I go back to the hotel and am relieved to find him up and showered. It transpires that he wandered off when I stopped at the cashpoint, thinking I was with him, and ended up in the small square outside our hotel. Well, when I say ended up in the small square outside our hotel, I mean he ended up in the strip club in the small square outside our hotel (Why did I not think of looking for him in there?). There he sat, drooling, in glitter-ball, Euro-disco heaven and paid 40 Euros a beer. Several East European beauties then approached him in turn offering him all sorts of depravity and squelching; their opening price? 350 euros. Eventually, though thoroughly hammered, even he realised how massively overpriced the beer was and crashed out of the place.

We go out determined to enjoy our last day. We need some lunch – wine and tapas would be ideal – and then we're off to meet Paul and Mick at the beach. But first we want to catch up with Tony Barrett to discuss the game. On our way we chance upon Olav and his mate sitting out in the sun. Olav is one of a long list of Norwegians (see also Bard, Roger Dahl, Paul Moller, Tage and Tore) who've spent that much time in Liverpool watching the Reds that they now sport impeccable Scouse accents. He's also sporting a couple of frightening freshly-stitched cuts to his shaved ginger head following an altercation with some chain wielding bouncers.

"You weren't with him where you …" I ask Olav, pointing at Nico. " … about 3 o'clock this morning?" Nico looks intently at Olav, just in case he might have been.

"No I was with some lads from Kenny. Got into an argument with some Turkish bouncers in Berlin after the Hertha game … tried to leg it." He looks at me as if to say "I know, I know … stupid.." I let it go; he doesn't need my patronising chastisement; not with those scars.

We spy Tony Echo at a pavement café having breakfast, and we join him for a beer and something to eat. Now we always say what a jammy bastard Tony Barrett is; that he has the best job in the world. He's a Kop season ticket holder who's now being paid to travel all over Europe and watch Liverpool play. Sounds perfect? Well I guessed yesterday on the slow train to Villarreal that he'd rather have been drinking beers with us than typing some article for Saturday's paper. And right now as we're trying to persuade him to come with us to the beach for a paddle (and maybe a few beers on the way), I know he'd love to come out to play, but duty calls and he has to go back up to his hotel room and thrash out another thousand words. And when you consider he's hardly travelling first class and staying in great hotels, and always missing out on the real craic in the bars, then it's probably far from the perfect job for a Liverpudlian. But it has its moments – like being able to type in your match report that Villarreal's new ground was paid for by their European Cup run; a run started by their defeat of Everton in the qualifier. "Get yer digs in when yer can," that's what I always say.

After half an hour Tony trudges off back to his laptop, his head filled with insults about David Moyes that we've given him and dared him to include in match reports. Meanwhile we finish our beer and tapas and think about getting to the beach. You can get the tram out there, but as it's such a lovely day we decide to walk. It's less than an hour's stroll away anyway, and the exercise will do us good. Barely ten minutes later though we're sitting on stools at a high-chrome counter having a small cold cerveza. We've covered maybe 250 yards but this bar – more a fast food café – looked too good to pass. Pretty young women are standing around drinking cold beers during their lunch break and smoking like laboratory beagles. One old guy comes in, orders a glass of cold white wine, necks it in 2 seconds flat and walks straight out again.

"I fucking love this country," declares Nico, reading my mind.

The phone beeps. It's a text message from Paul.

"R u coming the beach."

"Yes, on our way."

We drag ourselves away and begin the walk out to the promenade, El Paseo Maritimo, just the far side of the harbour. We've no guide book and are navigating by the maps in the bus shelters we pass. Every 2nd or 3rd bus stop seems to be outside a bar, and as it's another sweltering day (a digital display on a small traffic island showed the temperature at 2pm as 36 degrees!) we have to go in for a cold one. In so doing the walk down long deserted sun baked avenues, devoid of pedestrians with all windows shuttered, with frequent stops to take on liquids takes us 4 hours. Valencia doesn't have the best beach in the Mediterranean. It's pretty featureless and the buildings facing the prom are very modern and far from characterful. In fact when it momentarily clouds over it all looks pretty depressing and dull. Like Ellesmere Port. Nico and I take our shoes off and pad along the sand trying to find Paul and Mick. It's quite busy but there amongst the bronzed bodies two figures stand out: one is pale and wan, the other red and glowing like he's had Ready Brek for breakfast.

"I told him," says Mick as we approach, "Put yer t-shirt on."

"Alright!!" Paul comes splashing out of the sea towards us and as he gets closer I can feel the heat radiating from him. It feels like I've wandered too close to a 3 bar electric fire.

"Look at him – El Scorchio!" nods Mick.

Paul is standing in ankle deep water, every inch of him bright pink, wearing a Liverpool sun hat. He looks like one of Anthony Gormley's figures on Crosby beach.

"Did he put sun block on?"

"What do you think?" says Mick.

"It'll be fine," Paul says grinning, prodding and pinching at his flesh. I wince every time he does it yet have a sudden urge for some Peking Crispy Duck. He then splashes back out into the waves and plunges headlong into the foam again, emerging giggling with a long droplet of snot hanging from his nose. How all these Spanish birds can contain themselves around him is beyond me. They must all be lesbians. Nico is paddling, sandals in hand, telling me how he's lost weight over the summer.

"I haven't had a beer since May," he says proudly tapping a much reduced beergut, then adds after a small pause and without a trace of irony, "… just Rioja…"

After a stroll along the Paseo to dry out we retire to a small bar near the tram stop and have several beers, some tortilla, olives and nuts and while away a good hour or two discussing what we should do that evening. We agree to reconvene at Las Cuevas ("it's behind the Cathedral") around 10. On the way back to our hotel Nico and I emerge from the Metro into a busy shopping area, full of shoe shops and department stores, roads jammed with traffic. It's getting dark now. After neatly sidestepping a tramp trying to sell us a lighter he's just found, we can't resist one more beer, accompanied by a fried fish sandwich. We select a scruffy little bar populated mostly it seems by little old ladies stopping in for a sharpener on their way home from shopping. It's a hectic scene. The floor is covered with paper napkins, olive stones, prawn shells and cigarette butts. The waiters are shouting, laughing, whistling and singing. The television is blaring. There's no toilet paper. To call it unpretentious would be like calling Galatasaray v. Fenerbache "a bit of a tiff." Nico looks at me as he chews his sandwich.

"Yes, I know," I say to him, "you fucking love this country."

I'd hate to see him – and them – if we come back here for a real game.

JM

Glasgow Rangers (a)   4-0

Pre-season friendly   Sat 2nd Aug

Yes I know it's only a friendly but even us fans need our pre-season training and a night on the wallop in Glasgow is the perfect test of our fitness. All the ingredients for a decent run out are there. A big fat growling monster of a city with loads of dodgy boozers and the most partisan supporters this side of the River Plate. It's just what the doctor ordered. And so the day dawned. Even Danny Giles has been in training for it (two days off the ale). To him it's like Elvis fans going to Graceland. You see Rangers play in a part of the city called Govan, which is also home to the man who Danny has modelled himself on over these last 20 years. Yep, the unkempt, smooth-talking lush/fashion icon that is Rab C Nesbitt Esq. If you're not sure what Danny looks like, go to the kitchen and get a dessert spoon out of the drawer and look at your reflection in the back of it. Done it? Well that's him. That kind of fish eye lens, Jimminy Cricket type of vibe going on. Danny's another one who's partial to the odd beverage. In fact, if he ran for a bus he would probably fizz.

On board for today's shenanigans are, on the back seat, Paul (Muffa) Murphy – owner of the biggest hands in Birkenhead. You wouldn't want to take a crack off this lad – legs of mutton are smaller (and paler). Muff has an endearing habit of talking out of the side of his mouth – so much so that, after a couple of gargles, you find yourself shuffling around in a little circle, just to keep up with him and talk face-to-face. Co-passengers include Paul Stewart, outspoken, opinionated and owner of the cleanest house in Birkenhead. Stewy must have one of those mad syndromes where you can't stop tidying up; we'll have to rename him J Edgar Hoover. In many respects we're lucky to have Stewy with us at all these days, as he's fought a valiant scrap against throat cancer these past few years. Happily, he's in the clear –

fingers crossed. Less happily, his voice is reverting to its former, strident, permanently angry levels and, all things being equal, I may have to gag him at some point over the season. What are good friends for, after all? Next up is Paul Hendrick (Paul the Papers), the last pale skinned newsagent in the western world. Whereas Stewy always has a bee in his bonnet about something or another, Papers is calm, rational and focused. Britain's most selfless man Danny B. Nesbitt is in the front seat – of course – and the jockey for the day is muggins here.

It's a 3pm kick off on a Saturday which is almost retro, so we're on the road by 7.30 and we're looking good. By the time Gretna Green is breached, Murphy has already put a serious bid in for British 'Most farts in a car journey' record. That title has till now been held by today's front seat passenger on a drive from Seville to Malaga, after the Betis game a few years back. The phone hasn't stopped all morning and it's fair to say that all hands are on board for this one. We check in the Hampton Court B&B, which is just off Sauchiehall Street and without further ado – and to speak plainly we get right on it. Lo and behold at the bottom of the hill at our first port of call are my old partners in crime, Ally Atkin, Tony Gill, Tommy Sutton and Stevie Thommo, sitting there like butter wouldn't melt in their mouths. At this point I must digress and talk you, dear reader, through our cast of Tommys. We have many on this firm. There's Tommy Taxi, Tommy Trouble, German Tommy and Tommy Press-Ups for starters (Tommy Press-Ups aka Tommy Torso, aka Thomas O'Hagan, is the fittest 69 year-old in the world bar none. Many is the time he's entertained us with his crowd-pleasing Drunken Pressups act. He once did a hundred and forty four in Ned Kelly's before realising the last train was due; no doubt he jogged effortlessly to Lime Street without so much as pausing for a blow, and spent the journey doing chin-ups on the luggage rail). And the Tommys are nothing compared to the Johns – but I'll introduce them later. There's ale to be gargled the noo.

Fast forward four hours and we're in fine voice. Only problem is, we're miles from the ground and the match has already kicked off. We finally manage to negotiate the metro system and somehow get to the ground five minutes before half time. The away end is chocca. Loads of flags draped over the balcony, and get this! It's nearly all Scousers – 'sappenin lad? There was hardly a 'blert in a shirt' to be seen. It was commonly agreed that this would probably be our most blokey/Scouse away following of the season and it hasn't officially started yet. Liverpool won 4-0, if you're interested, and played pretty

L to R: Ally, some jock, Muffa, Stewy, Tommy, Gilly, Danny, Jegsy and Stevie

damn fine but if the truth were told, it was because Rangers were, well how can I put this? OK. Let's get the swearing out of the way. Rangers were absolutely shite. There, I've said it. I really don't want to lower the tone of this book so early but Rangers made me do it. Like Newcastle, they've got fanatical support but similar to those Geordie monkeys, their team is absolutely fuckin' awful. Just to confirm the point, the following week the mighty Rangers got knocked out of the Champions League qualifiers by a bunch of bricklayers and line dancers from the football hotbed that is Lithuania. Like I say – shite.

We're out of the ground and into a moody looking Rangers bar called the Stadium. The locals are obviously not happy by a) their teams performance and b) us breaking the 'no away fans' rule at their boozer, but who gives a toss? If it was the other way round, they'd be well in the Sandon, the Albert, etc. The Scots in general and the Glaswegians in particular are terrible marauders – they just take places over by sheer weight of numbers and noise and, by and large, they get away with it. Well here's a few dozen of Liverpool's finest returning the compliment and, much as they may not like it, we're here.

Fast forward and we find ourselves in the famous Sauchiehall Street and the night just becomes a blur. I've got vague recollections of Stewy making eyes at Thelma off Scooby Doo – and even vaguer memories of me, Danny, Muffa and Stewy getting ejected from Wetherspoons after arguing a little too excitedly over the contents of the kitty. For the avoidance of doubt, let me just say this: no kitties. Again, and louder – No Kitties, EVER!! Stag nights, football benders, Christmas parties, whatever – it only ever ends up one of two ways, both of them tearful. Either the fella with the kitty vanishes into the night, never to be seen until breakfast – or he claims the money's all gone after precisely two and a half rounds. This is what Danny and I were arguing over. Danny claimed the bunce was all spent less than an hour after taking stewardship. Wetherspoons staff, no strangers themselves to the occasional bout of hooch-induced fisticuffs saw the signs and chucked us out before the row had chance to escalate. Obviously they don't know me and soft lad. We've had this argument many, many times, all over Europe in fact. There's barmen and waiters called Luigi or Pierre or José who are probably still mentally scarred after witnessing The Kitty Rumble, and who'd fall to their knees and physically beg us to fuck off if ever we darken their doors again. Yet time and again, too, I succumb to the force of kitty's Sucking Pit, blacker than any credit black hole, vacuuming up any spare moolah it sniffs out. No kitties, I say – but Danny isn't listening. As usual all is forgotten in the morning.

We are awoken with what sounds like the last post being trumpeted from under one of the beds. It becomes apparent that Murphy is starting the day with a serious attempt at beating his own personal best. Hotel breakfast is missed, as usual, (a mercy, given the speed Murphy turns fried eggs into methane). Instead of a perfectly good, perfectly free brekkie in the hotel, we opt to wait five minutes and pay for a rubbish one instead. We go undercover to the 'spoons from which we were red-carded last night and order full growlers x 5. By some sheer fluke of nature, one of those million-to-one things happened. One of those occurrences that you could never repeat, no matter how many times you tried. Half way through the brekkie, someone cracks a funny and catching Muffa off guard, he half chokes and half laughs, which results in him coughing up a single baked bean, which travels at the speed of light and lands stuck to the middle of my forehead. I am sitting there like some Indian guru with one of Heinz's finest stuck to my swede and the lads are creased up laughing. Priceless.

We hit the road for the long drive home with a little stop off in a little place called Pooley Bridge in the Lakes. We only have a cheeky pint. There's about 30 birds on a hen day in the pub but the lads are visibly wilting. Time to crack on. Bucko's on the blower trying to get us to go to town but there's no takers. The lads are weighed in. Pre-season training see. We're nowhere near full match fitness yet. By September we'll be back in the swing of things. Mark my words.

JD

Standard Liege (a)   0-0

Champions League Qualifier   Wed 13th Aug

Since the Glasgow Rangers match there's been a major incident on the domestic front. I don't know how to put this but I'll cut straight to the chase and announce that I've moved in with me squeeze. It's been 6 long years since the dusky voluptuous princess was first touched by the Hand of Dodd. And now I've gone and done it. Obviously I'm taking a massive chance because it is a known fact that all birds are clinically insane but sometimes it's just gotta be done. Yes, I can hear the alarm bells, feel the cold feet and see the distress flares going overhead but sometimes I just want to hold her above my head like the FA Cup and say 'Look like what I've won!'. I've signed her on a free, given her a five year contract and if she puts in a decent performance each week, who knows? She might make the step up to the next level. As I always say, if she's got the passion, hunger and commitment, she could go all the way. But first things first, we've got a match in Belgium midweek and I have to go. I break the news to her and shock, horror, she's as cool as you like. Phew! Here's me expecting our first major dispute but no, she just calmly says 'oh good, I'll be able to do a bit of unpacking while you're away and maybe get a bit more organised. And anyway, you could probably do with a good blow-out with the lads.' Eh? I'm not used to all this. Usually in past relationships, it would've gone along the lines of 'Yes and you can stay in fuckin' Belgium forever with all those retards that you go to the match with because I won't be here when you get back' etc, etc, etc. But this is different. I know it's only early days but I'm thinking to myself 'Hey, this might just work'. Obviously it won't if I come home and find the whole house painted in pink. But I hope that's not gonna happen. She drops me off at Stewy's gaff at 10pm on Tuesday night. We're going to drive through the night and get the Channel Tunnel about 5am.

On board for this week's expedition, the runners and riders are Stewy and

Paul the Papers – welcome back. Our other companion on this merry outing is something of an unknown quantity – Steve Cottgrave, who's going out with Stewy's daughter. Steve stands 5'10," likes travel, enjoys good food, loves animals and would give all his money to charity if he won the lottery. Sorry. I went off on one there. No, Steve is an ex-boxer who looks likes he can go a few rounds with, well, anyone you fancy really. Didn't speak a word all the way to Folkestone. Probably just sussing us out to see where the land lies. It's always awkward when you're the youngest and you're with three elder lemons who think they know everything. Patience is everything. No one starts their first day at work ranting and raving, trying to make everyone laugh. You just take it all in until you're ready to stick your oar in. Tactics son, tactics – and the lad's doing well.

We arrive at the tunnel and enter France with the minimum of fuss. Usually my passport lights up like a singing birthday card when I pass through customs but not this time. I take the wheel and drive to the tobacco warehouses just over the Belgium border. We stock up and head down towards Liege. Hang on a mo! Paul the Papers is a reputable newsagent and an upstanding pillar of the community – but thinking back, he did purchase an unusually large quantity of cigarettes. No, surely not. He wouldn't, would he? We check into the Ibis by the ground and after a quick hour's kip, we take a 20 Euro taxi drive into town. First things first, I have to go to some god-awful Irish pub to collect my ticket off some Dutch bloke who Stewy knows. And why am I without a ticket, you may ask? Because the LFC ticket office have fucked up my application yet again. How, I honestly don't know. When I handed my application in at the window, the girl actually said 'Congratulations, you're the first one to put in for Liege (two hours after the draw).' I always physically hand the form in so it doesn't get lost in the post. So I wait and I wait and then go to the ground to pick it up. 'Sorry Mr Dodd, we've no record of you applying for the ticket'. 'Whaddaya mean, you've got no record. I came to this bleedin' window.' I call the manager who says the same and sympathises with me but tells me the remaining few tickets have already been boxed off back to Liege. Fuckin' marvellous. No wonder there's a sign by the ticket office asking people not to abuse the staff. It should be a god-given right to abuse such incompetence. What do they expect you to say? 'Hey, no worries. I've paid all this money to go to Europe and you've messed up again but it doesn't really matter. I'm sure there'll be a television somewhere.' Well I'm just about getting to the end of my tether with them. Anyway, I get the ticket. I quite like the away tickets in the qualifiers because they don't have to do them in that horrible, corporate Champions League blue with all those crappy sponsors names like MasterCard, Playstation, etc. They're just the real traditional ticket which is unique to whichever club you're playing. It goes without saying that we're on it by midday.

It's a long standing custom when British teams play in Europe that you have to be absolutely bladdered before you can set foot in the stadium. If they invoke the law where it states you cannot enter the ground under the influence of alcohol, our away end would be completely empty. Is that Bucko's voice I can hear coming from three streets away? David Buckley is officially the loudest man in Liverpool and quite possibly Europe's *grandest bruit*, too. He is the spiritual leader of the Red masses. For some reason he mysteriously disappears to London for a couple of days each week to 'do things'. My money is on him running a secret training school for town criers, street vendors and newspaper sellers. I've always thought he'd make a brilliant ventriloquist's dummy. Sit him on a big fella's knee and Bob's yer uncle. Let the show begin. It never ceases to amaze me how Her Maj has managed to so far overlook his obvious talents and not handed him a knighthood in recognition of his excessive drinking, incessant singing and that crazy little dance thing he does, when he comes boogieing towards you and then goes nimbly backwards, then forwards again with that manic grin on his face. A truly remarkable man and an example to any young urchin who hasn't quite mastered the art of getting up on the table and delivering a chorus or two of any Liverpool song you care to mention. An urban football legend. Our guiding light. Grown men look at him in awe and wait for a sign. Arise, Sir Bucko of Bootle. Lead us to the Promised Land and we will follow. For you are the chosen one.

Anyway the noisy bastard appears around the corner with his trusted generals, Richie Tierney and Mercer in tow. Richie is better is known to those who know as The Voice of Virgin Westcoast. (Think "hello, this is Richard your Virgin Trains Manager today welcoming you on board this 19.07 Virgin Pendolino service to Liverpool Lime Street..." Familiar? Well that's him. Dulcet isn't in it. I couldn't tell you if Mercer's dulcet or full-set as he rarely, if ever, speaks. Then just as it gets past three ay-em and you're starting to think of your cot he'll suddenly, you know.... Sing. I think we can just about call it singing though, for those who've met him, it's more like Mercering.) Bootle's Finest has his usual Pied Piper effect, with a bedraggled bunch of drunks, wastrels and wretches in tow – all in all, an excellent crew! We drink our own

Jegsy and Paul the Papers

body weight in beer and the suspension on our bus to the ground is pushed to the limits, as the Torres bounce hits frenzy proportions. Belgian beer is legendary and it comes as no surprise to discover that there are more alcoholics here per head than anywhere else on Earth (see also Villarreal – Nico from Antwerp). Even the Irish and the Jocks look at this country through bloodshot eyes with a mixture of envy and respect. We get to the ground and the teams line up. My ale goggles are playing tricks on me – there seem to be forty four players on the pitch, though as the game wears on and the ale wears off, that reverts back to the more traditional twenty two.

The match is dire. We are clueless and very lucky to survive. Pepe saves a penalty and we clear one off the line which probably, if we're honest, sneaked over. It is a classic case of underestimating the opposition. Keane hardly gets a touch and is subbed. It's our first competitive match of the season and to say we're lucky to escape with a draw is an understatement. There's a few moans after the game but that's soon forgotten about when everybody gets back to town. Near the end of the night I find myself involved in an incident which can only be described as bizarre. I'm drunkenly wandering around this big new open plan pub trying to find a loo, when all of a sudden I have a brush with death. For the life of me I can't figure out where the bogs are and I find myself in some darkened place full of building materials. I am just about to unzip my flies when I tread on a creaky floorboard and to my horror, look up and see a huge iron girder coming my way. It's one of those RSJ things which must've been balanced upright and I've just disturbed it enough to make it topple. My reactions are obviously numbed by what I've had to drink but I still manage to swerve at the last moment as it goes TIMBER.

It catches the side of my jaw and cuts my chin and must've hit my shoulder and my thigh. I'm like 'Where the fuck did that come from?'. It's only next day when I realise how lucky I was. I go back to the table where the lads are sitting and I'm greeted with a chorus of 'What the fuck happened to you?'. I've got blood all over me and my teeth have gone through my bottom lip. I take the lads to where the girder lay to prove that I hadn't been having a shady scrap with one of the locals. They are amazed I'm still alive. Stewy reckons that if it would've hit me flush on the head it could've killed me or at least, fractured my skull. It makes you think how fragile life is. You read about lads who are bevvied on stag nights who end up with all kinds of injuries. Some end up in wheelchairs and others pay the ultimate price. I reckon that's yet another one of my nine lives used up. There can't be many more before the Grim Reaper's dark index finger beckons me forward and this gruff, echo-y voice goes: 'Sorry Mr Dodd, that's yer lot. Your credit has run out and your time is up'. Anyway let's not get too morbid. We continue to talk a load of bollocks into the early hours and then get a cab back to the hotel. I discover next morning, after being questioned as to why I was anywhere near the iron girder, that there wasn't even a toilet in the pub after all. You had to use the one across the street in the other bar. So at least I'm not going mad after all.

We're just about to head out of Liege for the long trek home when we drive past the stadium. To our surprise, it's open. We can see the pitch through this big imposing gate. The sun is shining and the turf is as green as you like. It seems to be saying 'Come on in. Stand on me, why don't you? Take cheesy photographs.' Within minutes we're parked up and on the centre circle with hands on hips taking it all in. My head feels like it's been put in a blender. I am dehydrated, disorientated and nauseated but I'm still infatuated by standing here on the pitch where last night, the atmosphere was red hot as the Liege fans gave it the full bifters. It's a weird feeling as it's all so still and tranquil now. We need to get on the road but Stewy (who's football mad) is combing the press box for any form of memorabilia. He collects absolutely anything. He's like the cat that got the cream back at the car, with his laminated press passes and team sheets. We leave Liege and head back to the Channel Tunnel.

The journey is monotonous so we stop off at the booze and baccy place we visited on the way down. We're in a subdued mood when the silence is broken. A minibus skids around the corner and my old mate Sconch is hanging out of the window with a can in his hand. Uh oh. Put your crash helmets on. Sconch is in town. For those of you who are unfamiliar with him. Let me just say he is THE original hell raiser. Like an uncoiled spring. Absolutely anything can happen when he's around. He's ranting on about something that's just happened on their journey but he's just too fast. I can't take it in. It's all a hundred miles an hour and I'm still hungover. Sconch is a proper townie from the Bullring and knows just about every nut job in the city. To go out for a bevvy with him is like being in a hurricane or going on the Big Dipper without a seatbelt. Sensible, he is not. But entertaining, he certainly is. Put him together with Mr Noisy from Bootle and you have the perfect night of madness. On the numerous occasions I've been on the pop with them, I've probably only been allowed to interject with phrases like 'What are you having?' or 'Where shall we go after here?'. The rest of the time I can't get a word in edgeways, as the dynamic duo joust for vocal supremacy. It's a case of light the blue touch paper and stand well back. We make our excuses and hit the road, with Sconch and his crew about to do some serious shopping. We finally get home about 11pm on Thursday night, bedraggled, bloodied and tired. We mumble our goodbyes after yet another successful European jaunt. Paul the Papers gets quite rightly praised for his epic drive home. All I've got to do now is explain how I gashed my chin and how close Hot Lips was to having a cabbage as a boyfriend. Whaddaya mean she already has?

JD

Sunderland (a)   1-0

League   Sat 16th Aug

Friday is spent licking my wounds and recuperating. These European aways really take it out of you but we've got Sunderland tomorrow and there's frantic phonecalls to make. With it being a 5.30 kick-off and a decent allocation, everyone seems to be sorted. I've got a spare ticket and an empty seat next to me. I glance across the room to the mysterious lady with the big brown eyes. In one unaccountable sudden rush of blood I suddenly find I've asked her if she fancies it. Of course she fancies it. In fact she's overjoyed. 'What shall I wear?', 'anything.', 'Who's driving?', 'me there, you back', 'What time shall we leave?', 'early', 'Can we stay in the Lakes on the way back?', 'no', 'Why not?', 'too late', 'Is Torres playing?', 'dunno', 'Will the lads take the piss out of you being with me?', etc, etc, etc.

We go in her car and it's sound. A bit different, but a great day out. We park up and stroll to a boozer on top of the hill called the Halfway House. The weather's warm and there's pockets of Reds having a bevvy outside. Fitzy and Patto, both seasoned old pros, appear around the corner a little worse for wear with a big crew of old-school Redmen. They've all been at the unveiling of some sort of memorial to the late great Bob Paisley at a place called Hetton-le-Hole, which is a boss name for a town. 'Where are you from lad?', 'Hetton-le-Hole', bonnie lad.

'Is right!', lad.

We head off down the hill to the ground. Inside there are more than one or two who look like they haven't slept for a week. Obviously veterans of the Liege trip. Some of them look like they've just walked off the set of Michael Jackson's 'Thriller' video. I'm still conscious of being 'on the arm' as they call it and am waiting outside the Ladies when Richie and Mercer appear. 'Who are you with?' they ask. 'I'm just waiting for me bird' I say, which is greeted with the sort of expression that would only usually greet a very loud fart. A kind of puzzled look, with raised eyebrows, followed by insane grinning. Oh well, boys will be boys. We get the introductions out of the way and take up our spec right behind the goal.

The match is poor. We struggle to get any grip on the game. Dossena making his debut and Arbeloa on the other side are giving me the heebie geebies. Neither looks safe or composed. Time is running out, and we don't even look like scoring. It's all horribly reminiscent of another opening day fixture a few years back against Sheffield United. On that occasion we had to rely on a penalty awarded for the previously unheard-off category of "intending to trip Steven Gerrard." We were grateful for the point, but we were lucky. Today we're playing just as badly, if not worse. And then… and then… and then you thank God you've got Torres. He picks the ball up with about eight minutes left. He does his effortless thing of seeming just to go through defenders – I mean actually pass through their bodies like he's Jesus – which he is. He creates that little fraction of space he needs, and he hits it straight and true, into the bottom left hand corner and the travelling Reds go apeshit. It's mad celebrating a goal with your bird. You kind of don't know what to do. Usually with your mates, you're all diving on each other and falling on the seats like a gang of knobheads. But with your lady, it's more like, 'wahey we've scored' or 'get in there Nando lad'; a chaste hug and away we go.

We haven't played well but I'm well chuffed with the three points. Not every team is gonna come here and grab a win. We head back to the Halfway House to let the traffic calm down but this time we're the only two Liverpool in there. No need to worry though. Their lads were sound. We had a good gab with them. They wished us luck and a safe journey home. My god. I am turning into John Mackin. It's well know that Liverpool FC has supporters all over the world. There's the New York Branch, the Dutch Branch, the Belgians… well Johnny Mac is The Olive Branch'. He's always dead nice to opposing fans. Always swapping things with them, setting up mutual drink-ins with them in their boozers, always keeping in touch. Me, I've always been an absolute twat to everyone. I care about Liverpool FC full stop. John will happily collect money for teams in trouble, mop fans brows, run raffles and build bridges, etc while I just sit there telling them all to fuck off. Not that I'm a nasty person in real life. It's just that this is football and football is tribal. So therefore I couldn't give a toss about any other team's fans. And I'm glad I've got that off my chest.

We're heading south and she's driving like a loon. It's starting to rain and my girlfriend has morphed into a mini-Clarkson. She's hitting speeds of up to …. Oops, sorry can't say. Ian Kidd, the undercover bizzie, who follows Liverpool all over Europe, prying into people's lives, might just be reading this and she could get banned from the match for three years. He'll be in his superior's office the next day going 'Look, Jegsy Dodd's bird was doing 110 on the motorway (shit, I've said it) on the way back from Sunderland. Look, it's there in black and white. 'Surely it's football related? Let's ban her. Let's ban him. Let's ban everyone.' We reach Aldo's bar for last orders. Have a couple in Flannagans and head home, tired but content. The season is well and truly underway and for this weekend at least, I'm happy.

JD

Middlesbrough (h)   2-1

League   Sat 23rd Aug

Boro at home is traditionally one of my least favourite games of the year. I don't know what it is about Middlesbrough but just the sheer mention of the name makes you want to hook up the hosepipe to the exhaust and end it. Even the away fixture makes you feel like you're Bruce Parry off that Tribe programme meeting a remote group of people who've had no contact with the outside world. But hey – it's the first home game of the season and I don't really care if we play Bora-Bora… I'm excited.

We meet in Ned Kelly's in town. It's my first bevy of the new season with Parso, the much-loved and quietly sardonic wit that is Brian Parsons from Birkenhead. Tommy Trouble's already in full voice, and there's a fine array of oddballs all gathered to welcome the new season. It doesn't seem to feel like it though. Maybe we've been a bit spoilt with three decent away games already; one friendly, one European and one league. Another thing that makes it slightly flat is that more and more of the lads/diehards of my generation have decided to jib it. With the changing face of football, the money, marketing, sponsorship, the American ownership saga, the cynicism and all the other usual things it's becoming harder and harder to be a fan. It seems to be getting more geared to being a television sport now than a live spectator sport. Did I just say sport? How old-fashioned of me. It's now really one big seedy marketing circus of wheeling and dealing where the corporate pigs stand side by side with their snouts in the trough. Grunting and farting as they suck the game dry of any respectability. It's a sad fact that people like Tommy O'Hagan, Smigger from Kirkby, Dennis from Wallasey and numerous others have decided to call it a day. How much longer me and the other lifers will last is another question. But you can see by the creation of supporters' action groups like 'The Spirit of Shankly' that all is not well on Planet Football. More about S.O.S in a bit.

One of the maddest results of all the gradual erosion of LFC's male, local, working class fanbase is a new phenomenon that is happening downstairs in the Sandon – a half-brick's throw from The Kop, and the place where this football club, this institution, this Liverpool was founded. Every home game, The Sandon is packed to the rafters with all the old match heads while the game itself is being played out a hundred yards away. And it's not just a case of tickets being like the proverbial gold-dust at Anfield, and any spares being hoovered up by touts and cash-rich daytrippers who will get in, literally, at any cost. A lot of the ex-diehards don't want to be part of what they see now as a sanitised marketing ritual (later in the season, Commercial Director Ian Ayre will refer to Liverpool Football Club as "the product"). More of him later, too. In a weird way, by meeting up at The Sandon and having a laugh, this regular crew of 200 former Lifers still think they're kind of actually at the match but not really, if you know what I mean. I've had the odd spare ticket and offered it to Ally or Jimmy or someone and they've refused saying it's a better laugh in the pub where you can sit with your mates and have a few bevvies and even nip outside for a smoke if you want. The mad thing is though, if they watched it in town or nearer to where they live, they wouldn't class it as going to the match. So in their minds they're actually at the match but not wasting money on a ticket for The Product. Confused? So am I.

2.50 p.m. I enter the Spion Kop and head all the way up to the infamous Block 306, shaking hands and giving manhugs to fellow Redmen I haven't seen since last season as I shuffle my way along the row. There's little Mono from Halewood; him, Jeff Brittles, Gram, Spenno, John Nicko, John Garner, John Gaghan – all the Halewood Chains have been going home and away since the 70s, and they make up a good few rows of 306. Let's get some of the other Johns out the way, too. Leaving my esteemed co-author Mr Mackin out of the equation for a second – you can only leave Mackin out of equations for a second or he'll phone his agent and ask why Liverpool F.C are making a programme about fans without asking for his opinion – our immediate fraternity embraces John 'Mageye' Maguire, John Buchanan, John Joynt and little John the photographer, John Johnson. Also within hugging distance there's Gary Shaw, Danny Nicolson (John's young 'un, and co-creator of Boss mag with Maguire). There's Fat Paul Scholes in the form of Glen Monaghan, Tommy The German, Young Gilly (not to be confused with Tony Gill, one of the old school) and Wayno. There's the lads who make the big long banners – Ian Lewis, Joe, The Twinnies and Rimmer (aka the Skem lads, even though one of them's from Birkenhead). And there's the young lads who sit with Welsh Paul and Kev Moorland – this little firm deserve a medal and a free batch of Zoobs care of Liverpool F.C. Even if we're playing Notts County in the Carling Cup on a rainy Tuesday night, these boys sing non-stop for 95 minutes, and in the case of young Kev they keep it going in the boozers and in town for a good few hours more. His version of Horse With No Name has become a mainstay down at Ned's, and it's mainly down to him the song has become so popular with the Redmen once again. Just behind us there's the De Asha clan – Tony, Christy and Lee along with their mates Ronnie Dewhurst and Warren (Warren is famous for calamities abroad, and for his brother, the legendary Treeman of Taksin Square). And bringing 306 its air of worldy *savoir faire* there's a crew of luvvies and thesps that not even Chelsea or Man.U can match – Daily Mirror columnist Brian Reade, former crooner Peter Hooton, film producer Roy Boulter not to mention myself and Sammo, both known to grace the pages of Merseymart in our heyday.

Block 306 is full on. It's like a Kop within a Kop. It was created at the beginning of last season after a meeting between fans representatives and ironically fans enemy number one, Rick Parry. Poor old Rick. He gives them what they want, a section all to themselves to boost the atmosphere and what do they do in return? They sing naughty songs about Rick Parry all the match. He must be thinking to himself "Hang on a minute, what's going on here?" I suppose a lot of it is because he looks so cold and unapproachable, unlike one of those grinning, wild-eyed chief execs that you see on the telly, when their team's just qualified for the 3rd round of the FA Cup. Rick likes to keep his guard up at all times. Emotion is not a word in the Parry repertoire. He may look like one of life's pallbearers but I imagine when he's away from football he's a different animal altogether. I bet he's first on the karaoke in his local pub doing 'Satisfaction' by the Stones with his suit jacket pulled behind his shoulders. The life and soul of the party. All his mates are going "Come on Rick. Do your Rafa Benitez impression" and he's like "For sure," "We controlled the game," "Fact," "skwadd," "For sure," "Opportunities, possibilities, for sure." I can just imagine him acting in a really irresponsible manner. "Hey lads, have you seen my Frank Spencer?" "Ooo Betty!" What a bizarre thought.

Anyway, the atmosphere is pretty good for a Boro match – and the game's not bad, either. Middlesbrough are really up for it and attack at every opportunity. Gareth Southgate's done a good job up there. He's a likeable sort of bloke and one of a dying breed of young English managers. Boro score first through Mido, the big Egyptian lad who they signed from Spurs. Not a bad dig if the truth be known but Liverpool are woeful. There's passes going astray all over the place and Tuncay the Turk does a spectacular flick around Carra and collects it the other side and twats it on the volley only for Pepe to save. One of the best bits of skill you'll see all year. Time is running out and I'm beginning to think our miserable display is going to get what it deserves, when all of a sudden, right out of nowhere, Carragher hits one from about 30 yards. It takes a massive deflection but we won't let that spoil the carnage that ensues. A tumult of completely over-the-top celebration greets this first home goal of the season. We're back in it and of all people it's Jamie to the rescue. We press for the winner and deep into injury time, that man, the world's most complete footballer smashes an absolute piledriver into the back of the Boro net. Obviously the Kopites are delirious at the sight of Stevie G running towards them. He is an exceptional talent and last gasp winners are always the ultimate way to end a game. I'm buzzing but it's more with relief than anything else, because let's face facts, we were shite. We didn't play well at all and Boro must've felt absolutely gutted – they'll play worse than that this season and win, and their fans needn't worry. Carry on playing like that and they'll be knocking on Europe's door again next season after their unexpected run to the UEFA Cup Final a season or two ago. Anyway, at the end of the cliché, it's three points. Like Sunderland last week, it's a win and, in this dizzy, glitzy, world of premier league football, that's all that counts.

Time for a celebratory bevvy downstairs in the Sandon. Ally and the We're Not Really Here crew should all be there – always a tale to tell with those boys. I walk down with John Maguire, Danny Nicholson and the Boss Mag team. Boss Mag is different from all the other Liverpool FC fanzines in that it caters primarily just for Scousers and covers music, fashion and all kinds of nutty stuff. The after-match ritual for years has been upstairs in the Sandon, but unfortunately this season the corporate tentacles have spread like a virus to reach out from their smug private bars and enclaves within the ground itself and take over the upstairs room of one of our bastions of Scouse solidarity. Yes, there's bouncers in official club ties at the bottom of the stairs barring your way from what was, until today, our meeting place. It may not be the most earth shattering thing that's ever happened in the rich and glorious history of our club but it's still yet another brick removed from the wall of tradition that makes our club so unique. It's almost like the old upstairs/downstairs of the outdated

English class system. The corporate toffs quaffing above us while below the loyal peasants stand six deep at the bar waiting for a couple of jars to toast the boys in Red. Anyway it's only a pub and it'll probably go bust like the rest of them in a couple of years. I certainly won't be going back.

Taxis into town, a few in Aldo's and an early night. I'm starting to think though. What are we gonna do when Carra and Stevie retire? There's no homegrown players coming through. They were both there before the foreign influx, pre-Houllier and Benitez and there's no sign of anyone coming out of the Academy. It worries me. Will we just be like any other club? Foreign owned, foreign managed and filled with foreign mercenaries? Liverpool in name and nothing else? The clock is ticking and the future doesn't bear thinking about. Let's just get this 19th league title out of the way and then we'll have another look at it. I'd better get my head down as my mind is racing. Anyway, three points, could've been a lot worse. A win's a win, as they say.

JD

Standard Liege (h)   1-0

Champions League Qualifier   Wed 27th Aug

It's only a qualifier and there's really no justification for such an early start, but Sampson's having no back answers.

"This is Europe, John. The Liverpool Gentleman has certain standards to maintain."

Well, when it's put like that it's hard to say no to an early swallee in town. So it is with that that we meet in The Slaughterhouse at 2:30 to begin the traditional pre-European session. Sampson's in a chirpy mood and I'm suspecting he's had a stroke of good fortune; the film rights for some pseudo-intellectual gangster porn he's written being optioned by Guy Ritchie perhaps, or maybe he's had some gushing fan mail from Doris Lessing or Anthony Burgess? I know better than to pry, and so happily tag along as he first tries to buy me lunch in a Japanese place near The Strand, before settling on Scouse and Guinness in nearby Ma Boyles. We've been looking for a new pre-Euro ritual, and this might just be it. For years it was Tapas and Cerveza at La Tasca, a heady combo that saw us through epic campaigns, and triumphs in Dortmund and Istanbul. But after the disappointment of Athens and the reverse against Chelsea last season, we've decided that maybe the pre-match routine needs freshening up. The Champions League proper hasn't even started yet, there's a long, long, loopy mad road ahead and there's only me and Sammo… but Ma Boyle's by the Pierhead is as 'Pool as it comes. I come over all Brian Jacques at times like this: the squawk of the seagulls and the looming presence of the Mersey, a pint of the Black Stuff and a bowl of Scouse with red cabbage … why I can almost feel a sea shanty coming on.

It's my first game back after my hols, and I'm raring to go. After ten days of the finest seafood in Spain, I'm glad we've ditched Liverpool's noble, but ultimately futile attempts at Spanish tuck. My phone goes. The signal being crap, I pop out into the alley to take the call. I come back to see Sammo pushing his nose round an empty Scouse bowl, like a puppy. "Boss that," he says trying to lick his chin, by way of explanation.

"That was Sammy Lee," I tell him.

"Tell him dinner's finished."

"He was phoning about 'You'll Never Walk Alone'."

I'd contacted the club for an explanation as to why our anthem of 45 years had been shunted from it's traditional spot (played just before the teams come out onto the pitch) to just before kick-off. That query had been forwarded to Melwood, as the directive to move it had come from 'the manager's office'. Sammy said it was more or less an order from the Premier League, but he wanted me to come up for a chat and a cuppa, talk me through it all. How dare the Premier League make us move YNWA! Talk about the tail wagging the dog. I suppose if the next Sky TV deal was big enough the clubs would meekly agree to just about anything. I mean, if Sky insisted that the players made their appearance on the backs of brightly-painted unicycles, whilst the P.A. played "Glory, Glory, Richard Keys," we'd just say "Okay ... and could you make the cheque out to cash please?"

It's our turn on Union duty tonight, so at 5:30 we get a cab up to the Supporters Club in Lower Breck Road. We'll be selling coach tickets on the SOS bus for Villa at the weekend, as well as canvassing for new members. Sammo stays upstairs in the small bar on coach ticket duty (and quaffing the incredibly cheap Becks) and I grab a load of membership forms and head down to the main bar and lounge. It's not madly busy, perhaps 150 people in, 145 of who are wearing replica shirts, many over their jumpers, some wearing them over their coats. I'm informed it's the Bristol and the Grimsby branches. I assume they'll be fertile ground as the union exists to represent all Liverpool fans, no matter where they come from, I'm convinced I can do good work here. The plan is to get two or three on board on each of the coaches and they can distribute membership forms and leaflets and spread the word.

I'm met with blank stares or even people just avoiding eye contact completely: "Oi don't join things loike that," one bloke tells me.

"What? You're in a Supporter's Club? What 'thing' is this, that your SC isn't?" I leave a few membership forms and move on. One guy seems to be taking some attention so I try to engage with him.

"The SOS is fighting, amongst other things, for better deals on travel for fans, as well as a fairer ticketing system." Surely he can't argue with that, can he? No, he can't, but he's still not interested.

"Oi gets moine from the Zerbordurzzz Club. An me travel, an' all."

It's an I'm Alright Jack attitude of outrageous proportions. After another 10 minutes of further snubs and indifference I pack it in and buy an armful of bottles of Becks and join Sammo upstairs for an hour berating "them frigging wools down stairs." Sammo's had a few by now, and draws himself up.

"Watch and learn," he winks, grabs the membership forms and skips off downstairs. Ten minutes later he's back by my side.

"Give us a fucking bottle, will you…"

He looks ready to pop with rage – all red-faced outrage.

"What happened then, Casanova? The smooth talk not work?"

What happened is that Sammo had a similar response to myself – just didn't take it as a well. One lad in particular – who'd committed the cardinal sin of wearing an England shirt (an *England shirt*!!) to a Liverpool game, had got right up his nose. Whereas the table of lads he was with had stared at the floor and let Sampson say his piece, this skinny little ted in the Three Lions top had handed the leaflet back to Kev and started playing to the crowd:

"Not interested, lad. Heard it all before."

Sammo asked them to agree just to take the forms away and have a read on the coach home. England top snorted and threw his on the floor, prompting the storm upstairs and demand of an ice-cold bottle, immediately.

"He was a fuckin' Scouser, an' all," squeaks Sammo. I can't help chortling – he'd been so sure he could turn their heads.

The frustrations continue at Anfield later that evening. Such was the ineptitude of our team in trying to break down a stubborn and physically strong Liege side, that it's just short of the hour mark when we start talking about how great the UEFA Cup is. Plans are being made for how we'll get to all those mad out-of-the-way places, and tiny corporate-free grounds, free from the grasping Champions League circus.

"Much Chorzow… now there's a team I've always wanted to play," says Jegs.

"Go Ahead Eagles Deventer," counters Sammo. "Or any crack military team from the former Eastern Bloc…"

"Racing Boys Berne!" I say – not sure if they even exist. "They'll do…"

And just when we'd decided which obscure European outpost we'd be supping in, in a couple of weeks time, Dirk Kuyt ruins it by running smack into the path of a low cross from Babel, and somehow stubs the ball into the net. We survive a very late scare, when Liege miss a sitter in right in front of The Kop, and scrape through. Just. As The Kop can barely muster a round of applause for the Reds, Sampson is smirking like a demented gibbon. I'm thinking he must've been at J.B's Euro-flask again, but he rubs his hands together and slaps me on the back.

"That's it!" he beams. "It's meant to be. We're going to win this cup."

JM

Aston Villa (a)   0-0

League   Sun 31st Aug

The transfer deadline is fast approaching like an impending credit card statement. We haven't exactly set the world on fire with the scope and ambition of our signings. Why have we just shelled out £8m for Andrea Dossena? Fair do's, he's Italy's left back but by and large (and Dossena is a leeeetle too large for my liking) Italian players find it tough going over here. Besides, we have the ultra-promising young Argentian left-back Insua ready to make the step up as well as, when he recovers from his latest injury, Fabio Aurelio. (We still haven't really has chance to work out whether Aurelio is Fab as he seems to be 'out for three months' every time there's a bout of hay fever). Anyway – £8million for Dossena and £17 million for Gareth Barry – to my way of thinking that's £25 million we could be spending on Sergio Aguero or David Silva… on quality addition to the skwadd, rather than these piecemeal signings that never quite make it.

And the Gareth Barry fiasco has done no-one any favours, by the way – it's just embarrassing. What Liverpool fans found most puzzling was that in a team crying out for width, the manager was trying to strengthen the one area on the pitch where we had real class and strength in depth. The papers spin it whichever way their Liverpool bias fell: O'Neill was strong in resisting, or was it Liverpool refusing to pay his inflated price? Cash poor Liverpool didn't have the money, or was it Cash rich Villa who didn't need it? It was even rumoured that Randy Lerner, Villa's American owner, would not allow his club to fall victim to Gillett and Hick's pressure. Yet another version says that O'Neill agreed the transfer, then upped the price. Liverpool refused to play the game, and pulled out. Or was it that Rafa wanted him, but Parry didn't – or maybe it was George who didn't, but Parry did? Feck knows! To add further spice,

Juventus withdrew their interest in Alonso and the source of Rafa's transfer funds disappeared overnight, leaving all involved with messy, sticky egg on their faces. Not, as the cliché goes, the Liverpool Way. Whatever happened to opening the paper one day to find a photograph of John Toshack sitting next to Bill Shankly, pen in hand, with a paternal John Smith leaning over the two of them; or even the buzz that accompanied a Radio City announcement of a "press conference at Anfield at 11am," and genuinely not knowing what it might be about?

No, modern football is fast turning into rubbish, and it's doubly ironic that Barry might be lining up for Aston Villa against us today. There is only one immovable, unchanging Liverpool Way – and that's us lot. The fans. We still, and always will, do it right. It's 11am. I'm in a backstreet pub in Anfield watching a 5 year old girl in a pink frock, standing on a crate and pulling pints for half a dozen hardened Sunday morning drinkers. She takes their tenners and does the till with an aplomb I can barely believe. Its like a Fellini movie and I look outside hoping to spot The Pope leading a procession of naked nuns on zebras as confirmation. Nope! Just a steady drizzle. I'm a bit early for the bus to Villa and take the opportunity for this quick bevy. I'm of a mind to ask her for a vodka martini, just to see how good she is with the cocktail shaker, but think better of it. Men have had pool cues crocked over their noggins in here for less.

The draw for the group stages of the Champions League has left us all as underwhelmed as the game on Wednesday night did: Marseilles (again) and PSV Eindhoven (again)… yawn! The only thing to quicken the pulse being a trip to Madrid to play Atletico. It'll be our first ever competitive game in Madrid, a new ground to visit and an opportunity to thoroughly overdo it in some of the best bars in Europe. It's also a return visit for Torres to his boyhood club, so we expect some kind of Scouse-Madrileno love-in to take place. Never mind that Bolton went there last year and got royally booted all round the city by the Guardia Civil (far from civil in my mind); the return of El Nino and the adulation he shall receive from both sets of supporters will see us being carried shoulder-high around the city, festooned with flowery garlands, and plied with much Rioja.

This afternoon's game promises to be anything but a fiesta. It's a grey, miserable, wet day. Ten minutes after watching slack-jawed as our 'Barmaid of the Year 2022' poured the pints, I'm standing flush up against the wall outside the Supporter's Club waiting for the Union coach to Villa Park, trying to shelter from this morose and relentless drizzle. Large blobs of rain drip from the ledge above and plop onto my head before running down my neck. There's 30 or so lads here, standing round, no colours, hoods up, slurping from cans and bottles. It's a far cry from Sky Sports' adverts where family groups of New Fans kitted out in stripey scarves and bobble hats play head tennis in supermarket car parks, cheerily letting on to similarly-dressed Christmas trees from other teams. Our coach is already half an hour late and when it does eventually arrive the driver is just as miserable as the weather.

"No alcohol!" he barks – well, croaks truth be known as he's about 75, and whilst he chases one lad away who's carrying a Tesco bag full of beer, most of the others pass their carrier bags onto the bus, thus swerving the ale search.

Once underway it becomes clear that this guy drives by the rules. Our Union bus steward and all-round sensible fellow, John-Paul, comes back up the aisle to inform us that we've been doing a steady 52 mph along the M62, and he suspects the driver has set the SatNav to 'Stapeley Water Gardens by the slowest route imaginable'. One-stroke scooters, and even crisp packets blowing in the wind, are overtaking us. At this rate we'll make sunny Aston with 5 minutes to spare. Peter Hooton is sitting next to me, his complexion as grey as the sky. He's been to a wedding the night before and is refusing cans of lager as he tries not to spew out of his ears. He's also in a slight panic as his ticket is currently travelling north up the M1 with his mate Mick from London. Mick's also due into Birmingham around kick-off time so they're both cutting it fine.

After much cajoling from the rear of the bus ("Hurry up you cunt!"), and a more gentle reminder that he's actually allowed to go faster than a Stannah Stairlift, the driver presses his foot down a millimetre or two. The floodlights of Villa Park hove into view, clearly visible against the grey horizon, and luckily there's still a good hour to go before kick-off. Once off the bus Peter and I head to a local Jamaican café, 'JA REGGAE'. I'd visited this place a few times before, most notably with APB prior to the 2001 FA Cup semi with Wycombe. (Wycombe, by the way! And crikey how we struggled…) We were just back after a week in Barcelona for the UEFA Cup semi, and were ashen faced, baggy-eyed and swollen with beer. It took all our energy to just sit in JA REGGAE, sip Coca Cola and try and eat goat curry without heaving. Peter was looking similarly delicate, but the thought of a goat curry perks him up, and he even accepts a can of lager. I go for the Jerk Chicken with rice and peas, all served up by a huge – I mean HUGE – monosyllabic Rasta, which only added to the Kingston vibe. It's a perfect spot; the local pubs are rammed to the rafters with condensation running down the walls, and here we sit, having our Sunday lunch and listening to a bit of Bob Marley.

It's a noisy, almost rowdy, Villa Park that we enter at 5 to 4. We've got a good, young, boisterous support down the Doug Ellis-stand touchline, and the usually quiet Holte End seems to have roused itself for one, probably because its live on the telly. It's actually quite a decent atmosphere, and the Brummies have outdone themselves with one or two banners hanging from the upper tier of the Holte. One reads 'Villa: The Obsession" – which is just a bit too much like one at Old Trafford to deserve any praise. Then there's the 'You're Just a Fat Spanish Waiter' one. Pardon me whilst I split my sides and soil my bills. They're obviously irked about the Rafa/O'Neill slanging match, and have employed some of their finest comedy minds to come up with this riposte. Do I detect the hand of Jasper Carrot here? Perhaps a tweak from Lenny Henry? I tut-tut and shake my head at it, mentally unfurling a bedsheet with "You're just a four-eyed geography teacher" sprayed on it.

There's no Gerrard today: he of the last-minute wonder free-kick of last year, when we dominated but struggled to score. Hopefully that won't be the problem this time round. Keane has looked like he's trying too hard at times so far, but Torres has got off to a flier this season, and with Mascherano back from the Olympics, well, let's say I'm confident. Another 3 points here will set us up nicely for the upcoming visit of the Mancs. We start fairly well with plenty of possession and we're knocking it about crisply. Alonso is seeing plenty of the ball and is also getting plenty of stick from the Villa fans, whom I suspect bizarrely blame him for the whole Barry nonsense. (Add 'thick' to 'not funny'). The Liverpool fans respond with the predictable "You should have signed for a big club." which I hope is intended solely to annoy the Villa fans, as their captain, along with Xabi, is innocent in all of this. Then, barely mid-way through the first half Torres chases a ball out wide on the right and pulls up sharply – shit! He's touching the back of his thigh gingerly; please let it not be his hamstring again. He limps off, and along with him go our chances. Rafa sends on the lightweight Ngog, although the bloke in front of me was convinced it was Babel and screams "Go 'ead Ryan lad" for the next hour. He (Ngog, not the bloke in front of me) fails to make any impact against Villa's robust defence. Keane continues to "try too hard," though the more we say it the more it sounds like an excuse, and misses another sitter when clean through in the second half. Play gets compressed down a narrow 25 yard furrow, neither side capable or willing to use the flanks, and fizzles out into the predictable draw.

After the game our coach driver has come to his senses and lets the lads stock the coach up from the off-licence, so at least the journey home won't fizzle out into tedium. In fact we get nicely pissed and a sing-song ensues. The general feeling is that the game was there for our taking, but that we haven't got a squad that's good enough – no real strength in depth. It seems not so much like two points dropped, as one point settled for. We get off the coach on Lime Street and plan to hike over to Neds where we aim to sit cross-legged at the feet of Liverpool's sages and elders (the Jedi masters, Sconch and Bucko perhaps), listening to them dispense shrewd and perceptive reflections on today's proceedings. But we never get there. We decide to pay a visit to The Grapes on Mathew Street (having been assured by one of our group who looks far too young to know what a MILF is, that said Grapes has become the tipsy HQ for Sunday night hen parties). He's right. The joint is absolutely bouncing when we arrive, and a procession of hen parties do indeed come in, flirt outrageously with anyone with a penis and shriek like banshees. "It's like The Grafton in here…" Hooto says, his eyes alight. At this point someone on the karaoke is murdering 'Comfortably Numb', and feeling just a tad 'comfortably numb' myself I slope off for the train.

JM

Manchester Utd (h)   2-1

League   Sat 13th Sep

We all meet at the Supporters Club on Lower Breck Road on a gorgeous late summer morning. Since our 'ejection' from The Sandon, we've taken advantage of the nearby LFC Supporters Club, a ten minute walk from Anfield. It's a big enough space and the SC are supportive of the Spirit of Shankly Supporters Union, hosting fundraising nights and committee meetings over the summer. It's even more popular with those used to the Sandon's prices, and the combination of continental sunshine and £1.50 a bottle means the place is packed by 10am this Saturday morning. With the weather being so lovely, the large triangle of grass outside the club – Anfield's village green – is becoming packed with lads. Around their feet stand rows of bottles of Becks and Budweiser. There's also the odd bottle of wine as The Sandon Wall Wine Club live up to their promise that they'd be picnicking here today. The mood is good and expectations high. What's also drawn people in such numbers so early is that co-owner George Gillett is attending the match – the highlight of the domestic season. Funny how he's never here for Middlesbrough on a pissing down Tuesday night for a League Cup game. The Union has grasped the opportunity this provides, and have called for supporters to march in protest at Gillett and Hick's tenure, and the debt they've saddled the club with. The march is set to leave here about an hour before kick-off. There's a real buzz of anticipation in the air. Sammo and Keith Culvin are manning a stall by the front door, pressing people to join the Union and join the march and this time it's a completely different response. Everyone seems up for it. Fans from all over the country are joining up by the dozen, and Alan Kayll (whose Dad co-runs the SC with Richie Pedder) has to go out back and look for more biros.

Press, TV and radio are here by the bucket load for the match touted as Benitez's first real test of the season. The Union have been busy all week drumming up support for the march and have alerted the media. The situation grows more interesting on the Thursday evening prior to the march when Rick Parry calls me and asks if a small delegation of Union reps will meet with George Gillett. Parry implies that Gillett is the straight guy in the relationship and seems keen that we should hear him out. I get straight on to Paul Rice, the Union chairman.

"What do you think he's up to, Paul?"

"God knows? Maybe some P.R. Give us some bullshit...," he replies.

"What? Stroke our egos to try and defuse the protest?"

"Could be."

"Not gonna happen though, is it?"

"Is it fuck."

We agree the only thing Gillett could say to defuse the feeling of anger is to announce that he's sold the club that morning to a benevolent billionaire Kop season ticket holder, and personally paid off the debts himself.

After a quick beer at the Supporters Club, a small group of Union committee members arrive at The Shankly Gates. Apart from Paul Rice and myself there's Nicky Allt and the gravel-voiced Peter Furmedge. Stadium manager Ged Poynton, escorts us in through the players entrance, much to the curiosity of the autograph hunters and tourists waiting for a glimpse of a player. I suck my beer belly in and try and walk nonchalantly amidst this phalanx of 'muscle' hoping to see internet gossip that evening about Raul being spotted sneaking into Anfield ("He's put on a few pounds, I can tell you"). We're taken down the tunnel from the players' entrance towards the dressing rooms, escorted by stewards dressed in blazers and crisp white shirts and ties, rather than Hi-Vis jackets, one or two even have CIA-style earpieces in. We've clearly come up in the world. Half way down the corridor we are shown into a small office with glass walls made private with closed blinds. It's explained that this is Rafa's after-match room where he chats with opposition managers. The kind of low-key, off the record, place where he might discuss zonal marking with Roy Hodgson over a nice cup of tea, or offer to help David Moyes squeeze his eyeballs back into their sockets (that must be what that bowl of teaspoons is for). At worst, it's the perfect place not to offer Steve Bruce a glass of wine. It occurs to me that this private space for the managers to get together is a direct replacement for the famous old Boot Room. Managers from Shankly to Dalglish would offer opposition managers a cuppa, or a tot of Scotch, in that famous, old, cramped inner-sanctum. It was

Anfield's holiest of holies – the club's very soul. The Boot Room – its very name came to signify the ethos that ran through the club, an ethos of tradition, respect and simplicity. It was unpretentious and honest – things we thought our football club, though hugely successful, still was. We were hugely proud of it. However that decades-old icon was brushed aside in the '90s when Graeme Souness set about modernising the playing side at Anfield and stamping his own authority on the club. After a successful time at Glasgow Rangers during which the stadium and, to a lesser extent, the team's fortunes were rebuilt beyond supporters' wildest dreams (there was a time when their Ibrox stadium was the most modern in Europe and their team attracted the cream of European talent.). A similar transformation was intended at Anfield. Souness believed that the club had fallen behind the 'modern game' and its methods and values were relics of a bygone era. There was a drive to sweep away the old and promote, cultivate or if necessary downright impose the new. Well the baby was thrown out with the bathwater when the Boot Room was destroyed. Tradition and soul tossed onto the scrapheap to allow a brand new media briefing suite to be built. The Boot Room going was like the demolition of The Cavern Club: ridiculously short sighted, an act of vandalism to be repented at leisure. I fully expect any new stadium to include a replica... where tourists who wouldn't know the Boot Room from a broom cupboard will happily pay a tenner to have their photos taken next to holograms of Bill Shankly and Bob Paisley, who they probably wouldn't know either. This room we're in now, on the other hand, could be anything. It's identical to any small spare office in any office building. It is what it is: characterless and functional, and looks more like the lean-to conservatory attached to a Kwik Fit garage where you wait whilst your wheels are balanced. We are even asked to keep our voices down in case Rafa is nearby.

The situation is rich in irony for me. It hammers home what we've let slip out of our grasp as a club in recent years. Whoever owns the club – we'd prefer the term 'custodian' but that might be pie-in-the-sky romanticism - should have a firm grasp of the club's traditions; its core 'Boot Room' values. We are a million miles from that this Saturday morning. It also brings back into crystal-clear focus the very reason we are here sitting in front of this small, white-haired American multi-millionaire. This room is like the rest of this Main Stand: too small and cramped, out of date, clearly unsuitable for a club of our stature and aspirations. As with Rafa when it comes to his squad, this meeting room screams 'make-do and mend', and there sitting opposite us is

George Gillett, the man to whom the club had been sold for the sole reason of providing the investment to build a new stadium. The man who clearly has no intentions of providing the financial wherewithal that has been promised. Well, not from *his* pocket anyway.

Gillett is looking all cuddly and avuncular, a picture of homeliness in beige. He's even wearing comfortable, lived-in walking boots – every bit the genial host who's invited you in for a nip and a natter. He's sitting just in front of a small fridge with Carlsberg in and, on its top, several bottles of decent Rioja. Ha! So they knew I was coming. I'm gasping too. It's not often a game against the Milltown scruffs is attended without some form of pre-match gargle being consumed in some sort of quantity. Gillett clears his throat, and we make the introductions. We briefly tell him who we are, then Gillett introduces the club's Chief Executive, a mildly troubled looking, Rick Parry, and a long time business associate of the Gillett clan, Jim Skidmore. Jim, in blazer and chinos, is looking the most uncomfortable of the three by far. He looks like he belongs in boardrooms or on sunlit patios introducing senators to hedge fund presidents – not here facing four Scousers who smell of lager, all itching to tell his 'buddy' what a twat we think he is. I'm chomping at the bit for a sharpener from the Carlsberg fridge behind him and find myself not listening to the opening pleasantries. Alas, these introductions are as far as the formalities go, and we're not offered any refreshments.

Just as well really.

"Jim's an old family friend and business partner... he's certainly not my bodyguard," laughs Gillett. I look across at Nicky and I know he's thinking "too fucking right he's not your bodyguard George." In fact, Paul Rice, on my left - who makes Luis Garcia look like Martin Skrtel - could easily chin him and he'd have to stand on the chair to do so. Despite the anger we all feel, we are also upset that it's come to this. Never mind Jim not wanting to be here; we don't want to be here. I don't want to be here. What's become of just going to the match, and having a few pints and a laugh with your mates? Since last winter it's become a succession of protests and interviews, press releases and condemnations. We were never the type of supporters who'd call for the manager's head or chant 'Sack the board' after every cup defeat, even in the dark days of Souness' reign. Had we been Geordies then the FA Cup defeat by Bristol City in 1994 would have seen Anfield laid waste by suicide bombers. But no. There were mutterings and dissent, but the very real anger was suppressed. Washing our dirty linen in public was not 'The Liverpool Way'. It was unseemly and beneath us, but more importantly we'd be attacking our own. However, in May 2007, the Athens ticket fiasco – where Rick Parry had 'refused to play the numbers game' and account for where tickets for the final had gone - enraged many Liverpool supporters. It was a terrible time. Here we were, the 'Famous Kopites', three weeks before a European Cup final, marching on Anfield calling for the Chief Executive's head on a platter. Sponsorship and hospitality, it seems, had eaten its way into LFC so ravenously that the club were obliged to supply countless corporates with cup final tickets (literally – the club couldn't or wouldn't count them!) This in turn had deprived many season ticket holders of the opportunity to go the final. And you had to feel sorry for Parry; UEFA's ridiculous insistence on playing the greatest club game in the world in stadiums that were too small in the first place, then reducing the number of tickets available to the competing sides in order to cater for the "UEFA family" and their advertising hoardings was at the nub of the problem. But Rick Parry took the wrong route in dealing with the issue. Rather than engage with the support and explain the mechanics of divvying up a minuscule allocation he battened down the hatches and sidelined the fans. From that moment forward he was painted as 'the enemy' as the hardcore home-and-away mob marched on Anfield for the first time ever to demand that Rick play "The Numbers Game." And when it became apparent that Gillett and Hicks (Who had been cheered to the rafters at the final, and lauded in the streets prior to the semi-final against Chelsea at Anfield) had been plotting to get rid of the sainted Benitez and hire Jurgen Klinsmann in his place, the marching season began in earnest. We sent round an email to every single Liverpool fan we knew entitled S.O.S – Save Our Soul – beseeching them to mob up and march in favour of Rafa before the Champions League game against Porto that the Americans seemed to hope would be his last. And almost a year down the line, here we are ready to go again – this latest march the biggest we've planned to date. You want to defuse our ire, George? Here's the floor…

Paul Rice opens the discussion in a calm and blunt manner. He lists one by one the promises made and subsequently broken by the owners. He goes on to demonstrate how the club has nose-dived from a position of comparative stability to this current seething madhouse of financial chaos and divisive acrimony. Gillett listens attentively with an apparently sympathetic air as Paul proclaims them unfit to own the club. He blasts their inability to give the club direction or leadership, and criticises the levels of debt now sitting directly on the club itself, showing how this financial incompetence has lead to compromise in the transfer market and a halt on the new stadium build. He's equally scathing of their failure to respect the position of the manager. Finally, he makes the point we've all got things we'd rather be doing than remind George Gillett of his promises and his duties as co-owner of this magical, celebrated football club. Instead of looking forward to the biggest league game of the season, all we'd been talking about was the mess the Americans had got us into. Football hadn't even entered my head this last 48 hours – and I resented that – but we just had to use this opportunity to let Gillett know what we felt.

"We've never needed to demonstrate and protest," I say. "Because in the past we all seemed to be pulling in the same direction: the players, manager, staff and fans – all together. But that's been ripped to bits by you fellas..."

"We've crossed the Rubicon... a very big step for all of us." Furmo adds. "We've never done this before – but that old relationship has been absolutely betrayed."

Gillett looks surprised – or rather he looks like he's *trying* to look surprised.

"That old relationship was us all pulling in the same direction.," I explain, "Us behind the club. Totally. The flip side of that coin was that the club was always behind us: always there for us. We were never just turnstile fodder. We were never just there to be exploited. But that's changed and there's a feeling now that the club doesn't care who the fans are as long as they've got money. Take this as an example..."

I get out my fancard.

"You are aware of what one of these is?"

George shakes his head, "No."

"This is my season ticket. But nearly all fans have one – they're called fancards – our membership cards for the club."

Furmo chips in, "These new cards replace a card we got 3 years ago that we were told was 'a card for life'. They were £3 back then. Now supporters are being asked to cough up £29 per year for one, just to have the chance of applying for a ticket for the game. No guarantees – just the privilege of being able to apply for a match ticket."

George looks like he's about to shake his head in disbelief – it can't sound like much of a deal even to him, I'm sure.

"No other benefits?" he asks. Perhaps he's been briefed. Maybe he's ready to rattle off a lengthy list of wonders that the 'Belong' scheme provides - added virility, free car insurance and the like...

"No. None." I tell him. There might well be, I haven't actually read the leaflet that came with the invitation. I tossed it aside in disgust at the inference that you could BELONG to the club, made to feel part of it and given priority for match tickets, simply if you were willing to part with £30 a season. What about those who really and truly already belong? What about the generations of kids and relatives of lifelong Reds who've already been so disenfranchised by the system that they meekly accept they'll never get to see the team play? What about those fans who make the effort to support the team whenever and how ever they can? Who sit with the phone in their hand waiting for someone to answer, a computerised voice telling them they're number 39 in the queue and their business (their *business*! Fuck off.) is important to the club and to please hold on while an imaginary telephonist flicks the v's and plays computer games on their mobile? What about the fans who scramble around the websites and ever-diminishing sources tickets on a weekly basis? Those who have been attending games home and away games for years but won't pay this... this ransom? Where do they belong?

"There are no other benefits," I add.

"Hang on," remembers Furmo. Then he adds, straight faced, "You also get a pencil case."

It seems to us that not only are we being milked these days but also paying for the privilege of being milked. 'Adding insult to injury' it's called. What's more galling is that the cream from our milk is then going to pay off the debt heaped upon the club by Gillett and Hicks. We are, in effect, paying for them to own our club. Furmo then accuses the Americans of being "leveraged buy-out merchants." George pulls a face at this – we've got to him at last. Call him a two-faced, lying bastard and he'll make eyes at you, but call him a Leverage Lout and he's all prickly and wounded. We produce a print-out, quoting, one of Tom Hick's many astonishingly dumb statements, this one likening the acquisition of Liverpool to his acquisition of Weetabix.

"When I was in the leveraged buy-out business we bought Weetabix and we leveraged it up to make our return. You could say that anyone who was eating Weetabix was paying for our purchase of Weetabix. It was just business. It is the same for Liverpool."

Even now my stomach turns at those words. It also turns at the thought of Weetabix, these days.

Gillett says nothing and continues to scribble his notes. Furmo goes on,

"But the debt you put on the club, means we are (a) in debt to the tune of hundreds of millions (b) we have no new stadium, and (c) we can't compete at the top end of the transfer market." Gillett's still examining his own notes and doesn't say anything. "And," adds Furmo, "we now have £30m interest charges which have to be met.."

Suddenly George bolts upright. He's doing his surprised thing again.

"*How* much?"

"Thirty million – in interest."

Gillett feigns a combination of shock and incredulity. I say 'feigns' as this figure has been openly accepted by the media for months and has been confirmed by independent accountants familiar with Liverpool's business model. Is he hoping we'll go out of here, flushed with this dramatic inside info, and tell people "Hey, we've got it all wrong, put the pitchforks away – it's only £25 million!"

"Who's telling you this?" He asks.

I'm tempted to blurt out, "Don't you read the papers, Dickhead? Everyone!" He won't be drawn on the figure but tells us its nothing like that amount. Well what's it 'like' then? Is it, like, nearer £25m? £20m? Gillett takes a metaphoric step back.

"Look guys, I'm not going to change your minds today. You guys leave here today as pissed as you wanna be at me and Tom – that's up to you. But at least I'd like you to be pissed off at us with THE FACTS!"

Furmo takes the opportunity to draw him.

"Fire away then – how much debt *have* you thrown on the club?"

After the metaphoric step back, Gillett now jogs down the corridor, as far away from the subject of debt repayments as he can.

"Ok, guys, lets see what we got...," and he examines his notes and lists the points we've brought up, the promises broken, so far. "Err... We're not fit to run the club...60 days promise, spade in the ground... No debt on Liverpool FC... dishonoured the club even after our claims to honour 'The Liverpool Way'...." and so it went on for a couple of minutes. Finally Gillett reaches the end of the list and says:

"Is that it? The list?"

"Yes."

We sit and wait for his response. He tries look us all in the eye simultaneously, and then begins...

"As far as the debt and the interest... we are in decent shape. Compared to the other top clubs."

We try and get him to elaborate, but he won't give specifics.

"When we took over, we did say no debt on the club, and for a year it was okay. But then came the credit crunch.." He pauses as if to underline the point. Then says very deliberately, and slowly, opening his eyes wider as he gets to his climax:

"The world financial crisis is here. It...is... real!"

He's warming up now and goes, for the first time, into some detail.

"The banks, they reneged on commitments. And we are looking at lawsuits. But the notion that we lied or reneged doesn't stand the test.... This club was debt-free – it had some transfer debt and that was it – and it was like that for the longest time after the transfer." (I'm guessing he means transfer of ownership as opposed to players here). He pauses again.

"It... was... the... banks; the institutions. They changed the deal... and there IS debt today. But the debt, relative to the operating profit, is lower than any major club except Chelsea... including AC Milan and AS Roma..."

"Why them two?" I think. "Why not Man Utd or Arsenal?" He then adds strangely, "In fact, I just saw the books on AS Roma...," as if this would lend credulity to his claims. But all it does it make me ponder why he's looking at their books and not just concentrating on ours.

"This club – is in very, very healthy shape," he says, apparently drawing the issue to a close. "The fact that we lied is inaccurate. The fact that the market changed is 100% accurate. When I read that we had lied... of all the things you can accuse me of, well that broke my heart the most. It was external circumstances that I had no control over."

I have to admit that at this point I'm almost feeling sorry for him. Almost. But not quite.

"Everyone uses debt in combination with equity as a way to further the use of their own money" he offers. Then after a pause, "Sure, DIC is fabulous... but the intermediary is the most dangerous human being that I have met."

"Amanda Staveley?" asks Furmo. George smiles.

"I didn't say that."

We've already been told by a good, reliable source that Gillett believes the SOS are being seduced by Staveley on behalf of the DIC bid. He's way off the mark, but continues to get his digs in at the DIC bid.

"If you look at the documents – which I have – DIC's original plan had all sorts of debt in it. It had debt for the purchase of the club; debt for the new stadium; and it had a return rate that would have required a number of 'operational changes' substantially in excess of what has occurred under our tutelage. Even this paragon of wealth called DIC – that was their plan."

Then there's a sudden change of tack.

"We spent a couple of hours yesterday with Rafa." He calls him "Roffa" in such an amiable way it feels like he's about to add, "Yes, my old buddy, Rafa." But he doesn't. He just wants us to know he cares about the team, not just the business. George reminds us of the money the club has spent in the last few years, and then bizarrely adds.

"If your problem is with the quality of the players... then please – Sweet Jesus! – don't blame me for that!"

George tells us as far as transfers go, "All major clubs – the top four – have restrictions in their debt agreements that prevent them from spending money... and you guys won't let this process go through!"

He finishes quite forcibly.

"We are winning the battle!" he declares.

"How much did we spend this year?" Furmo asks him.

"21.7 million," George replies, remarkably accurately.

Parry then speaks for almost the first time, adding "Plus Mascherano. Plus Skrtel." He goes on to outline how over the last 5 years we've outspent almost everyone in the league, except the obvious club – Chelsea.

"And whereas Man U might spend nothing one year and then splash out £30 million on one player the next... we, for whatever reason, spread it more thinly."

I find that last caveat ("for whatever reason") unnecessary and it makes me uncomfortable. I feel he's playing this card for Gillett in his battle with Rafa. Parry closes with, "Don't blame George for that (who we spend money on). That hasn't been his decision."

So, the players we buy or don't buy is purely down to Rafa then? That has to be the point of this latest diversion surely, as we haven't come in here to quiz the owner on the players. We haven't even alluded to the players. Gillett is, obviously, making sure we get his version of events.

"What about Gareth Barry?" I ask.

"What about it?" George replies.

"Well it was all leaked to the press in May. Then it's been all over the papers, all summer. And then it all fell apart – it's a fiasco."

"The club looked like it didn't know it's arse from its elbow," adds Furmo.

"Okay," says George, warming to the task, "Let's talk about Barry."

He seems more than keen to let us in on the whole affair. Though it's just one player, the on-off-on-off transfer perfectly illuminates the dysfunctionality within the club and we're all curious to know more.

"This family," I assume he's talking about the Gillett family business here, "has a budget. A strategy. A plan. Now for 18 months we have asked *'the football side of this operation'* for a plan. To this day we don't have it. There's no plan. We have become a 'transactional club' – whoever's the latest and greatest."

Why he doesn't just name names and get done with it is beyond me. We all know who he means. I'm sure even Jim who's day-dreaming, no doubt, about giving Governor Sarah Palin one, knows who George is alluding to.

"You see," George goes on in a similarly cryptic manner, "certain people figured out how to operate within the disagreements within the club."

He's keen that we get his inferences, and pushes home the point.

"You understand what I just said, Peter?"

Furmo nods. Having apparently made his point and satisfied us with his cunning innuendo, Gillett then returns to the Barry issue with renewed gusto.

"We were very supportive of (the) Gareth Barry (signing) when this started even though it wasn't part of any plan. Now I'm not naive enough to know what this football club needs... but *a fifth midfielder?*" A pause for emphasis. *"Another holding midfielder?"*

I'm beginning to feel a bit confused now. He admits to not knowing what the team needs, and yet almost spits out in disgust at the idea of another holding midfielder? As if someone had suggested playing Osama Bin Laden in front of the back four.

"And the reason – no, *the excuse* – we get is that *'we can play him wide'*, which is not a position he either likes or is very good at."

Frigging hell! This is a footballing masterclass here. I'm all ears. I look at Nicky. His eyes had narrowed in concentration, his brow furrowed. He's either trying to visualise Barry skipping down the left wing, or he's about to launch a deadly attack on all three of them.

"And then to have the price almost triple at a time where we'd already purchased Keane...well, it didn't work."

He and Parry go on to describe how the valuations of Barry and Alonso fluctuated wildly over the summer, basically killing the deal stone dead in their eyes. They had an initial agreement in place with Juventus to pay £16 million for Alonso. Rafa told them Barry was going to cost £12 million – we were going to make money on the transaction, the way it all sounded back then. But bit by bit Juventus cooled on Alonso (how they must hug themselves at the inspired signing of Paulsen, instead) while Martin O'Neill hiked Barry's value up to £18 million in retaliation to what he saw as Liverpool's bullying methods.

"When the Barry deal got ridiculous we said to Rafa, 'Your own scouts say Shaun Wright Phillips is brilliant.'. We encouraged him to take Riera on the left and Wright Phillips on the right." He pauses again as though he's expecting us to be nodding in agreement. We remain silent.

"Let's fix this frigging club once and for all… we want to force people to play us wide!" he announces with a grimace of determination.

This couldn't get any better I'm thinking, it's like listening to Arrigo Sacchi playing Championship Manager on the Xbox.

"I mean…," Gillett enthuses, "… two goals in his first three matches!"

With that he sits back, widening his eyes as if to emphasise just how quickly he's picked up this football malarkey. I'm impressed. I mean, Rafa, what the fuck are you playing at? Why didn't you sign Wright-Phillips? With that scoring record he could… Whisper it quietly but he could yet be the new Nigel Clough!

The meeting is beginning to wind down now, we've been here an hour, and George checks his list and returns to a point Ricey made about leadership and direction from the top; about how in the vacuum created by the absence of a controlling voice, press conjecture had run wild. What's more, in completely untypical fashion, the Gareth Barry fiasco was all conducted out in the open, in the pages of the press. Rumours had been allowed to flourish with little or no counter PR from the club. We'd become tabloid heaven. A joke.

"You asked: 'Why no PR? No statements?' That's because this family is highly respectful of The Liverpool Way. We wouldn't conduct business like that." Again, another pause to build up to a point he wants to get across clearly,

"*We* never leaked any of this to the press…." He says this in a manner that leaves us in no doubt that he's implying that the leaks came from *'the football side of this operation',* and finishes with, "You guys gotta hear – we're not the ones leaking information. We're not the ones causing the vast majority of the embarrassment."

That said, the meeting quickly comes to a close. We shake hands and thank him for his time. The time for the protest march is drawing close and we have to get back to the Supporters Club as quickly as possible. Although they'd tried to delay the march until we could report back about the meeting, the sheer weight of numbers and the desire to *do* something means the S.O.S organisers can't keep it back much longer. Like Canute holding back the tide they'd tried to contain it, but in the end had to let the thousands stream past, over the Village Green to the Cabbage Hall pub and then up towards Anfield. I've just reached the petrol station near Flagpole corner of The Kop, when I first spot – and hear - them. Looking down the length of Walton Breck Road I can see the melee - a sea of people, flags and banners. Brought up in a city with a boisterous and active marching tradition (both St Patrick's Day and the Orange Lodge) it sends a thrill through me. All that's missing is the echoing BOOM! BOOM! BOOM! of the drums. However, this march has its own soundtrack. Alan Kayll and Jay McKenna are working the crowd from the front, sharing megaphone duties and whipping up the atmosphere:

> "They don't care about Rafa,
> They don't care about fans.
> Liverpool football club
> Is in the wrong hands"
> "Get out of our club! Get out of our Clu-uuu-ub!!!
> You lying bastards!
> Get out of our club!"

Alan could be on the picket line at Orgreave, or outside the shipyards at Gdansk, such is the passion etched into his face:

> "What do we want"
> YANKS OUT!
> When do we want it?
> NOW!"

As if to underline the parallels Sammo's new banner, a massive **Scouse Solidarnosc** written in the same iconic lettering brings up the rear of the marching legions, half a mile down the road.

At the margins, all along the pavement as the march passes, stand tourists, day-trippers and other bemused family groups. They are taking photos and clapping though it's clear they don't know what's going on. They're indicative of a huge swathe who've come to Anfield today (and most weeks) to spectate, rather than support. They are as emotionally impassive out here on the streets as they will be inside the ground. I don't want to be uncharitable, everyone deserves a chance to find their feet and acclimatise to the way we do things here but you just know these bystanders will always be just that. To them, we are part of the day out – part of the entertainment. We encourage them to join in, to step off the pavement and take part. But they don't. I feel they don't really know what they're joining. There's lots of Liverpool flags and lots of noise and its something to do with the owners, but they have no real opinions either way about the situation, so they stand there in their Torres shirts and spectate.

It's like we're the cast and technicians on the set of a blockbuster: Jay and Alan are the choreographers, Gary Shaw's the set designer,. The rest of us are the Gaffers and Key Grips, Directors of Cinematography and Continuity Assistants. Whoever's marching next to Nico is the 'wrangler' or monkey handler (Please note that no Belgians were harmed in the making of this motion picture spectacle). The crowds along the pavement, well, they've paid their ticket money to come along gawp, gape, scream, shout and clap and toss popcorn down their throats, then go home and show all their friends footage on their camera phones of Stevie G taking a corner and some Scousers shouting about the owners being 'Cunts'.

Rogan Taylor and supporters from the ShareLiverpool group are marching down one flank as the raucous mass of protest passes me by, just outside The Sandon. He's been banished to the margins after attempting to steal pole position and march at the very front behind their 'ShareLiverpool' banner. Politely reminded that the march wasn't his to command, he seems to have sulked way to the edges, albeit still happy to be here. As they approach I catch his eye – well I'm standing on a garden wall taking photos – and he nods at me, but his face says he's thinking: "Who's that?" I've known him for almost 20 years, since the earliest days of the Football Supporters Association - but still have to re-introduce myself whenever we meet. I don't know who that says more about: him or me.

"Mackin! Yer dick! Stop taking photos like a bleeding tourist and get down here!"

It's Joynty and bloody hell, he's right! I jump down and barge into the proceedings. Just as well as they're all carrying cans and bottles. Giulio Canetti – one of the Union founders – clasps me on the shoulder and offers a swig from his hipflask; something mad, like Grappa or Tequila. It makes my eyes water. He laughs and says:

"Sammo's looking for you, he's at the back."

I look around hopelessly. There's thousands of faces.

"With the Solidarity flag." he explains.

I bob and weave my way to the rear where Sampson and John Buchanan are holding aloft the 'Scouse Solidarnosc' banner. Sampson offers me a can of lager and asks about the Gillett meeting:

"It was weird."

"How come?"

"Gillett – he's weird. He looks like an kindly old uncle and he's very, er, nice, if you know what I mean...," my voice trails away unsure of what to add, where to start.

"But?" Sampson prompts me.

"But he doesn't half talk a load of bollocks."

Sammo roars laughing.

"According to him we're in great financial shape, and he never lied – its all the bank's fault. The debt – he didn't want to do it. The banks made him." I hand the can back to Sampson, he takes a swig. "And whoever's leaking intimate details of transfers to the press – it's not him." I add.

"Got you," Sammo adds draining the can. "So let's make sure he knows, hey?"

"Yep," I say. Then in unison we both go – "And then let's fuck Man U."

The tail of the march at last turns past the corner at the petrol station and swings onto the main road running down the full length of The Kop. The noise is incredible. Stretched ahead of us are thousands of heads.

"What do we want"
YANKS OUT!
When do we want it?
NOW!"

I need to see what's going on and so weave my way back down to the front again. The main body is motionless. The flags are fluttering in the breeze, the chanting getting louder. We're within earshot of The Main Stand now. Maybe George Gillett can hear this. I suspect Ged Poynton certainly can judging by the stewards jogging round looking concerned.

"What do we want?"

YANKS OUT!"

"When do we wannit?"

"NOW!!!"

The police have been escorting us en route, and the march was supposed to disperse alongside The Albert pub, on the waste land in front of the Main Stand gates. The police are guiding the front of the march onto this open land. Just in case, however, the club are taking no chances and the gates to the car-park are blocked by two rows of stewards in orange hi-viz jackets. They're double checking tickets and no-one's getting past without a ticket for that part of the ground. A few hundred slip away from the march and head noisily towards the Main Stand, chanting. The police and stewards struggle to head them off. However, they eventually prevent the hardcore from getting close to the gates and after some noisy chanting everyone disperses to watch the game either inside the ground or in the pubs around Anfield.

'We Love You Liverpool!' is now being belted out with gusto by those queuing at the turnstiles and milling around The Kop forecourt, around The Shankly Statue and Paisley Gates. After all – this is what it's all about: this football club; this team and its manager – The Holy Trinity. Its also a great relief not be protesting, not be chanting against anyone and everyone involved with the club. As necessary and as important as it all is, it still hurts to do so. From now until the final whistle everyone is concentrated on supporting the team.

We've made our point – its been a huge success: the turnout exceeded all expectations, it's bound to get the media coverage that the issue warrants, and it seems to have wound everyone up for the game. Still buzzing from it all, a few of us gather outside the HJC shop to drain cans of lager and psych each other up for the 90 minutes ahead. This shouldn't really be necessary seeing as we're playing those horrible bastards from up the East Lancs Road. It's like saying you need the services of a fluffer before a steamy session with Holly Valance. However, with all the focus on the protest, the game hasn't had its normal week-long build up to heighten the sense of occasion: this clash of the 2 biggest teams in the country. Today is important too for purely footballing reasons. Dropping a couple of points at Villa, when we really should have won means that we can't afford to come out of today's game with nothing. Everyone - the players, Rafa and the fans – has to be up for it.

Inside, The Kop is bouncing. All the banners from the march are in here and down the front of The Kop, spread along the front, are the 'wavers' making The Kop the only 'continental' end in Britain – ironic given that the Kop is revered throughout Europe and has inspired so many foreign clubs to establish their own 'end'. Your 'Curva Sud' and your 'Pena' and so on are all modelled on the original… Anfield's Spion Kop. The players are on the pitch lined up for the benefit of Sky TV's cameras, going through a rigmarole that at one time would have been deemed over-the-top even for a World Cup Final. It won't be long before players come out on the backs of baby elephants or hover down from the sky on magic carpets. The PA system then sends the three words that never fail to thrill me, booming round the ground, "*When You Walk…*" and 35,000 scarves are suddenly hoisted aloft. I can see Julian Lane struggling manfully to keep his 'Liverpool – The Originals' waver aloft. Poor lad. He's been parading outside for over an hour with it, hollering and marching on the protest and here he is giving it loud and proud with that massive flag, flying it high, waving it lustily. Jules is a big lad, but he must be knackered now. As Sammy Lee was at pains to explain to Ricey and me, this season 'You'll Never Walk Alone' is being played just before kick-off rather than the traditional ten to three. I hated the idea of mucking with our traditions at first, but having seen it in action now I've got to say this new way works even better. Both teams are out on the pitch to witness it, rather than cocooned in their dressing rooms, and this will serve to intimidate the opposition as much as it inspires The Reds. The crowd will attack the song more forcefully too, seeing our opponents out there in front of them. Today it works beautifully and the anthem is given a roaring rendition. Try as they might – and they've tried, believe me – United will never have an anthem that comes close to being as famous, as rousing and as well-loved as this. They can wheel out their end-of-pier crooners to belt out that laughable 'United Road' (sorry, but even the mention of that has poleaxed me with laughter. United Road – hahahahahahahah! That's just… *shite*!) – but they'll never have a YNWA. That, coupled with the worldwide renown of The Kop is a source of great envy for them.

The early omens aren't promising: both Gerard and Torres are out. The attack is led by the less than promising trio of Robbie Keane, Dirk Kuyt and Albert Riera, none of whom have looked 'up to it' so far this season. Still, we've dug in before and got great results with top players missing. All we have to do is keep it tight early on, don't concede, and play ourselves into the game, building confidence as we go.

The game gets off to a cracking start, both sides approaching it like the derby game it really is. We survive an early scare when Skrtel blocks an effort from the lank-haired Berbatov... handball? Who cares! What does Berbatov wash his hair in? Lard?

"It's about time we had some luck against these when it comes to penalties." says Jegs. "We NEVER get them and these are just nailed-on to get a really fucking spawny one..."

"Last season they would have been given that.." adds Lou Lou. For her sins the poor girl's seat is right in front of ours. She's next to Tommy Keiner, Tommy the German, who's a wonderful source of amusement for Jegs and I and, well, virtually everyone else around. He has a knack of saying exactly the wrong thing at the wrong time – always. Without fail. Tommy's about 6 foot 3 and built like a *powerhaus*, yet his face is as smooth as a baby's bum. He doesn't look like he shaves and Sammo regularly nudges me during slower passages of play and mutters.

"Tommy. Bird?"

It's an absurd, surreal and frankly rather distasteful thought, the idea of our very own Scouser Tommy actually being a lass, but so daft and always delivered at such a time that you can't help crying with mirth.

"It could be our day..." adds Tommy nodding. "The Gods are on our side...."

With that Berbatov wriggles free again and crosses low behind the defence to an unmarked, even more lank-haired, Tevez. Tevez may well resemble a warthog impersonating Richard III with his head on back-to-front – but he's not going to miss a chance like this. From 15 yards out plants it comfortably into the corner of the net. Right in front of us. Right in front of The Kop. Bastard! We like to say of Man U that they are 'forever in our shadow'; well today the early sun sits low in the sky and as the Anfield Rd end faces south, most the away following have their hands up shielding their eyes. Most of them can't see a bloody thing. Good. The majority of them won't have seen the goal they're celebrating. Its only a crumb of comfort but it's the tiny things like this – these little victories – that prevent us from slitting our wrists. As the Mancs go beserk down their end, all we can do is hope a load get lashed out by the stewards, or maybe slip off their platform shoes and do themselves some injury. All around me the goal is greeted the same.

"Bastard!"

We're looking at one another – here we go again. Another false dawn.

But within a few seconds there's a rumbling from behind and someone roars "Come On!!!!" It's taken up and fists are shaken as the chant booms out: LIV-ER-POOL! LIV-ER-POOL! It's at times like this I'm known to say: "It'd rather they go in front 3 minutes from the start, than 3 minutes from the end.." So I say it now, but no-ones listening. Everyone is punching the air and screaming their support for the team. All that is except Dodd who's taken advantage of the hullabaloo to drop to his knees and smoke a fag ('for his nerves'). He's looking up at me, grinning. It's being naughty like this that compensates for the thrills he's lost in football; namely running round the Road End as a youth, punching people.

Liverpool hit back, and Kuyt goes close twice. But he really should have gone closer.

"Torres would have buried that.," says someone stating the bleeding obvious just behind me. I bite my lip. Maybe I'm just upset I never said it. Kuyt is supposed to be a centre forward and he scored, oooh, about a thousand goals in Holland but has never looked like a natural striker here, always needing two touches before getting a shot in. As Gary Shaw's always reminding me: "His first touch is that bad that his second touch is always a tackle.." I turn to look back up half a dozen rows to where Gary's standing shaking his head. I catch his eye, nod to concur, and then switch quickly back to the play in time to see Riera working his way into the box only to be brought down. We scream as one:

"PENALTY!"

Howard Webb ignores the appeals, aware – no doubt – of not seeing Skrtel's earlier handball.

"You twat Webb!" I angrily shout.

"Told you!" shouts Dodd, "We never get a penalty against these!"

"No-one does. When did they last concede a penalty?" asks even-tempered, reasonable and well informed Brian Reade. "1906 wasn't it?"

It looks like they've done what they always do here: ridden their luck and taken their only chance. Then just when it seems our counter offensive might just be running out of steam, Ferguson's inability to spot a decent goalkeeper is exposed again. A speculative cross-cum-shot from Alonso on the right is fired into the Mancs' penalty area. The strangely orange Wes Brown moves to cut it out, just ahead of Albert Riera, who's lurking at the far post with all the menace of my mum waiting for a bus. Brown should have no problem hoofing this clear until Van Der Sar dives foward and attempts to punch the cross clear.

His rapidly approaching presence causes Brown to falter and Van Der Sar succeeds only in palming the ball against Brown's legs. It rebounds and bounces, far too slowly for my bloody nerves, into the unguarded net. Of course, from up here, 200 yards away its difficult to see exactly what's happened, but no-one gives a fuck. Jegs just goes.

"YISSSSSSS!!!!" and bear hugs me. All around 306 people are splayed over the back of seats, demented, delirious faces grinning up at me. Sammo has somehow got his feet in Row 57 and his head in Row 54, twisted round like Janus Stark as half a dozen of them piley on in a mass, delirious group hug.

We re-group, act as though that didn't just happen and exchange curt, formal, manly handshakes.

"Goal," says Sammo.

"Hurrah!" I reply.

"Top hole!" says Jegs.

And the truth is the goal was as jammy as fuck – but we'll take it all the same. It's about time we had some luck against this shower.

Louise is all ruddy cheeked and her hair is all over the place as she's been in the midst of some joyous hugging, hair-tousling and buttock squeezing celebrations. There's still 20 minutes left of the first half but she's already collecting the orders for half-time bevvies. We're all dropping pound coins into her cupped hands and by the time she's made it to the end of the row she's mouthing to herself. "Fourteen Carlsbergs and a Coke." Louise is extremely keen for a sharpener. She's been in town since 9 this morning with Gary Shaw and Paul Jones, who in true Wine Club traditions went straight on the Vin Rouge in The Welkin. They've had 4 bottles between the 3 of them in an hour. As pre-match appetisers go, that takes some beating. No wonder she needs something to freshen her palate; a Brillo pad maybe?

The half-time whistle goes and is greeted with a mixture of relief that the game hasn't followed its usual pattern, and appreciation for the way we've fought our way back into things. Instead of a quarter hour of recriminations and 'Windows' preaching his 'Rafa's-worse-than-Roy-Evans-well-at-least-as-bad-as-Houllier' mantra, I can actually look forward to enjoying my half-time beer. When we get to the concourse Lou Lou is standing guard over a dozen or so bottles and for two minutes at least she is the most popular person on The Kop. We stand around, smiling, some are still buzzing from the march, some buzzing from several early morning beers: and everyone is buzzing from the goal. It is always nice to score against that lot. It's time to dispense wisdom and observation and dissect the morning so far. I'm getting quizzed on the meeting with Gillett. Word has got round very quickly, but I have to remain vague as we've promised to brief our members first. Most of the chatter, though, is of when Benitez will unleash Gerrard and Torres on the Mancs.

"They're not that good," says the sage and mentor Tommy Keiner. "I haven't seen that Ronaldo touch the ball once."

Joynty, who has a PhD in sarcasm, cuts him a sideways glance.

"He's not playing, Tommy man la," explains John Maguire. He of the Scouse accent so thick you could stand lamp-posts up in it.

Tommy looks at Mags, says nothing, and downs some beer.

"Torres would kill Vidic here," Joynty announces, "He's a carthorse."

"He's not fit though, is he?" Gary Shaw says. " Or he'd start him."

These two are never far apart at the match: one tall and slim, the other... er... not so tall and not so slim. They are the Laurel and Hardy of Block 306.

"Then why's he on the bench?"

Gary thinks for a moment.

"So, only to be risked if we get desperate?" he offers.

"Is right!" declares Joynty

They clink their plastic bottles together in agreement.

"He's more likely to risk Gerrard though. He's had more time to recover..."

He has a point. Rafa has vowed that to close the gap we have to start beating the top three. Maybe if we're looking like coming away with nothing, again, he'll risk either or both of them and then rest them against Stoke, against whom Gary and Joynty could probably score. Gives them a fortnight to get fit for the derby. But I hate all this second-guessing. If a player's fit – he should start. If he's not then leave him at home. But what I hate more are international games, especially those played right at the start of the bloody season. We get injuries to our two most influential players and risk not getting off to a flier. Because as sure as anything we'll hit that mid-season, winter bad patch and we need to be up there challenging, to have any chance come May.

"He'll go for a draw now, as usual." proclaims Joynty to whoever's within earshot. The second half is just underway and people are trotting back upstairs to their seats. A few hardened socialisers are still here nursing their beers.

"Who? Rafa? Course he will." barks Windows.

"Noooo... arl Bacon Face. He's done that for the last few seasons now. He nearly cacked himself with surprise when Tevez spawned that one last year. And that useless twat O'Shea the year before…"

I seem to be a lot more sober than most of this lot, as indeed does Jegsy. He's been up late cabbying on the Wirral, ferrying drug dealers and clubbers the length and breadth of the peninsular. He's very sensibly had a lie-in which means he'll last the pace better than most. We leave Joynty with Windows and whoever's daft enough to be still listening to him and return to our seats.

Joynty was right. As the second half progresses its all Liverpool. United seem content to pack themselves behind the ball and try and stifle us. Our lack of width seems apparent to old Bacon Face too - he's making us play it long and he's managing to concentrate our attacks where they are best disposed to deal with them: the aerial strength of the camel-faced Ferdinand and psychotic looking Vidic. To digress for a moment – was Rio Ferdinand's top lip designed with dissent in mind? All those photos of him putting the Respect Campaign into practice as he hunts down the referee, snarling and vituperative, and all you can see is that weird, weird, freaky top lip of his curled back on itself, ready to spit out the Wigga invective. Anyway. Ferdinand. Funny looking cunt.

We keep coming at them and it actually does feel like we're going to break them down. Keane misses another good chance and almost immediately, and to a thunderous welcome Gerrard comes on. There's 20 minutes left, and it's all Liverpool.

"ATTACK! ATTACK! ATTACK-ATTACK-ATTACK!!!" screams The Kop.

Ten minutes to go. We've pulverised Man U second half. It's looking like a draw now, but come what may this is a moral victory. United will be glad to get off the pitch, get their white slacks on and get off down Brasingamens for a couple spritzers and a lurch around the dance floor. But what's this? An attack down the right seems to have fizzled out and the Manc defenders try to shield the ball from the advancing Mascherano and usher it out for a goal-kick. Mascherano, as ever, is playing like a man possessed. With Gerrard now alongside him in the midfield, he's thrown caution to the wind and is chasing down every lost cause, harrying the shaky Wes Brown and making life difficult all round. His persistence pays off as he slides in behind Brown, scoops the ball back before it crosses the line, and screws the ball back to the edge of the 18 yard box. Kuyt flashes it across the box towards the on-rushing Babel and it seems an eternity from his connecting with the ball and it arrowing into the roof of the net. The truth is, as MOTD later shows, it didn't "arrow" anywhere. It scuffed! It bobbled. It both looped and loped into the roof of the net, but do any of us deranged, slobbering loons give a shite? Do we fucking fuck! Jegsy launches himself on top of me sending me sprawling across the seats, screaming in my ear:

"YEEEEEEEEESSSSSSSSSSS!!! YES!! YES!! YES!!"

It is, quite simply, that only word that'll do in these giddy circumstances, and the only one needed, too. All I can see is legs and arses and general mayhem all around. Someone reaches down and helps drag us both to our feet, where we continue to slap backs and hug people as if we were on the pitch ourselves. But as Kopites, affecting what happens on the field of play is what we're supposed to do, so it's only right we should celebrate like players, too. At the end of the row poor Matty Mwanje is standing in the aisle looking dazed, holding his hand over his face like he's just remembered he's left the iron on. There is blood everywhere, his nose almost broken by a stray elbow in the mad celebrations. But he doesn't care and after disappearing for a few minutes to mop up the blood, he reappears to join in the taunting of our fiercest rivals. Bill Shankly once said after a memorable derby game that had he been dead he would have instructed his coffin be taken to the game, propped up and had a hole cut in the lid, so I'm sure Matty isn't going to let a small broken bone get in the way of a few choruses of 'Always Look on the Bright Side of Life'. The vocal support has been brilliant today so I suppose we've done our bit and deserve to take some of the acclaim for what surely must be a victory now. Within minutes the entire Kop is bouncing to 'Ring of Fire'. I look around and see most of Anfield joining in, scarves being twirled in the air. The Mancs down the other end, however, are motionless and quiet and have been quiet for the last hour. Its an intensely satisfying sight. They can see that they haven't really turned up today – a fact compounded when Vidic gets sent off right at the end to much delight from a hooting, baying Kop.

It hasn't been a classic, but – without Torres and Gerrard, remember – we've got stuck in and recovered from an early set-back; something that's been beyond us in recent years against the Mancs. The final whistle is greeted with a lusty roar of satisfaction, a clearing of throats in anticipation of the liquid celebrations to come. All the way down the switchback stairs at the back of The Kop the air is filled with an excited chatter, laughter and occasional bursts of singing. We regroup outside the HJC shop, checking what everybody's plans are though suspecting that everyone is planning to head back down the

Supporters Club where we can stand outside in the sunshine and enjoy the rest of this glorious afternoon.

On the walk down towards the Supporters Club, we pass The Flatiron pub which stradles the junction of Walton Breck Road and Anfield Road. Outside are about 50 or so of the younger Urchins. They look ready to move at a second's notice and are probably waiting to hear that United have been let out of the ground, whereupon they'll trot up to the Arkles to wave them off and wish them a safe journey back to Devon, Sussex and South Wales.

Back at the Club I have to hunt down the bag I left here first thing this morning. In it is a bottle of Rioja, a wine glass and a corkscrew. I go back out onto the 'village green' to be met with envious stares from Joynty and Gary Shaw who hand me the cold bottle of Becks they've just got me.

"You've got wine!" Gary blurts out accusingly. "I want wine."

Him and Joynty turn as one, and march across the green to the local shops. Returning with several bottles of 'wine', costing from £1.99 (Joynty's) to £3.50 (Gary's). Gary's a wine buff and obvioulsy won't touch the plonk that Joynty's screwing his face up at, as he take's his first mouthful.

"How can you drink... *that*?" Gary snaps, "... its got a donkey on the label."

"Lovely!" declares Joynty, his teeth turning pink. He grins at me.

"You seen Teasdale? Kip of him. Looks like he's going Speed Dating." I just smile at him and go, "Oh aye, yeah!" but even now I have no idea what this might actually mean. Tony Teasdale's a mate who lives in London and spends his days in a Nathan Barley world of Hoxton arts and media types, as he works (if you can call it work) for several trendy men's magazines. I mean, he drinks in Soho House for chrissake! When I find Tony he's looking smartly turned out as usual, wearing flannels and a bespoke shirt, but Speed Dating? I don't get it. Maybe just a touch of the "JFK at the beach" or a "weekend on Long Island" look about him – or maybe it's just that Tony isn't wearing Adidas trainees that's caused all this mirth at his attire.

"You know its days like this, results like this, that make you pine for the Footy Echo." he laments. "It'd be about now that the guys would be coming round the pubs with them and you could look at the result again in black and white..."

"Black and pink," I correct him.

"... in black and pink. Always used to get a thrill from seeing the league table in the Footy Echo when we went top."

With the Supporter's Club prices being so low, people are hurriedly getting rounds in before we move anywhere more expensive – i.e Town – a cheap ploy, and ultimately self-defeating as everyone's getting so pissed that they'll soon forget who's bought what. I've soon got half a bottle of wine, and 4 or 5 bottles of Becks at my feet. It's getting a bit hot now for red wine now, so I give Paul Jones a glass and concentrate on the Becks. I need to pace myself, I mean it's barely 4 p.m. and her indoors isn't expecting me home until midnight. Gary, however, is merely topping himself up, and doing so rapidly. Within half an hour he is soaring, and we amuse watching a well-known and stunningly good-looking female Red called Rory doing drunken keepy-ups on the green, much to the approval of the merry throng.

We are joined by a journalist from a national broadsheet, a Liverpool fan, who's enjoying a pint in the sunshine before heading back to both his laptop and his deadline for Monday's edition. I suspect he might also be fishing for a hint of what went on between the union and George Gillett. However, he's getting nothing sensible out of anybody, least of all Gary.

"Arhhhh! You're him. That fella." slurs Gary, grabbing 'hims' hand and shaking it furiously.

"You're good you are," he continues.

Him is smiling to begin with but as Gary's arm-pumping handshaking shows no sign of letting up after 2 or 3 minutes, the smile slips into a worried grimace. Gary , meanwhile, is manically grinning – it's like Jack Nicholson's face through the bathroom door in The Shining - and making noises that almost sound like words, but not quite. He then breaks off and leaps into a boxing stance delivering a flurry of right-arm jabs at 'Him's' chin before tucking his elbows in and ducking, avoiding an imaginary counter assault before dramatically unleashing a second series of jabs at an immobile 'him' who's is now standing motionless, smiling faintly. He's either incredibly cool or absolutely terrified. Gary dances around on his toes delivering swift one-twos before losing his balance and staggering to one side.

"Whoopsy daisy, yer daft bastard!" says Joynty catching him.

"Here, drink this" he adds, handing Gary another Stella. This is tantamount to giving moonshine to the Indians on the reservation, and I suspect Joynty is conducting a serious social experiment here. Gary turned up this morning looking smart, well groomed: urbane and intelligent. He's barely coherent now and beginning to slobber. In fact, if we had an Oxford English Dictionary to hand we could look up the word 'Shitfaced' to read "See: Gary

Shaw." He's soon collapsed across a concrete bench on the 'green', like a puppet whose strings have been cut.

'Him' has taken the opportunity to escape and hails a cab back to the sanity and the safety of the real world, that far off place that we, in the Land of Swallee, occasionally visit between football matches. Others too are beginning to slope away now, into town in dribs and drabs to continue the celebrations. Sammo is the master of the invisible slope. He's been doing it for years and years and years, yet we never see it coming: no 'goodbyes', no handshakes – he just vanishes, and today is no different. He's been the life and soul of The Party On The Green, approaching people he plainly doesn't know and engaging them in group hugs and singalongs, poncing their spliffs and telling them lies so immense that they must actually be true – but then he's gone. Not even a little puff of green smoke or anything, just – gone. Teasdale's next. He gives us a jaunty 'Ta-ra la, se ya!' and heads off back to that there London town and a night-cap in The Ivy with AA Gill. Then there's Joynty and Jegsy mouthing destinations like 'Neds' and 'The Yankee' as they hail cabs. Gary somehow manages to rouse himself and actually say goodbye before turning to wobble off down Lower Breck Road. I assumed he was looking for a taxi but he continues walking, and walking... and walking the full 7 miles home to Woolton. Across fields and parks, over fences, through bushes (narrowly avoiding stepping on a couple, out dogging – as they do in genteel Woolton. "What shall we do this evening, Prudence?" "I don't know, Badger. Shall we go and bang the arse off some chubby rip in a dim-lit car-park?" "Excellent plan! Don the sex wellies!"). Gary stumbles off pavements and meanders down cul-de-sacs on estates that weren't built the last time he walked this way, and eventually falls asleep in Breck Park. It was a magnificent display of drunkeness, only pipped as highlight of the day by the result of the match.

Ah yes, the result. Well we finally did what we said we needed to start doing – beating the top 3 teams at home. This is important in its own right, as a statement of intent, but it's also made up for dropping points at Villa last week. We have to keep the momentum going now – and thumping Stoke next week will be the ideal way to prepare for the Goodison derby. Talking of which: any spares?

JM

Marseille (a)   1-2

Champions League Group Phase   Tue 16th Sept

There are few things in life that really, really annoy me: anyone who refers to the league as 'The Prem' is one; then there's that programme Jegs calls 'Britain's Got Dickheads' – that's another. I can't abide drivers who don't indicate on roundabouts – can get quite apopleptic about that. Also any programme with that albino numpty dwarf Patrick Kielty in – definitely cause for ire. As is 'Patrick Kielty'.

Oh, yes – and Ryanair. Ryanair badly, badly, badly do my head in.

In spite of all the added charges: (what can they 'tax' us for next? Seat-belt surcharge? Seat tax? ("Well, sir, we are encouraging passengers towards greater self-sufficiency, sir, and we **are** rewarding passengers who bring their own seats. Sir.") What else? Safety demonstration levy? Clothing tax? ("No fee for naked passengers"). But in spite of all their snidey add-ons, taxes and hidden charges, Ryanair's flight to Nimes was still the only reasonable way of getting to Marseille. So, drawing a deep breath (£3.50 extra), we had to bite the bullet (£5) and book on-line. After 15 minutes spent removing numerous surcharges for unrequested, and completely unwanted insurance, sports equipment, hold luggage, heavy coats, and actually physically checking in, we had relatively inexpensive flights at reasonable departure times. The flight itself was the usual hard-sell of scratch-cards, useless gifts and overpriced refreshments, all played out in a cabin plastered in so much advertising that it looked more like a tube train than a jet plane. The journey was made even more uncomfortable by the awful landing (the pilot made two approaches and pulled out before finally landing at the third attempt) to be greeted by a fire engine on the runway. There was an audible sigh of relief from all on board – including the cabin crew, one of whom dropped her rosary beads and vomited into a paper bag – as we came to a halt, and a lone voice cried, "Thank fuck for that!" I think it was the co-pilot.

"I don't care if we have to walk next time, we are not going with them." someone said as we queued in the cow-shed to show our passports.

We're to spend the night here in Nimes, and we have train tickets (£17 return!) to Marseilles at 10 in the morning. We've done the Nimes trip several times before – both for Marseille itself and Barcelona, so we know the score. Outside the airport there'll be the usual scramble for the one shuttle bus and four taxis. (Nimes airport makes Liverpool's JLA look like Heathrow). We make sure we're first out of departures and head straight for a cab, bag it, and advise the driver to scramble her HQ and get them to send out a flotilla of taxis. She nods, smiles – and does nothing. In the Irish pub later we hear tales of woe from Scousers who've waited over an hour for taxis to get them into town.

We check in at the Hotel La Baume on Rue Nationale. This hotel is superb. We'd stayed here last time and couldn't believe how great value it was. It's a typically French boutique hotel in a converted 17th Century townhouse. It's the kind of place that's keen to make it into photo-spreads in style magazines and colour supplements. Bare stone walls, cool recessed lighting, dark wood. Too good for us, its the type of romantic place you take a bit of strange to in order to impress her drawers off. So, I make sure that Jegs and Sammo are sharing and bag a nice double room, all of my own. Very cosy – just me and my snoring. Just as well really, as many a previous room-mate has shied away from co-habiting with myself after being exposed to the Mackin Thunder. APB, not a man to squander his pennies recklessly, has long since opted for single room soundproofing, and top warbler Luke Daly from Cork still bears the emotional scars after one particularly brutal night's noise-torture in this same hotel. He said it was like sharing a room with a horse – and he should know. I made sure he told that story next time he was holding court to LouLou and co: "Hear that, girls? Johnny Mac's like a horse in bed."

After a dinner of steak (possibly horse) and frites, wine, beer and pastis, we go for a wander looking for a local bar, seeking out some authentic Languedoc colour and atmosphere; perhaps a gentle game of boules whilst Jegs puffs on a Gitanes and plays the accordion. We come across a small square with a fountain and large crocodile statue.

"Is where Lacoste got the idea from, then?" asks Jegs. Sammo gives a potted history of Crocodile logo that at least half the Liverpool following will be wearing tomorrow night – based on the nickname given to tennis player Rene Lacoste. So the great crocodile of Nimes is, sadly, nothing to do with tennis gear.

"So what's this one then, John?" asks Jegs. "Go 'ead. You know things."

I raid the deepest recesses of my mind, puff myself up and let rip.

"It's the emblem of Caesar's legions of the Nile...they helped transform the place from a little hick market village into a cosmopolitan town."

"Oh aye, yeah. Fuck do you know that?"

I draw myself up again, suck my alegut in and wrinkle my forehead, ready to dazzle him with statistics. I pull out a pamphlet.

"It's all in this guidebook – free at the hotel reception."

Sammo cracks up. Jegs snatches the pamphlet.

"Well sod this. Get that guidebook out and find us a fucking Irish bar..."

This is news to us. Jegs, as a rule, wants to swerve Irish bars, Union Jack bars, anywhere where there'll be hordes of English shouting loudly and lighting their farts. Not that he's anti-English – far from it – but he is notoriously, how-you-say... "frugal," and Irish bars are a licence to tear you a new arsehole and sit back chortling as you cack Euros. But Jegs has heard on the grapevine that there's this one bar that'll be full of all the old faces and Road End loons. But when we find it, its quiet; no-one there we know. But then it's no real surprise. With nothing much riding on this game, we'll take a fraction of the numbers we've brought to Marseille before. We decide that the bar'll have to do, and settle down for a few beers. At least Jegs can smoke without having to go outside so it's not a complete waste of time. We chat briefly to two lads who were on our flight, then decide to have an early one and head back about 1 am.

We get up early with plenty of time to make the train but not enough time to make breakfast in the hotel. It costs extra anyway, and fearing Ryanair-like prices we head straight out for a taxi and have a great breakfast instead at Nimes station – proper fresh juice where they just tip sacks of oranges into this Perspex pulping machine – mmmmmmmm! And hot, buttery croissants in the thick of a crowd of schoolgirls and office workers, all getting their priorities right with a fag and an espresso. The train to Marseilles is a pleasant enough journey through interesting scenery, the last ten miles or so being a coastal line with the still-blue Med below. We lay off the ale for the trip as we don't want to peak too early, plus we remember that the local rattler (the cheap train we're on) doesn't have a toilet. Well it does, but it smells like a dolphin's been dead in there for a fortnight.

"Did you know that Nimes is twinned with Preston." I say, breaking the silence, as we watch the countryside roll by.

Jegs looks up from yesterday's Liverpool Echo.

"How do you figure that out?" he says "... or is *that* in your guidebook too?"

"Sign outside the station."

"What? Preston station?"

"No, yer divvy! Nimes. When you were queueing for coffee, there was a sign on the wall."

"Why's Nimes twinned with Preston."

"Absolutely no idea. Its not like its an old Roman town like Colchester or York is it?"

We ramble on and discuss the possibility of Liverpool being twinned with Marseille. Both great old port cities with a rich mercantile and militant tradition. They both treat the capital city with a disdain bordering on pity for the unfortunate souls who have to live there. They're both a bit rough round the edges. They're both passionate and lively. And they both love their football. Our footy team is better, we concur, but they've got better seafood restaurants.

"I can live with that," declares Jegs.

"And," adds Sampson, "unlike the capital city they both got teams that have won the European Cup!"

"Ah, but they had to hand theirs back didn't they? Match fixing and all that ...," pipes up Jegsy. Its his turn to come back with 'The Facts' now.

"Nah, that was a few years later," Sammo corrects him. "Think they were banned or something, might have had a French title taken away, but they defo didn't lose the European Cup." Jegsy snorts and looks at us both like we'd just told him his new haircut makes him look like Fred West, before returning to his newspaper in silence.

We arrive at Marseille's massive Saint Charles station bang on time, expecting to bump into some Liverpool fans who might have travelled here from Paris, as it's only 3hrs on the TGV. We'd looked at that option but the train alone was £75. There are a few Reds around wearing scarves, one or two with replica shirts on. There's no-one we know though, so we set off for our hotel.

As we march down the platform, Sammo and I, hands in pockets, bags over our shoulders, are chatting. Jegsy then suddenly warns us both:

"Beware of pickpockets. Keep hold of your bags, Don't make eye contact with Arabs. Don't get in a cab if it doesn't have a meter.," His eyes are scanning

Jegsy having a reviving cup of coffee

the forecourt ahead of us. Looking for... well what? Ambushes? Snipers? Gangs of marauding Tuarags and Berbers looking to pick off lone pasty-faced Scousers?

"Shall we stick to well-lit thoroughfares and only drink bottled water, too Jegs?" asks Sammo. "Kinell, la – it's not like we don't know Marseille can be moody..."

Jegsy does have a point though. On our first visit here in March 2004 a dreadful display under Houllier saw us knocked out of the UEFA Cup. And this was despite taking the lead in the away leg through an Emile Heskey goal. They then needed two goals to win. But after scoring we simply collapsed. It was pitiful. It ruined what promised to be an utterly fabulous European campaign (possibly one to even rival the 'Around The World in 80 Days' jaunts of 2000-01). We'd had trips to Ljubljana, Bucharest and Sofia – all equally untainted by 'modern football', all hot beds of debauchery and fun. The Marseille defeat, sealed with an offside 'goal' from Didier Drogba, was compounded by some hairy scenes both before and after the game as we'd tried to get to and from the stadium from the Metro.

Right outside the ground, right before kick-off there was a pitched battle outside a big bar where the sky was blotted out by the bottles, ashtrays and beer cans launched at us by the Marseille Ultras. In spite of the police keeping us back for an hour or more after the game, the walk back to town was "on your toes" as little mobs appeared out alleyways every few hundred yards. One positive note from that 2003-4 UEFA Cup was that it was won by Valencia, who completed a League and UEFA Cup double, thus virtually ensuring that their manager, Rafa Benitez, would be recruited by Liverpool that summer.

But that was then – and today is today. It's a lovely day as we walk down the massive main street, 'La Canebiere', running from up by the station right down to the old port where our hotel is.

"La Canebiere," pronounces Jegs, grinning. He says it again, slowly.

"La Can o' beer," he winks. "I'm here all week."

It takes us all of 4 minutes to check in to the anonymous, modern, concrete Novotel-type monstrosity down by the port, drop our bags, and get back out onto the street.

"Gerronit, la," laughs Sammo, taking up the Boss Mag mantra. "Get *rar* on it."

No-one's arguing with it. We head towards the harbour where we're bound to bump into people we know. And we do. O'Malleys, an Irish pub just off the quayside, is rammed. There are lads standing out in the street with pints, others foregoing a trip to the bar and drinking from cans bought from local shops. It's a nice day and standing outside isn't too bad. As we're feeling a bit peckish I suggest finding somewhere to eat and call the 'Gentlemen's Dining Club' to order. There's only two of us present (Sammo and I)but that's enough for a quorum. Jegs pulls a face. He doesn't fancy going to a restaurant when he can get a burger here in O'Malleys.

"Besides," he adds "I just met this lad from the Nocky I haven't seen since 1983 when we got legged up the escalator at Euston by some Tottenham skins. He got a pasting on the concourse. Then he joined the army. Got shot at by the IRA in Belfast. I'll catch up with you later, just going for a natter with him."

"You'd better hurry then," I say. "Before the French Foreign Legion come and take a pop at him as well.."

We leave Jegs and find a restaurant in the streets behind O'Malleys and enjoy a lunch of fish soup, Salad Nicoise and two bottles of local Rose. Attempts to contact Jegs prove futile as he probably can't hear his phone ringing. I mean we can hear the lads singing and we're 2 streets away.

"Allez Les Rouges! Allez Les Rouges!"

As the waiter brings the bill he asks. "Liverpool?"

"Oui" says Sammo. "Le Kop…. Errr….. Spee-On.

He gurns at the waiter and thumbs-ups him. The waiter listens to the distant singing, ear cocked.

"Ah, c'est bon!"

We leave the restaurant and return to O'Malleys to look for Jegs, but he's nowhere to be seen. There's no response from his phone, either. I go inside and check every nook and cranny but the boy's vamoosed. Back outside I remark how close we are to the water's edge…

"He could have fallen in drunk, or been kidnapped by Barbary corsairs." I say.

"Or just gone for a bevvy with his old hooligan mates?" suggests Sammo.

"Always a possibility…"

"Danny Giles has probably rung him and told him there's a pub selling lager for half a Euro a litre on the other side of town."

"Well he certainly isn't going to be in any of these gaffs, is he?" I add, surveying the ranks of posh seafood restaurants that line this side of the 'Vieux Port' quayside. "Probably about 10 Euro a bevvy."

"And the rest. Come 'ead, young Mackin," he says. "Follow yer Uncle Sammo. Let's you and I go and get drunk."

The bar we're in is up a side street just off La Canebiere. It's not far from the Metro stop we'll need to get out to the Velodrome, but far enough away from the main road to be quiet enough. It's got a smattering of Marseilles fans in their pale blue and white, but they're friendly enough. And if they're drinking here, I have a hunch it'll cheap. We're right: its far cheaper than drinking by the harbour so we get stuck into several beers before switching to pastis.

Sammo has some good conversational French and asks some of the older fans about our first trip in 2004. They mime a bit of boxing and then one of them performs a grand comedy gesture of pretending to draw a knife, and adds: "Algerique!"

We all laugh. The Algerians tried to run us all over the shop that night. So different from last time; the last game in the group stages in December 2007. Marseille needed to win in order to qualify, and we needed at least a draw, too. It was like a cup final: the ground was packed and bouncing. Our end was chocker with over 4000 Reds braving the biting wind that whipped over the roofless stands. Within ten minutes we were two up, including a glorious Ian Rush-like goal from Torres to make it 2-0. We coasted the remainder of the game and ran out 4-0 winners. And their fans? Well they were gracious losers that night, staying behind to applaud and chant 'Liverpool!'.

"Wait till they get us outside and stab us," Jegs had said, watching them wrap up their banners and empty out into the streets. We expected something from them after 2004, yet when they finally opened the gates, and the wall of Reds spilled out into the car park... there was nothing. No-one. The Marseilles fans had just drifted off home. We had a quiet journey back into the city centre, and when we arrived back at the old port, notoriously dangerous after dark, there was, again, nothing but Redmen – and the mother of all parties.

An hour and a half before kick off Sammo and I leave for the metro, and within 2 minutes of finding a seat on the train he's asleep. I shake him as we arrive at the stadium stop and when we're out in the fresh air, he livens up again. As our end is under capacity its quite easy getting through the ticket cordons and searches and we actually make it in for kick-off. As we're moving around the large open section they've put us in we find Jegsy.

"Where've you been?" he demands, "I've been ringing you for hours!"

Despite us both producing our phones showing no missed calls from his number he insists he's been ringing every 20 minutes for at least 4 hours.

The Stade Velodrome is a marvellous stadium. I love the two massive identical elliptical stands at either end – twin Kops that most grounds would die just to have one of. Each of these is packed with competing Ultras keen to outdo their fellow fans opposite them. Tonight there's a mosaic at each end. At the far end to us is a huge blue and white roundel, it could be the club badge, but I'm squinting with one eye closed just to focus on it. The end adjacent to us has a mass of silken banners held above their heads, undulating like waves. Both ends are making a tremendous racket. Despite the twin ends being packed, the ground isn't full. The Main Stand opposite is empty at the sides, and I suspect our side of the stadium is similarly under capacity. The away enclosure is far from full, and many Liverpool fans are sitting down and have banners draped over the empty rows of seats. It's this aspect of this competition I hate: The Champions *League*. The tension and, thus, the real dramatic allure of a knock-out competition is absent. It means that these games are seldom played before capacity grounds. Liverpool fans, knowing what the next couple of away games are, can decide not to 'do' Marseilles and save up for Madrid instead. And having been here 3 times now in 5 years, who can blame them?

We start well and nearly score when Babel collects a pass on the edge of the box, spins away clear and then blasts the ball narrowly over the bar. Cue for much derision from Dodd who thinks Babel is a complete waste of space. Shortly after, Gerrard shoots from 25 yards and brings a great save from the keeper low to his left, pushing the ball out for the corner.

"We're all over these. Shall we fuck off and have a bevy?" Sammo yawns, floodlights reflecting off his match goggles.

"Awake are yer?" Jegsy adds, grinning. We're all laughing and joking about how easy a ride this will be, when Marseilles break away, the ball gets lofted over the back four where Skrtel just stops dead and looks at the linesman. I mean, even Sammo can see the lad's onside. He tucks it away with aplomb and the place erupts. One-nil.

"Aw... Just play the bloody whistle, will yer!" wails Jegsy, before shouting, "Oh fuck off!" at the 15,000 Marseilles fans going nuts behind the goal next to us. He lights up a cigarette before muttering cliches like, "Schoolboy error! Schoolboy error!"

As we're shaking our heads and looking around in a mixture of disgust and anger, I catch someone's eye. It's Mick Smith from Huddersfield, with several of his regular travelling companions, Nicky Boothroyd and Phil Robinson. I've known Mick for years, and I'm surprised we haven't been in touch today about meeting up for a beer. Mick goes absolutely everywhere with Liverpool, and plans his entire calendar around the match, booking days off within minutes of the fixtures being announced. He clambers across several empty benches and says:

"Why doesn't he just play the bloody whistle?" and shakes his head.

Mick swaps 'Hellos' with Jegsy and Sammo, and we agree to meet up later back by the port, and off he goes over the empty rows of seats.

"We'll have these, just you wait!" I shout after him. He looks back as if I'm nuts, just as we break and attack down this near side, right in front of us. The ball is played back inside by Kuyt, into space just outside the box, where

Gerrard moves to meet it; he swings his right foot at it and curls a delightful – no, a fantastic – shot, beyond the keeper, into the far top corner. It's world class finishing from a world class footballer – a strike of sublime skill and execution.

Now its our turn to go nuts. I hug Jegsy, Jegsy hugs Kevin, we all hug some bloke in front of us. I dance over the seats down to Nicky, Phil and Mick and we indulge in a group hug from which the smell of Pernod is staggering. I'm still down with these three, asking them about how their day's been when we break away again. Babel – looking amazingly like a real international striker now – latches on to a great long ball from Jamie Carragher, skips into the box and brilliantly earns a penalty with a little step over and a dummy. I turn and look back up the steps to Jegsy. He's standing with arms out, palms facing up, as if to invite explanations as to how that could have possibly happened. Gerrard tucks it away and we have the lead our early play deserved. We can relax.

I say 'we' but I mean us, the fans. What I don't want is to see the team relax. Unfortunately we seem to sit back in the second half and invite Marseilles on. Babel wastes one glorious chance to seal it from six yards out, blasting the ball straight at the keeper.

"See! See!" says Jegs. "Told yer."

"At least he's been better than Lucas." I say to him.

He looks at me with a simple patronising smile that says, "*Well that's not hard, is it?*" In the end we're glad to see the game trail off and we're both more than happy with the night's proceedings. As, indeed, is Sammo, who – amazingly – has stayed awake all the way through a European second half.

"Can't ask for more than that," he declares. "Away win. Three points...."

He nods in a "Garth Crooks' saying-the-bleeding-obvious" kind of way, grinning at me and Jegs.

"Is right!"

We get the metro back down to the Old Port, looking right and left and all around as we hit the side streets and jiggers. One moment Sammo's there, trotting out his favourite away game-ism "this is where they get you" – the next thing he's sloped. Kaboosh! Gone.

"They must've got him," smiles Jegs.

There's singing coming from the same backstreet bar we'd been in earlier. Jegs and I go inside to find Mick, Phil and Nicky. Mick's laughing.

"Was this the one you meant?" he says. "We were in here all last night.

A night in Nimes after Marseille

It's a madhouse. They won't let you out."

Also in there are two pissed Liverpool fans from London, awaiting the 6:30 flight back to England. They say they're going straight the airport from here. There's also a collection of old men, playing board games and arguing amongst themselves. Everyone's drinking pastis. Jegs has met Mick a few times before, but he doesn't know Nicky or Phil, so I make some introductions.

I'd met Phil in Seville when we were playing Betis. He was on his own at a bar and we invited him to join us, so for a while he was known as 'Seville Phil. After just one or two away trips with us it soon became apparent that this was insufficient to fully describe him, so he was re-christened 'Calamity Phil'.

"Why?" asks Jegs. 'What's he done?"

Mick starts sniggering.

Well, where do you start? There's so many. Collapsing sideways in a pub in Sultanhamet, Istanbul from a standing position and having to be dragged like a corpse back to the hotel at 4am covered in his own piss, only to regain consciousness, struggle free from our grasp, and send himself sprawling into the gutter – not once but several times – is a particular favourite of mine. He woke up next morning covered in cuts and bruises, stuck to the sheets with his own blood, asking what had happened.

He saved his piece de resistance for the World Club Championship in Tokyo. We're in Shinjuku and its late, very late. We're looking for another bar. We've been told there are several good places in the district on the far side of a huge main road; what looks like a 10 lane motorway. There's a pedestrian crossing, so we press the button and wait, standing with a crowd of patient locals. The traffic's hurtling past like its the rush hour, though its well gone midnight. Phil's beginning to wobble and get impatient, muttering "Rioja, Rioja!" to himself. Unable to contain himself any more he suddenly flings himself out into the traffic, with a loud "Waaargh!" and ploughs his way across to the central reservation in a wild zig-zag, hardly able to keep his balance.

Cars are screeching to a halt and the pedestrians are pressing their hands to their face in a silent Munch-like scream. The drivers sit behind their steering wheels similarly shocked. It's not because he's nearly killed himself that they're like this. No, it's because he never waited his turn. He took things into his own hands and acted alone. Having neither the necessary social graces, nor the self control, to cross the road in a polite and proper fashion he has brought shame on himself and his family.

Whilst we're screaming laughing, a small Japanese man next to me looks to me as if to say, "You must tell him. He must do it.." I nod to him, sombrely, realising he must mean that Phil must retreat to the privacy of his hotel room, at once, strip to his underpants, tie a Liverpool scarf around his head, and silently fall upon a small ceremonial disembowelling sword.

Then his family shall have honour again.

I considered passing this information on to Phil later that night/morning when we were all slurping noodles and drinking warm saki, but I knew full well that he could kneel on the hotel bedroom floor, grasp the short sword to his navel, and slowly fall forward. But he'd still miss.

Nicky Boothroyd: what a grand Yorkshire name is that! Aye, 'appen it is. Nicky, has the thickest accent of anyone I've ever heard. He's from Huddersfield, same as Mike, but his accent is so thick that I often have real trouble understanding what he's actually saying. I know its English as (a) I can recognise certain rhythms and nuances in his cadence, and (b) he's English, but I can't understand a sodding word. I'm left having to rely on specific facial ticks, certain looks or verbal cues to let me know what to say when he's finished saying whatever it was he was bloody saying.

"Oh, is right Nicky!" or "Oh that's awful." Sometimes I just guess. But he's a lovely, lovely bloke, and a regular at all these European games so I'm just going to have to buy myself a 'Learn Yourself Boothroyd' phrasebook pretty soon. Jegs is similarly flummoxed by Nicky's accent and is reduced to giggles when asked anything and excuses himself to go out for a ciggie even though everyone's smoking in the bar.

Mike's getting another round in but has had his fill of pastis. The barman pours Jegsy a lager then starts filling our pastis glasses.

"No, no" says Mike, "I can't take any more of that... (he thinks)... er... Vodka and coke, s'il vous plait."

The barman grabs a huge tumbler, tosses two large chunks of ice in, then almost fills it with several huge glugs of Smirnoff. He then, almost as an afterthought, delivers a few splashes of Coke. It's not even enough to change the colour.

"Oh fuck," Mike says, "That's me done for."

At some point soon after this we realise the two pissed Londoners are gone. Is it that late? Jegs has had enough lager, and I'm knackered, so we leave the bar in the safe hands of Calamity Phil who's now sprawled across a table, and a pissed Frenchmen who's nodding furiously and laughing at whatever it is Nicky is telling him. We take to the night, thoughts already turning to Stoke on Saturday, and the very real possibility that this could be our year. Teams like Stoke, though – you've got to twat them. That's the mark of champions, just as much as beating your closest rivals. The Stoke Cities of this world have to be put to the sword – starting Saturday.

JM

Stoke City (h)   0-0

League   Sat 20th Sept

Well it seems my new 'lucky undies' worked a treat last weekend. I was only giving them a bit of a test drive just to see how 'lucky' they could be and look what happened. We only go and beat those Manc wretches 2-1 and play them off the park. I don't think Anfield has seen the last of these new, red, slightly fetching, boxies this season. Now the thing about lucky undies is that you can't wear them for just any match. Oh no. They are only to be given an airing at derby matches, cup finals, grudge games and the like. Today we're playing newly promoted Stoke City and I've reverted back to my run of the mill bills. After the Man U game I was telling anybody who'd listen that we'd win in France at Marseille and that it was nailed on we'd fuck up against Stoke this coming weekend. You didn't need to be Gypsy Rose Lee sitting behind her scarlet curtain on Blackpool pier to know that Stoke would come to Anfield and shut up shop and try and frustrate us. Which is exactly what they did.

I'm no clairvoyant but me and 40,000 others saw it coming. Time and time again it happens. The Rafatollah gives all the right soundbites in the Echo about how we'll treat Stoke with respect and approach the game the same as we would against a big club, but we don't. We never do. Except that this time, with the sun shining hard and The Kop responding loudly to the rousing support of the Stoke City blerts in their stick-o-rock shirts, the team come tearing out of the blocks, all guns blazing. Within a minute we're a goal up and I'm already thinking in terms of the last time we played these – a 7-0 win in a League Cup run that took us all the way to Mickey Mouse glory in Cardiff. Except it's not. Even though we can all see that the ball has clearly crossed the line, the ref has ruled it out for I-don't-know-what. This happens sometimes – referees, who more and more have come to view themselves as part of the 'show', will give a controversial decision against the likes of ourselves or

Arsenal (but never Man.United) just to show that they're strong. They can't be intimidated. Now, I like my referees just the same as I like my drummers and bass players – invisible. You only know they've been any good after the event, because you hardly noticed they were there. Once you start talking in terms of so-and-so being a cracking bass player or a boss little drummer, you're halfway to the purgatory that is Mark King of Level 42 (aaaaargh! No! Not a plonky-funky Mark King "bass symphony!") and Cozy Powell. Sack it.

Anyway, the goal is inexplicably disallowed and, rather than being fired up by the injustice of it all, we seem to drop a level. Then another. So that, in the end, we resort to hoofing long, high balls to a Peter Crouch who is plying his trade approximately 250 miles away – having been sold to Portsmouth in the summer.

We end up dropping two points at home against a team that contains Salif Diao in midfield. That just about sums it up really. Newly promoted team's fans are a fuckin' nuisance as well, with their rosy cheeks and silly songs. Wandering around outside the ground in awe like starving refugees who've just been invited to feast at the king's banquet, waiting for discarded crumbs to be dropped from the captain's table. And today's crumb was a massive two points dropped and one gained by the wide-eyed scavengers from Stoke-on-Trent. These types of fans are like the ones you come up against in the 3rd round of the FA Cup. It's their first visit to Anfield for about a quarter of a century and they treat it like it's the last day on earth, knowing they probably won't be coming back next year. It's one crap song after another. They even sing our 'Burning Ring Of Fire'. Kopites shake their head at the unoriginality of it all. On their coaches back to the Potteries they probably talk about the day they outsung the famous Kop. But fans, like the team, can find it hard to get motivated against the smaller defensive teams after a Champions League week and a Man U win. And this was one of those days.

I didn't even stay out after the game. Sammo and John Mac and all the Supporters Union type geezers have had an early start due to a bucket collection for the 'Free Michael Shields appeal' which is ongoing. Sammo is down under the bowels of The Kop, helping count the coin mountain. The last one of these raised £20,000 towards bringing Michael back from Bulgaria, so let's hope this one's another good 'un. Kev has give his ticket to Gary Dempsey, an old mate of Johnny Mac's from Bootle who emigrated to Texas when he was a kid and now lives in Paris. In any one given sentence his accent veers from coarse, seafarer's Scouse to Maurice Chevalier back to John Wayne

– and he's the spit and image of Popeye Doyle of that French Connection. It's Popeye Dempsey's birthday today, too, so we head along to The Stanley after the game.

We get a call from Sammo to see where we are. He's gone straight from the money-count to the Supporter's Club, but we've gone the other way, back towards Scotty Road. As he's on, Kev says it's going off with Stoke. It's mad getting a running commentary of something like that, something that has supposedly died out of the game but still goes on (and off) under the radar, sometimes hours after the game has finished and miles from the ground itself.

I slope off into the evening, shoulders hunched, muttering under my breath about missed chances and Gerrard's disallowed goal. Even the likeable Stoke manager, Tony Pulis (who looks like an extra from Emmerdale Farm), concedes it was in, but that is of no consolation. It wasn't given and that's that. Although if a decision like that was given against our dear neighbours from across the park (but not for long – ah-nyahahahahaha!), we'd still be hearing about it in 15 years time. It's a good job we have a bit more class and humility than them Bluenoses. What's done is done, and if we can turn to Football Cliché Number 113, these things do tend to even themselves out over a season. If we can get back to winning ways next week, this will all be forgotten under a tide of ale and a thunderous gust of celebratory singing. Why? Well funnily enough, we play the Kings of Injustice next week at 'Castle Doom'. I wonder what they'll be moaning about then. Another small team with delusions of grandeur, only marginally bigger than Stoke. An early kick off at the home of bitterness. Can't wait.

JD

Crewe (h)　　2-1

Carling Cup 3rd Round　　Tue 23rd Sept

Crewe Alexandra at home in the Carling Cup on a Tuesday night? Come on, give us a break. It's like being back at school when the PE teacher announces that you're all going on a four mile cross country run and you're standing at the back going "F' fuck's sake Sir. Do we have to?" Most normal people with the exception of the star-struck Crewe fans would answer the call with the same stock reply as in "I really can't be arsed." You know Rafa is gonna play his fringe players and you know it will be close because the Crewe team will give everything in the hope of getting noticed. And you also know that they will be praying that Torres or Gerrard will come on for a few minutes so that they can swap shirts at the end. Then when the lucky one or two recipients get back to their Cheshire semis at one in the morning they'll say to their bargain basement WAGs "Get in the bedroom and hide your eyes, love. I'll tell you when you can peep." Then they pull Fernando's soiled shirt out of their man bag, hold it up with both hands and smell it before pulling it over their head. They shout from outside the door "Keep your eyes closed till I say it's ok. Are you ready? Ok, I'm coming in." They then stand at the foot of the bed with their arms outstretched like the statue overlooking Rio de Janeiro. They remove their underpants and say "Ok Tracey. You can look now." Then bursts into a chorus of "His armband said he was a Red, Torres, Torres. You'll never walk alone it said, Torres, Torres. We bought the lad from sunny Spain. He gets the ball and scores again. Fernando Torres, Liverpool's number nine. Na na na na na na na na na na na na. Na na na na na na na na na na. Na na na na na na na na na na na na na na. Fernando Torres, Liverpool's number nine." Then they swoop on top of her and make mad passionate love. When the dust has settled and they both lay side by side, she whispers in his ear "By the way, what was the score?" and they say "We got beat 2-1 but at least we had a go. Daniel Agger scored a free kick early on but Michael O'Connor equalised for us to make it 1-1 at half time. They had loads of chances and that Lucas Leiva scored the winner with a header early on in the second period. You knew they were taking the piss because Lucas Leiva is never gonna score the winner for them in a proper game when it really matters. But I've really enjoyed myself and I think that the Fernando Torres shirt has brought us a little bit of added flair in the bedroom, don't you love?"

"Yes love. You don't mind if I try it on, do you?"

"No love, of course not. You can even sleep in it if you want." "Si señor, si"

And with that Liverpool progressed to the next round of the Carling Cup. And a little corner of Crewe lived happily ever after.

JD

Derby Day – Everton (a)   2-0

League   Sat 27th Sept

Ah Everton, dear old lovable Everton. Our bitterest rivals. And when I say bitter, I mean BITTER in letters as big as your house. Derby days at the rickety old Castle Doom are quite poisonous affairs these days. Long gone are the misty old traditions of pre-match banter and sing-songs in the pubs. Nowadays it's designated as a category 'A' fixture on the police calendar. On a par with the Man U game but if the truth be known, it's far worse. It's almost like Merseyside's best kept secret, because the majority of post-match incidents are in the city centre, so they're not directly connected to the match. It must've been hard being an Evertonian these last couple of decades watching your rivals, as they conquer Europe and gather admirers all over the world while you're left in that dilapidated old monstrosity of a ground moaning about transfer funds season after season. Blaming Liverpool FC for basically everything that ever goes wrong. If it rains at Goodison, somehow it will be Liverpool's fault. Take any normal run of the mill Evertonian (he doesn't have to be a scally or particularly aggressive) and sit him on a psychiatrist's couch and just utter the words Liverpool Football Club to him and watch him morph spectacularly from ordinary, bloke-next-door type to demented gibbering wreck, foaming at the mouth, shouting abuse and accusing Liverpool of being the root cause of all things evil. It's almost a form of mental illness and for the poor old season ticket holders it's a kind of ongoing self harm.

The thing is, this siege mentality is not going to change unless a rich sugar daddy comes along with more money than sense. And even then will they be happy? Of course they won't. They're Evertonians for god's sake. They're never happy. Anyway I could bang on about the inadequacies of our downtrodden friends forever and a day but the 208th derby match is upon us and I'm restless. I always struggle to sleep the night before we play the bluenoses. The same with United but more so Everton. LFC TV did a survey once asking who Liverpool's main rivals were. 70% said Man U and 30% said Everton. You can bet your bottom dollar that the 70% were from Thailand, Tunbridge and Timbuktu, while the remaining dirty thirty were from where the derby really matters, on the streets of Merseyside.

I'm up early. Hot Lips drops me off at the Albert to meet up with all the faces at 11am. Normally the Albert by the ground is 'Wool Central' and is to be avoided at all costs but today is different. The vibe is good. Sammo's in there, Hooto and Mono roll up, as do loads of other people with O after their name, looking smart, keen and lively. It's too early to really get 'on it' but I have a couple of swift ones to relax the nerves and lubricate the vocal chords. I sidle up to John 'Mageye' Maguire and whisper in his ear "Don't worry lad, I've got them on." He looks at me with a blank expression then I hook my thumb inside the elastic of my ruby red boxies and pull them up. "The lucky bills, John. I didn't forget." He grins and calls me a mad bastard. Danny Nico just stares at me, more than a little confused.

The sun is shining as we walk to the ground. Confidence is high but you never know in these games how it's gonna go. Anything can happen. Me and Sammo cut through the Park doing that slightly-louder-than-natural talk that you do when you're a bit tense. We get onto the cinder path and just below, right opposite The Abbey pub, all Liverpool's young lads are walking to the ground. As they get to the boozer they start giving it "We won't be like Everton," one of the old hoolie songs from the late 70s that commemorates a famous Bluenose drubbing – say no more. Sammo turns to me, a bit worried.

"D'you think they know how little that mob is?"

I pat him on the back.

"They'll be sound. Look. No-one's coming out..."

"You know what I mean, though. When you're that age and you've had a drink, you think no-one can touch you. It feels like there's loads of you..."

He pulls out his mobile, phones one of the lads, puts on a 'formal' voice.

"Stanley Park police surveillance. We have you in our sights..."

I'm laughing as I can see the lad looking round. He checks his phone – maybe he can't see the screen too well in the sunlight coz he holds his hand over it to see who's phoning him and laughs, looking around again. We wave to them. They hurl a volley of abuse at us. PC Sammo again:

"Please be aware that you are only twenty strong – and your language is appalling. Over."

Got to give it the young firm. They don't care. As they get nearer the ground they sing even louder, taunting Everton about their planned move to Kirkby.

"Fuck off to Kirkby – this city's all ours!!"

The butterflies have started as we approach the back of the Park End where a big poster informs us that Everton are the People's Club. Mmm, dunno about that – surely they mean Pauper's Club? We enter the ground and go on a journey back in time. Up the cranky old wooden stairs to the back of the Lower Bullens Road Stand. The whole place is made of wood. The floor, the seats, only the big iron stanchions that obscure your view and the tiles above your head are not wooden. It's like being downstairs on a pirate's galleon. They should run stadium tours here to show people what football grounds were like before the wheel was invented. Not much has changed since 'Dixie' was a lad.

The teams come on to a deafening roar as both sets of supporters trade the usual insults. There's the odd witty ditty but most of it is just bordering on plain hatred. I think the derby has reached its lowest ebb – it really can't get any worse than this. The match kicks off and Liverpool dominate from the start. We look good. We're quick, precise and confident but you always worry when you've had so much of the play and you haven't scored. Half time comes and me and Sammo meet the rest of the lads downstairs. We all agree we're playing well. The whole team looks good with the exception of Dossena who seems to have the first touch of a rapist. He may well come good – but so might Ronnie Biggs. Keane, Riera, Kuyt, Gerrard, are all turning it on. All we need is a goal. The second half kicks off and we attack the Gwladys St End. Chances come and go and it's all starting to get a bit nervy. The longer we dominate without scoring, the more Everton's confidence will grow. The unthinkable might happen, here....

And then Keane gets to the byline and delivers a peach of a cross to our boy Torres. Most other players would've needed at least a touch to bring the ball under control, probably allowing the opposing defender time to recover as they brought it down and lined up a shot – but with Torres it's all instinct. His first touch is a laser-guided volley that simply flies past Howard in the Everton goal. Pandemonium breaks out as it hits the back of the net. There's fat blokes falling over seats. People going mental all over the place. You're giving hugs and kisses to people you wouldn't normally pick up with a pair of tongs. The whole away end is rocking as people who haven't seen their shoes in many a moon bounce up and down in celebration of Liverpool's Number Nine. Just as I pause for breath after about 10 choruses of the 'Torres bounce', he fuckin' scores again. Oh my god, I'm gonna die of a heart attack in Goodison bastard Park. Everton have gone now – they've wilted. All around me lads are screaming at the team to go for jugular. My good companion Sammo, as smiley and reasonable a fella as you'll ever meet is stood precariously on the lip of his seat yelling:

"Humiliate them! Rip them to bits! Rub their fucking noses in it!"

It's a good job that skinny little 'ne'er do well' Mike Riley disallows Torres' third goal because that would've been it. I'd have run on the pitch or exploded or re-claimed The Streak.

There's still about 25 minutes left and the infidels are already leaving their seats. As usual Everton have their player sent off in the Goodison derby. This time it's that little non-entity Tim Cahill. You know the one, the snide who always wants to have a fight with the corner flag. Australian fella. Only little but fancies himself a bit. Anyway, it doesn't matter, only that it gives them a bit of 'If it wasn't for fuckin' Riley' bile to spit back at us when we rub it in later. The whistle blows and we're bouncing. We've outclassed the enemy and it's our best start to a season since the Premiership began.

We circumnavigate Stanley Park and end up back at the Albert for a bout of manhugs, pats on the back and celebratory drinks. The mood is euphoric. Songs are sung and pints are downed as maniacally grinning Redmen enter the legendary old pub which over the years has become a shrine to followers of the greatest club side on earth. All those grizzled old faces you know so well from down the years seem to look ten years younger as the glow of victory animates their features. It's amazing what wins against United and Everton can do for a Redman's soul.

We get a cab into town and head for HQ (Ned Kellys). It's heavily policed with riot vans parked outside and newly installed bouncers on the door. Although it's got a fearsome reputation as the Liverpool Hooly pub, you don't really get any trouble in there as everyone knows each other. The police obviously keep an eye on it, on the off chance that a renegade bunch of disgruntled Blues might try and make a name for themselves – but that would be a pointless exercise as Neds on a derby day is almost impregnable. A Scouse fortress manned by some of the city's most colourful characters. Next door is Aldo's bar. Owned by John Aldridge who, in my opinion, was the most underrated striker to play for us in generations. It's more cosmopolitan in there. There's Irish and Scandinavian fans mixed in with the Scouse overflow from Neds, and Pat and Faye behind the bar make you feel welcome. Fuckin' hell, I sound like Paddy Shennan from the Echo's Good Pub Guide. Anyway, both boozers are bursting at the seams. Paul Stewart is bladdered as are all the ones who couldn't get a match ticket. They're all about 5 pints ahead of us because they've had to watch it in the alehouse.

One of my best mates 'Frankie boy' appears out of the mist. He's not a big match-head, supports the Reds, but he's not that arsed. He's one of those who likes to see us win but he's not an obsessive like the rest of us. Put it this way, if we get beat, he's not going to stick his head in the oven. He'll just say, 'Oh well, there's always next week.' He's in town to try and get me to leave the madness of Victoria Street and to go and meet some of our mutual bluenose mates, always a joy after a skinful and a derby win. We stagger across town and walk into the Revolution Bar on Wood Street and are greeted with the sight of TC and his fellow blues looking like they've been to a funeral. 'Oh no! What are you doing in here Dodd? You smarmy Rednose twat'. 'Hello lads. Have you had a nice day?' 'Fuck off. If you're coming in here to gloat, we're going home.' Obviously I can't help myself and I poke a bit of fun and they take it on the chin. I try and console these broken men but for some reason I can't seem to get rid of that inane smug grin, which has been etched on my face for these last six hours. We make it to the Jacaranda on Slater Street but we are flagging. The early start, lack of food and copious amounts of lager are beginning to take their toll. The Blues have managed to shake us off somewhere between the Jac and Central Station so me and Frank have one for the road in The Globe, down Cases Street (mysteriously known locally as "Casey Street") Dava Hardman is having his 50th birthday bash in there with the regulars off the Wilcox Tours bus, but by now I've lost control of my limbs and have begun to speak fluent Hungarian. Time to go methinks.

I awake in the morning in the spare room to the strangest sight. I seem to have subconsciously pushed a load of boxes together and placed a pole in the middle with my now legendary lucky undies as a flag at the top, reminiscent of that famous statue where the American soldiers raised the 'Stars and Stripes' at Iwo Jima. I peel my tongue off the roof of my mouth, have a cup of tea and realise that I have been blessed to have born a Red.

JD

PSV (h)   3-1

Champions League Group Phase   Wed 1st Oct

After the underwhelming showing against Liege I decide that maybe Ma Boyle's isn't the talisman it needs to be to host a pre-Euro get-together. We were minutes from possibly being in the UEFA Cup, and whilst we'd have convinced ourselves how great that might have been as far as the craic was concerned, we're in the big boys cup now. So we need a more reliable gathering place if we're going to go places in this season's European Cup. The pre-match swallee should be for building camaraderie and confidence: not for fretting about whether we're actually jinxing the team or not.

So, after a brief discussion, we fall back on an old favourite: 'Shenanigans' on Tithebarn Street. Known as 'The Rising Sun' previously, it was bought by two brothers from Dublin, Conor and Darragh, and revamped as Shenans in the mid 90s. It's authentically scruffy and 'Oirish', homely and welcoming: it even has an open fire. Up until recently the toilets also had some the best sectarian graffiti in the city, but it's gone now; Shenans obviously doing its little bit for the peace process. Any good pre-match HQ, where we may be gathering from noon, also needs to do food, and Shenans does some of the best Irish Stew in the city. It sells beer – which helps, and has its own wine list. It also has its own bus stop right slap-bang outside the door, for the 15 minute journey on the number 27 up to The Kop. It's so well placed, in fact, that as the bus pulls up to the stop you have time to finish your pint, adjust your cravat whilst wishing all a fond and cheery farewell, before climbing aboard and tendering the correct fare.

When I arrive at Shenans, late afternoon, there's already a fine collection of match going regulars – all good, solid Reds – assembled. This lot were also here after last Saturday's derby when we'd enjoyed an hour or two's celebration before dispersing around the city to sing anti-Everton songs, compose love letters to Fernando Torres, and generally gloat ourselves into a coma.

"I've had a bet," I tell Paul Stewart. "Keane. First goal. Twenty quid."

"Well you've fuckin' thrown that down the bog, haven't yer?" he scowls, "That pikey little Irish bastard couldn't hit a cow's arse with a banjo.."

Paul – as you now should be vaguely aware - holds some forthright opinions; most of them unrepeatable and certainly unprintable here. His anti-'Oirishness' though is the one constant in his twisted view of the world; a view so twisted in fact, that he doesn't seem to see the irony of being a regular in this pub.

"Nah," I counter, "He's had - what – a dozen games? He's due a goal."

"Is he fuck!"

"Under floodlights, European game? He'll score." I add, or mutter, to myself.

"That'll pay for my beer in Madrid."

Stewey just ignores that and lets rip with a truly terrifying tirade during which he dismisses all of the Liverpool team as being 'useless twats', but especially Keane, Kuyt and Lucas Leiva, for whose uselessness he invents several new adjectives to describe. Its a good job most of the lads in here know him otherwise someone would be ringing the RSPCA to have him put down. It's worse when someone we don't know catches his eye and, knowing he has an audience, he raises the invective to new heights.

"... and don't get me started on that fucking fat Spanish bastard, Benitez..."

Most of us who do know him have long since learned the futility of disagreeing, or engaging him in logical argument. We just smile and shake our heads. I shut him up for a few short minutes by buying him a Guinness. Silence. Bliss.

I have to declare an interest here. Liverpoolfc.tv – the club's satellite TV channel – asked me to go on a fans' show before the season started to discuss the coming campaign. I can't recall exactly what I said, but it was something along the lines of...

"We relied too heavily on Torres last season. We need someone to weigh in with their share of goals, and Robbie Keane is exactly the type of striker who'll get you 15 or 20 league goals. He's a natural poacher, a great finisher...with his contribution then, yes, we can win the league."

With each passing game I'd been reminded of his impotence in a red shirt. Not even my comparisons with Peter Crouch's start at Anfield could deflect the barbs of criticism aimed at Keane. With every scuffed shot straight at the keeper; every time he miscued and kicked fresh air rather than the ball ; in fact, every bloody time he touched the ball I'd be reminded, by those around me, of my confident assertion that Torres and Keane would, like Dalglish and Rush, win us the league.

Over the next hour or two Shenans fills up nicely and most of the familiar faces are there: Charlie Sheen lookalike and professional dispsomaniac Ian Roughley; there's Billy and Mark Harrup, sons of Erin, for whom Shenans is a home from home; Simon Morris and Peter Hewitson – long suffering drinking companions of Stewey, who've given up all hope of getting any sense out of him; the lonesome and lagubrious travelling Red, John Duffy, who'll turn up quietly in Moscow after travelling across the continent on his own, to appear alongside you – out of nowhere – like he's just popped into his local; and my old mate Stevie Wright, clasping a pint of Guinness and smiling and looking for all the world like a young Rev. Ian Paisley (which, for someone who flew to Rome to see the Pope lying in state, the day before we played Juventus at Anfield in 2005, must surely hurt). All are enjoying bowls of stew and a bevvy, discussing last Saturday's win at Goodison or contemplating what will happen tonight. PSV are no pushovers but we should get the win without too much trouble. PSV are another side we've played all too recently in this competition. They should hold no surprises, and, as 7:15 comes, we all pile onto the bus confident about tonight's proceedings.

PSV do indeed hold no surprises for us, and it's not long before we take the lead. Just a few minutes into the game we get a corner on the right at the far, Anfield Road, end. Robbie Keane is handily placed in the six yard box, lurking dangerously, in my eyes, and sharpening his boots. Torres is out near the penalty spot trying to lose his marker as Gerrard drills the ball over to the edge of the six yard box. Bursting free, the wonderful Torres thunders over to meet it with a side-footed effort that the keeper saves brilliantly.

We all throw our hands to our heads in disappointment, especially me – as the ball rebounds nowhere near Keane. It falls, instead, to Kuyt who drills it hard and low such that the keeper can only fumble it into the net.

"Yes!"

All around me people are punching the air, though there's none of the crazed spectacle of recent celebrations. I'm applauding too, but slowly and shaking my head. John Maguire leans over and asks,

"Wassup lar?"

I hold up my betting slip.

"I had Keane, first goal."

He turns back, still clapping, but now laughing as well. I slowly tear up the betting slip and toss the pieces into the air. It's a familiar sight, seen all over The Kop, after the opening goal, when so many betting slips suddenly become obsolete. Then I notice there's just one other tiny shower of paper, about fifty feet down towards the bottom corner. There's only me and that fat bloke down there, who've bet good money on Robbie Keane to score the first goal.

I settle down to await the avalanche of goals that must now ensue, but despite a few near misses, especially a flashing header from Torres, PSV look to be hanging on until half-time. Until, that is, Torres bursts down the right wing and clips a wonderful cross into the box where Robbie Keane expertly sidefoots it across the face of the goal from 12 yards, and into the bottom corner. It's a cracking move and a great finish from Keane. His acrobatic celebrations are as much in relief as they are in joy, and I can't see anyone begrudging him this moment. Some of the more curmudgeonly onlookers, however, of which there are many in the rows behind me, snort and scoff at his theatrics, no doubt preferring to see the simple, manly handshake that served Albert Stubbins and Billy Liddell so well down the years.

A large proportion of the crowd take up the song:

"Keano! There's only one Keano,
There's only one Keano,
There's only one Keano
There's only one Keano"

It's poo-pooed by a good number, including myself. It's an awful song that's followed him around his career, and is as especially rampant at Ireland games as it was at White Hart Lane – though how Spurs fans can gaily take up a song that Man.United followers patented for a different Keane is beyond me. Have they no wit, no originality…. No shame? It's the type of thing people who know nothing about football *expect* football fans to sing. It's to be abhorred, as is anything that's sung to the tune of 'Winter Wonderland', and anything that ends in "till I die" (typically preceded by the name of a supremely shit place whose residents are uncommonly proud of belonging to said shithole. See "Barnsley till I die, I'm Burnley till I die, I know I am, I'm sure I am, I'm Mansfield till ARR-DARR!" No, Robbie Keane needs something better; much, much better. Trouble is we haven't come up with anything yet, and the longer he's taking to become a real goalscoring hero, the less likely it is that we will. In fact all we can come up with so far is a riposte to those singing, 'There's Only One Keano':

> (To the tune of Let It Be):
> "Robbie Keane, Robbie Keane, Robbie Keane, Robbie Keane,
> His name's not fucking Keano!
> Robbie Keane."

He's wearing the famous No. 7 shirt as worn by such legendary luminaries as Kevin Keegan, Kenny Dalglish and Harry Kewell: he needs a simple, classic chant of salutation that befits such a legend. I turn to Sammo, clap once and shout:

"Keane!"

He gets it. He's almost crippled with laughter, the simpleton. Maybe this could catch on. I'm not holding my breath though.

After the game, which we eventually and very comfortably win 3-1, we all re-assemble outside the HJC shop. We're satisfied with a performance that leaves us joint top of the group, on 6 points, with Atletico Madrid, who we play in the next game. The group is shaping up nicely, and we're all discussing how we're getting to Madrid, where we'll be staying, drinking etc, when I feel a hand on my shoulder:

"Mackin you gobshite, told you that was a wasted bet." The gravelly, pirate-like voice of Stewey cackles down my ear.

"Well at least he scored," I say turning to him..." just wasn't the first one.."

"Oh behave!" he cries, waving his hand as if to dismiss anything else I might add, "He mis-hit it! He's shit!"

"Oh, alright then. Maybe you're right," I say sarcastically. "Maybe next time I'll bet on 'Keane to score first goal with a 25 yard diving header from his own cross."

He pretends not to hear.

"I'm going the Stanley," he snarls, and then storms off through the crowds pouring back towards the city centre. Peter Hewey and Simon Morris shrug almost apologetically, then trot off after him. The poor old Stanley. I wonder if its too late to phone them and get them to close the place up?

JM

Manchester City (a)   3-2

League   Sun 5th Oct

It's a beautiful day and we've got Man City away. They are this week's world's newest, richest, biggest and fattest club. Can football get any madder? What next? Accrington Stanley owned by Bill Gates? I don't think anything can surprise or shock me anymore. At least I did think that until 'fan friendly' John Mackin strolled across the Lime Street concourse wearing a slightly unsettling black double breasted U boat commander's overcoat. I think Dave Hewitson of the '80's Casuals' football fashion label can sleep soundly in his bed tonight, knowing that Herr Mackin's match-going attire is unlikely to catch on amongst the Scouse trendsetters.

There was also a bit of a shock late withdrawal yesterday afternoon. When I say shock, I don't really mean 'hold the front page' shock because he has been known to pull a muscle in the warm-up once or twice before over the years. But it's still a blow to hear that our resident writer, hesitant fighter and early-nighter, Kev Sammo has failed a late fitness test and won't be joining us on the Ordinreh to Citeh. An irreplaceable member of the firm whose organisational skills are beyond compare. He's the type of person who achieves more before breakfast than most of us do in a week. Put it this way. Before I've been to the loo to drop anchor, he's already saved the world, penned a modern day classic and booked all the flights to the next European away game. Only this time I think he may have just slipped up. Because I have an uncanny feeling in my water that today against Man.City we are gonna witness something very special. I know we've been spoilt these last few weeks with memorable heady triumphs against our two most annoying rivals but I got dat feelin' baby!

"Day return to the Darkside please mate." "Manchester?" "Yeah! You got it mate." Wow, even the ticket bloke knows. He'd have ruined it if he'd have just gone "Where?" but he didn't. It's gonna be a good day. I just know it. The train's a bit of a mixture of footyheads and the run of the mill shoppers. Me and John just grab a seat in the front carriage and plan the day ahead. We get off at Oxford Road but most stay on to Piccadilly or Victoria or wherever it goes. I know the Darkside quite well as the dusky, vivacious one (otherwise known as Hot Lips) spent the last ten years of her life here in the city centre before I drugged her, tied her up, lobbed her in the car, then drove her up the M62, opened the boot and said "Hey Baby. Welcome to the Pool of Life." Ok, ok, I'm exaggerating a bit but you know the score. Suffice to say that I kind of got to know the area a little bit. Been to loads of bars and clubs and stuff around here. Always undercover of course, you know, wig and that. Can't be too careful when you're behind enemy lines. Even used to put a false voice on. Kind of James Bond one. "Pint of Shtrongbow, pleash and a glash of chardonnay and a packet of peanutsh if itsh all the shame to you."

Anyway, we're off the train. There's no spotters at the station so we're not gonna get hopped on by the local divs, which is always a great weight off your mind on awaydays. We go left out of the station and head up to one of my favourite bars, a cracking little indie bar in a Victorian toilet, called The Temple, but this being Sunday morning, it's closed. On to the Circus, which is a Wetherspoons pub further up the road. The phone's going and it's Captain Bucko wanting to know where we are. I tell him there's too many Mancs in here for him and his platoon to go unnoticed, so we head back down to meet them in the first boozer to the right of Oxford Road. Ideally you don't want to be walking around Manchester with someone with Bucko's heroic lung capacity, but you just can't help loving him. He's infectious. We place a gag on him and the ten of us walk on as inconspicuously as it's possible for ten people to walk. We hit one of my other favourite Manc bars, situated dead opposite the BBC, called Odder. It's the perfect place for a few pre-match scoops but even better in the evening. If ever you are lost in the North West's second city and you fancy a swift one, dive in there, ignore downstairs and go straight upstairs which is the place to be. A weird and wonderful bar for the discerning drinker, almost a throwback to times gone by when the odd, the arcane and the just plain freakish was considered fair game as entertainment.

We get two cabs up to the ground not knowing what might lay ahead. There's loads of City fans wearing kind of Arab headgear and getting all wacky about their new billionaire owners from Abu Dhabi. Fancy dress at the match – what the fuck's all that about? Don't wanna sound like a killjoy but fancy dress is only ever even remotely justifiable if it's last day of the season –

and even then it's for divvies. I remember seeing Birmingham fans invade the pitch at Crystal Palace one year, all in fancy dress. Henry the VIIIth, Batman & Robin and Scooby fuckin' Doo, Bananaman fighting toe-to-toe with The Grim Reaper. Oh, they were all at it. Imagine at the ID parade the next day where the Smurf who they've caught on camera is trying to swap hats with the Viking and asking if he can borrow Zorro's mask? One time up in Newcastle, a Giant Panda walked past me as cool as you like, as if it was the most normal thing in the world. Can you imagine the scene in Panda man's house just before he leaves? "How do I look Pet?" "Wor, you look fooken lush pet." "Let's just check; keys, ciggies, lighter, season ticket, money. Is me head on straight, well?"

And don't get me started on those "Scouser" wig monstrosities. When we won in Istanbul I taped everything so I could relive it all again and again when I got back. The morning after the night of all nights it switched to Breakfast TV and I couldn't believe my eyes. Both presenters had black curly wigs on grinning inanely at the screen. Is this what national television thinks the people of Liverpool deserve as a tribute to one of the greatest sporting achievements of all time? Is the Harry Enfield wig now indelibly synonymous with our city? If it is I, for one, am not amused. There's even the odd one on show at Anfield every so often but they'd better beware because if I ever happen across some gurning out-of-towner with a "Calm Down" wig on, they are going to get cheese-wired. End of story.

Anyway, the City fans are enjoying their five minutes in the spotlight and, living next door to the unspeakable ones, who can blame them. The match kicks off and the atmosphere is a bit flat. The travelling Reds downstairs are making all the noise but up where we are it's pretty sedate. Stephen Ireland puts the sky blues ahead on 19 minutes and the City of Manchester Stadium comes alive. It gets even madder when Garrido curls a free kick past Reina's near post. The omens don't look good. A Vicky Pollard lookalike in a cheap tracksuit top is screaming abuse at us across the partition. Various extras from 'Shameless' are going off their heads with delight about 20 yards away from us, too. Thinking that all their birthdays have come at once and the golden egg has finally been laid, they're dancing, cavorting, doing that weird, woolly, drying-your-back-with-an-imaginary-towel routine that they do and – and this is the thing that marks them out as relegation fodder rather than title contenders – they *goad*. It's a silly, petty small-team mentality, goading, and it's generally the preserve of the newly-promoted minnows. They'll come to

Bucko and Jegsy in Odder

Anfield in early September, before all the joys of the big time have been battered out of them by a succession of 7-0 reverses and they'll sing:

"Worst support we've ever seen…," or "It's so quiet at An-fee-yuld" or other tiresome ditties about how they, Shit Town, are loud, tattooed and proud while you, the spoilt, decadent big-timers are dead, dead, dead, dead quiet.

City are like that now and, 2-0 ahead, are suddenly very smug, and very full of silliness. Vicky Pollard is conducting a puppet show without puppets as she wobbles to the edge of the divide and gives it a fat, flabby, "calm down" routine. Calm down? Oh dear me, Man City – we haven't even got started yet…. as you are, unfortunately, about to find out. I don't usually like to see people broken hearted and close to tears but when we leave this stadium I am going to absolutely revel in it.

The half time whistle blows and the oil rich Mancs are loving it. We're subjected to songs along the lines of "We'll buy your club and burn it down."

Hmmm, that's nice of them – as is: "We'll buy Torres and Gerrard too" with a little bit added on saying "you can keep Dirk Kuyt." Oh the boy Dirk will make them pay for that little ditty. We're downstairs at the break and there's heated discussions about the formation and why Rafa has changed a winning team, dropping Keane. I reckon if we can pull it back to 2-2 it'll show we have the character to go all the way this season. We've already come from behind to beat Middlesbrough, Marseille and Man U and this bunch of no-marks begin with the letter M, so why not? Kev texts me from his sick bed saying: "These are shite. 4-2 to the Redmen." I wish I shared his optimism.

The second half starts and we go at them right from the off. Kuyt gets dropped in the area. No pen. Unbelievable decision. It's a blatant foul. Ten minutes in and the golden boy Torres slides the ball home in goal which had 'Rushie' written all over it. Game on. Come on Reds. We'll have these. We'll have these. City are on the rack and Zabaleta gets red carded for a two footed challenge on the much improved Alonso. There must be an Alonso's Ankle Sweepstake among the professional footballing fraternity, the amount of no-marks who target him and try to break it.

The Redmen can smell blood now, and we're going for the kill. 15 minutes left and we get a corner. In it comes, a flash of golden mane as Liverpool's Number Nine hones in on the ball like a heat-seeking missile and BANG!! YESSSSSSSSSSSSS!!!!! Fernando scores a peach of a header and the Mighty Reds are level. Last ten minutes and there's only one end of the ground singing – in fact it's positively bouncing. Vicky Pollard is now the focal point of the travelling army's songs as the siege on City's goal continues. Even some of the Mancs are laughing at the severity of the abuse directed at the blonde, bloated, Burnage bombshell.

"Fat Vicky Pollard! You're just a fat Vicky Pollard!"

"Are you one of Rooney's Grans?"

"Get your gut out for the lads!"

"Vicky, Vicky wobble yer arse – Vicky, wobble yer arse!"

And to the Man.City anthem 'Blue Moon': "Too soon, you started bingeing too soon…"

It's cruel but you know the saying 'He who laughs last'. Then calamity strikes. Chasing down a hopeful ball over the top from City, Martin Skrtel turns awkwardly and goes down in agony. You can tell it's a bad one as the attendant medics are giving him oxygen. How does that happen to fellas as fit as these? For the best part of 20 years I turned up once a week for a game of footy in the park, no exercise at all other than that through the week, and the pitch was a liability too, full of pot holes, craters and broken glass – yet the only serious injury we saw in all that time came when one of the lads head-butted another in temper. Yet the fittest of the fit seem prone to these "non-injuries," if you get what I mean – real serious casualty gear after minimal if any contact. That's not to trivialise what are some horrific, career-ending accidents but blimey, they don't half take some tumbles. Skrtel is off on a stretcher and we've used up all our subs, so it's back to 10 against 10. The board goes up. Five minutes injury time. If we can pull this off it'll be one of the best comebacks for decades.

It's one of them where it just feels like our destiny to do this now, and the whole Liverpool section is up on its feet willing the boys home. Last attack. This must be the final few seconds of an absorbing match and, if you'd have asked us at half-time we'd have taken this point, no problem. The ball comes into the box – hit it Yossi lad... bury it! Aaaaah, fluffed it Benny la...but it bobbles loose to Kuyt and there isn't even time to connect there's only seconds left and he smashes it high into the fucking net and oh my giddy fucking aunt I'm going to pass out with sheer joy and relief and that mad, mad, mad, mad ecstatic fucking euphoria that only a last-minute winner can ever give you! I mean that. Sit back and add up all the greatest moments of your life. We all know the ones we're *supposed* to say... but did you summersault over six rows of plastic chairs and dance round and round and round in a circle with a sweaty fat fella you'd never met before when your first kid was born? No you didn't. Only football delivers such moments of unbridled celebration, and we Redmen are among the chosen ones for whom such moments are many and legendary. This one, for now, is just the latest – another legendary, beautiful, ecstatic moment. I've just witnessed one of the great football turnarounds of recent years. For us, everything now will be forever compared with Istanbul but forget that, for now. This was wonderful. As Tony Barrett wrote in the Echo after the PSV game. "Dirk Kuyt is like a married man on a stag night. He only scores in Europe." Well not today, Tony lad, not today. No-one – and I mean no-one – deserved to score the winner more than Dirk.

This win is just massive for us. I'd say as big as the two against the unmentionables, just for the sheer intensity of the way we rose from the dead. We pile out of the ground and it goes off almost straight away. Obviously the Mancs aren't too happy and it's full on, toe to toe, fisticuffs right next to us. I'm on the phone at the time and it gets knocked out of my hand by a copper who dives on some Scouser next to me. Kev, who I'd been speaking to, obviously thinks I've been attacked, but a wily old veteran like me can smell trouble a mile away. I recover the phone and me and John walk to the city centre speaking in hushed tones. We'd be fucked if Bucko was with us.

As I say, I know Manchester quite well so I'm in charge of proceedings. We reach the top of Whitworth Street and walk briskly past the gay village. Don't want to be stopping off there for a quick one. It's bad enough getting man-to-man marked on the pitch but you don't want it while you're having a bevvy. I remember years ago, coming down the stairs and saying to my mum and dad "Listen, I've got something to tell you and you'd better sit down because I'm not sure if you're gonna like what you hear." You could see the shock on their faces. I was about 16 at the time. I said "Mother. I think I'm a heterosexual."

We dive into O'Shea's which is not too bad for an Irish pub and watch the bluenoses struggle to a 2-2 draw against crisis club, Newcastle. Then head up to the Temple Bar, up by Oxford Road. Best jukie in town, mad posters on the walls – a real indie feel to it. It's time to get the train so we go to the offy and stock up. It's been a beast of a day and the train journey is full of boisterous, happy Redmen. We finally arrive at Ned Kelly's HQ to be greeted by all kinds of deliriously, deranged people. A very drunk Danny Giles, Marty Bannan, Vinnie Hoo Har, Tommy Trouble and Bucko and his merry men. The list is endless. It's been a long day. I slope outside for a smoke, never to be seen again. Somehow I just evaporate into the city's dampened streets and awake next morning thinking to myself, "Fuck me, that was some day out." And I hate to say it but if we carry on this, we might just go all the way. What a scary thought.

JD

Wigan (h)   3-2

League   Sat 18th Oct

After all the excitement of the last few weeks with late goals and unbelievable comebacks it came as no surprise that I was hardly straining at the leash for this one. Just say it quietly to yourself 'Wigan At Home'. See, it hardly gives you a semi-on does it? But these are the games that make a season. In days gone by, teams containing Dalglish & Rush, Keegan & Toshack, Barnes & Aldo, Hunt & St John, would have absolutely battered teams like this into oblivion. But times have changed. Nearly every team in the Prem is capable of causing an upset and Wigan are no different. Because of the English league being the best in the world, there are all kinds of great players emerging at clubs everywhere. Everton obviously being the exception to the rule but Wigan have an absolute gem in a player called Amr Zaki. More about him later. Today I'm going to the match with 'the dark mysterious one' for her first home game of the season. Yes I know what you're thinking, bird/match, match/bird; it's always a hot topic amongst the dyed in the wool hardcore match goers. But hey! As long as they're polite and they don't perve too much in my line of vision, it's ok. I'm not naïve enough not to know that when my back's turned there's not the odd sexual reference and a bit of undercover blimping going on. But that's the price you pay for having a boss bird and you're foolish enough to take her on a testosterone filled Kop. Luckily today it's only Wigan so no-one is too hyped up or under the influence of alcohol. We stand next to Joe Corrigan. Joe looks like a magician. Shock of white hair, piercing blue eyes, dark clothing. I can imagine him saying "Go on, pick a card, pick a card! Look into my eyes, look into my eyes!" Lives in Holland but drives a London taxi two days a week and manages to still get to all the LFC games. Now that's what I call magic.

The game kicks off and Wigan come at us like Real M' fuckin' drid.

They're all over us and take a deserved lead on the half hour. Daniel Agger, who's back in the team at the expense of the injured Skrtel, has a rush of blood and makes an absolute howler of a mistake and that bloke Zaki nips in and scores. 1-0 Wigan. You're thinking to yourself "here we go again." Small team full of ambition and ideas and the Reds getting clogged up in midfield. Mind you, this wasn't like Stoke where they just came for a draw. Wigan were right up for it. Kuyt pulls it back on 37 minutes after a good run and ball in from Agger who could have easily let his head drop after his costly mistake but to his credit he kept going. It's just on half time when right out of the blue that cheeky little twat Zaki hits a spectacular scissor-kick past Reina. It has to be said, it is an absolutely stunning goal. In fact it has 'Goal of the Month' all over it. Maybe I'm a bit harsh calling him a cheeky little twat but let's get it right, if you don't play for us you're a twat. Harsh but true. Hotlips goes down at half time. I don't mean down, down. I mean she goes to the loo while I stay up gabbing to the lads. Lulu who is probably the only female in Block 306 asks me how I managed to get such a young beautiful girlfriend. Obviously she is insinuating that I am not worthy or not up to scratch. I have to remind Lou that she should never underestimate the Power of Dodd.

The second half kicks off and Wigan are still at it. Steve Bruce may have a barnet like an exiled Eastern European leader but he can still manage to get a team going. Valencia, the player not the place, gets a red for a tackle on Alonso on 75. That's the third match in a row that our opposition have had a man sent off for a tackle on Alonso. Little memo to managers of our next few opponents; 'If Xabi is in possession, don't touch him. Ok.' It's harshish, not hashish, no it's a bit harsh but as I've told you 'stay away from Xabi'. Ten minutes to go and Riera gets the equaliser. Since we've signed him we've heard no more about the word 'width'; which I was getting really sick and tired of. He deserves his goal and the Reds are going for it now. Surely we can't come back from the dead yet again. Oh yes we can. Dirk Kuyt volleys it in off the bar with 5 left. Oh happy days. Last season Dirk couldn't have hit Steve Bruce's head with a frying pan and now he's won us the game for the second week running. Get in there Dirk lad.

We give it toes to get out of the ground but Hotlips looks in distress. "I'll tell you when we get out the ground" she purrs. Only Joe Corrigan (pick a card, pick a card) has elbowed her in the mouth. Anyway I'll be seeing him in Madrid. Fancy elbowing my bird. I'll saw him in half or throw daggers at him or maybe even make him disappear. That should sort the cabaret out for our

Spanish trip. So, the march continues and we keep coming back from the dead. Guess who the next league game is? Chelsea away. Should be a piece of piss. They haven't been beaten there for four fuckin' years. Well d'you know what I think? I think we might just do it. Now where did I put those lucky undies?

JD

Atletico Madrid (a)   1-1

Champions League Group Phase   Mon 20th Oct

'UEFA: fucking fans around since 1954' – there you go Michel Platini, put that on your business cards. The mess that was created by UEFA's decision to punish Atletico by forcing them to play this match at least 300km from Madrid is only now subsiding. Their reaction to the trouble at the Atletico-Marseille game was to slap this punishment onto the Spaniards a little over a week before the game was due to be played. That makes it about 2 months after most of the independent travellers had booked their flights and hotels. We'd pondered what to do if UEFA were true to their threat, and forced the game to be played in Valencia or Seville. Jegs and I considered getting the train or a flight from Madrid. There was even a suggestion that the game would be played in Mallorca, several hundred miles off the coast.

"It'd be mental. There'd be thousands of Atletico fans trying to do the same. Prices would go through the roof," mused Jegs.

We decided that should UEFA move the match that we (and probably hundreds of other Liverpudlians) would stay in Madrid and watch it a bar as close as possible to the Vincente Calderon Stadium. We'd be there in spirit' as it were; almost like the real thing.

However, sense – a word not usually associated with UEFA – eventually prevailed. Rick Parry had said that he'd been on the phone pleading our case, and told UEFA that at least a thousand Liverpool fans would be in Madrid on the Tuesday afternoon, the day before the game. He said that UEFA had presumed that the vast majority of our fans would be travelling on chartered flights on the Wednesday, and that these flights could be easily re-routed to Andalucia or The Balaerics. In my role as Fan Liaison officer for S.O.S, I spoke to Parry for an update.

"UEFA haven't got a clue, have they?" I said to him.

"It would seem not," he said, sounding like someone who's given up all hope.

But amazingly, at the 11th hour, UEFA do something they haven't done for a long, long time and put the fans first. Or, if they don't quite do that, they don't put us last, this time. The game is on – and it goes ahead in Madrid.

Jegs and I are staying at the Asturias Hotel in central Madrid on Calle Sevilla, a 5 minute walk from Puerta Del Sol. It's got a turn of the century charm, but it's a bit frayed round the edges and could do with an overhaul. However, seeing as its just a place to sleep and shower, and in a fabulous location, then it'll do nicely.

We arrive around 3pm, and Jegsy is thinking of having a quick kip, but I talk him out of it and drag him out for a beer. Just round the corner, on Calle San Jeronimo, is the fabulous ' El Museo Del Jamon'; or at least one of them. 'The Museum of Ham' is one of a small chain of bar-cum-butchers shops throughout the city. On one side there's a gaggle of old women in headscarves, all buying ham and bacon for 'his tea' from a fabulously well stocked meat counter. All around the walls and ceiling hang dozens of hams (jamons) giving the air a slightly sweet and nutty aroma. On the other side is, well... it's a bar. There's no seating, just a horseshoe-shaped zinc bar, with glass chiller cabinets, crammed with croquettes, sandwiches, anchovies and sausages. Behind this stand half a dozen barmen in waistcoats waiting to serve you coffee, cerveza and tapas from 8am until the early hours. Everything from egg on toast to fried squid. For the footy fan on a budget – it's a godsend.

After a short pub crawl Jegs decides he needs a teatime kip in order to set himself straight for the evening's onslaught, and after a sticky cake from a pastry shop he heads back to the Asturias. Left to my own devices I head off for a sightseeing stroll and a few beers in the bars on Calle La Cruz. When the draw had been made I'd watched it live on the UEFA website. As the little national flags of the clubs involved moved across the screen from the 'Seeding' boxes into the little 'Group' boxes I kept an eye out for who we might get, mouthing 'Jammy bastards' as the Mancs got Villarreal, and Chelsea got Cluj. I knew that at work Mick Smith would be beating the top of his desk in frustration at these same draws. We'd had a boring set of clubs so far, with the oh so familiar faces of Marseilles and PSV, and only team left to go. However, the red and yellow striped Spanish flag of Atletico was still there. My focus narrowed in on it, in anticipation of seeing it slowly cross the screen to settle in Group D.

When it happened I let out a triumphant 'Yes!' and leapt into action. Holland and France could wait, this was the priority. It's long been an ambition to watch The Reds in a competitive tie in Madrid, one of Europe's greatest 'going out for a bevvy' cities. The Spaniards love a drink as much as they love their football. We have at least *that* much in common. Add to the equation that, served as it is by dozens of budget airlines, Madrid is one of the cheaper places to fly to, and it was certain that we'd be bringing *thousands* out here, with tickets or without.

In the early evening I meet up with Mick Smith, along with Nicky, Calamity Phil and few others, including Big Andy, the monster sized farmer from Nottingham, with hands the size of hot water bottles. He has the appetite of a grizzly bear and I once watched him demolish a 3 course meal in Bordeaux, then call the waiter back and order an extra pudding and a plate of chips. They're in the Taberna Real, a great old tiled tavern opposite the Royal Opera House. We have a few, then move on to a restaurant over the road. I order a steak and a bottle of Rioja. Everyone's pleasantly half-cut by this stage, and Phil's already spilled one bottle of wine over the tablecloth, and in bending down to retrieve a lost spoon, cracked his head on the table, almost knocking himself unconscious. Knowing that the game is still 2 days away gives us all a real holiday, devil-may-care, rather silly feeling. We're having a raucous time. We've necked about six bottles of wine, when someone mentions my impending appearance on Liverpoolfc.tv. Shit! I'd completely forgotten about this. They're going to ring me at 11 so I can go live on-air and give the viewers a taste of what it's like in Madrid tonight. Worryingly, I'm pissed as a fart, but I've got half an hour, so we pay-up and leave. Mick and I go over the road to a small cafe where I order a coffee. Well, it's a *carajillo* to be fair, a staple of Spanish nightlife (and day life) which consists of a coffee with a brandy top. I reckon the caffeine might just jolt my brain into life.

When they do call it takes an almighty feat of concentration not to swear, so I can't really remember what it was that I said, bar for something about there being loads of Liverpool fans around the centre of Madrid already, and to bring a coat as the weather will change on Wednesday. Oh, yes, and I called a Jegsy a puff for going to bed. Media call over I decide it's time to wake Dodd up and introduce him to the madness that is Madrid at night. I phone him, arranging to meet on the main street up by the hotel. When I see him, he throws his hands in the air.

"What have you been saying about me? I've had all sorts of text messages saying I've just been called a puff live on the telly."

"Don't know what you mean mate."

"Gilly and Ally and everyone just said Johnny Mac said Jegs is a puff. He's in bed," he complains.

I may well have called him a preening, cat-napping jessy but he's obviously done the sensible thing. We've got four nights of this before we fly home and I have a feeling that maybe I've jumped the gun. Still, I can't help myself – I'm a veteran of many a great Euro night in many a strange city but I'm excited, damn it! *I'm excited.* We could do this for another 30 years and I'll still be excited. I decide that Jegs needs to start catching up and I tell him I'll take him to a real – REAL – Spanish bar.

La Taurina Cerveceria, near El Museo, is a bullfighting beer hall. It's tiled in the Andalucian fashion, with cast-iron ballustrades and old black and white photographs of Spain's great bullfighters. One would imagine Ernest Hemmingway in here, sipping a carajillo and making some notes for 'Death In The Afternoon'. All around the walls, high up, are stuffed bull's heads, mounted like the hunting trophies I suppose they are.

Jegsy is studying a small plaque beneath one of the bull's heads. On it is a collection of names and dates.

"I think it's the name of the bull... er... the farm where it was born," I say. "Er... and that must be the year it was born."

"Go 'way," he says, smiling and licking a Rizla that he's about to fashion into a roll-up.

"And that, I think, is the name of the bullfighter who killed it and the date..." I add.

He thinks it's amusing.

"So it's like saying: Kenny Dalglish. Born: Glasgow 1951. Glasgow Celtic. 1971-77. Liverpool 1977-89," he suggests.

"Yeah, 'spose so," I say. "Something like that. Only they wouldn't have his head up on the wall."

He pauses to digest that. "No.... No 'heed'. Not just yet. He hasn't finished with it."

"They're as famous as footballers or pop stars in Spain, you know. They take it all very, very seriously," I tell him. "...and the bulls live a pampered life and are revered almost as much as the matadors are."

"Yeah, until they cut their balls off and eat them," he says.

In the bullfighting bar in Madrid before Jegsy threw the lips on El Toro
and had to leave in a hurry

"I bet that's only put on the menu to frighten tourists," I add. "I bet no-one really eats them."

"Well you couldn't put something's balls in your mouth, could you?" he says, and fixes me with a look that tells me this conversation is about to stray wildly off course. So I pay the bill and we move towards the door.

"Oh hang on," says Jegs.

He jumps on a table and grabs a bull by the horns and kisses it on the snout.

"See ya, Kenny!" he says.　And the bar goes silent. It's one of those *Deliverance* moments. The staff look on horrified. Its as if someone had gone into the Glasgow Rangers Supporters Club, stood on the bar and drawn a moustache on the portrait of The Queen.

"Jegs!" I say, as one of the barmen appears to be reaching for something under the counter. "Come 'ead – let's go!"

We cross the busy main road and head back to Calle La Cruz, a more serious drinking area; I mean, there's an Irish pub there for a start. In one of the bars we strike up a conversation with a little bloke who talks in a faint, soft Merseyside accent. He laughs at our gags and asks if he can hang around with us.

"Yeah, of course mate," I tell him. With that, our new best friend heads off to the toilet and Jegs says to me:

"As long as he gets the ale in." Then after a pause:

"Do you reckon he's a Queg?"

Got to say, that's not impossible. The guy's too well groomed for a football fan out on the ale. And he speaks too nicely; not particularly effeminate but, I dunno. He has a hint of lavender about him. He's also wearing a brightly coloured, striped top; the kind of thing that would get you chased out of Kirkdale, and you wouldn't stop running 'til you collapsed panting into the foyer of Garlands. We think about it.

"Yeah," we say in unison. "He's arse."

Anyway, turned out it was his first time in Madrid and we got to quite like our new mate. He was funny and talkative, and he bought the next round so he was fine by us. With a multitude of places to drink in the immediate vicinity we decided to go on a pub crawl and see a bit more of the area between Plaza Santa Anna and Plaza Mayor, but for the life of me I can't remember why we went into the bar we chose next. It might have been the blaring Salsa and Samba sounds from the band crammed onto a tiny stage in the corner, or it might have been the beautiful, scantily clad Latino girls. Yes, Jegs and I could letch and leer in here, nudge each other like Sid James and Kenneth Connor, and generally prove how heterosexual we were, whilst Lenny Lavender could eye up the Antonio Banderas lookalike behind the bar.

I fling caution to the wind an order a Caipirinha, a Brazilian drink made from Cachaça, distilled from sugar cane, and get Jegs and our pal pints.

"What the hell is *that*?" asks Jegs, eyeing the colour, the glass and the *straw* with pure disdain. Maybe the combination of gay boys and Samba music has brought out my sensitive side. I mean, it's a well-known fact that I use moisturiser and this drink most definitely has a straw – what more proof do you need? The band is in full swing and the place is almost bouncing, inch by inch, down the street, such is the volume of the music. Jegs is still my poking my glass as though it contains crystal meth.

"It's a Caipirinha... Brazilian. Never had one before. Seen it on the telly," I shout down his ear

"And...?"

I take another sip.

"Wish I'd never bothered. It's shite. Too sweet.... Serves me right for trying to go native." I'm considering asking the barman to tip a large vodka into it when we both see our new friend: we've been in here a matter of minutes and he's already chatting away to an absolutely stunning looking bird. Honestly – she made Penelope Cruz look like Ann Widdecombe.

"She's barking up the wrong tree there," Jegs says with a knowing nod. And we're feeling a bit smug. But then she suddenly drapes an arm around his shoulder and two minutes later she's sucking his face off.

"Fucksake, would you look at that!" I say to Jegsy. "We never saw that coming did we?"

And all we can do is sit back in wonder and watch them swap tonsils, so we order a couple more pints and tap our toes to the increasingly irritating music, looking all pale and English amid this throbbing melee of Latin American sensuality. Face facts boys – this is not the place for two ageing Scousers with day-on-the-ale complexions and a genetic disinclination to dancing. We drain the pints and head off out into the night.

JM

Day Two   Tue 21st Oct

I know I've mentioned the link between drinking and going to watch the football before but the Atletico Madrid bender was of Vesuvian proportions. Yes, we're all partial to a few bevvies and a bit of a knees-up over a long, hard season but Madrid was almost one step beyond. This morning I swear I woke up to find my liver sat next to me having one of those miniature cups of black coffee.

"How you doin', Jegsy lad?"

"Shite, liver. Shite."

The question is – why do we do it? You don't see Italians, Spanish, French and the like drinking themselves to death staggering around Liverpool city centre pissed to the eyeballs. They just come here, go to the Beatles museum, have half a lager in the Cavern, go to the match and fuck off home. Not us though. No sirreee. We have to get leathered. It's the law. There is no escape. Even if you sneak back to the hotel, lock the door or nail planks across it, like in the Tom & Jerry cartoons. There'll still be a load of your mates banging on it, screaming "Come out you lightweight. If you don't open up, it's going in." You reluctantly open it and there's six Shane McGowan lookalikes grinning and gurning at you like you've just been outed as a mere fifteen pints a night man. Normal blokes from decent families who have got responsible jobs touch down on foreign soil for an away match and turn into slobbering monsters. Horns appear out of their heads and bloodshot eyes dart from side to side surveying the scene. Take Professor Andy Baker, for instance, a fine upstanding man, and one of Europe's foremost economists who waves tatty-bye to his lovely wife flies in from Belfast where he now resides and within 24 hours, he's lost his phone, lost a tooth, lost a lens from his glasses and lost his mind. One minute he's a quietly spoken, thoughtful, reasonable Liverpool supporter, next minute he's like a zombie flesh eater roaming the darkened streets of Madrid, looking for a one-way ticket to the twilight zone. That film *The Hangover* was based on Andy Baker, I mean it.

Mackin is in my bad books after his announcement, live on LFC TV last night that I was a big poof and had gone home to bed early. The truth being that I'd just legged it back to the hotel to change my bills and t-shirt and indulge in the Euro-necessity of a shower and have a quick half hour. But the viewing public think that I have taken the knock early, which is evident later tonight; shouts of "where's yer fuckin' pyjamas?" and "isn't it past your bedtime lad" are directed at me from the Kirkby Commandos; big Chris, who lives in Brighton, Smigger and little Darren and various other dodgy looking geezers. I shout back: "Not guilty, your Honour. All I did was freshen up, sir." But in the eyes of the viewing public I had taken the knock and for that, for a hardline supper like myself to have to take that from someone like Mackin… well it's just not on.

I am beginning to get flashbacks of a mad Cuban club, the sort of place you'd see in a Bacardi advert, all jazzy trumpets, bongos, smoke and mad Latin dancing. Certainly beats going to O'Shea's or O'Neill's or O'Shite's and drinking overpriced lager with embarrassing Liverpool fans from places that are not even on the map.

I bury my head in my hands. We make a feeble and unworkable promise not

Bucko reveals his secret weapon to the Spanish

to drink before evening as we won't be able to keep up this pace for four solid days and nights. We even discuss going to a museum or a gallery to steer clear of the demon drink. But this pathetic attempt to stay off it lasts less than an hour – just as we are about to go off in search of culture, we are sidetracked by shouts from a side street. Not for nothing is John Mackin known as a bit of a Fan Fagnet. This time it's John's Yorkshire friends hollering him (he has a slightly annoying habit of smiling when he's telling you who the latest batch of strangers are – like he's saying "Yep – I know *everyone*, me." You'll be just about to give it toes from some pigeon-toed tosser in a Beatles wig and there'll be Mackin waving gaily, saying "there's Mad Marvin from the Ramsgate Branch." John's weird pals are always called Mad or Mental... and they're never from Liverpool. Begrudgingly though, I'd say most of them are alright.) The Mad Yorkies are sitting outside a café bar in a picturesque square. We make a half-hearted attempt to keep it brief and non-alcoholic, but resistance is futile. As a sop to sobriety that's so pathetic it's hilarious, we order those brandy glass-sized third-of-a-pints. The old lady brings them out on a tray with olives, and the beer's so cold it forms dewdrops that you just want to lick off the glass and in that split second the world could not get any more perfect. I'm with mates, abroad, drinking cold, cold beer in a far foreign square and I'm here to see the Redmen. It's exactly 2 p.m on the day before the game. The sun shines down on my grizzled gob and as that first golden cerveza slides down the hatch I just know it's going to be a long, long, long, long road to bed.

We move on to the Museo de Jamón, meekly accepting that we are now, once again, officially On It. Joe Corrigan with a few Dutch Reds with him, then Nico and the Belgians arrive. As the old pin-stripe scarf used to boast: Liverpool FC – Supporters All Over The World, and I'm half expecting the Democratic Republic of Congo Reds to march in next or the Ashby-de-la-fuckin'-Zouch contingent. Mackin absolutely buzzes off it and I suppose it is a good thing. There are no rules on who or why you should support a team. You just come along and join the family and swear allegiance to the Liver bird. We are an equal opportunities organisation. But obviously if you decide to wear silly hats or wigs in the mode of the what the identi-kit Sky TV football fan looks like, you may get a tap on the shoulder and a verbal warning. We do have our reputation as the coolest fans in the world to uphold. A few of our newer supporters from around the country have had to be reminded that when following Liverpool away in Europe that it is not in any way like going abroad to watch Ingerland. There's no place for Nazi salutes and Rule Britannia's on

Andy Baker the life and soul of the party

our firm. Because we are global, man, with the epicentre centred around the mean streets of Anfield, Liverpool 4. There's no need for us to mob up, kick off and abuse the locals. No, no, no. The secret is to embrace the culture, get pissed and enjoy.

Our only problem in Madrid is the amount of Scousers getting pickpocketed. Yes, I know – Scousers getting dipped. We're meant to be streetwise, and all that. But seriously, it isn't just one or two of the lads who've been relieved of their money, cards and passport. It's literally dozens. Everyone you bump into has a story to tell, most involving ladies in headscarves jostling around them on the crowded tube trains. Some of the sums of money mentioned are eyewatering but the most surprising thing is that a lot of the victims were some of the most seasoned duckers and divers ever to follow the men in red. Of course, not even the legendary Diego Dip, whispered to be the greatest pickpocket in all Iberia could capture that most elusive wallet of all – the fabled Danny Giles Pouch of popular myth. Such a mainstay of Scouse folklore is the Giles Wad that its size and whereabouts remain, to this day, a matter of fierce conjecture. Is it so vast that he carries it in a manbag? So sacred that it has to stay close to his skin in the form of a sweaty waist pouch. Some still say that Danny's bed hovers mysteriously above the ground, so immense is the stash he's shovelled underneath it. Wherever he keeps it though, the pickpockets of Madrid are going to have their work cut out as the King of Kitty and his slummy are not easily parted. Should the dipmeastros manage to breach security and delve among the skulls and carcasses of Danny's loose change pocket, they'd probably find a few pesetas he's slotted from the 1976 UEFA Cup kitty (or was it EUFA back then?) when Toshack scored the winner in Barcelona.

And is if by magic, the great one materialises out of the ether.... It's Danny blinkin' Giles and I'm made up to see him. It's like something off 'Stars in your Eyes':

"Tonight Matthew, I'm gonna fire the ale in."

Danny's up on the train from Malaga with Stewy, Cavo, Hendo, Paul Randals and all the Birkenhead crew. Every bar you go in you know someone. The gaff is rammed with Redmen. And it gets better… the aforementioned Mad professor, Andy Baker strolls in, all genial smiles and formal.

The Irregulars, as always, are there in force, as is "Eurolad" – the name me and Sammo have give to all of those faces you've let onto over the years that you just haven't got a name for. You shared some amazing experiences all over Europe with some of these people and you don't even know who they are. "A'right lad, a'right mate, how's it going kidda, man, la, lid," etc, etc. You see them season after season, year after year and you haven't got a scooby if they're married, divorced, sane, sectioned… what they do for a living or where they live or anything. But it doesn't really matter. They are your match mates and over the span of your life on God's scorched earth you'll be seeing more of these boys than any of your supposed old school mates. Mad isn't it. Anyway – myself, Prof Baker, Johnny Mac, Danny Giles and his extended Birkenhead clan have a ball getting drunk and teaching the locals the full red repertoire. Can't be beat.

On the way back to our hotel, we stumble across quite a famous face from the match, who shall remain nameless. He is walking arm-in-arm down the road with a prostitute who looks like Didier Drogba in a frock. Let's just hope our man doesn't go down in the box as easy as Drogba does. He may live to regret it.

JD

Day Three   Wed 22nd Oct

Match day. After 2 successive nights on the swallee, including yesterday's mega bender, I wake up simultaneously hung-over and roaring drunk. It's about 10am. I take great succour in knowing that it all awaits me again, and that we have another couple of days of this ahead of us. Can't wait!

What can I remember …? Wine. Lots of it. Joe Corrigan going round the bar dispensing alcoholic largesse like a Russian oligarch at his daughter's wedding. What else? Sampson, yes, no – he's not here. So who was that? Oooer! … Oooh, dunno. What the feck happened? I try to rouse Jegs who is lying face down on his bed in his boxer shorts and t-shirt looking like he's been shot. "My lord, my lord," I shake his shoulders. "Your carriage awaits.". He shoos me away like a fly so I switch on the telly, in the hope that this gets him into the land of the living, and head for the shower.

As I stand under the lukewarm dribble of water, fragments of last night creep back into my head but the overall evening remains beyond me. Errrr …. nope, nothing, *nada*. Not a clue. I feel like Guy Pierce in Memento, trying to piece my life back together again. After a quick shave I return naked to the bedroom hoping this might frighten El Dodd into action. I stand in front of him brushing my teeth. He's upright now – no, not THAT way. He's sitting on the edge of the bed trying to remember how his legs work.

"Wharrapened?" I ask.

He puts on his glasses and suddenly beams: "Oh Mackin, Mackin, Mackin… you were bladdered, my friend. You were gone."

"Yeah?"

"Oh yiss. 3 bottles of wine and a shed load of ale. Corrigan had to take you home."

I laugh.

"No, honest, he did. Your eyes had gone. You were, in short, utterly fucked"

That might explain why my mouth feels like sandpaper yet when I look in the mirror it's Johnny Depp staring back at me. There's only one possible explanation: I am still pissed. Tremendous!

It's grey and wet when I hit the pavement twenty minutes later. It's also bloody cold. I'd woken up in the middle of the night and put on a t-shirt, a pair of footy shorts and a pair of socks in order to keep warm. Yesterday's sun bathing in the Plaza Santa Anna seems like an age away. The Spaniards are all wrapped up in overcoats and scarves, and the forecast is for heavy rain. I can see a messy afternoon holed up in bars ahead of us. Blast!

Jegsy, meanwhile, is stumbling round the room trying to find articles of clothing, brain cells etc. so I've arranged to meet Joe for a coffee and he tells me how he had to guide me back to the Asturias as he feared I'd get lost walking the 100 yards back to the hotel. I have a wee chuckle to myself; that hasn't happened since Norway in '97 when a little old Norwegian woman, 80 if she was a day, had to walk me back to my hotel at 5am. Why she was out wandering the streets at 5am remains a mystery: she was either off out to milk the goats or she was Bergen 's most optimistic prostitute.

Joe and I decide that having a beer right now would be fatal, and opt instead for a walk up towards the Teatro Real, the Opera House, in an attempt to see slightly more of Madrid than the world that's enveloped in these same four streets. The rain is now beginning to lash down in earnest and the walk unfolds into ten paces on slippery paving stones, followed by 5 minutes sheltering in a doorway. A tiny Chinese woman has been watching us – the only idiots on a busy main street without either hats or brollies – and sidles up to us, grinning, and tries to sell us umbrellas. They're gay little tartan things that collapse, when folded up, to the size of a tube of Smarties. After a quick haggle we hand over 5 Euros for two and continue on our way. Another ten paces ... This is ridiculous, we agree. It's simply ruining our hair. I've a black trail of 'Just For Men' slowly trickling from my left temple and down my cheek, looking like a map of the River Nile. A quick glance shows the sky darkening. I look at Joe, Joe looks at me.

"Fuck it!" and we beat a retreat back to the Museo Del Jamon and order 2 'fatal beers'.

By the time a full complement of gentlemen has assembled in the 'Jamon' it's getting on for 1 o'clock. Nico is there with a couple of Belgian buddies, Marc and Dirk, and Joe's been joined by his lad, Jack. Irish Liam, that's Liam Carpenter from deep in the Wicklow mountains where he still lies in wait to

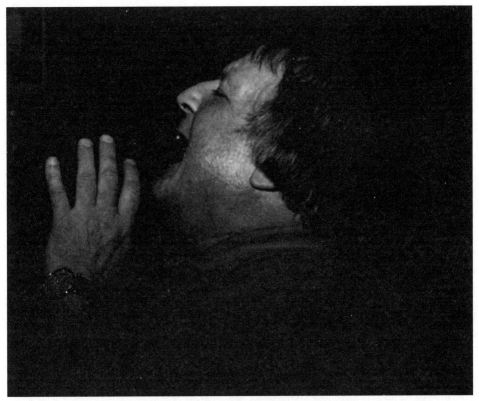

'The call of the wild'. Lenny Woods in full voice.

ambush Black and Tan convoys, is sat back, watching it all unfold, roaring with laughter at anything and nothing. He's wearing a 2001 Alaves shirt – a change from his usual five-sizes-too-small 1965 Cup Final jersey. Doddy and Baker are engaged in quiet conversation. Everyone's on the cerveza and eating a variety of tapas, except for Dodd who's opted for bacon on toast. The rain has, quite literally, dampened any intention we may have had of striking out and visiting bars further afield.

We move on to the streets around Calle Victoria. More and more Reds are appearing and the Irish pub up the street, is getting noisy. The rain finally stops and this prompts us to amble further afield. Mick Smith and his crew of Hobbits (So called as they come in all shapes and sizes, and enjoy a minimum of 12 meals a day) are in a restaurant where, I am assured, "the wine is the gear." However, this recommendation comes from 'Calamity' Phil, whose wine tasting faculties have been eroded like a Dorset beach from years of over indulgence. I pop my head in – he's grinning like a children's TV presenter – and he brandishes a glass at me in salute:

"Rioja!" he bellows across the restaurant, "Fantastico!" Seconds later he's spilt its contents all down his shirt and over Mick's jeans. The look on his face was as if he'd accidentally flushed a winning lottery ticket down the toilet. 'Calamity' Phil's idea of hell on earth would be a repeat of the 13 hour flight we shared to Tokyo for the World Club Championships. The Alitalia cabin crew were incredibly mean with the wine, and Phil had to somehow make just 3 small bottles of 'cooking Chianti' last him the entire journey. I even gave him my rations to see him through his cold turkey as we flew over Siberia, Phil sweating and mumbling as I watched 'Sleepless in Seattle' for the 3rd time that night.

He refills the glass and offers it to me – it's not bad at all. I promise to join them all later. I had back across the *calle* to a tiny bar – stuffed with all us 'arl arses' quaffing Mahou lager. The place is decorated with colourful ceramic tiles and looks more like a fish and chip shop – with it's high zinc counter – than a pub. And that's probably because it is a fish and chip shop; well, a fish and patatas bravas shop that also sells draught Mahou. There's a right motley crew assembled: old school, hard-core travelling Reds sheltering from the drizzle, and several local octogenarian alcoholics trying to sell us forged tickets for tonight's game. What we all have in common is our stratospheric blood-alcohol levels – we are all children of a common bond known as 'the swallee'. Half of Bobby Wilcox's regulars are in here; Philly Aspinall in particular is having problems standing upright, as well as a clutch of old Anny Road-ers that Jegs hasn't seen in years. Steve Sullivan sits, beer in hand, grinning as usual and looking dishevelled like he's just climbed out of the boot of someone's car after a 48 hour road journey from Bootle. He has strange, wiry hair growing out of the top of his crumpled t-shirt, and from his every crevice and orifice. To small children I imagine he looks very, very scary – to us, he is the twinkling weasel known to all and sundry as Sully.

We're regaling each other with tales of last night, of bars visited etc. when there's a kerfuffle out in the street. I take a peek, expecting to see Calamity Phil sitting on the pavement, holding his head, as a waiter tosses his coat out after him. What we actually see is an old woman, lying in a puddle. She's wailing in Romanian. The cause of this wailing is probably because she's got two Scousers sitting on top of her. It transpires that she'd just snatched some woman's handbag and managed to sprint just a few yards before being sent sprawling by the two blokes. Once on the ground they affected a citizen's arrest by jumping on top of her, twisting her arm up her back, and recovering the handbag. The bag is then swiftly returned to it's owner, a middle-aged Spanish lady, who – clearly shaken – stands over the old woman chastising her loudly. The two blokes sit there, awaiting the arrival of the police who don't appear to have been summoned. They are beginning to look uncomfortable. The Romanian is now screaming and a small crowd has gathered to take photographs and point. The Scousers look to the Spanish lady to move things along.

"Phone the bizzies, love. We'll keep 'er 'ere. But hurry up, will yer! She stinks!"

However, the Spanish woman, having had her rant, just rams her bag tightly under her arm and marches off. The two Scousers have now become the focus of attention, much to their unease. They have no option but to get up and let their Romanian hostage wriggle free and scamper away, to much abuse from the Spanish crowd, one of whom throws a small orange after her. Disappointed that a lynching now looks less and less likely, the children of Franco shuffle off into the afternoon. What with the Madrid police and the Atletico ultras both on their best behaviour tonight, and the bullfighting season still months away, the slowly dispersing mob have seen their only chance of a bloodletting evaporate before their eyes. The Scousers, meanwhile, stand there sniffing their hands and pulling faces of disgust.

"What's the Spanish for 'Fabreze'?" one of them asks.

* * * * *

Around 3pm we decide that it's lunchtime and Joe calls the 'Dining Club' to order. He's selected a Basque seafood place called 'Xabriero' just over the road from the 'Jamon'. It's a long, narrow, dark-wood panelled room but the owner has let us brighten the place up by putting all our flags up. 'The Gentleman's Dining Club' one is draped over the front window which only serves to make things inside even darker. Nico's 'Rioja Gran Reserva Por Favor' flag adorns one wall inside, and seems to be well received by the Spanish couple enjoying a quiet lunch at a nearby table. We're just settling in and studying the menus, the table already groaning with wine, beer and Asturian cider, when Gary Dempsey arrives from Paris with his mate Godfrey, a Belfast lad. They've come direct from the airport when they heard we were having lunch, determined not to miss out. Gary's dad Stan was one of the great old school Reds, and even though he'd been exiled out in Ohio for 30 years his love for Liverpool FC never wavered and he'd make it over to Anfield every season. Gary's a Scouser too, but he's lived in New York for years, and is now living literally in the shadow of the Eiffel Tower in Paris. He has a habit of ringing me up from inside football grounds all over the world: Moscow Dynamo, Boca Juniors, Red Star Belgrade... and saying: "You'll never guess where I am?" When I ask what he's doing there, it's always; "Oh, it's work!" Some job. Godfrey Deeney is something of a nutcase: an Oirish rake, a wastrel, a libertine... and I love him. He works in the fashion industry in Paris and has the phone numbers of the likes of Naomi Campbell and Karl Lagerfeld in his mobile. Beware of a drinking session with this man. He is seriously bad for your health.

We're crowded round the tables on small stools and we order everything on the menu – twice. Or so it seems. Plates of razor clams, prawns, squid and fried fish are piled on top of one another. People are wandering in and out all the time from the street to have a pint with us – it seems most of 306 Block are in here. John Buchanan and Mags are ripping the shit out of poor old Loz Gray, The Rattle webmaster. He is on the receiving end of a sustained tirade about his choice of footwear. Ironically, it's the fashionista Godfrey who saves him with a:

"Don't you listen to all these dickheads – Adidas is shoite!" Loz is well into his 30s, yet could pass for 15. As Baker once remarked: "He has the skin of a teenage girl." To which Jegs replied, "Yeah... but, it's in a suitcase under his bed."

Sammo calls – he's just checked in at the Asturias, where his unfeasibly fast metabolism (he farts all day and all night) have forced him, yet again, to book himself a single room. I volunteer to go and get him and bring him back to the bar. I arrive at his room in time to find him spreading straw over the floor.

"Come 'ed then, you've got serious catching up to do."

"Just give us a sec," he says, patting a rubber sheet into place and securing his nappy. "Okay. Let's have it."

It's 5 pm now, and we regroup over at the 'Jamon'. More beer is drunk and arrangements made to meet up after the game. We split up into small groups and head off to Vicente Calderon stadium, some by metro, some by taxi. Baker and I slope off for a few quiet beers up the road, ending up in the Taberna Real, drinking wine, about an hour and a half before kick-off. Deciding that the 'rush' will have abated by now we hail a cab and set off. The roads seem very quiet and it looks like we'll be there in plenty of time, however a couple of hundred yards away from the stadium, with the floodlights glowing high up in the damp night sky, we grind to a halt in the traffic.

"This'll do, mate" says Baker, and we tumble out onto the pavement directly outside a small bar. Forty minutes, and several beers, later we're approaching the Calderon.

"This must be our end – coppers everywhere"

Over the road a group of about 250 Liverpool fans are being held back about 10 metres from empty turnstiles. They are protesting about not being allowed in. I decide to stand back and see what happens as there's a line of police on horseback just behind us, slowly stroking truncheons strapped to their thighs. Things could be on a hair-trigger, and I'd rather not get beaten senseless for simply trying to get into the ground. Baker, meanwhile, is impatiently bobbing around and scanning the scene like a meerkat. He hasn't been baton-charged since Athens and I suspect he's becoming impatient. He loves the smell of teargas in the morning. After a few minutes he decides to take matters into his own hands and turns to what we assume is the Spanish copper in charge.

"There's no need for all this, kidder. Not all Liverpool fans are hooligans you know." He then looks at me and nods, before adding, "We are, though."

Feeling pretty smug he folds his arms and leans back against a fence, which slides unexpectedly backwards leaving him flat on his back in the street looking up at a row of mounted coppers, all dressed like Darth Vader, atop snorting horses.

"Well done there, mister," I say, helping him to his feet, "I think we've got them worried."

Just behind us Ged Poynton stands on the back of a police lorry watching us. Poynton is Liverpool FC's stadium manager and organises the security at our away games on the Continent. He's flanked by English police spotters in yellow tabards with Crosses of St George on them.

"You wanna gerra grip here Ged," I helpfully proffer, nodding at the fracas unfolding at the turnstiles. He looks less than pleased with this advice and raises his hand to shield his eyes from the floodlight glare. Then with his eyes hidden from view so I'm not sure who he's addressing he says something about people arriving late and forged tickets. I'm just about to remind him that it's the Spanish police preventing us, and several hundred others, from getting into the stadium when the police suddenly move away, allowing the Liverpool fans to eventually have their tickets scanned and enter the ground.

Ged's an ex-copper, and boy does it show. I'm sure he sees fans as unnecessary interferences to keeping his stadium nice and tidy. In an ideal world ('Gedworld') Liverpool would play in front of four empty stands, echoing to the barked commands of the players as battalions of stewards marched around the perimeter of the pitch, never breaking stride until they reach the corner of The Kop and the Kemmy. There they'd snap their heads sharply towards Ged in his police control room eyrie above the scoreboard ("Eyes … right!") and salute him. Ged would remain motionless throughout this with his binoculars pressed to his eyes like one of Rommel's Panzer commanders. After a suitable pause he'd say:

"Stand down operation Anfield exercise."

We get in about 20 minutes after kick off to find the concourse rather busy. The match is underway and we are already a goal to the good but there's dozens of Liverpudlians just standing round chatting or eating burgers or trying to get coppers to swap their riot helmets for scarves. Keane scored as we were queueing outside, leaving some fans remonstrating with the police to be let through. Why? He's already scored, hasn't he? Running in now won't let you see him score it again. It's gone – forget it. Buy the end of season DVD or something. It hasn't, you may have guessed, been the first goal I've missed in my years following The Reds abroad. An example: Nico and I were in a bar opposite Real Betis' stadium in September 2005. There'd been a kerfuffle with nervous/over zealous Spanish police who'd been somewhat truncheon happy as kick-of approached (Sammo took a good thwacking to the legs for his troubles). So Nico and I decided to avoid the possibility of a beating and come back in 15 or 20 minutes. So, we're in the bar and the barman has asked if we were Liverpool fans and we said 'Yes'. He then said, in a rather welcoming and generous gesture, or so we thought: "Betis – zero. Liverpool – two."

We smiled and thanked him for such optimism thinking he must be a Sevilla fan predicting the score, but he then clarified the situation by pointing behind us, towards the looming stadium across the road, and said again:

"No! There! Betis – zero, Liverpool – two... NOW!"

And he was right. We were 2-0 up after fifteen minutes, eventually winning it 2-1. We meet Jegs and Sammo milling around this concourse. Sammo's in luck – he's avoided a thrashing from the police and seems relatively sober. They say that its packed "up there" and you can't see anything.

"Seems overcrowded," Jegs says, "People in the aisles, everywhere. Standing on seats."

"Jibbing it?"

"Nar. We're here now, aren't we? Pool!"

And in unison we give him the answer call he's waiting for.

"Mighty Reds!"

We follow them up and it is as they say – a terrible view of the pitch. We're right down at the front by the corner flag. I squeeze to the very front so as to take a photo of the pitch. This could prove useful in the morning if I can't remember whether I actually got in or not. But there's no room for the four of us so we move about a bit, as the game continues, trying this spec and that, all to no avail. We move up an aisle trying to get higher, and as we try and move in on a row where there looks like there might be a bit of room, we are told off by some bloke.

"Eh!" he says, puffing up his chest. I recognise this as Stage 1: Territory Defence Mode.

"... we were here first!" he adds. He's wearing a replica shirt over his coat and a Torres baseball cap. I look at him. He looks very, very wrong. His bird's not much better, she's wearing one of those truly, truly awful *pink* Liverpool scarves that some marketing genius decided would be cool match-day attire for our female following.

"We can't see anything from anywhere else." I tell him, thinking he might budge up and let a couple of us in. I mean, if his bird buggered off we could all get in.

"Well you should have got here earlier."

"We did. We got here Monday…."

The lads chuckle heartily, and thinking this has melted the ice Sammo burrows in further.

"Come 'ead lad – we're all standing up anyway…"

But the superfan is having none of it. He puffs his gut right out to block the way.

"We were here 2 hours before the kick-off – and these are our seats…" He says this as if he thinks it's deserving of a medal. His girlfriend nods at him with a look in her eye that says "That's right, Bomber, you tell them Scousers. Why can't they get here 2 hours before kick-off, too – like it says on the ticket?"

After a pause, Baker pipes up, in all seriousness: "2 hours before kick-off? Why the fuck would you do that?"

We give up and head back down to the concourse. The half time whistle blows and people stream down the stairs from the terracing, jogging to the toilets, looking for food. A few head up to the security staff and ask to be let out. The stewards shake their heads. No-one's allowed out at half-time. Sammo's noted this No Exit policy and I know what he's thinking. It's a challenge he can't turn down, even if he wanted to.

He's a veteran of the half-time escape to victory. At Porto in 2001, he pretended to be blind, donning Roy Orbison shades and holding on to his brother's arm as their Neil explained to the police how he had to leave the stadium, half an hour from the end, so as to avoid the crowds ("It is not safe for him. He is blind."). And it worked – the police chaperoned him right to the perimeter exits then looked on slightly baffled as he skipped across the road into the nearest bar. Whilst we were kept in for almost an hour after the final whistle, in the drizzle, Neil and Kevin sat with the locals supping SuperBock.

"Come 'ead then, young Mackin," he says. He pulls an Asthma inhaler from his pocket. "Props department."

"Oh God, not again," I say.

Baker and Jegs, knowing what's coming, say they'll meet us back in town later. I almost falter, I should really stay and watch the match, but the 'naughtiness' gets the better of me and I put my arm around Sammo's shoulders and guide him towards an exit. As we near the stewards, he droops, as if about to faint. It's a masterclass. I say something that includes the word "hospital" and they open the gate and usher us out. As soon as the gate 'clanks' shut behind us, I know we should have stayed inside. Idiots! Nothing to do now but go find a pint.

There's nowhere round our end of the stadium, no bars, it's all quiet. So we go round to the far end: the Atleti end. The end we'd been warned about by the police back home. This is where Bolton fans had been attacked by both the Spanish police and Atletico fans. We'd been advised to avoid this area completely. But, I mean, let's face it: it was only Bolton after all, and sometimes they just deserve a pasting. No?

We find a bar about 200 metres from the ground. As we enter no-one bats an eyelid. They're all glued to the TV showing the second half. We order a couple of beers and when they hear our accents, a few glances are exchanged. But they look alright; they're not exactly Ultras in here. They're just normal fellas. Even when they think they've equalised (it was ruled offside) they're pretty good about it all, ignoring us and just celebrating. So when they do eventually equalise – and it was a cracking finish from Simao – we just smile to ourselves and order another beer. They probably deserved that. As the clock ticks towards 90 minutes we decide to get away and beat the crowds. We jog up the steep hill to a main road and jump in a taxi back to Puerta Del Sol.

Back in the Xabriero it seems that the owner is only just finishing clearing up from the afternoon session when the bar starts filling up again with Reds. He's delighted. He must have taken a fortune today. By about midnight the place is absolutely rammed. The flags are up on the walls again and the three blokes working behind the bar are constantly pouring beers and cider, or opening bottles of wine. The main source of conversation seems to be the pick-pockets on the metro, who appear to have had a very productive evening by all accounts. They were dressed as Liverpool fans so they could mingle in the crowds. Wallets and match tickets went missing by the dozen, most of it blamed on Eastern European professionals, several of whom also took a bit of a pasting for their trouble. As one 50 year old Scally who really should know better commented: "You can't rob a robber."

There's a bit of a sing-song going on, and some of the Belgian contingent are looking on in awe as classic after classic is aired. From supporting Liverpool from afar to suddenly being in the middle of this must come as something a shock to them. Nico's mates, like Marc, Bert, Dirk, Cola and Stefan know all these songs (some even have great Scouse accents) and have been regulars at European aways for years now; but there's a few others from the 'Official' Belgian branch who I don't know. There's one big guy called Fabian: massive. Turns out he's a professional cage fighter. He's arseholed and shouting "Yes, Yes, Liverpool," at every opportunity between songs. Some great old Kop favourites are getting belted out but Sampson, though, has gone very, very quiet. We've both had a couple of hours start on most of this lot, and even now some stragglers are just getting back from the match, and he's beginning to wane. In fact he hasn't touched his pint in ages and eventually he starts nodding off and mumbles:

"John, John... I'm done for lad..."

I pull him to his feet and guide him out of the bar and along the main road. Without warning he goes completely limp, as if he's collapsed and I struggle to keep him upright. I can see the hotel about 150 yds away across a wide junction and so I sling him up and over my shoulder in a fireman's lift.

"You okay mate?"

"Awwwww...fer...gol...bar...mmmmm...awwwww...," he slobbers.

"Okay then, off we go to Bo-boes."

For the first 50 yards it wasn't too bad: he's only a tiny, wee slip of a lad after all. But then the weight begins to increase, as if someone was dropping lead ingots into his pockets. After 100 yards I'm covered in sweat and breathing heavily. The hotel is tantalisingly close yet I can only take four or five steps at a time. Sampson is slumped like a dead weight; I can't even feel his wiry frame breathing. Eventually I reach the hotel and stumble to reception.

"Three Oh Four," please I pant.

The night porter passes me the key. I stagger to the lift where I can thankfully put him down and prop him against the wall as the tiny cabin clunks and whirs slowly up 3 floors. It shudders to a stop, whereupon I draw back the metal grille and and manouevre Sampson out into the corridor, to be met by a worried (not 'concerned') looking manager.

"Is okay? Is okay?" he asks, seemingly panicked.

"It's okay mate. He's not dead."

He then follows us down to Room 304 and watches me push the door open with my foot, drag Sampson inside and drop him face down on the bed. I take his shoes off and half cover him with a sheet. The manager watches me in silence as I leave the room key by the bed, and close the door behind me.

"Right pal, thanks for your help. I'm off for a swallee," I tell him.

Back up by the Xabriero. I meet Joe Corrigan who's come outside for some fresh air. It's a wise move as it's getting rather mad in this bar now and the owner is making noises about it being time to close. It's 2am. Perhaps we might look for what other bars might still be open and find somewhere quieter. We've been running up a hell of a tab too. I ask Joe how much he reckons we owe.

"Nothing."

"Eh? Are we doing a runner?" I ask looking over my shoulder.

"No, that mad cage fighter from Belgium – he paid the bill."

"What? The nutcase? How much?"

"200 euros."

"What? Why?" I ask. Why the hell would he do that?

"Says he enjoyed our company so much. Loved the singing," Joe explains.

"Pissed?" I ask by way of explanation.

"Twatted," says Joe. "But he wouldn't take 'No' for an answer. Not that anyone actually said 'No', mind you...." The next morning in reception Joe tells me that The Cagefighter had an even more expensive evening after he'd left us.

"The daft bastard came back to the hotel at 5am completely stark bollock naked. Just his shoes on. Didn't know where he'd been or what happened.

Phoned his credit card company to report his cards missing and discovered he'd used it to spend 750 Euros somewhere, verified by his PIN number! Has no idea what he did."

"Maybe he met The Irregulars and paid their bar bill as well?"

"That might explain the 750 Euros," Joe says "... but the stark bollock naked thing?"

Meanwhile, back outside the Xabriero, we hear a wailing and a shouting and Phil Aspinall comes tottering round the corner. Phil's a great old-school Kopite, a friend of Bobby Wilcox and a top 'Globe Rat Pack' drinker, and author of some brilliant Kop songs. He's looking bewildered and emotional.

"Phil, Phil! Wassup?"

"I've been robbed, robbed!!" he wails.

"Mugged?" Joe asks, and we look around for signs of someone making a getaway.

"No, No, I think I've been dipped.," he continues. "Its all the ciggie money, Gone! Gone!... It's all gone!"

"How much?"

"A grand... more... 1200 Euros," he splutters. "It's all the ciggie money." The 'ciggie money' is the kitty used to buy cheap cigarettes abroad – and Spain is one of the cheaper countries for tobacco in the E.U. – that are sold back to subsidise your travelling costs. It's fair to say, that the 1200 Euros was not all Assy's and that several blokes would now be severely out of pocket.

"I'm skint," he goes on, clasping his forehead in his palm. "Do you know where Bobby is?"

Joe and I haven't seen Bobby all day, and we tell Phil that. I can sense Phil beginning to panic. He looks lost and we try and reassure him that it's okay now, he's among friends.

"Can you get back to your hotel? You got money for a cab?" we ask him.

"No! No!... it's all gone. I've been robbed!" I give him 20 Euros and tell him, "Look Assy, just get back to the hotel, Bobby might be there."

A small crowd of concerned Reds from the nearby bars has gathered, including Roy Bentham, from up by us in Block 306, who also hands Assy some money, 2 or 3 other passing lads who recognise a fellow Red in distress abroad also give him 20 Euros each. He's got more than enough now to get back to his bed, no matter where in Madrid he might be staying.

Then, thankfully, Paul Rice appears; he's more than likely travelled over here with Wilcox's crew. Ricey might know where Bobby is. And he does. He

The legendary Bobby Wilcox (left) duets on yet another bar room ballad

turns and heads off up the top of the street to where Wilcox Tours are ensconced, warbling mad old songs and drinking Madrid dry. A few minutes later a sight to behold hoves into view. Bobby comes trotting down the street out of the darkness, puffing and panting, wearing a pair of green dayglo plastic sunglasses with flashing lights set into the frames.

"Assy! Assy!" he cries, "Worrapened?"

"I've been dipped, lad. I've been dipped!"

"How much?" says Bobby.

"All of it. 1200 Euros." says Phil. He looks like a frightened kid trying to explain something awful to his parents.

"ALL OF IT? ALL OF IT!" wails Bobby, throwing his hands up and his head back, "How? How?"

"I was dipped. Some bird in a bar, I think," he says, then – reading Bobby's mind, as we all were too – he adds… "She weren't a brass, was she?" his voice almost trembling.

"Oh you stupid bastard!" Bobby roars. And I get the feeling that wise old

Wilcox has warned Assy about straying from the group, or carrying so much cash around; and Phil's not listened. It's becoming a 'bit of a domestic' now. Bobby's berating Assy in a way that only Bobby can – a way that makes grown men cower, telling him that its his own stupid fault for carrying a wad like that whilst drinking absurd amounts. We cringe, and thank fuck it wasn't us. But, thankfully, Phil's safe now, he's with his mates so we disperse back to our pubs and bars and continue to drink the night away.

JM

Day 4   Thurs 23rd Oct

It's the morning after the match and we think back to the madness of yesterday. I remember the 'love in' at the end of the game with all the Atletico fans chanting 'Liverpool' and us returning the compliment with everyone swapping souvenirs and shaking hands. It goes back to what I was saying about going to watch England abroad. You don't have to punch fuck out of your hosts to gain a bit of respect. You can still have a laugh and do mad things without losing your credibility. I got the feeling last night that the fans of Madrid were almost honoured to have us in their ground, which is really quite a weird kind of feeling. I certainly hope it doesn't spread to the Premier League. That would be very wrong indeed. Imagine going to Old Trafford and both sets of fans applauding each other. No, no, no, no, no. What a nightmare scenario that would be. In fact, that would be the end of life as we know it. That thought must leave my head, never to return again. Just the words Manchester United make my slippers curl up at the end, my brow furrow and my knuckles whiten.

Mackin looks worse for wear. I mean seriously worse for wear. Three big, big nights on the pop and the boy don't look well. I knew God would pay him back for bubbling me to LFC TV. His jovial smear campaign against the staying power of yours truly has spectacularly backfired as it is he who can't hack it after all. Oh thank you Lord. The boy Mackin looks in trouble. He yearns for the peace and quiet of home and the warmth and reassurance of his good lady. All he wants to do is clear his head and detox with scented candles and ambient music. Not today Johnny boy. Not today....

For the show must go on. We haven't quite finished yet – oh no siree... we are about to embark on the final leg of the journey. We are going to Lisbon for the night. Yep, you heard right. Lisbon. It's cheaper to fly back to the Pool of Life from Portugal than Madrid. We can get a hotel for the night and flight back to Liverpool for about £70 each, so Lisbon it is for our final night of debauchery. We bag a couple of taxis to the airport after a late, late breakfast and reluctantly part company with Andy Baker who is a shadow of the man we hooked up with on Tuesday. This gibbering wreck of a human being shuffles off in a daze to try and find his way home via Paris. We wish him luck. He is going to need it. He is fucked.

We arrive in Portugal and somehow manage to find the Zenith hotel which is shockingly brilliant. On this leg of the journey there have been a few team changes. I am still sharing with Johnny Mackin but we have been joined by our chief negotiator, Kevin Sampson. Peter Hooton, lead singer of, Mersey pop sextet and style icons, the Farm is on board, as are John Maguire and John Buchanan, a fine pair of upstanding young men. Last but not least, a young couple called Alex (female) and Michael (male); and a fella called Les with a flat-top.

Me and The English Patient (Mackin) have an hour's disco-nap (not so gay now is it Johnny Boy, the sneaky siesta!), and then go down to the harbour in search of the rest, who are already on it. You don't have to be a clairvoyant to see what state we are all going to be in in six or seven hours time. Darkness falls and we head up the hill to the famous Barrio Alto area. The cobbled streets are alive with people out on the town. Everywhere you go there are family-run bars dotted about playing really good music like The Doors, Talking Heads, The Stones or more modern stuff like The White Stripes or Arcade Fire. Imagine that in Liverpool. No chance whatsoever. It's the usual diet of funky bastard house and cheesy R'n'B shite, force fed to the Scouse nation every night of the week, all year. There is no alternative. I think Liverpool's had a good dig at being Capital of Culture for Europe in 2008. There's been some mistakes and some success stories. But you come here and think, this is culture. This is the real deal. The place is alive with sound and life. The cosmopolitan feel is boosted by the close links between Portugal and Brazil. The thing that really stands out for me is the distinct lack of pissed, fat, orange-faced birds staggering around with no shoes on, shouting at the top of their whiny, irritating voices. Also, an absence of gaunt looking smack heads trying to beg off you in that over-polite way that they do. Too many pleases and insincere thank-you's for my liking.

"Arright there mate, sorry to intrude on your personal space but my situation is this… I was on me way to hospital to see me Nan who's only got a few hours left to live…."

Stick to the facts smack heads. Tell me what you want in a normal manner- then I can tell you to fuck off in a normal manner back. Anyway. Lisbon. Absolutely brill.

L to R: Nico, Jegsy & Andy Baker. Three lads who shook the world. Intoxicated air guiitar. Don't ask.

We have a sit-down meal in this proper football-themed restaurant. Not some Hard Rock type of gaff or glossy sports bar (sorry Jamie lad, don't mean yours, honest) but a real independent footy restaurant. Pennants and scarves and photos everywhere. Hooto gets the sherries in and we're off. Tastes fuckin' awful but it's a start. Beer arrives, food arrives, Mackin departs. He admits defeat. He's hardly spoken all day. Off his food and hasn't been near a bevvy. Kev, who's just starting to take it up a level after finding his line and length, is goading the poor boy – he even gives him his money back, telling Mackin it'd be a disgrace to Redmen everywhere to accept money for his pathetic non-indulgence. There is no comeback and Mackin is deposited into a taxi for his own sanity and safety.

We finish up, tip them handsomely and troop over the road to a small, empty bar that boasts the unlikely combo of greatest jukebox in the world (Stone Roses, Iggy Pop, Talking Heads, The La's and, er, Andy Williams all went on) – and the two oldest men in the world sat next to it. Give them their due though, these two arl fellas haven't got a tooth between them yet they're grinning over and thumbs-upping us like they're in a Dentabrite advert. And then a bizarre scenario unfolds. Sammo winks at John Maguire and Hooto:

"Tune up, lads."

They're on it straight away, all three of them devoutly sat over imaginary guitars, holding them up to their ears to check the pitch. Young Alex and Michael stand stunned with mouths agog as men their father's age let rip. It's bad enough playing air guitar in front of people twenty five years your junior but to stand there for five minutes tuning up first must've been worthy of the firing squad. Hooto's bouncing. Me and Peter go back a long way and it's been years since I've seen him this animated. He's really letting his hair down and it's great to see him so happy. It's infectious. I suppose when he's in Liverpool it must do his head in when, every time he goes out, people are saying "Aren't you that bloke out the Farm?" No-one knows him here so he can do whatever he wants knowing that he won't end up on YouTube the next day. The same cannot be said for Kev Sammo who has never been worried about what might be said of his behaviour. He loves to act the goat and tonight he is madder than ever. In fact, he is stark raving bonkers. Completely off his chunk. A group of students hover by the door, unsure whether to come in. Like a Club 18-30 rep who's seen better days, Sammo bounces over, grinning like a loon. Blissfully, The Undertones come on at this precise moment, and Sammo utters the immortal words: "Come on kids – let's pogo!!"

The whole place goes up, but no-one bounces more enthusiastically than the oldest men in the world – Hooton and Sampson, that is.

To make matters even more bizarre, a hawker comes in selling Comedy Specs... big, huge, gaudy-coloured plastic shades that spark up with flashing disco lights every time you move. Me, Kev and Les bounce around to The Jam wearing ludicrous gigs and even dafter grins. I love seeing Sammo in this state. That 'knowing but vacant' look which says 'everything is under control' when it so obviously isn't. I take a breather and sit with the two remaining Johns who are just grinning at the whole stupidity of it all. It's getting late and I have to try and get Kevin back to the hotel. Only problem is, how am I going to manage to get him down off the ceiling? Half an hour later I miraculously get him into a taxi and give directions to the driver. We drive through the crowds blocking the roads. Kev, who has been slobbering gently, suddenly sits bolt upright and goes: "Drop us by ours."

Now this is going to be quite a difficult manoeuvre because we are in a cab in Lisbon, Portugal and Kevin thinks we are in a cab in Liverpool, England. We get him back and he's deposited safely at his room. Johnny Mac is still awake, wrestling with his demons when I tap on the door. I've got an inkling I'm not gonna feel too tickety-boo myself when I wake up, but tomorrow's another day. Come 'ed Redmen. Make us dream…

JD

Chelsea (a)   1-02

League   Sun 26th Oct

If it's not sodding UEFA, its frigging Sky TV. How they expect travelling fans from the North West to get to London it time for a 1:30 kick off on a Sunday quite obviously never enters their minds. I'm in a bit of a pickle: there's no direct train at anything like a reasonable hour, and to get there for 1:30 means driving to Crewe and catching the through train to Euston. I can drive to Halewood and pick up either the SOS union coach, or John Garner's LBU bus (LBU: The Leather Bottle Ultras, The Leather Bottle having been a legendary old pub in Halewood that's sadly no more). Either way meant not being able to have even one beer as I'd have to drive home again.

"Couldn't you just not have a pint and drive yourself?" Alison wonders out loud when I cheekily suggest she drops me off in Crewe and picks me up again that evening. What she meant was 'Sod it, mate, I'm having a glass or two of vino while you're out gallivanting with your drunken mates all day.'

"Not have a pint? Not have a pint? We haven't won there in years, what if we *do* win? I'm not going all the way to London and back, watching Liverpool be the first team to beat Chelsea at home in the league for almost 5 years, go clear at the top of the league, and NOT HAVE A PINT!"

Was she mental? What *if* we win? That hasn't happened since early 2004, a generally poor season that eventually saw Gerard Houliier get the chop for effectively taking the team backwards. That win, along with Danny Murphy's penalty that won us the game at Old Trafford, was acknowledged as the highpoint of a forgettable season. Not many of our usual crowd had travelled to that game as we'd called for a boycott when the ticket prices had been announced: almost £50 for a midweek game in London that was also being shown live on tv. Fifty quid for a normal league game! It was just after Christmas too, and everyone was skint. We decided to watch it en masse in a pub. We had mock match tickets printed up for 'Chelsea vs Liverpool, at Shenanigans Pub, Tithebarn St. L2. Admission £5.' Profits went to the HJC. We'd ordered food and sold about 80 tickets before finding out 15 minutes before kick-off that the satellite telly in Shenans had gone on the blink. We picked up the trays of food, took our pints, and decamped en masse next door to The Brunswick, where a delighted landlord took a week's money in one night. As the teams were announced the dreaded words, "and with Steven Gerrard out injured, into midfield comes Bruno Cheyrou…" brought howls of derision. "That's it, we're fucked!" announced Joynty. Someone tried to defend his inclusion in the team, only to be reprimanded by Joynty with, "I'll tell yer what – if Cheyrou scores I'll show my arse.." On the half-hour Emile Heskey crosses into the box where Cheyrou – described by a straight-faced Houllier as "the new Zinedine Zidane," well the physical resemblance was indeed remarkable, but I'm certain that's not what he meant - slides in to volley into the net. At the moment he WAS Zidane. And Pele. And Cruyff. The pub exploded in a volcano of joy and flying beer. It ended a dismal run of 7 consecutive defeats at Chelsea, and left us all enduring the site of Joynty standing on a table, in a packed pub, displaying his hairy arse.

So I've got a decision to make, and in the end the easiest option picks itself. I get the direct train from Chester which won't get me into Euston until just around kick-off time. From there it's going to have to be a mad sprint on several tube trains down to Fulham Broadway and a gentle jog the ground. On board are a couple of dozen Liverpool fans all bemoaning the fact that this country's third world train service and a satellite television company had conspired to prevent them getting to London on time to watch a full 90 minutes. There were two Irish lads – Tom and Damo – from Dublin who'd come over on the early boat and who were travelling back to Holyhead immediately after the match and would only spend about an hour actually stationary, in the ground, amidst 24 hours travelling. And they didn't even have tickets – they had to pick them up from a friend outside the ground. They asked about the tube trains, and I suggested sharing a cab as it seemed the better option given the time constraints. They normally travel to Anfield for most home games with a travel company from Dublin, but this fixture – and the ones at Everton, Arsenal and Man Utd – had sold out at the start of the season.

"I don't know where they get the tickets from," says Damo, cracking open another can of cider. "But they're always in our end. I think they took 25 to

Un-oit-ed last year an' all. Cost 230 quid, with a hotel in Warrington."

"That's scandalous," I say. "I didn't spend that much in a week in Madrid."

"They always get them, but these big games, they're expensive and they sell out quickly."

"You lot must be mad spending that sort of money for league games."

"Its alroight for youse Scousers," he laughed. "Youse can get tickets. We can't."

He's right of course. And it's probably Scouse touts passing on tickets for today's game to travel agents in Dublin and Belfast and Oslo that are at the root of all this.

"There's one fella we heard of in Dublin who gets 15 tickets for every home game from someone in the ticket office. Fifteen tickets. Every game." Damo chips in.

"From the ticket office?"

"Aye. Every game."

If that's true, I wonder how many tickets go missing and end up in the hands of touts or travel agencies for each big away game. Sections of our end at the supposed glamour games like Man. United have looked like the crowds at Madam Tussauds in recent years. Tourists, obviously attending their first ever game of Association Football anywhere ever in their lives, who've cheerfully forked out two or three hundred rips to sit among lads who've qualified on 14 or 15 credits, and whose mates are wandering around outside looking for a ticket, any ticket, somehow. It's wrong. A few years back we had to have a word with the stewards there as two Japanese tourists came into our end at Old Trafford, both wearing United shirts. I actually felt sorry for them – it would have been like throwing Christians to the lions. Tickets for these matches are sold on the basis of the number of credits you have from attending previous games, and yet here are 20 or 30 seats – in a block – filled with 'fans' who barely know the simplest of songs and chants, more concerned with taking photographs than watching the match.

"Who's the Number 9, Nigel?"

"That's er…" (consults match day programme, £5.00). "That's Torres, silly."

"Right." (Pause). "He's pretty cute, isn't he?"

Damo and Tom don't fit into that category of clueless daytripper, and I have a deep admiration for the lengths they're going to, to follow their team.

Our team. I even feel sorry for the tourists too, at times, but at the end of the day there's no doubt that your diehard, long-standing, seasoned Reds are being elbowed further and further away from the match day action as our club shamelessly drops her drawers and turns tricks for the high rollers. The Irishmen and myself jump a cab at Euston, just as the game's kicking off. The driver's got the radio on, and as he's an Arsenal fan he's as delighted as we are when Alonso scores after ten minutes.

"I hope you fack these today, mate. I fackin' hate Chelsea."

"An attitude that does you great credit, driver" I tell him. "Can you turn the radio up!"

We're still MILES from the ground and I'm wondering if we'll get in before half-time. The driver does some sterling work down the back streets around Earls Court and just on the half hour mark – we've just gone close to scoring again and the three of us are chomping at the bit to get in – we are dropped off on the Fulham Road, a short jog from the away end. The lads are supposed to be meeting their pal, just outside our turnstiles but he's nowhere to be seen. I tell them I'll see them here at this very spot (I'm pointing at the tarmac as I say it) after the game and we'll go back to Euston together. There are surprisingly quite a few Liverpool fans knocking around the concourse; lads without tickets, lads waiting for other lads with tickets, and lads with tickets but apparently too drunk to be let in and eating hot dogs trying to sober up. I show my ticket to two separate coppers, and when I approach the turnstiles a steward just waves me in, through an open exit gate, without checking my ticket. I'm supposed to be in the upper tier, and this is the lower. Its cheaper, but the view is generally crap. I'm considering asking for a refund as I make my way out into the seats, when an arm clasps me round the shoulder. It's John Pearman, editor of Red All Over The Land. He hugs me and asks which pub I've just stumbled in from.

"Do you *ever* get in before half-time, Mackin?" he grins.

"I'll have you know it's a very reasonable five-past-two, John!"

"Yes. We kicked off at half-one!"

I explain the travel problems and ask him how it's going:

"Sounds like we're all over them on the radio." I say. "Chelsea've done nothing," he says.

"Did we nearly get a second, just before?"

"Gerrard... brilliant effort, just tipped over the bar," he says.

To say I'm delighted is an understatement. I'd hoped at best that we'd come away with a nil-nil. With Torres still out injured I thought we'd struggle to create any chances at all. But with Drogba not playing they're not posing much of a threat, either. I say as much to John. The words have just left my lips when Deco thumps a great effort goalwards. That's it – my nerves go. I need to shut up and not tempt fate. It's a difficult task indeed to keep quiet, as this is one of our noisiest away ends in years. There are young 'uns baiting and taunting the Chelsea fans across to the right with an unbridled optimism that I'm afraid my advanced years will not allow. I've seen this type of thing come back to smack you in the face before.

"Too soon – you started singing too soon….," is one the older fans will know too well.

Its a great relief when the half-time whistle blows and we're still a goal ahead.

The second half holds no better luck for my nerves. The longer it stays at 1-0 the more I get paranoid. If we win this, we go top. If we win this it really does 'send out a message' or 'lay down a marker' or whatever Lee Dixon says on Match of the Day. Is this team really good enough this year to be 'sending out messages'? We might be. But facing up to the fact that we might be good enough to win the league only sets you up for the ultimate pratfall when you blow it somewhere daft like Hull or Stoke. As long as we stay just the one goal in front, then the longer this promises to be just a false dawn. All it takes is one second's lapse in concentration and you've thrown 3 points away. And that's very easy to do somewhere like Chelsea.

We get a free kick in a dangerous position just outside the box. Alonso lines it up – and he looks confident. He lets fly, right against Petr Cech's post. From where we are, very low down and to the right hand side, we're convinced that it's rebounded into the net. I grab the bloke next to me whilst hundreds of us all around leap up and down in celebration, shouting 'Yes! Yes!'. My utter elation at that moment is returned with interest – as a defender hoofs the loose ball over the crossbar for a corner – with a deeper bout of paranoia. That false outburst of relief was there just to exacerbate the dejection that will come when Chelsea surely equalise. As the clock ticks nearer and nearer to 90 minutes all around me, coltish young fans are singing "We're gonna win the league." The fools! The idiots! Don't they know that its moments like this when God loves to remind you who's in charge and deliver you an almighty smack in the kisser? Even at 89 minutes, as our support is in paroxysms of joy and singing their lungs out, I'm convinced that Chelsea are going to score. I can't sing. I can only stand there – the pressure building in my temples - and chew my nails and, yes, look at the clock. I consider turning on my heels and legging it, that way when they do equalise then at least I know I won't miss my train.

But I don't go. They don't equalise. Jamie Carragher and Daniel Agger have been 'immense' – another expression I believe Lee Dixon uses with an awestruck shake of his head to describe displays like this. At the final whistle I can only punch the air and grin like an idiot. I can feel the tension drain from my brain and my leg finally stops shaking. I let out an exultant, "Get in!" and look around for John Pearman, only to see him at the top of the steps leaving. He waves and shakes a fist at me in delight. I shake hands with complete strangers and slap them on the back, and we all pour out of the exits singing our hearts out. Outside, I stop and look around for the Oirish lads. Its extremely crowded where I'd said I'd meet them and I hang back for 5 minutes before having to go for the tube train back to Euston. They didn't turn up. Nor are they on the train back to Chester, North Wales and ultimately, Holyhead. I even spend the last 2 hours of the journey in the buffet car in the hope of seeing them and buying them a cider in celebration.

It gives me time to reflect. We really have thrown down the gauntlet now haven't we? We've been the first team in almost 5 years to win at Stamford Bridge in the league. We're still unbeaten: 7 wins out of 9 matches and 3 points clear at the top of the league. We've seen off Man.United and Chelsea with some style and guts, and we've buried Everton, too. It's Portsmouth next up and, while they provide us with a different sort of challenge, it's a game we've just got to win. I know that on Wednesday the temptation will be high on The Kop to proclaim this team as potential champions, but it's still only October. I make a mental note to keep an eye on John Garner who's been itching to sing "We're gonna win the league," since we scored the late goal against Wigan and recall on old saying: "There's many a slip 'tween cup and lip."

Not sure if that's one of Lee Dixon's or not.

JM

Portsmouth (h)   1-0

League   Wed 29th Oct

God it's freezing. I'm walking down Castle St. looking like an urban Ernest Shackleton. I quite like midweek games on a winter's night. They seem to have a certain magic that you just don't get for an afternoon fixture and even less so for one of those ridiculous lunchtime kick offs. I meet Danny Giles and his mate John who's home for a few weeks from Oz. Danny, who is technically a brickie but hasn't laid a brick since Rudolph Hess was in Youth Custody, greets me with "Fuckin' hell lad, who got you ready?" You guessed it – sin of sins I'm wearing a parka on a very cold night. I get called everything from Eskimo Nel to Kenny off South Park by the man whose fashion sense wouldn't look out of place in a televised darts match audience. We have a couple of scoops and pick the bones out of our separate Madrid experiences. We get a cab up to the ground just in time for 'Walk On'.

Pennant, Lucas, Babel and Hyypia all come in to the team as Rafa decides to rest Agger, Keane, Mascherano and Riera. It's a tough old game as Portsmouth pack the defence and combat anything we have to throw at them. Kuyt hits a post on 10 minutes. Half time comes and it's still 0-0. Downstairs Joynty gives me an enamel badge that says 'Huyton Fatties LFC', where the Liver bird looks pregnant. The badge is sound but something is wrong. Señor Joynty is how you say, well, slim. OK, well not exactly slim but you know, he's not fat anymore. I don't want to start taking the Huyton Fatties to a Trade Descriptions tribunal but you can't play the fat card if you're not, how you say, fat. I suggest he goes to the bar and gets himself a couple of sausage rolls and a beer. I mean you can't have anyone on the firm looking fit and healthy, can you? We've always prided ourselves on having a mish-mash of supporters who have broken noses, beer bellies, funny eyes and cauliflower ears. What on earth would opposing fans think if we all turned up at away games looking toned, tanned and trim. It doesn't bear thinking about. I have a quick word with Gary Shaw, who does the Mersey Boxing books, a quick chat with Brian Reade and his lad Phil, and head back up for the second half.

It's one way traffic and Sami Hyypia strikes a post on 59, and you start to get the feeling we'll rue these missed chances and shots off the woodwork. The fans are getting nervous as the chances come and go. At last we get the breakthrough on 76 minutes when Papa Bouba Diop, thank the Lord, takes all leave of his senses and volleyballs a harmless cross away. Papa Bouba Diop, now there's a name to conjure with – and we salute him for his crazy, double-handball kind of manoeuvre. It's a definite pen and I bet Tony Adams who was in charge for his first game must've done his nut at him in the dressing room after the game. Step forward Mr Gerrard with the perfect penalty. Hard, low and precise. He is invaluable to this Liverpool team. A true leader. There's a few minor scares but we get over the finishing line and remain three points clear at the top. We leg it out of the ground and I bum a lift off Sammo into town. I dive into Dr Duncan's for a quick pint and bump into Dave Kirby and Andrew Schofield who've been doing rehearsals for Dave's new play at the Royal Court. I only stay for one and get the train back to Dodd Towers where I catch the end of the midweek version of Match of the Day. I've enjoyed myself tonight but I just hope we can keep this momentum going. It's hard not to get too carried away but calm is what's needed now. Harry Redknapp's just taken over at Spurs and they're beginning to look a different side. We've got them on Saturday at the Lane so we can't ease up and think the hard work's done. We have to believe in ourselves. Sweet dreams.

JD

Spurs (a)   1-2

League   Sat 1st Nov

It's the day after the Portsmouth game and a minor catastrophe has occurred. For some unknown reason my back has gone. I've no recollection of picking anything really heavy up or feeling any twinges. Nope, I just wake up and can barely move. Tottenham away is severely in doubt as the day wears on. Those of you who've never suffered from the old dodgy back will probably be saying "He's just trying to get out of going all the way to London for an iffy kick off time (5.30pm Saturday tea time)." "He can't cut the mustard; he's a part-timer." Well nothing could be further from the truth. I was genuinely looking forward to it but I'm walking round the house looking like a potato-picker who's just had an accident in the trouser region. I manage to offload my ticket on the Friday and resign myself to watching it on the box. Only problem there, is that I don't/won't have Sky in the house, which means I have to venture out to the pub looking like Max Wall. If you're too young to know who Max Wall was, he was a bloke who did a cabaret act walking around with his arse sticking out. Not his bare arse of course, just his arse kind of jutting out like a monkey doing a silly walk to a jaunty drumbeat. People would pay good money to see him and then piss themselves laughing. Well no-one's paying to see me but I swear I heard a few sniggers behind me when I waddled into the pub, but I was that done in I couldn't even turn around to give 'em the 'Kop Eye'.

Inside I meet Frank, Chris and Cal, and they're looking after me like I'm a geriatric dribbling granddad. "Do you want a bag of nuts?" Now are you sure you're alright going to the toilet?" The thing is they seem to say it in a louder voice than normal. I'm not fuckin' deaf, I've just got a bad back, that's all.

The game kicks off and Dirk Kuyt scores almost from the off with a cracker, an absolute thunderbolt of a shot from an acute angle, right into the Tottenham net. I resist the urge to jump up. I just flutter my eyebrows a bit and shout at the screen. I hate watching matches in the pub because there's always some knobhead close to you who hasn't got a clue what's going on but has to express his ill-formed opinions louder than everyone else. I wouldn't mind but he's even calling all the players the wrong names.

Although Harry Redknapp has arrived from Pompey to save our North London opponents from the Abyss, the fact is, we're all over them. We should be four up at half time but we have to make do with a flimsy 1-0. The retard at the bar is getting on me tits now. Gerrard has hit the woodwork twice and has been dead unlucky when he screams down my ear "Fuck off Gerrard, you're shite!" I can feel myself going but then I'm thinking 'keep a lid on it, lad'. I can barely walk, never mind go 15 rounds in the car park with Billy Big Bollocks behind me. Frank calms me down with a quiet word:

"Look at the positive side, Jegs. At least he knows which one Steven Gerrard *is*."

Frank can always take the sting out of a situation with his surreal, sarcastic take on things.

But against all odds and completely against the run of play, in the 70th minute disaster strikes. Spurs get a corner and it skims off Carra's head past Pepe and into our net. We have totally dominated play and to drop two points here would be an injustice of gigantic proportions – but worse is to come. Spurs are on a high and they plug away and plug away and of course the inevitable happens. In the last minute Pavlyuchenko scores from close range after some panicky defending in our box. Ouch! It's like we're all in a submarine and the oxygen has suddenly been cut off. People slump into their seats with heads in hands as everything seems to go into slow-motion. Billy Big Bollocks, the voice of pub punditry gives one last glowing piece of football insight before shuffling off to his stinking bedsit.

"FUCK OFF LIVERPOOL! YOU'LL NEVER WIN THE LEAGUE IN A MILLION YEARS…"

I hate people like him supporting our team. All of a sudden I have a strange desire to murder him but when I weigh up the pro's and con's of it all – these being five minutes of satisfaction versus life imprisonment – I err on the side of caution and give him a walk over. He turns to leave and I can't help noticing he's got GERRARD 8 on the back of his Liverpool shirt. The irony of it plunges the dagger even deeper into my wounded heart.

Anyway we're all a little deflated not to have won and the papers tomorrow will be full of stories about Harry Redknapp's magic touch but even Harry knows that lady luck has smiled on his team today. We've got to try and remain positive. We sneaked it ourselves against Boro, City and Wigan when we looked dead and buried, so you've just gotta take it on the chin when things go pear-shaped. It's not easy but that's the way it goes. My main worry at the moment is getting this back of mine sorted before Tuesday's match with Atletico. We made it through to November before our first defeat in the League, and we've just got to treat it like a bad day at the office. Keep the faith brothers and sisters, keep the faith.

JD

West Brom (h)   3-0

League   Sat 8th Nov

When I was a boy, football was played at one of only two possible kick-off times. There was the traditional, the eponymous, THE footy kick-off time of 3 o'clock on a Saturday afternoon. This is the proper time for football to be played. 3 o'clock gives blokes the opportunity to get a few bothersome chores out of the way first before attending the match: a morning at work perhaps; taking the missus to do a 'big shop', or mowing the lawn/painting the skirting boards; or maybe even playing a game themselves on a local pitch against the cocaine crazed, drug-dealing psychos from that mad pub on the estate. But whatever the morning threw at you, there was still ample time for a bevy two before the game and a walk up to the ground with your mates.

There was also the more exotic time of 7:30 in the evening; but only on a Tuesday or Wednesday. This was when League Cup football would be played, as well as F.A Cup replays and the occasional re-arranged fixture. And for the lucky few clubs, it was when European Cup football would be played. However, since Sky's stranglehold on the English game took a grip in the early 90s we've seen kick off times at all sorts of hours and on every day of the week. A weekend game could be played at any time from 7pm Friday to 8pm on Monday evening, and for a variety of reasons, too – ranging from 'Police Advice' to Far-Eastern TV audiences ("don't complain, Liverpool F.C – 11am is prime time in Singapore. Think of the replica shirt sales!").

By far the most agreeable of these TV-oriented kick off times has to be the 5:30 home game on a Saturday. This gives everyone the chance to do a variety of things before the game, and also to enjoy an evening's entertainment in licensed hostelries with one's chums afterwards. Should the 'variety of things before the game' translate as 'variety of pubs to visit before the game' – then you've scooped the jackpot. She should expect you home in a very messy state no earlier than 1am, smelling of beer and chips.

I get out early for this one. It's a lovely day and the sun is shining. I'm in town early – around 11am – and drinking pals are thin on the ground for the next hour or so. I decide to go somewhere I've never had a pint in before and hit upon The Lady of Mann, a new bar in the small paved square behind Rigby's on Dale Street. I'm the only customer so it only takes 20 minutes to get served by a young girl who'd rather polish the optics. I take my Guinness and settle down with The Daily Post and The Mirror. Everton are away at West Ham and the Post quotes their manager, Gianfranco Zola, thus, under the headline 'Zola looks to follow Goodison example':

> *"Last Year Everton did very well and they are certainly a very good team. I like the manager who has done a great job- and they can be one of the examples we can use: a small team that has got good results."*

So, the Daily Post can say that the 'Goodison example' is "a small team getting good results," eh? Yet this same paper goes apoplectic on behalf of its Blue readers when anyone from the Red camp uses the 's' word. They are SO touchy when it comes to that word. I even had a cover on the 'Red All Over The Land' fanzine that featured a PORG (person of restricted growth, aka a dwarf or midget) in an Everton kit, playing football. The caption?

"Everton: The small, people's club."

It got us a rather nasty solicitor's letter accompanied by a faxed copy of the 'offending' cover that originated from inside Everton FC. It was not the reaction I expected from our mighty, sleeping-giant neighbours, those Mersey Millionaires who never miss an opportunity to lecture us all on how they like to do things "with a bit of dignity, a bit of class." Rather it was a petty and small-minded response from a petty and small minded club. It cost us £1500 in damages, which I believe paid for their pre-season tour of Lilliput.

The MTV awards have been held in Liverpool this last week. All the Merseyside Glitterati were out in force which meant only those rich enough could attend (footballers and gangsters), while the rest of us roundly ignored it. One photo appeared of Robbie Keane and Gary Barlow from Take That. I could see our next cover already taking shape before my eyes:

Gary Barlow: "I know another Robbie who's also being paid millions for doing fuck all."

Cruel? Maybe, but the sword of satire is a sharp one. I've um'd and ah'd before this game about putting another bet on Robbie Keane. If you're a striker desperately searching for your first league goals what do you really, really need? That's right: West Brom at home. In the end I decide against it; I'm carrying enough guilt already without putting the mockers on players and results. We need to win today if we're going to challenge – properly challenge – for number 19, and nothing, not even 'Keane: First Goal at 4/1', can come in the way of that. Losing in such ridiculous fashion at Spurs only underlines how important it is that we take maximum points from these home 'bankers' as, no matter how well you're playing, you'll come unstuck somewhere when it's just not your day.

After a marathon pre-match supping session that included some baiting of Man U-supporting students watching their team get beat by Arsenal in The Railway; some spilling of pints and general drunkenness in Rigby's with Sammo and Mick Potter; and ended with Billy 'The Arab' Harrup signing copies of the LFC magazine in Shenans as he'd been featured in close-up on the back cover of the latest issue, we descended upon Anfield at 5pm.

Its the nearest game to Remembrance Sunday, and just before the kick off there's a minute's silence. German OSTY looks very sombre and, as a sign of respect, takes off his baseball cap and bows his head.

I can't resist the opportunity.

"That's not good enough, Fritz." He looks up. I think he's wondering if I'm being serious.

"On your knees."

This elicits a fit of giggles from John Maguire as OSTY blushes, head bowed, still mulling over whether or not he's the victim of a joke. He probably still is.

It's all too easy. We don't play particularly well but are still streets ahead of West Brom, which is what I've come to expect from any side managed by Tony Mowbray. They have Relegated Already written all over them. Despite actually 'having a go' here at Anfield they look pitifully short of class. That said we take a while to break them down. Keane's first goal, on the half hour, comes from a glorious, curling Gerrard through ball, played in just behind the centre halves. Keane breaks free and bears down on Scott Carson – after whose debut in the European Cup game against Juventus in 2005 I had expected great things. Carson just makes it easy for Keane. He comes rushing off his line, leaving Keane the relatively simple task of rounding him and clipping the ball back into the unguarded net. I say simple, I'd have broken my ankle attempting the strike, but then I'm not on about a quarter of a million quid a month to do so.

In front, at home against West Brom, I'd have expected us to hammer home our advantage, but it fails to materialise. In fact we are fortunate to snatch a second, just before the break, to and our general inability to score more here against poor opposition is beginning to worry me. Our (and Keane's) second is remarkably similar to the first. A long ball from Aurelio on the left is played in beautifully just behind the central defenders allowing Keane to use his pace, knock it past the (again!) onrushing Carson (knowing that any block, any foul, will see the keeper sent off) and turn the ball back across the box and into an empty net. If West Brom had had quicker defenders and a slower keeper they may well have gone in at half-time at 0-0.

As it is the whistle blows, it's 2-0, and it looks relatively respectable, I suppose. But you can't help feeling ManU or Arsenal would be 4 up by now. It's a point being discussed over bottles of Carlsberg (I yearn for the day we are sponsored by Becks) on the concourse: "Do yer think that's Keane finally up and running, then?" I ask Joynty. "Reckon his legacy starts here?"

"Spose so," he says morosely.

"Don't sound too enthusiastic will yer? Lad's on an 'at-trick!"

He fixes me with a cold stare and states, slowly:

"It – is – West – Brom."

I feel chastised. I've allowed childish exuberance to override common sense. I'm desperate for Keane to be a success. For one, it will vindicate my gushing – and very public – praise of him on LFC TV. But above and beyond that, Keane firing on all cylinders could also give us something we badly need – a counterfoil to Torres' brilliance. The Dalglish to Fernando's predatory Rush. Having 2 brilliant, different yet complimentary strikers is something we've not had for years, probably not since Fowler and Collymore for that all too brief a period before Robbie got fat and Stan went mental. Having cover for Torres too, given that he's had an injury stricken start to the campaign, is essential if we're to sustain any reasonable tilt at the title.

The second half continues in much the same vein. Keane comes close to a hat-trick twice on the hour with disallowed goals, so I'm confused when he's substituted with 20 minutes to go. Does Rafa not want Robbie Keane to get a confidence boosting hat-trick? That aside, why not substitute the ineffectual Kuyt or Riera? Neither of them has done a tap, today. Are we to be that concerned about keeping some rigid 'shape' or system for the last 20 minutes? At home? Against West Brom?

In the end it's a last minute goal from Arbeloa that gives the scoreline some reflection our domination. He cuts in from the full back position and curls a shot in at the far post, much in the same way Phil Neal used to do back in the 70s. At 3-0 with a minute to go, John Garner does the unforgivable and bellows, as the cue for a song to begin:

"Liverpool, Liverpool – Top of the League! "

He's rounded on immediately.

"Noooo!"

"Not yet!"

It's a bit cruel on JG. Yes, he's right, we have just gone back to the top, and it should be celebrated, but it seems far too premature to be crowing about it on live TV. It's tantamount to taunting the Gods to knock us back with another stupid defeat at Bolton next week. John looks a bit miffed, but he of all veterans should know the score. We've made a decent start in the league, let's not tempt providence. In any case, Chelsea are playing Blackburn tomorrow and barring a freak result will return to the top.

A freak result, like ours at Tottenham, maybe?

No, No! Don't even think about it.

JM

Spurs (a)   2-4

League Cup   Wed 12th Nov

It's a Carling Cup match on a wet, windy, Wednesday night in North London. Rafa will put out a virtual reserve side and the tickets are full price and there's a credit crunch. Now, the question must be asked:

"Do we have mental health problems?"

Because no-one in their right mind would blow a hundred quid on travelling all the way down to bleedin' London to watch the second team have a run out and then get home at 3am. Well, we've just done it and I'm seriously thinking about phoning the doctor and asking for some sort of brain scan. I suppose it's my punishment for failing to go to Spurs last week with my bad back. 3,000 fans made the trip down there tonight. That's a hell of a lot of loyal fans to travel so far and to be let down so badly by the club. It is blind faith beyond the call of duty. So if we go on and do well in the League, all will be forgotten but when you're 3-0 down at half-time in a shite competition and you're 200 miles from home on a freezing cold night, you do think to yourself 'What the fuck am I doing here?'. We've got no intention of trying to win the game. It's obvious that Rafa sees this game as an irritation and just wants a damage limitation job. Get beaten, get on the team bus and get home. He'll do all the predictable soundbites of how we tried hard and how we should have had a penalty, but really he just wanted out. So where does that leave us, the fans? There should have been 3,000 medals cast that night. Or at least a guarantee that all 3,000 mugs who were there should be the first to receive tickets if and when we reach our next Cup Final – and the chances of that happening lie somewhere nil and zero. I well recall some of the militant types having a meeting with Rick Parry years ago – there was still a Safeway by ours it was that long ago because I remember them coming back and telling us they'd asked Parry why loyal fans couldn't have something like a Safeway 'points' card, with extra points for going to the likes of Boro away in the League Cup. Well if that system had ever come into play, all those who went to Spurs tonight should have been given triple points – almost as an apology for the shambles that we witnessed. There will be those 'one game a season' types who showed up in Istanbul and Athens who wouldn't even have known that we'd been playing tonight, let alone the score. But you can bet they'd have been at Wembley if we'd have got there. Pisses you off, doesn't it?

And the day started off so well, too. A nice early pick-up outside Ned Kelly's at eleven bells. Big Ian Mac, who is our jockey for the day, turns up in a brand new hired people carrier. I am travelling down today as a guest of the much loved Bootle Battalion, whose Commander in Chief is the softly spoken David Buckley. On board we have Steve Mercer on drums; on lead guitar we have Darren 'Dadger' Patterson; bass guitar is Neil Bucko (no relation to you know who), Ian Mac himself is on keyboards and on lead vocals (no mic necessary) I give you David "Hear Me Now" Buckley. On the return journey we'll be joined on backing vocals by Ritchie Tierney whose larynx has been challenged by a week's consecutive shifts on the rattler so he could get time off for this intoxicating experience we're about to endure. Ritchie may well work on the trains but he's been completely off the rails for many a year.

The crack is good. The jokes and the surreal conversations are coming thick and fast. The ale is flowing and Big Macca is doing a sterling job of negotiating the streets of Norf Landon. It's with disappointment and no little regret that I have to report that those very same streets are not actually paved with gold at all. They're paved with cack, KFC wrappers and chewy. We're safely parked up outside a boozer called the Elmhurst by 3.30pm, which gives us plenty of time to have a couple of scoops and a bite to eat. We're joined by Darren Fessey who just slopes into the pub looking as Scouse as Scouse can be. Short hair, dark clothing, no colours. You know the dance – no explanation needed. We have a mooch up the road and come back to the pub to be greeted by a couple of moody bouncers. They're searching everyone, so I ask them what they're actually looking for. They say it's not weapons, it's just alcohol. Apparently the previous week when we played here in the League all hands had been smuggling their own ale in. Shock. Horror. Whatever next? We nip out the back to the beer garden for a smoke to find John Macdonald and Steve Davis, two of our very finest, getting slabs of lager passed over the fence. I really don't know what the world is coming to. We slope off to a boss little boozer called the Antwerp which is down the edge of a park by the ground.

David 'the Voice' Buckley outside The Antwerp at Spurs

Bucko has to meet a few old Tottenham Skins he knows. The aforementioned Quiet Man is lucky enough to know everyone in the world. You could be in the Amazonian rainforest and there would be remote tribes pan-piping their welcome down from the trees which, roughly translated, would say:

"Alright Bucko lad, how's it going?"

Or you could be lost in the Siberian wilderness and a ragtag band of goat herders would go:

"You haven't seen Bucko have you? He promised us three front row stalls for the Cheeky Girls at the Vladivostok Megadrome."

We get near the ground and Bucko decides he can't be arsed going in – he'd rather stay on it, which in hindsight is the wisest decision of the day. I don't know where to start concerning the match. The first half was like

L to R: Ian Mac, Neil Bucko, Dadger, Jegsy, Darren, Mercer, Ritchie, and last but not least, Bucko

watching a car crash. No, worse still, it was like being in one. Philipp Degen who was signed in the summer along with Dossena had one of the worst games I have ever seen from a player in a Liverpool shirt. Tonight, there's only Agger and Torres who you'd call an automatic first choice, so you'd want players like Babel, Lucas, Plessis and Ngog to be giving it loads in games like this – nail their names to the shirt. El Zhar looked okay in spells but overall it was painful to watch.

I stood next to famous 'Liverpool face' Marty Mullen in the ground. Me and Marty go back many moons – over 30 years and counting from the days we were skinny young men in the Road End. Marty puts a proposition to me. He's seen my 'Huyton Fatties' badge and would like to own it. I try to change the subject going oooh and argh at the game but he's having none of it. He wants the badge. Seeing as I'm neither fat, nor from Huyton I decide it would be in my best interests simply to hand the badge over. Knowing Marty as I do, the alternative could well have been that I ended up in a 'Reservoir Dogs' scenario, taken to a disused warehouse on the outskirts of town, strapped to a chair in an empty room, hands tied behind my back with the flex of a ripped-out telephone while Marty paces around the room going:

"Come on Jegsy boy. For the last time, where's the Huyton Fattie's badge? I want that badge, lad!"

I give him the badge. Like I say, I'm not from Huyton.

We leave the ground slightly traumatised at our fortunate 4-2 defeat. It could have been even worse. We sack the boozer and we're back on the road to the Promised Land within minutes of the final whistle. There's a quick stop off at the Offy to replenish the stocks and its tallyho all the way. Bucko, who by now is delirious with alcohol, is becoming increasingly unstable. He demands to know where Ian Mac is taking him and where we are. Big Macca calmly tells him we are on the M1 motorway. Bucko insists we drop him off on the hard shoulder for some unknown reason. He has decided he doesn't like the route we are taking. He's beginning to repeat himself and I'm praying he falls asleep soon. No such luck. It's a long journey home but we make it in one piece. Dadger has had me in bulk and the quieter, more reserved Bucko (Neil) is always there with an understated one-liner. Mercer and Ritchie have both contributed to a day that's been weirdly enjoyable given the result, but the award for outstanding achievement goes to Big Ian Mac for keeping a cool head while all around are losing theirs and getting us there and back without any hiccups. Yes, it's been a thoroughly enjoyable awayday, spoilt only by what was the main reason for our journey – the bloody football.

JD

Bolton (a)   2-0

League   Sat 15th Nov

This isn't one of the more eagerly awaited away games. I think, in fact, I'd rather go anywhere than Bolton: I'd even prefer Crystal Palace for a midweek cup replay. It's just such a boring day out. They've built their new ground (stadium is too grand a word for the plasticky Reebok Arena) out in the middle of nowhere, close to a motorway junction, miles away from the town centre, as if it was an Asda or B&Q. Its only redeeming feature is that it's nestled in the armpit of the Pennines; the mildly interesting scenery is all that makes this place preferable to Pride Park or The Riverside. There are no pubs worthy of the name for miles around, and those that are close enough are definitely off-limits to visiting supporters, especially us. To gain entry requires Scousers to try and warp their nasal brogue into some baffling Lancashire vowel sounds that render most Liverpudlians helpless with laughter. Nah – we'll stick to a few cans in the car park, thanks.

It's another kick-off rearranged for live television coverage; this time at the other end of the spectrum, at 12:45. This, ironically, is not unwelcome today. Why? Because it means the day isn't a complete waste. I can be home and in my local before 5. There's also neither the time, nor the opportunity, to go for a few pints before kick-off, which means I can bring a packed breakfast of 10 bottles of chilled Spanish lager and a bag of Pickled Onion flavour Monster Munch.

My neighbour Alan Diamond is coming to pick me up at 10:30 with his 2 boys, Josh and Greg. I smile ruefully as I sup my cuppa and anticipate the typical car journey rows between between two young brothers:

"Dad he's sitting on my side of the car."

"Dad, he said Riera's rubbish, but I say he's great."

"Dad, he won't give me back my Gameboy / iPod / copy of Razzle."

Although when I'm there they tend to fall into a trance – part horrified, part fascinated – by this oaf smelling of San Miguel at 11am and telling outrageous stories about how much their dad has had to drink at various Liverpool games.

We park up about a 20 minute walk from the Reebok, close to the motorway junction, and around 11:30 I'm stood around outside looking for one of the lads who has my ticket. It's sunny but cold, and inside – in the shade – it'll be freezing. John Pearman, in fingerless gloves, is selling the fanzines and shouting "Buy a Big Issue – help the homeless please!" He gives me a copy of 'Rotation, Rotation, Rotation' by the former Through The Wind And Rain editor, Steve Kelly. It's a compilation of his pieces that appeared in The Irish Examiner last season, and is a brilliant showcase for Steve's eloquent cynicism, described to me later by someone who'd read it as "Rafa-bashing ranting." It's far from a rant, it's just that Steve's reluctant to join in any bandwagon that he himself hasn't started, nor will he subscribe to any stereotypical, blinkered Liverpudlianism. According to Steve, Rafa needs to earn his idol-like status by winning the title, and winning it in style; he's been living on his Istanbul laurels for too long now.

It's games like West Brom last week that trouble Steve – this cagey philosophy of playing just the one out-and-out striker at home. In Kelly's world (and mine too, truth be told) we should be tearing sides like West Brom apart, end of story. The shackles, need to be cast aside – especially at Anfield. In a nutshell, Steve Kelly wants it to be 1979 again. We scored 7 goals against Bolton that season, 4 of them away at Burnden Park.

Rafa has a lot to live up to then, so what do we get today? We get Keane in a lone striker's role. I'm looking at the Bolton team and I've never heard of most of them. There's a sub with the magnificent name of Danny Shittu, but seriously – this match is crying out for Torres and Keane together. Nando, supposedly not "match fit," has only made the bench. To get Match Fit I suspect players need to play, you know, matches – so how sitting in tracksuit does this is beyond me. I put this preposterous theory to the fella sat next to me.

"Rafa knows what he's doing."

He says, and it's almost an incantation, so spontaneous and so dogmatic is his belief. And so long as we keep winning I suppose most other fans will also think this way. I'm wavering into the Kelly camp here, though, and I'm worried we're beginning to pay the opposition too much respect. I want us to think about *us* first and foremost – to play like a Liverpool team. And if we do that, we don't even have to know who's playing for teams like Bolton.

We start well and have almost total possession, Alonso enjoying free rein and pinging the ball about at will. Bolton are so ineffectual that even Riera is looking quite handy, and has time and space to knock over a series of good crosses. But there's no end product, no real threat to Bolton's goal. I moan to the fella next to me about our cautious approach and question Kuyt's credentials as a goal threat.

As if to spite me, he almost scores at this point, rattling the bar with a thumping drive from just outside the box. It doesn't take long for us to actually go in front, though, and it is, of course, via the industrious Kuyt. If ever there was a word that describes Dirk Kuyt, it's that. Not 'magnificent'; not 'deadly'; but 'industrious'. If was a car he'd be a London Cab. Anyway, the industrious Dirk converts Arbeloa's great cross with a fabulous looping header. Thank God for that! Perhaps we can relax now, push on and really take this game to Bolton with a bit of *brio*. And we almost do. A few minutes later Keane (why did it have to be him?) contrives to miss a chance that if he'd just stood still, and shut his eyes, would have gone in. How did he miss that, though? *How*? Everyone's heard the cliché about the chance that's easier to score than miss, but this one is just… a *doddle*. It's crazy that he's fluffed it. My head's whirling now; what is it with Keane? Is he trying too hard? Has he left his contact lenses out? Or, is Paul Stewart right? Is he just shite?

At half time the guy next to me says he's going for a slash and never comes back. So I stand there and examine this ghastly football ground. Down at the opposite end, the Bolton home end, at least a dozen cross of St George flags are proudly hung, onto which their owners have imaginatively put B – W – F – C in the four corners. It looks like a Combat 18 rally down there, or a Chelsea away end in Europe. Same thing really, no?

Bolton begin the second half with their tails up, in the knowledge that despite our monopoly of the ball they are still very much in this game. We all know it too and are beginning to suspect that what should be 3 easy points cannot be taken for granted. Our unease seems to have transmitted itself onto the pitch and we're losing possession and being forced to defend. If anyone's looking likely to score now, it's Bolton. And they really should have done, when substitute Ricardo Gardner rounds Reina and shoots wide of a gaping net. The away end bursts out laughing – as much out of relief as anything else, although it may have had something to do with Daniel Agger running into a post and knocking out a tooth as he desperately tried to get back and cover the open goal.

Rafa seems suddenly to realise that we're not going to be able to defend this slender lead and warms up Torres.

"About sodding time!" comes the cry.

He replaces Keane, which comes as no surprise, after all he'd played his contractual 70 minutes – although I'd like to have seen Torres replace Riera instead, who seems to have run out of steam. It doesn't really affect the pattern of play much and Bolton still seem the more likely. Until that is, with about 20 minutes to go, Torres chases and wins a lose pass wide on the right of the area and then plays an impudent ball across the 6 yard box, with the outside of his right foot, onto the head of a diving Gerrard who guides it across the face of the goal, and into the far corner. Its a touch of pure class from 2 truly World class players, and they know it. They run together and celebrate in an almost homo-erotic fashion. A manner I suspect that'll have these Lancastrian patriots throwing down their Burberry caps, tearing at their gelled hair and cursing these 'Scouse Pooftahs'.

The rest of the game is played out amidst chants from the Liverpool fans about being 'Top Of The League' and about telling Bolton that they look like going down. There's the usual banter to-ing and fro-ing between the corner section where I am, close to the scoreboard, and the appallingly badly dressed Bolton chavs in the paddock next to us. This brings a couple of stewards and several coppers running up the aisle to where we are on the back row. I can hear their radio crackling: "Back row, black jacket about 10 seats along..."

Black jacket – that should be an easy arrest then...

"Out the way," barks one of the stewards as they barge down our row and confront some guy in a black coat. The coppers hang back in the aisle. There's a heated exchange between the stewards and this guy about exactly what it was they've taken exception to.

"You can't use that kind of language about Hotpot...," one of them says. I kid you not. And suddenly all hell lets loose and Stewgate bursts out into a full-on scuffle. This is Scouse v Hotpot and I try to restore calm by chiming in with some advice: "Go 'ead lad, lamp him!" but it's too late. Half a dozen coppers stream in and carry him off kicking and shouting. Fascists! Free the Bolton One!

Back in the car Alan and I dissect the strategy we appear to have adopted of 'keeping it tight' and refusing to throw caution to the wind and just attack teams like these.

"Maybe he's just playing to the strengths of the players he's got?" I say.

"Players he's bought!" Alan reminds me. Does he mean Keane? Or Riera? Or Babel? Or Dossena? Or...

I decide to change the subject and ask the lads what they thought was the best part of the match.

Josh: "When Agger ran into the post."

Greg: "That player called Shittu."

Out of the mouths of babes, eh? In the end we conclude that we're happy enough; we've got the 3 points and we're top of the league. And I'm extra happy as my beers are still cold.

JM

Fulham (h)   0-0

League   Sat 22nd Nov

I am the world's worst pundit. Really. Utterly crap. I was back on LFC.tv this week to assess the season so far. The 'Kop Talkin' show features supporters giving their views on the team. I'd been on the pre-season show to talk about my hopes for the upcoming campaign, and they've asked me back for an update. Well, what could I say? I re-iterated my belief that Robbie Keane would take the weight off Torres and chip in with his share of goals; and that despite some unfathomable – often laughable, in hindsight – misses recently, he has, at least, begun to score. This is what strikers need. Goals breed confidence which in turn breeds more goals.

"Robbie Keane will," I assured the watching dozens of viewers, "only get better."

The show's host, Matt Critchley, is smiling and nodding like I'm uttering pearls of complete genius. This urges me on to continue with this nonsense and I churn out my ill-thought through reflections, and analyses, of the opening 3 months of the season.

As for the Fulham game, there could be only one possible result, I tell Matt.

"We have Torres coming back to fitness and, well, we are playing as potential Champions do, and winning whilst not actually playing very well."

My fellow pundit, Peter 'Evo' Etherington (think 'Buster Bloodvesel from Skelmersdale') agrees.

"Is right John lad, Is right."

"However," I add, "it all depends on which Liverpool turns up on Saturday: the tentative, nervous Liverpool of last season or this solid, resilient new Liverpool churning out the wins that see us top of the league well into November."

Matt's all ears. Though his teeth are nice and shiny too.

"We've been traditionally stronger in the second half of the season. In the past few years we've fallen too far behind by the half-way stage to mount any real challenge later on. I said at the start of the season that if we could stay in touch, say, to within 6 or 7 points of the leaders at Christmas, then I'd have some real belief that, come May, we'd be close."

And here we are – joint top in November. It's about this time of year that Liverpool have always had a bit of a dip in form: the November Collywobbles. During this period of stuttering, incoherent football we'd occasionally lose a match – maybe two – and stumble to a few draws and get to Christmas just in touch of the top. Then, as if a switch had been flicked, we'd go into overdrive in the New Year and go on a 15 match unbeaten run or something (usually all wins with a drawn game somewhere just to prove we were human) and end up Champions. The ultimate example of this was 1981-82: 5 defeats by the New Year, including the nadir, the 3-1 home defeat to Man City on Boxing Day, that left us mid-table in 12th position. We then won 7 out of the next 9. Then after the defeat at Brighton in early March, we won 13 out of the last 16, drawing 3 times. This included 11 straight wins, including beating United and City, both away, within 4 days of each other. Happy, happy days! Then, just as now, we were blooding a new striker – Ian Rush. I keep reminding myself of this: that history often repeats itself.

The first thing I hear as I push the door open in Shenanigans is the voice of Paul Stewart: "Saw you on telly the other night, Mackin."

"Yeah? You alright, Paul?"

"You were shite!"

The ever-affable Simon Morris, and the ever half-bevvied Ian Roughley, though are far less damning.

"Alright mate. Saw that thing on that LFC tv thing...," says Simon still smiling at Paul's vitriolic critique. "Thought it was good."

"Oh thanks mate," I tell him.

"I'm not sure about Keane, though," he adds, almost apologetically.

"Truth is," I confess, carefully checking that Stewie can't hear, "...neither am I. I keep saying it in the hope that it comes true."

Ian Roughley drains his pint and adds: "Self-denial that."

I nod in agreement. It probably is.

"I'm very good at that meself," he adds. "Do you want a bevvy?"

Whilst we're in the pub the team news comes through and despite

Gerrard's absence (he took a knock at Bolton) it looks promising – Torres, Keane, Kuyt and Riera are all starting.

"It's about time we did that and put out a really attacking team at home." Ian says.

"Well, Kuyt and Riera are really in midfield, but it's only Fulham so I expect them to push on into the attack." I say, and for the first time in ages I have a really good feeling about the game. Let's knock in a few goals, get the place rocking and really grasp this opportunity to show that we really want this league.

"Oh, for fuck's sake!" Simon interrupts my inner pep-talk, "He's playing Lucas!"

From the end of the bar Steweys 'I told you so' voice booms: "There you go Mackin! Told you – that Spanish twat hasn't got a clue!"

"Alonso's on the bench. Mascherano and Lucas in the middle." Simon continues.

"Dossena?" asks Ian.

"Er... on the bench.," Simon says.

"Thank fuck for that," we all say at once.

At half-time there's a simmering discontent amongst the critics of Block 306 as they take their half-time refreshment.

"That was shite," Jegsy offers. "Utter and complete shite."

"It wasn't even that good," says Lou Lou.

"Oh and you were right Mackin, Robbie Keane CAN only get better!" he snaps at me.

I wince. He's been shit again, missing the easiest chance of the half when clean through eight yards out. With 24,000 Kop eyes imploring him to score, he blasts the ball wildly, straight at the keeper, Mark Schwarzer.

"What the fuck is Lucas doing on the pitch?" Jegsy continues.

"Garbage!" says Sammo, "has been all season."

"So why's Alonso on the bench?"

Joynty comes over and recognising the atmosphere asks, "Who you talking about?"

"Lucas!" we say in unison.

"We've got the only fucking Brazilian in the world who can't control the ball, can't pass and can't shoot," says Joynty before turning and walking away.

His inclusion is certainly strange, especially given that Alonso's been playing so well and that Lucas' form has been, at best, indifferent. We're struggling to create anything here. Mascherano rarely gets forward anyway, but Lucas has contributed nothing. He's constantly giving the ball away or playing harmless 5 yard passes. The centre of midfield is offering nothing. Then as if it couldn't get any worse, Windows comes barging through the crowd, his face as grim as thunder.

"Did you hear that? That chanting for 'Alonso'?" has asks.

We had. After another misplaced ball from Lucas parts of The Kop had begun chanting for Xabi.

"He won't bring him on now. You watch. He's played Lucas to show us that he's right and we're wrong. He's worse than Houllier."

No-one's arguing. That's not because we agree with Windows; it's because to challenge him would result in a statistics-packed lecture on money spent versus results obtained. It could take days.

"Its worse than Houllier. This team is worse than it was in 2004," he proclaims.

Then as we drift back up to our seats, he shouts,

"He's got to go!"

If anything the second half is worse. There are just too many of the team not performing: Keane and Lucas, naturally; but also Kuyt, Riera who are also failing to make any sort of impact. Mascherano too is lying too deep to be any threat to a Fulham side who've looked lively and dangerous on the break. This leaves Torres, alone, to make any sort of fight of it. His pace and tenacity is causing problems but he can't do it alone. It his first start since the win at Man City and he must be frustrated at losing Gerrard, his talisman, only to find him replaced by Lucas who's drifting round the periphery of this game like a little girl.

The Kop are growing impatient. This clearly is not working. The chants for Alonso are increasing and I look back along the row behind us towards Windows. He's shaking his head frantically at me, going "Just watch! Just watch! He won't do it...." The only real chance of the 2nd half is one that Torres creates for himself down at the Anfield Rd end, cutting inside from near the corner flag, he bursts electrically into the box and lets fly a shot that Schwarzer barely sees but manage to parry away.

Finally, finally, to much ironic cheering and genuine applause, Alonso is standing on the touchline waiting to come on. But when he does – and to great disbelief (and not a little vocal disapproval) – he's replacing Mascherano. I daren't look at Windows now as his blood will be boiling. I let Jegsy, instead, try and articulate what we're all thinking.

"Why? What? How? What the fuck?... How the fuck is Lucas still on that fucking pitch?"

As substitutions go, it's baffling. If we really want to win this game we have to change it's shape. The Lucas issue aside, all this has done is replace a deep lying Mascherano with Alonso who'll have to cover the same position. The game needed something different.

"Why wasn't that Babel for Lucas, or Benayoun for Riera or... something?" I ask.

"He's stubborn.," Sammo says. "He's put his team out to play a certain way and all our complaining isn't going to make him change his mind. He's picked Lucas and he's not admitting it's a mistake."

And so the match fizzles out into a draw, the final whistle greeted with a mixture of swearing and applause – though the latter is far from appreciative. It's the applause of habit; of duty.

We stand around, hands in pockets, kicking at the litter, as matchday announcer, the gravelly tonsilled George Sephton, reads through the full time scores from elsewhere. Chelsea's draw at home with Newcastle only makes things worse and elicits a few groans of, "Aw for fuck's sake!"

A few people actually cheer this result, "It keeps us top!" they say.

But they don't understand. It's not wasting the opportunity to go clear at the top that's the disappointment, its that the nagging doubts may be becoming a reality: that we've been riding our luck, and this team might not be good enough to last the pace.

After the game we walk silently back to the La Rouge bar on Walton Breck Rd. Since The Sandon turned its back on 'the likes of us' to chase the corporate dollar, La Rouge has taken over as the post-match drinking haunt. It's far from ideal – it's not a pub, just a large empty room with a bar in it. But unlike The Albert or The Park it's not crammed beyond comfort, and its full of like-minded souls. After the disappointment of the day though I don't really fancy staying out on the swallee, and head off to town for a pint or two before getting the train home. I share a cab with Danny Nico and John Maguire who tell me of a graffitti attack after the West Brom on The Sandon.

"Its 'ardly guerilla warfare tho' like," says Mags. "Just a birra graffitti."

"Saying what?" I ask him.

"Er... 'The Death of LFC'" he says.

"A bit over the top, no?" I ask them.

Danny smiles and adds, "And there was one saying 'You corporate bastards'."

"Well then... that's a bit more accurate.... So where are we going then lads, Neds?"

JM

Marseille (h)   1-0

Champions League Group Phase   Wed 26th Nov

I know my dear friend and co-author Senor Dodd loves to scoff at my wide and cosmopolitan circle of Red friends who hail from all corners of the globe, but even he is finding this hilarious. We're in the Big House on the corner of Lime Street, just facing the infamous Adelphi Hotel and in front of us sits an smiling, personable Eskimo.

"Kevin Sampson," he smiles. "Here to meet Kevin Sampson of S.O.S. I am Nils from Greenland…"

The big house has, temporarily, become Town HQ for the Union, and Kev has asked a few of his overseas pals who are here for the game to drop in and see if they're interested in opening a local branch of the Union in their own countries. We've all met his mates Mauro from Turin and Jussi from Finland before, but none of us was expecting a full-on Inuit – that's got to be a first! Jegsy persists in making comedy scuffs at the floor, as though he's trying to dig a hole in the ice with his heel. He mimes unwinding a fishing line down the hole then squats patiently by his imaginary hole, waiting for a fish to bite. One by one the lads come over to say hello to Nils, who tries to buy everyone a beer before getting down to the business in hand. He produces a list.

"I wish to speak with Mr Paul Rice, please…" he pauses, then reads on. "I wish to meet grumpy bastard Paul Stewart." He squints at his own writing – presumably Sammo has set him these tasks – "And I wish to perform one Torres Bounce."

Everyone buzzes off him and by the time Sampson shows up off the London train, we're all completely hammered. The mighty Finn Jussi Ahokas is here, and we're slightly scared to note that, after a year on the wagon for health reasons, Jussi is tippling once again. This could get messy. Jussi's an ex-punk who fell in love with the Redmen at the same time he discovered the

Pistols, and moved over here to live in a squat, fuck tha police and catch as many games as he could. His English is impeccable – when he's sober – but for Jussi an all-day bender means a several-day bender and he's been on the ale since Monday. He's leering, slurring, hugging, swearing, madly excited to be attending another Euro night at the world's most famous footballing citadel, and determined to turn the Big House into his own little mini Kop here and now. Poor old Peter Hooton looks stir crazy as Jussi grabs him round the neck with one hand, shakes his hand interminably with the other and sings "London Calling" into his ear with all the woozy passion of an old Clash fan. It's a picture to behold.

We take a convoy of cabs to the ground and bail out for a quick snifter in The Albert – just this once. The place is, as always, packed to the rafters and it's usually a no-go zone before any home game at all, let alone a big European night. But we get served quickly and easily – Jussi just shouts until he gets served – and we're all set up for another night of high jinks and goals.

Except the goals don't come. Ourselves and Atletico have got this group sewn up already, and it's Marseille's fans who make most of the noise as we have to settle for a one goal win, Gerrard nodding in the winner at the Road End.

After the game, everyone legs it back to Shenanigans for a sing-song that becomes so raucous that Jussi nearly misses his overnight coach back to Stansted. Jegsy pushes him into a cab and, with Jussi now incoherent with drink, tells the driver to make sure he gets on the right bus. We all toast him off as the taxi disappears, and toddle off our separate ways not long after. The season's nearing the halfway stage and things could hardly look brighter. Qualified from our CL group as Champions, barring a disaster. Barging our way past all comers without really getting into kind of run of form, yet. And only just beaten for the first team in the League. Whatever next? Top of the League? Perish the thought!

JM

West Ham (h)   0-0

League   Mon 1st Dec

The morning of the match sees about 20 turn up at Anfield to lay out 12,000 red and white cards on the Kop seats. When held aloft at kick-off they'll spell out: "Free Michael Now."

It was a message that has to go out loud and clear during the TV coverage, and it's part of an orchestrated demonstration tonight that's been organised between S.O.S, the Shields family and Liverpool Football Club – particularly Rick Parry and David Moores. Before the club got involved in Michael's case (and, even though they've been superb they still took their time), Michael faced a long, long stint in a Bulgarian jail, serving a sentence for a crime he patently did not commit. In an act they considered merciful, the Bulgarian judiciary agreed to allow Michael to complete his sentence in the U.K – but it was going to cost his family an £80,000 fine. By the time interest had been added, that figure was closer to £100,000. Various fundraising initiatives started to bring the money in, but being absolutely blunt about the situation, it was the intervention of LFC that made the difference. A bucket collection (ironically before the West Ham game in 2006) raised £20,000 and the players themselves donated significantly after Parry invited Michael Shields Senior along to Melwood to speak privately with the squad and make them aware of Michael's plight. Again, in an ideal world, the players would have had the nous and the soul to do it the other way round – come to Michael's house and speak to his family. But they got there in the end. They did the right thing. And a huge big step was taken on the road to justice when Michael was finally moved from Bulgaria into the U.K prison system.

Next week there's to be a Judicial Review of Michael's case. Justice Minister Jack Straw has insisted that he doesn't have the power to pardon Michael Shields as his sentence was handed down in another country. He says that he has all sympathy for the Shields family (he should do, having once had to intervene in the justice system himself, this time to help his own son out of a sticky situation). He says that, if he had the power and the right, he would push for Michael's release.

Jack Straw's constituency is Blackburn. We play Blackburn on Saturday and we've been considering a demonstration on his home turf – he still likes to play the earthy socialist and speak from his soapbox on Saturday mornings… such a man of the people. Tempting as it is to bring this case to Straw's doorstep, we can't risk anything that might backfire. A match-day demo populated by Liverpool's hardcore might easily become a target for Blackburn's hooligan fringe, none of which would do the Shields family any favours, so we pour all our energies into making as big a noise as possible around this last televised home game before the Judicial Review. Local Echo reporter Greg O'Keeffe, a devout Evertonian, has come up with the inspired idea of asking the players to wear Free Michael Now t-shirts during the warm-up. It's an amazing coup – every single player wears a t-shirt and their message is captured by the media hordes covering the game and goes out far and wide – way beyond these shores. The S.O.S have made a huge pro-Michael banner which is unfurled at the front of The Kop during "You'll Never Walk Alone." The team walk towards the banner applauding it, then look up to applaud The Kop. That is what this club is about. It's what this city is about. We stand together, shoulder to shoulder. I'm proud to be a Kopite tonight. Or I was, until the game kicked off.

* * * *

Now I've been going the game for a long time. A long, long, *long* time. I've watched sides managed by Bill Shankly through to Gerard Houllier, and now Rafael Benitez, go top of the league. But I'm struggling, really struggling to recall the last time a Liverpool team went clear at the top and yet was subjected to Liverpool 'fans' booing them. Maybe it was the time in 1976 we lost 9-0 at home to Ipswich but because QPR were beaten 16-2 at West Brom we went top on goal-difference?

It was either '75 or '76 anyway.

I've been harping on all season that if we could see through the inevitable 'November collywobbles', then I could see our expected second-half-of-the-season-charge enabling us to make a decent challenge. Well, here we are, going top by a point in early December and – unbelievably – people are jeering, even booing at the final whistle. It is just embarrassing. Booing the team for any result is just not on. If we are supposed to be the 12th man, then those players on the pitch are our 11 brothers.

That's what being a 'supporter' is: you support, you encourage, you breathe confidence and belief into the players. You're not a cinema critic. It would be like jeering a child at their school Christmas play because they fluffed their lines. You've given up a cosy night in front of the telly, to see a class of 9 yr olds perform a Nativity scene, and that little girl from down the road can't even pronounce 'Frankincense' …

"Gerroff, you're shite! Booooooooo!"

But then the type of person becoming more and more common at Anfield these days is less a 'supporter', and more a 'spectator'. In fact, they're not even that – they're just parasites.

There I've said it. Parasites.

They turn up and expect to be excited, entertained and made to feel smug and superior because they follow a top team. They've been sold the dream, and now, by taking part in satellite TV's glamorous and spectacular live Premier League 'event', they feel they belong. Belong where though? To whom? Certainly not to me, or people like me.

They just take, take, take from the game, and put nothing except their money back. They've paid their ticket money and expect value for money. They expect victory. But they won't put themselves out and help influence the outcome. They want a win for their money, but it's not up to them to help get that win. They're customers. They've paid. They have rights. Well get this, customer. At Liverpool, we're all in this together. It's Anfield's Holy Trinity: manager, players and supporters. If you don't do your bit, then you're not fulfilling your part of the bargain and you do not belong here.

'306' were doing their bit almost constantly tonight, making a considerable and constant racket for the first half hour at least. Meanwhile, most of The Kop just sat dumbly on their arses waiting for a goal feast. Like bloated Roman emperors in The Coliseum they sat waiting for West Ham to be put to the sword before they'd even consider rousing themselves from their torpor, putting down their jumbo hotdogs, and joining in – probably with the Torres bounce or something else they'd seen on YouTube.

Right behind me sits, or stands, Daily Mirror columnist Brian Reade. When there's a misplaced pass or a miscontrolled cross, he'll bark

"Unlucky,son!" He's constantly willing the team on, encouraging players to tackle, to head or shoot even when they're having stinkers. At one point, midway during the second half we've had a shot deflected wide for a corner. I clasp my forehead in my palm, a combination of frustration and the fear that this game is becoming a manifestation of The Collywobbles. Readey leans over and with his hand on my shoulder assures me: "No trouble. We'll score from this. 3-nil this. Easy."

It's as if he's reassuring a small child. And like a small child I place all my trust in him, I believe him – because *I want to believe him* despite what my eyes are telling me. Imagine 45,000 like him inside Anfield. There are many, many like Readey (I'm one most of the time I like to think) but there's also the moaners, the 'experts', the critics – those who tell you that Benitez will never win us the title.

"He hasn't improved the squad from Houllier's set-up at all."

There's those that tell you Arbeloa, Lucas, Dossena will never make it and are "not Liverpool players."; that David Ngog should, well, "N'go!" and that the midfield maestro that is Alonso, he of the "passes are so delightful" also has "shooting that's fucking frightful." These experts will tell you that Babel is no longer "a young lad still learning about the English game" – he's just "fucking lazy." And my comrade and editor Sammo just won't have it that Dirk Kuyt is anything other than a "yard dog." They're all too quick to let these feelings be known, loudly, whenever someone messes something up on the pitch.

Meanwhile, from the back of The Kop, comes the cry, again: "Unlucky son! Head up...."

With 45,000 like Readey inside Anfield we'd be unbeatable. Robbie Keane would have 15 goals already, Dossena would be playing like Carlos Alberto and Xabi Alonso would be having the occasional shot on target.

We all have a gripe about a player over a pint, make a few jokes about his dreadful performances, but that's where it ends. Once you're 'out there' you have to support them. You support the team, not just which ever players take your fancy. Otherwise you stop being part of the solution and instead become part of the problem.

Which leaves us where? 18 corners, nearly all the possession, 20 shots, top of the League... but booed by a section of the crowd. Played 15 games: 10 wins, 4 draws and one very, very flukey defeat at Spurs.

And booed.

Best ever start to a Premier League season.

And booed.

Top of the league.

And booed.

Not even the half-hearted chorus of "Liverpool, Liverpool, Top Of the League!" could gloss over it. This crowd has become spoilt and rotten. What was most galling about this act of treachery was that it played right into the hands of the press. Almost every headline the following morning referred to the booing. Every story used it to prop up their reports that despite climbing a point clear at the top of the table, all was not well at Fortress Anfield. Liverpool have somehow stumbled to the summit, fluked their way there, playing unconvincing football and are leaders almost by default. It must be so, they proclaim – even their own supporters ON THE KOP think this way: they booed them! And rather than use this as an example of our true title credentials (if it was Man U they'd herald for playing poorly but "grinding out the result" they needed to stay on top) it was used as proof, instead, that we won't be there long. As soon as Chelsea or the Mancs get their act together we'll be where our football belongs: fighting with Arsenal, Villa etc. for a top four spot. Rather than forcing journalists to think about the situation, the booing gave them an easy headline.

And what it also did was to sideline, if not to downright undermine, the public show of support for Michael Shields' judicial review inside Anfield tonight. The reaction of the crowd to the final whistle became the big story tonight, rather than the huge gesture of Solidarity with one of our own in need of our help. The booing became the story instead. Tempers were fraying as we left The Kop and strong words exchanged between the admittedly small number of boo-ers and the rest of us. It left a sour taste in the mouth, one that I didn't even want to wash away with a beer or two, choosing instead to head straight home. A bad, bad night – and one we need to get out of our system as soon as possible.

JM

Liverpool Boys are in Town Book Launch

Static Gallery   Fri 5th Dec

As he always does, Alan Kayll has tomorrow's team on his mobile. He's never wrong, Alan. Whether he perches himself up on the tower block overlooking Melwood or he's just a clairvoyant we may never know – but Know is what Alan K is In The. So Robbie Keane is to be on the bench at Blackburn tomorrow, the sort of game he might have expected to start. In fact sod that, we paid nearly £20 million for Robbie – he should expect to start *every* game. But Rafa's patience has snapped, it would seem. He's cutting his losses on this one.

We're in The Static Gallery in Liverpool city centre, at the re-launch of Dave Hewitson's brilliant book ('The Liverpool Boys Are In Town') about the birth of 'Football Fashion' back in late 70's Liverpool. Half of Block 306 are here – well, the older half to be precise – because they're in the book. It's fascinating, and not a little funny, to see 30 year old photos of these near middle-aged guys. Here they all are tonight, slightly balding and greying, with beer bellies and faces that tell a thousand tales, while in the book they're all whippet slim, with ridiculously long fringes and tight jeans.

But the talk here tonight is as much about Robbie Keane as it is about Adidas Trim Trab and the 'Ordinary to Chelsea'.

"He'll be gone in January. Defo! Take my word for it..."

"Where?"

"Problee Spurs – we still owe them the money, so its easier that way."

"I expect Rafa's just decided it's just not working and we need someone else instead...."

"Stop intellectualising it all.," Joynty advises me. "He's just shit. End of. Move On." And he hands me a can of Red Stripe.

But it doesn't seem right to me. Surely, we just wouldn't pull the plug on it half-way through the season? Not unless Rafa has a replacement lined up. That has to be it. He'd be mad to weaken the squad at such a vital time. We're top of the League, we're through to the knock-out stages of the European Cup and we'll be hoping for a decent run in the F.A Cup this year, after last year's pathetic showing at home to Barnsley. Rafa *must* have another striker in mind. We start into our favourite game, You – The Manager.

"Peter Crouch," says Joynty. "Half the team think he's still here, the amount of high balls they bang in..."

"Too Eeengleesh for Rafa," says Sammo. "It'll be Sergio Aguerro..."

"We can't afford Sergio friggin' Tacchini," I say.

Sammo strokes his chin. He likes to think of himself as a bit of talent spotter does Kevin, often reminding us that when he wrote *Extra Time* in 1997 he suggested we sign the 16 year-old Rio Ferdinand but curiously neglecting to remind us of his other tip-top recommendations in the book – Kevin Davies and Carl Serrant! Exactly.

"Know who'd I'd have in a flash," muses Sammo.

"Bette Midler?"

"Betty Turpin?"

He gives us a patient smile.

"Thierry Henry. Serious. Can't get a game for Barca. Knows the English League inside out. Still the greatest player in the world... and he *loves* Liverpool. You with me?"

It's fair to say that Thierry Henry did stare gob smacked at The Kop during his last game at Anfield, an F.A Cup tie remembered more for our prolonged, 6-minute chant for Justice for the 96 than it was for Arsenal's easy 3-1 victory. I'd *love* to see Henry here. Whoever it is though, to raise the cash for a replacement, Rafa has to offload Keane. Well, like I said, its all about the team, not individual players. If Rafa can strengthen the team then any sentimentality about Keane has to be put aside. I say this to several people over and over until I convince myself that this is the case. Only then can I finally enjoy the evening and have a few beers.

Photos of Fila tennis tops, Lois jeans, Kickers and Transalpino train tickets are being projected onto the walls. What with the terrace fashions and the DJ set of classic Jam, Clash and Joy Division sounds, it seems I'm in Steve Kelly territory again and wishing it was 1979 once more.

JM

Blackburn (a)   3-1

League   Sat 6th Dec

Another lift from Alan Diamond, this time without the antagonistic atmosphere generated by Josh and Greg, who are as quiet as Jack Straw these days. It must be the proximity to Christmas, and the threat of a possible last minute confiscation of potential presents, that's forced these two into an uneasy truce. There's the odd elbow jab and murderous glare (and that's just from their dad), but on the whole it's a pleasant dash up the M6 and M65 into north Lancashire.

Unlike the recent trip to Bolton, this similar short hop - easily there in an hour – is a pleasure. Bolton's just a tedious drive up the motorway to Manchester's grim northern satellite towns; there's no sense of being anywhere other than 'somewhere near Mill Town'. Blackburn, on the other hand, is a bracing trip into the real north of England: moorland hills, limestone walls, cotton mills and snow; and with both the reborn Accrington Stanley, and the sadly defunct Colne Dynamoes, just up the road, it's a footballing Mecca.

"Nil Nil today," I tell Alan. I'm convinced the wheels are about to come off the challenge. As much as I'd love to believe all these points amassed from indifferent performances are signs of title-winning form, it all smacks of 'luck' to me. Perhaps I'm just too scared to believe? Maybe I just don't want to get my hopes up and then have them dashed by a Chelsea side I abhor for representing all that's wrong with modern football; or worse, still, a Man Utd side equalling our record of 18 titles, would be utterly crushing. I would have to go out and buy a cat so that I could kick it. No, fuck it, I'd buy some hand grenades...

Alan's smiling, however, and he's normally the pessimistic one – though he'd call it 'realism'.

"Nah mate... I work with a Blackburn season ticket holder and he said it's so different this season. Ince has changed the way they play – not the rigid 4-4-2 of Mark Hughes had them playing, all solid, boring but safe. Ince has got them playing open, flowing football."

"You are talking about Blackburn aren't you? They haven't flowed since 1995."

"He says they'll be wide open. Honest, he told me we'll score 4 – easy," Alan reassures me.

I ponder on it.

"Nope, it'll be 0-0," I insist. Especially if Keane and Torres aren't playing, I think to myself.

The recent dropping of silly points at home has got me paranoid. I'm still grasping at my 'touching distance' at Christmas scenario and in that case a draw here wouldn't be a bad result.

We park just off the M65 in the shadow of Pendle Hill, just on the border between Blackburn and Darwen. Before the motorway extended this far, this was always a good spot for a pre-game pint of Thwaites and a plate of pie and peas in The Golden Cup, a tiny local hostelry. But the motorway has seen this once quiet pub overrun on matchdays with hundreds of Liverpool fans spilling out into the car park. Inside there's sweat running down the walls and it's 4 or 5 deep at the bar. I'm lucky to have brought a few bottles of San Miguel with me ('The taste of Spain', all Flamenco dancers and Torres' volleys; except it's brewed in an aluminium and concrete, Kennedy Space Centre-lookalike, chemical plant near Hereford). Ole! Futball con Passion!

The motorway flyover looms up over the pub and casts a permanent shadow. Its absolutely bloody freezing. The pub and main road are still frozen, the frosty car park cobbles a deathtrap, so I pick my way gingerly down the hill towards Ewood Park. Down at the bottom of the hill is The Fernhurst pub. If I thought the Golden Cup was packed, this place makes it look as busy as the Everton ticket office on the first day of Season Ticket renewals. The Fernhurst is bulging at the seams, bouncers and police are stopping people from getting in, and there must be a thousand fans in the car park. Empty cans are crunching underfoot and the police are busy confiscating footballs that periodically appear and get launched high into the air, like an Arsenal defensive clearance, to come hurtling back down to earth like meteorites. This little game has become a staple diversion at away games, especially abroad, its sole purpose being to piss off the police as much as possible whilst looking like harmless fun. Even by our standards of fanaticism though, Blackburn has become a madhouse of Liverpool away day over the last few seasons. With away tickets now next to impossible for most fans, Blackburn's proximity, and the generous 7,500 allocation, means that everyone makes a day of it. I see Peter Hooton outside with his lad, Tom.

"You'll never get served in there," Peter says, swigging on a can of Stella. "Probably easier in the ground."

"I guessed as much. See you in there!"

Once inside it's not too difficult to get a pint and a Potato and Butter Pie (a new one on me). The TV screens are showing the team news. Keane is on the bench, as predicted. Maybe he really is on his way. Almost everyone I know is here in the Darwen End and each and every bloody one of them is telling me the hot gossip surrounding Robbie Keane. Mad rumours now abound of a supposed troublesome private life - all originating from the usual utterly reliable sources, of course. Maybe Rafa hasn't got anyone else in mind at all, then? Maybe all our gossip-mongers are right this time and Keane just HAS to go, replacement or no replacement.

It's confirmed that Torres is still injured, and it's the 'Industrious One' leading the attack. "No Torres? Mind you, it worked against Man U...," I say to myself lapsing into that blissful self-denial that Ian Roughly so admires in me. The good news is that we're playing Insua at left back He looks a belting prospect.

"We'll see the best of Kuyt now he's at centre forward."

It was the mantra repeated by almost everyone I met on the concourse under the stand. A mass out break of self-delusion only rivalled at St James Park whenever Newcastle sign a forward.

"He played there for Feyenoord and scored about 400 goals; Rafa's got him dicking about on the wing, just watch him now he's playing up front."

Well they can't have been talking about today, obviously. We may as well have just had a 6 man midfield. No outlet, no pace up front: no surprise it was 0-0 at half time. To be fair the ball was generally just lumped up to Kuyt or he was coming deep to deep to pick it up and finding, obviously, no-one to aim for further up the field. Alonso needs to start playing higher up in games like this, especially with Mascherano covering so well. He's not creating in dangerous areas, and he's not shooting. Then there's Babel.

"He needs a run of games to build up his confidence," is Sammo's assessment.

"He needs a start" or "he's never given a chance," the other experts tell us. Well he was given one today against some of the league's least impressive defenders and he shit out completely. Sorry, but if you want a word to describe Ryan Babel then try "disinterested." Insua did more in one 20 second spell on that left flank than Babel did all game. There's real hunger to impress in that young lad.

At half-time I need more food to soak up the beer, and some more beer to wash down whatever stodge I might buy. In the queue for a pie fellow S.O.S lifer Steve Monagahan (Mono) sidles up to me, and pretending to talk to me about some incredibly important Union business, bunks in behind me. The very pretty girl serving me is trying to explain the different pies I'm having with my two pints of lager, her East European accent making it an amusing interlude.

"And dis is shteak unt kidknees."

Mono takes the opportunity to get even further to the front of the queue by barging in, under my armpit, and leaning on the counter.

"Alright love, are there many Polish girls in Blackburn?" he asks her in a jaunty, neo-East End, cheeky boy manner.

"Yes. Many," she answers, very straight faced.

"4000 Poles in Blackburn Lancashire, eh?" he beams. "Eh?"

She looks at him blankly.

"You know – The Beatles?" he explains, miming what looks like George Formby playing a ukulele.

"Sorry?"

"Kids today eh?" He looks genuinely crestfallen. "Two lagers please, love."

He joins me for a pint and we discuss the first half. We agree that Insua's had a handy 45 mins and looks keen to get forward, something we've missed from the full backs this season – ever since Riises's first couple of seasons to be precise. And there was Reina's brilliant save from Pederson – one of many this year – to keep it goalless.

"Yeah but he still gives you kittens when he won't come for crosses." I say, "Especially corners."

"Its that zonal marking shite," Mono says. " Everyone hates it."

I follow him back to his spec to the rear of the lower tier, on the aisle. There we (me, Mono, John Garner and Roy Boulter) stand for the second half, enjoying a little moan amongst ourselves. The second half is panning out much like the first, and we can't see where a breakthrough might come from.

Benayoun feeds Gerrard on the right as we attack the home end, Kuyt lurks in the centre.

"Here we go," groans Garner loudly. "End of attack."

Then the ball is crossed. A static Kuyt swings his boot at it, the effort is blocked and the ball somehow squirms out to Alonso, about 20 yards out. Apparently at a loss for alternatives, he calmly sidefoots it - 'passes it', is a more accurate description – into the bottom corner. One -nil! Blinkin' eck!

The entire Darwen End, both upper and lower tiers, explodes. It's pure relief, and Xabi feels it as much as we do. He hares off to the corner flag, like an incontinent dog suddenly let out of the back door, punching the air in sheer joy. I meanwhile run and up and down the stairs, whooping like a Red Indian, and hugging anyone I see, whether I know them or not. Oh me! Oh me! Oh me of little faith! How could I ever doubt them?

Chelsea are winning 2-0 at Bolton, and we all expect Man Utd to cane the rudderless Sunderland. The 3 points are vital here. Yet the one goal lead, ironically, has made it even more nerve-wracking here in the stands. But we needn't worry. The goal transforms the way Liverpool are playing, and confidence suddenly surges through the team. Down the right flank Yossi attacks the defence on the edge of the box, skips past our former left-back Steven Warnock and hammers it home. It was quick, decisive and penetrating – the type of play we've been lacking for weeks now.

Cue more mayhem in the Darwin End with people ending up on their backsides in the aisles.

"That was pure Beardsley," I shout at Mono, who just nods and goes "Yiss!"

With under 10 minutes to go 'The Kop on the move' are opening up their lungs to celebrate. We'll be staying top of the league tonight and the crisp Lancashire air resounds with the cry,

"Liverpool, Liverpool, Top of the League,
   Liverpoo-ool!
   Top of the League!"

And Garner's happy we're singing his song again. It's still too early to crow about winning it and we generally avoid singing anything that might... Shit! And that's why...

Blackburn play a short corner right here in front of us, the cross is nodded on towards the far post where Santa Cruz dives to head in. That sodding zonal marking again. All it had taken was for a little bit of movement in the 6 yard box from Rovers, and at least 2 Liverpool defenders ended up not knowing who or what to mark. We went to sleep there and now the last 5 minutes are going to be nail-biting rather than the celebratory sing-song we'd been gearing up for.

"What did I tell yer!" Mono reminds me.

"No-one on either post for that. Would have easily cut that out," I concur.

"Why does he insist on it when most of the players seem to hate it as much as we do?"

He's right. Gerrard and Alonso looked at each other after that as if to say, "Was that your ball or mine"?

In response Rafa brings Riera on for Benayoun, perhaps hoping to stretch Rovers wide at the back, to keep the defence occupied and keep them from coming on to us for the last 5 minutes. But shouldn't that be Keane's role? We look at each other and agree – that's it, Keane must be finished at the club. Riera, to his credit, is instrumental in creating our last attack, and setting Gerrard up for the goal that comes from it. It lifts the slight air of irritation among the travelling fans that we'd made an easy job hard for ourselves here. And Keane's absence spoke volumes here today, too – no, it spoke libraries. Whatever is going on appears to have come to a head.

On the brief journey back Josh and Greg are delighted at the 3 goals, the 3 points and the fact we're still top of the league. They're happy enough to leave each other alone and to play on their Playstations. I'm quietly confident too.

"Was that it then?" I ask Alan. "Were Fulham and West Ham it? The blip? The Collywobbles?"

"Well we weren't that good today," he says. "Made them look quite useful at times."

"Yeah, but we won. Not playing particularly well and winning. That's not the 'collywobbles' is it?"

"It doesn't sound like it. We needed a result and we got it."

"I declare myself mildly satisfied..."

And far from staying 'in touch' at Christmas, we're a point clear at the top. With an easy 3 points next week against Hull before the Christmas game away at Arsenal I'm starting, against my better judgement, to feel a little confident. Dare I suggest it?

JM

Hull City (h)   2-2

League   Sat 13th Dec

The last Saturday home game before Christmas and everyone is up for it, everyone wants to be out on the swallee after a good win. With us today is Andrew Baker, our dipsomaniac Wirral academic chum, last seen staggering away from us in Madrid airport after a spectacular display of tipsiness. Baker's quite probably the most intelligent bloke in our midst. He's a very highly regarded senior lecturer in Political Economy at Queen's University Belfast, who's regularly invited abroad by monetary think-tanks to give his (highly expensive) overview on international financial affairs. He's also a perfect example of the modern academic: intellectually brilliant in his field but not an ounce of common sense. I'm watching him, Guinness in hand, berating all and sundry for 'giving it toes' at Cologne station in 2002, when the 'Koln Skins' ambushed a trainload of Reds heading back from Leverkusen. "Stand! Stand!" he yelled on the station concourse, adopting one of those Victorian boxing poses: bolt upright and both fists held stiffly up in front of his face. All he needed was a waxed moustache.

He's my mate. A good lad, boss drinker and top Red. Just don't get him started on Governance and Constitutionalism in World Politics and the role of the elite's causal beliefs and divisive societal interests in determining the G20 states' monetary and financial policies. I did once, when we were drinking vodka outside Old Trafford, and very nearly hurled myself under a bus during a lull in the ensuing 2 hour rant.

Today, however, he's catching up with mates he hasn't seen since Madrid. I often wonder how he can travel the globe dispensing wisdom to finance ministers and international bankers, and yet also end up utterly paralytic in European capitals, having lost his phone, one lens out of his glasses and yet another coat. Did he do this out in Dubai, when lecturing to Gulf States' financial institutions, as he did last year? Suddenly turning up the next morning to meet Sheik Mohammed bin Rashid Al Maktoum, with only one shoe on and a prominent dark stain down one leg of his trousers. He says not, but DIC walked away from the club soon after. Go figure.

He's over this weekend as he can't make my birthday piss-up next week and we're determined to have a good one. It's an early start, therefore, at 11am in Shenans, with all the regulars in attendance; all similarly keen not to waste the last really decent drinking day before Crimbo. Next weekend, the official start of the holidays, will be a mess: town absolutely full with pissed-up office parties and frantic, panicking shoppers. Bar staff will be knackered or envious at missing out themselves. As such elbow room, general bonhomie and festive goodwill will be in short supply. Add to that the prospect of Everton at home next weekend, and the possibility of debauched Evertonian mongs screaming 'MUUUURDEREEEERS!' at anyone they identify as being a Red (i.e the vast majority of the city), and town needs to be given a huge body swerve in the week before Crimbo. Best to stay in and watch 'A Miracle on 34th Street'.

Ian Roughley, meanwhile, looks like 'The Miracle of Tithebarn St'. He's been up all night but seems remarkably chipper. Got the constitution of Oliver Reed that lad. We muse on the other miracle – that newly-promoted Hull City are not only not languishing at the foot of the table in that specially-warmed hatch marked Straight Back Down, they're actually enjoying themselves, playing very decent football and, for a good long while, held down a top 6 slot. They're starting to slip a bit now though – we should snot them. Baker slaps me on the back.

"Come on, Chief, drink up. We'll miss this otherwise."

We leave Shenans at 2:20, there's still a good 20 or so lads in there who'll be following us on one of the next 4 buses between now and kick-off.

Up on Row 56 in Block 306, John Maguire is standing silently, hood on his coat up, half covering his face, like a contemplative monk. He notices us 3 looking at him.

"Its me lucky hood." he explains rather sheepishly. "I had it up at Blackburn."

Ah, that explains it then. Relax everyone, Mags has his hood up – the points are in the bag.

* * * * *

This game isn't going to plan. We are top of the league and playing at home. They are Hull City. And they're two up and playing some good football. Their first goal was the result of some truly terrible defending. About ten minutes into the match, a free kick from out on the right wing is allowed to sail over and actually bounce in the box, before being returned from the left into the 6yd box. Here, the completely static Dossena seems surprised, if not downright shocked, that an opponent might actually jump off the ground to head a ball. And head it they do – past Reina and into the fucking onion bag!

It gets worse, and we're soon 2-0 down – but you've got to give them credit, this was a beautifully-worked goal. A searching cross-field pass stretches the back four and, again, exposes Dossena who they've clearly identified as the weak link. He's left for dead by the winger who fires over a low cross that Reina really should have collected – he doesn't like these low hard crosses, Pepe – but instead the ball arrives at pace at Carra's feet about a yard off the line. He appears to try and sidefoot it wide for a corner, completely fucks it up, and knocks it into the net.

"For fuck's sake, Dossena!" someone shouts.

John Maguire, pulls his Lucky Hood back slightly, screws his face into his Firm But Fair persona then offers the following observation.

"You know when we said last week that Lucas is the only Brazilian who can't shoot or pass... well Dossena is the only Italian who can't tackle or defend."

There are silent nods of agreement

"Tellin' yers," adds Mags.

Brian Reade takes this as his cue and roars: "Come on Reds! Let's get into these!"

The call to arms ripples around and Block 306 tries to get the rest of The Kop going. And The Kop does indeed rouse itself and get behind the team. There's barely 20 minutes gone and plenty of time for us to wake up and start playing. In fact the response comes sooner than expected and we hit back almost immediately when Gerrard slides home after collecting a loose ball following a great cross from Kuyt. Why weren't we pinging the ball about like this 15 minutes ago?

The Kop's in full voice now, roaring the team on, and they in turn now appear to throw caution to the wind. We pour forward, and by the half hour we're level: Gerrard again coolly half-volleying into the roof of the net from a Benayoun pass. There's an hour to go. The noise level increases and Hull are on the ropes. Now's the time to turn the screw and take them apart.

But we don't. After having 'had a go' we revert to our previous shape and allow Hull to play themselves back into the game. It's infuriating. We've shown that when we don't care about what the opposition might do and just attack them, we get results. But here we are reverting to a more cautious approach and the game's back in the balance. I don't get it.

At half time we troop down to where Louise has all our 'interval refreshments' lined up – beers galore, along with a couple of dangerously-smoking pies. 20 minutes later, Sammo's still blowing his pie, recoiling each time his lips get close enough to touch it. In the States, a lawsuit would follow. Lou's looking very fetching today, she's obviously just had her hair done and is dressed for a Crimbo night out.

"So Lou," I ask her. "You out on the pull tonight?"

"Might be..." she blushes.

"You've got all these young lads after you, you know. You're their favourite MILF."

"I'm NOT A MILF!" she protests.

"Hang on... you're 30-odd, you're a single mum, and you know all this lot would (*gestures around the concourse*) **love** an older woman," I explain. " So face it. You are a MILF!" I finish off my beer and toss the bottle into the bin. Lou's still weighing up the pros and cons of Milfdom.

"... I've been for a wax an' all," she admits.

"Copping off knickers?" I ask, purely out of academic interest.

"Might have...." She blushes again.

Professor Baker weighs up the academic evidence.

"MILF," he declares, drawing the subject to a close.

As we trot back up the aisle to our seats, Joynty says:

"Am telling yer boys, another half like that from Dossena, and Lou Lou won't be only one getting fucked tonight."

Luckily for Dossena, he's a bit better in the second half. But overall we're struggling to create any clear-cut opportunities. The Kop would normally be chanting for Robbie Keane by now – that's if we'd have come up with a chant for him by now. The 'Keano' one is still getting regularly booed down and its proponents castigated, but there's been no proper replacement. No real song for Robbie. There was a desire, early in the season, not to rush in and pen something silly that our famous number 7 would then be stuck with for years.

You know, like that stupid Peter Crouch one. I'd often feared him scoring the winner in a European Cup final and have to listen to such schoolboy, internet-fed, drivel, as:

> "He's big, he's Red, his feet stick out the bed.
>   Peter Crouch! Peter Crouch!"

It needs something simple, catchy and dignified. But the more and more it looks like Keane's for the chop, the less and less likely it is that someone's going to waste energy thinking a good song up. So with 20 minutes to go, and with us looking no more likely to score again this year, we all stand there and attempt a mass mind probe from Row 56; all concentrating on beaming our thoughts deep into Rafa's consciousness.

'Get. Him. On. Get Keane on now!'

Mag's face is all screwed up, deep in concentration.

"Careful there, Maggi," says Andy, one of the Skem lads who make the banners. "You might poo yourself."

"I'm tryin' too 'ard.," says Mags.

"He probably can't speak Bootle," says Baker. "Try it in Spanish."

There's some sudden activity on the bench. We see a tracksuit top being discarded and wait, with baited breath, to see if it's worked and whether or not Derren Brown has anything to fear.

"Who is it…?"

"Who's dah…?"

"It's… it's… fuckenell, it's El Zhar!" bemoans Lou Lou.

"That doesn't even *sound* like Keane," complains Mags.

"Told yer," says Baker. "It's yer accent. You keep schtum next time."

"Well 'ow duzee understand Sammy Lee then?"

"Sammy speaks Spanish," Brian Reade chips in. "Otherwise Rafa'd be fucked."

Well at least we got the timing right. No matter how badly it's going Rafa will wait until, at the very earliest, 70 minutes before making a change. It's as if changing things earlier means admitting his starting XI was the wrong in the first place. But how that wasn't Keane is beyond most people here. To be fair, El Zhar's at least a bit more direct than Benayoun.

"At least it wasn't Lucas on for Kuyt, or something…" says LouLou, fully realising what such a change would have precipitated amongst Windows and his disciples. Down the row I can see him jabbing his finger to make several equally deranged points simultaneously. He's deep into conversation with Mono, Mick Potter and Peter Hooton. None of them looks particularly happy.

As the clock ticks away Hull are giving as good as they get. But we are, at last, creating chances, and it looks like we've won it when Sami Hyypia rises above everyone and thumps a header full..... against the post. I can't believe it – everyone thought that was in!

Gerrard's faded as an attacking force, Riera's been quiet most of the game and Kuyt seems glued to the right touchline – I hate to harp on about it but the game is screaming out for Robbie Keane. 10 minutes from time, more touchline activity. Could this be the moment? Could it feck! It's Ryan Babel, on for the ineffectual Riera. Well we could see Riera going off, but Babel??? Once again, the substitution is aimed at just introducing a fresh pair of legs with the accent on preserving the overall balance and shape of the team. The shape, that is, that's been as blunt as Tommy Keiner's attempts to start a song this past half-hour. Why not just go for it, Rafa? We love you, man, you'll never be anything less than a legend here so, come on – off with the brakes, for crying out loud!

As the game enters its last few minutes it's clear that Robbie Keane has no future at the club. We're minutes away from dropping another 2 home points – that'll be 8 points dropped at Fortress Anfield against the international heavyweights of Stoke, Fulham, West Ham and now Hull - unless, hang on... unless this last substitution...

"You've got to be fucking joking!" sighs German Tommy at the sight of Lucas Leiva replacing Mascherano.

"Just what is the frigging point of that?" I ask Baker. "There's only about 3 minutes left?"

He just looks at me blankly. See, he may well have the enormous intellectual dexterity and versatility that results from a training in Politics, Philosophy and Economics, and he may also be an enormous professional and intellectual asset, valued and trusted by governments and policy makers the world over; but – can he explain how Lucas Leiva got on the pitch just then?

Can he fuck.

* * * * *

After the match, over a few Crimbo beers in Neds, Baker does indeed attempt some kind of explanation for all these dropped points.

"Its a kind of erectile dysfunction," he says.

"Yes doctor."

"Not one with a deep rooted physical cause... no. This is more psychological. An inherent lack of confidence that make your cock go all floppy."

"Speak for yerself."

"I'm speaking metaphorically here," he insists.

"Winning the league is something that's taken on an unnatural, an overwhelming importance."

"I agree. We've won loads of things in the last decade. We've won the European Cup... but we're told that we're nothing unless we win the league."

"Well, now we're top at Christmas and people start speaking about it more and more... journalists and the like. The players are starting to think about it and it's building up this big, mythical presence in their minds....the pressure, the spotlight, all that emphasis on The Big Shag...it's getting to them."

"And the fans," I add. "You saw today how cranky it's making everybody when it looks like we're pissing it away with these stupid draws."

"Exactly," he says putting down his empty glass, and pausing.

"It's like you've been after this really fit bird for ages and you finally pull her... take her out a few times, the odd fumble, but then one night she tells you she's wanting the big love with you and... 'Tonight's the Night'!"

"Of course! But what took so long?"

"But you immediately start to panic. Are me undies clean? Can I get a 'ard on... all that nonsense...."

"Did I shave me plums in the shower? Yes? That type of thing..."

Baker looks at me askance.

"You shave your plums, Mackin? That's just... sick."

"Go on... finish up your ludicrous analogy if you must..."

"So, you get her back home and get her kit off... right?" he asks.

"Hang on," I say, narrowing both eyes, "I'm just imagining that... okay, carry on!"

"Then just when you need to be at your best... it's not happening.... nothing... Just hangs there like a piece of rope."

"Wouldn't know," I say, smirking.

"And it's all because you've wanted this so much, for so long, that when it's presented to you – you panic. Are you good enough? Can you perform? Will you be a better shag than her last fella...."

"You need to relax. To not dwell on it." I tell him with a surprising insight into such issues. "Just let it happen. Then when you know you can do it, and she's loving it, then you suddenly become the world's greatest shagger."

"That's what's happening in these games. It's got too close now, too real. The team know it's time to perform – especially at home against these lesser sides. They need to step up and prove they've got what it takes to be the world's bossest shagger, but they're afraid of failing. And what do we get?"

"A piece of rope. When what we need is something you could open a tin of paint with," I say.

"Exactly," he says triumphantly. "I rest my case."

We clink glasses and toast 'The Mighty Reds'. I think back to his meeting with D.I.C.

"So, Andy – is this what you told the Sheik, then?"

JM

Arsenal (a)   1-1

League   Sun 21st Dec

It's a biggy. Arsenal away at the Emirates. I quite like going to the Emirates but something's bugging me. I just can't believe how easily everyone in football has accepted the name of an oil rich state as the home of Arsenal, one of our oldest and most respected clubs. The thought of the Gunners coming up here to play at the Abu Dhabi Stadium or the Bahrain Bowl is enough to give you nightmares. Nothing is sacred anymore. Highbury was Arsenal and Arsenal was Highbury. Like Anfield is Liverpool. There's no immediate panic though regarding our new stadium because they've been banging on about it for over a decade and the builders still haven't moved in yet. I'll probably be pissing my stripey pyjamas in some minty nursing home before the LFC Red Sox run out at the Oman, Showman, Go Man Arena.

That's the beauty about getting older. There's less chance of seeing your lifelong passion sink any lower into the money grabbing pantomime that it has already become. The way I see it is, it's like the woman you love being wooed by the big, fat, greasy billionaire at the end of the bar. You discover her two days later in a hotel room, a half drunk bottle of champagne in a bucket by the bed. There's dollar bills scattered all over the pillows. Her eyes rolling, her cheeks flushed and clothes torn, confused and silly, she doesn't know whether she's had the greatest weekend of her life or been the victim of some glorified date rape. Drugged up to the eyeballs on a cocktail of marketing, money and mismanagement – that's the state of play at the moment. Football doesn't know whether it's coming or going. It's speeding down the highway ignoring all the warning signs and if it doesn't put its foot on the brakes, there's going to be casualties.

I'm just back from sunning my pretty little persil white arse on the beaches of East Africa – Kenya to be precise. Just a bit of an unofficial mid-season break to get some sand between my toes, sun on my back, see the animals in their own backyard and to recharge the batteries. There are many words in the English language which are overused, misused and exaggerated. Love and hate are two of them. "Oooh, I'd *love* a cup of tea" or "God, don't you just *hate* it when the lights go on red." Awesome is another word which is just thrown into conversation to describe things which are really not awesome at all. Buy an American a drink and they'll say "wow, that's really awesome" and you're like "no, it's just a bevvy" – there's nothing awesome about it in the slightest. But when me and Miss New Brighton walked in and opened the curtains of our room in the hilltop safari lodge, it was like "FORRRRKIN 'ELL MAN." Awesome doesn't even come near to describing how amazing it was. Wilderness as far as the eye can see. The best view I've ever had in my life bar none. And that includes peeping through the curtains of the pub when I was eleven to watch the 'Stripper at the Clipper' do her thing and nearly having a heart attack.

Out there in the wild there's all kinds of mad stuff going on amongst the bushes. There's things eating other things and eagles circling around as leopards sit nonchalantly up in the tree waiting for the elephants to pass. It's just another normal day in the 'cradle of civilisation' we call Africa. Yet up there on the menu along with Safaris and jeep trails, we have the option of an accompanied trip out into the mean streets of Kenya proper and watching the footy in a bar full of fanatical African Reds.

The lads who took us out for the Blackburn game didn't have a pot to piss in, if the truth be known, but mention LFC and they'd start salivating and getting all animated. Fred, Snoop and Samson (no relation) are not their real names but people like me would struggle to pronounce, never mind spell what's on their birth certificates. So they just adopt a name which tourists can say. Liverpool are on telly every Saturday and Sunday here and then repeated about three times during the week so there's nothing they don't know about the Mighty Reds. I amaze them with tales of what it's like at Anfield and show videos on my phone of demonstrations outside the ground and of us lot in the San Siro. I show them photos of me and Carra and Stevie G and they lap it up with childlike amazement. I'm basically showing off and probably acting like a right prick but I'm miles away from home. No-one knows me and the natives are buzzing. I feel like I'm Dr Livingstone on a mission to spread the word of Liverpool FC across Mother Africa – or Johnny Mackin with less hair. Is right lad!

We get taken to this bar which can only be described as shady. Hot Lips has had reservations all day about us going but sometimes you've got to live a little. We're both aware that last year there was a bit of unrest in Kenya and loads of people were macheted to death but hey, can it be any worse than going to Man U? Health & Safety would do back flips if they walked into this bar. I know I'm gonna get scalped on the drinks but as long as we win and the lads enjoy it, I feel like it's my treat.

It's weird watching the match on the other side of the world when you know it's your duty to be there. But when you weigh up the options, Ewood Park, Blackburn, Lancashire in deepest midwinter, or Tsavo East National Park in ninety degrees of heat is not the toughest of toughies. Life throws up many hard decisions, but this wasn't one of them. We won 3-1 and everything was cool but the maddest thing that I'll remember is when we scored. Normally you and your mates just shout "Get in there!" or "Yes!" or whatever, but not here. The whole place jumps up and down making animal noises. Absolutely bizarre. When Alonso slotted the first it sounded like I'd stood on a parrot, volleyed a hyena and pulled a monkeys tail off – the place just went off its head. Some fellas were yelping and squealing like pigs and others were just sitting there inventing new noises. It was a great experience, albeit a strange one. Chelsea were on the other telly the other side of the bar and I found it heartwarming when the Kenyan Liverpool fans started giving the Kenyan Chelsea fans stick. It made me think that wherever those phonies from the Fulham Road are in the world, there will be Redmen breathing down their necks, whatever colour, creed, nationality they are, they will never be free from our shadow. Warms the cockles of your heart, doesn't it?

Anyway I survived and I'm back but I'm faced with a choice. It's four days before Crimbo. Tickets are sold out. No trains back after the match. Everyone is either sorted or not going and funds are very low. The other more attractive option is a big all day blow out in town to celebrate Johnny Mackin's Big Five O surrounded by fellow Reds. Sounds well tempting. I'll probably save over a ton by not going to Arsenal, and most probably have a better laugh in the company of about thirty good Redmen. I can't believe I just said that "I'll probably have a better laugh watching it on the pub telly instead of going." Oh my god I'm turning into the dreaded Sky Guy. Here's a quick pointer for you. If ever you see me with a replica shirt on (which you won't) in a pub telling proper fans who've just got back from an away game that it was a penalty or an offside because I watched it on telly, you have my absolute permission to

Jegsy with the Kenyan Reds. Fred, Snoop and Samson after the Blackburn away game

drag me out into the car park and beat me about the head with a blunt instrument until I beg for forgiveness and promise not to be such an annoying twat again.

The only downside is that Johnny Boy wants to celebrate his big day in – wait for it – Shenanigans. Actually it turns out to be brilliant. Sammo has sorted it so we have a sit down scran at 2pm with wine, sherry, whatever the Good Doctor has ordered. With the match starting at 4, that gives us time to tuck in and give the Big Fella a good day. We raise our glasses and give him a toast.

"To the Redmen – is right, lad!"

The food is a Christmas roast with all the trimmings (the full bifters) and is very nice too. Mackin has his usual array of match mates in party hats and one or two I don't know. His global (okay, Liverpool-wide) appeal is impressive, and there are appearances from Paul Rice, Chairman of the supporters Union, Gary Shaw and even Sampson Junior (aka Arr Neil) shows up and gets into the spirit of things by ordering 4 bottles of red wine as soon as he hit's the bar. Some of my old mates like Ally, Gilly, Stevie Thomo and Neil Heron turn up just for a bev and to watch the game. Even Frankie Boy Boundy shows up. This has the potential to be an absolute stonker of a night. Normally watching it in the pub is a bit of a pain in the arse but this is great. There's no stray bluenoses making wisecracks or worse still, no embarrassing Reds shouting for players we sold three years earlier.

Sammy Lee takes charge today as Rafa is still recuperating at his gigantic Caldy home after a kidney stone operation. It's a fairly open game for a 'big four' clash with both sides going close but it's the Gunners who break the deadlock in the 24th minute. Robin van Persie is the scorer and sometimes you've just gotta hold your hands up and say "Yes, no complaints lad – great goal." He takes a long ball down on his chest, turns two of our lads in one movement. Chest, left foot and bang with the right. We looked really comfortable up until that point but after a nervy five minutes or so, we begin to get back in it. Then a couple of minutes before half time we get the breakthrough. It's a bit route one but with a thunderbolt of a finish. Robbie Keane, who's endured loads of stick off the Arsenal fans due to his recent Tottenham past, races onto a long ball off Agger that's bounced right over the hopeless Senderos. Robbie steadies himself and you're thinking to yourself, either this is gonna knock Nelson off his column or it's going in, and praise the Lord it's the latter, a perfect volley past Almunia and into the net. The pub erupts into an explosion of joy. There's ale going everywhere, people dancing on tables and plates getting smashed, the whole caboodle. Keane's made up and who can blame him. But we haven't finished yet. In the remaining two minutes to half time we nearly score twice more. Gerrard slides in at the back post but misses by an inch. Then just on the whistle Dirk Kuyt brings a fingertip save from the Arsenal goalie. Half time and we're looking good.

Fabregas doesn't come out for the second half due to a knee injury and it's us who start strongest. Lucas goes close. Agger heads wide then next minute all hell breaks loose as Adebayor is red carded for his second offence, this time on Arbeloa. Arsenal look vulnerable, now. Down to ten men and their best player off injured. The noise in the pub is deafening as everybody to a man urges the Redmen over the finishing line. We hold all the aces. Everything is in our favour, but what do we do? We go all cautious and start knocking it sideways again. It's as if we're scared to take a chance in case we get hit on the counter attack. Arsenal are in disarray and they're there for the taking, but we seem to just settle for a safety first attitude and a solitary point.

This is the part of Rafa's masterplan that mystifies me. We won't get many better chances than this to finally get three points here but we blow it. The final whistle goes to mild applause from the assembled Reds, and murmurs of "not so bad" etc, but it's obvious that everybody's disappointed. Don't get me wrong, a point at Arsenal is always a decent result but all the lads know it could have been so much more. I suppose it's better than a defeat but the mood is of frustration because we know that if the team got the nod off Rafa they could have gone for it. Anyway it's good to see our mate Johnny Mackin enjoying his first half century with that vacant grin on his grid. He's even got prezzies. Bottles of vino and even a cheeky hair dye thing that Sammo has customised so that instead of Just For Men it says 'Just For John', and underneath he's written 'Burnt Mahogany'. I give John some old footy memorabilia as I know he loves a bit of merchandise. John's three old chums from The Irregulars, Si Morris, Peter Hewitson and Ian Roughley slope off but the rest of us, including John Maguire, John Buchanan, Wrighty, Stewy and the crew all head over to the White Star to meet up with my old Aigburth mates.

God, I used to have some laughs with those lads when we bounced around the country in the late seventies and eighties. We were the original football casuals, long before all these identikit clones copied our every move. You used to go to Leeds or wherever and they'd say "Eh up Scouse, why are you wearing training shoes? Is it so you can run away after the game?" Now they're all writing hooligan books saying how cool they were and how no-one would ever come near them. If the truth be known, Scousers were that far ahead of the average football fan, it was as if we'd evolved to walking upright while the rest were still walking on all fours – that's how big the gap was. Thirty odd years of so-called Terrace Culture later and finally the penny drops. Anyway Johnny Boy is dispatched onto his train with his armful of gifts and a face that says "Okay lads, I give in." We stick around till about ten-ish as the South Enders want to finish up in the Allerton Road area, but once they've give it toes we start to split up and go our separate ways. It's been a good day out but if Rafa would've take his safety belt off it could've been even better. John Mackin – fifty not out. Is right old fella.

JD

Bolton (h)   3-0

League   Boxing Day

Boxing Day – so called because we often used to play Man Utd on Dec. 26th – is one of football's best days as far as fans are concerned. Festive cheer; escaping the claustrophobic clutches of the family; and a fair bit of sherry coursing through people's bloodstreams, usually means today's going to be a good laugh. This year, however, I end up driving to the match because Merseyrail won't pay the overtime and there are no trains. This puts a real dampener on things, as I never discovered this until late last night. However, it does mean that I can have a bit of a lie in and sleep off some of yesterday's alcoholic excesses. If I was on the swallee today I'd be dragging myself out of bed before 9, out onto a 10 o'clock train, and be in The Lion or The Globe at 11 wishing barmaids 'Happy Christmas' and humming of Jamesons.

Instead I'm parking outside Sam Dodds bar on Oakfield Rd, just a couple of hundred yards from The Kop, around noon. My head's a bit thick, the sprouts are working overtime in my bowels, and my breath smells not of whiskey but of mouthwash. 'Tis the season to be jolly? My arse.

What to do? I've got 3 hours to kill. I can't drink so I'm not standing in a crowded pub with backpackers from Stavanger standing on my toes or spilling lager down my back. Ho-hum. Everyone else is either in town having a Crimbo swallee or coming straight here shortly before kick off. Yawns. I know – I'll go for a walk. Clear my head.

Sam Dodds is a relative newcomer to the Anfield pub scene compared to The Albert and The Sandon, both of which have been here for over 120 years. Every time I pass it, Dodds seems to be slowly expanding – like Rapid Hardware on Renshaw Street – and filling the whole block. There's only the Sandon standing between Dodds and world domination.

The Sandon – walk on by. Enough said.

At Flagpole corner I take a right turn and wander up into the Kemmy (
now know as The Centenary Stand, but still The Kemlyn to everyone over the
age of 35) car-park. At the top end are lined up a parade of top of the range
4x4s – Mercs, BMWs – some with Spanish number plates. No guesses whose
they might be. Nice to see our heroes using these workhorse cars when they're
on duty, and leaving the Ferraris and Astons at home. You wouldn't want them
rubbing your face in it would you? It's the modern day equivalent of Billy
Liddell coming to Anfield by bus.

At the top of the car park I turn left by the burger stalls and the 'hat-cap-
scarf-badge' man shivering in the shade. The Anfield Road is always freezing
on days like these, being in almost permanent shadow. There are a few Bolton
fans around already, queuing at closed turnstiles, standing idly by and leafing
through the match programme, or patting police horses. Seems I'm not the
only one who's here far too early with sod all to do. At the end of the Road
End, is the Hillsborough Memorial and The Shankly Gates. The Memorial
has even more flowers on it than usual. At Christmas time all our thoughts
turn to lost loved ones and the Memorial is bathed in red and white floral
tributes with fans paying their respects and taking photos in silence. I always
stop. And I always make sure I read the name of a good pal's younger brother.
I simply cannot imagine the pain he must have felt at losing him, and the
subsequent horror of having to endure the lies, the slurs, the deceit and the
cover-up that followed. If anyone ever questions why the fight for Justice still
needs to be fought, I always think of this one young lad.

Turning into the Main Stand car-park, out of the darkness, the sunlight
is dazzling. I buy a programme from the shop in the corner. I used to be an avid
collector, a completist. But after filling up half of my mum's house with
programmes, and with shoe-boxes on top of wardrobes and in the loft back
home, I've had to cut back. I buy all the European's of course – home and
away – and if I had to really reign it all in, I'd sell everything except the
European proeys. I also buy all cup ties, proeys from derby games and Man
Utd and a few other big games. Then there's the odd, impulse programme
buy – such as today's.

Halfway down the car park, around the players entrance, a large crowd is
gathering. These are the football groupies or 'Stage Door Johnnies', willing to
stand in the cold for hours just to catch a glimpse of a millionaire getting off
a bus listening to his iPod. This crowd is where you'll see the greatest
concentration of what some people, unkindly, call 'whoppers' or 'beauts'. The

'whoppers' are the tourists; the out-of-towners; the Sky TV generation; those who are classed as 'fans' as opposed to 'supporters'. They're the type most likely to turn up in fancy dress, or with a replica shirt with their own name on, worn over their coat. If 'BBC Wildlife' were making a documentary about this ridiculous and clueless sub-species then you'd point them here on match days to set their tripod up. Behind the steel barriers the 'Whoppers' congregate like Wildebeest at a watering hole, regular as clockwork from 1pm on match days, craning their necks to look at anybody walking past who isn't dressed like them. After all, it might be a player, or an ex-player? Maybe someone employed by the club? Or Sky TV? Maybe it's an actress from Hollyoaks, or that Annabelle Tiffin off the telly with the rectangular head? Maybe it's just Ged Poynton, parading round Anfield inspecting his troops like General Eisenhower, pre D-Day? Whoever it is, the 'whoppers' will stand with their mobiles at arms length taking photos (as they seem to do inside the ground at every corner, throw-in, free-kick etc.). I'm just being bitter, of course, as not one of them, ever, stops me for a pic. Sampson and Dodd are always being hassled, wherever we go:

"Quick picture, Sammo? Will you sign this?"

Fuck's sake! Haven't they seen me on LFC.tv?

At the bottom of the Main Stand, outside the gates and amidst the wasteland created by the demolition of several streets of terraced house, sits The Albert. Like an inner-city 'Little House On The Prairie', where once it nestled cheek-by-jowl with the walls of The Kop and the surrounding houses, it's now isolated, surrounded by a tarmac car-park. I know better than to try and get any sort of drink in there at 1pm on a Boxing Day. The windows are already clouded with condensation. They'll be packed so deep at the bar that there'll be people barely inside the door, shouting out for pints, who won't get served until just before 3.

Directly across the road from The Albert is the Hillsborough Justice Campaign Shop – the HJC – and that's where I'm headed for a cup of tea. As usual Gerry and Kenny are behind the counter and I offer to make them a brew. If I'm in luck there might be some biscuits. Even better – some supporters club branch has been in and brought some cakes. Tea and cakes – this beats drinking lager in Neds any day. Jegs doesn't know what he's missing.

And what he is missing is the team news: Keane is playing. I don't know how to take this, is this Rafa playing mind games on us? Or on Keane? Why is he okay to play against Bolton, but not Hull? Is he staying? Is he going?

Chelsea have already beaten West Brom today, so we need to win to stay on top. So, with the continuing absence of Torres, the fact that Keane is playing is welcome news. As is the fact that Shittu is again on the bench for Bolton. I do hope he gets on: we could sing "You're Shittu, and you know you are...." It's certainly childish enough to tickle Mr Dodd.

In fact he didn't need to bother coming on. Bolton were Shittu, all of them, and this was one of the easiest games of the season. So easy, in fact, that Riera shone for most of it, scoring midway through the first half to ease everyone's nerves. In the second half Keane adds two goals (a "brace" I believe broadsheet journalists call that; see also "the table" upon which transfer requests are "slapped" by "want away" players. Not to be confused with the Treatment Table, which I like to imagine as being not unlike a fancy wallpaper table, but nowhere near as flimsy). Both Robbie's goals come from great knocks played just in front of him, just beyond the last defender; one from a cross following a brilliant counter-attack started by Pepe Reina. It seems that given his preferred service he will slot them away. Its a matter, I suppose, of whether Rafa thinks Keane's demands of the team, dovetail with his ideas for how we should play. And more importantly, how we will play when Torres returns?

It must be over 10 years since I went home from a Boxing Day game with my team top of the league – and stone cold sober. It's a funny old feeling, one I'd almost forgotten about: a feeling of pride and self-satisfaction, smugness even, at looking down on everybody from 'our perch'.

All's well with the world, even if it has been a 'dry' day. And I'm slowly – don't say it too loudly – coming round to the notion that this could be our season. And with that, I also suspect that I have quite royally put the mockers on it.

JM

Newcastle (a)   5-1

League   Sun 28th Dec

Brrrrr. It's -2° and the alarm goes off at 5.30am. I'm on a mission to get to the 'Rocket' at the start of the M62 by 7am. Initially I was supposed to travel up yesterday with Nico & the Belgians and stay overnight in some fellas gaff, but things went a little pear-shaped. 'Nico & the Belgians' sounds like some obscure Indie band that John Peel would've played on his show back in the day. Anyway Bucko has booked me, him, Richie and Mercer on John Garner's Renegade coach. Bit of a last minute thing, but I'm just glad we're able to get up there and watch the boys in Red whup those cheeky little Geordie monkey's arses. Hot Lips is with me, checking I've put my shoes on the right feet and I'm tucked in where I should be and hanging where I should hang or the other way around. She gains maximum girlfriend brownie points by scraping the ice off her windscreen and driving me through the darkened, empty streets of town to the 'meet'. I stand there on me bill like one of those downtrodden blokes you see waiting for their lift to do another early shift of drudgery down on the soulless factory floor, dreaming of that two weeks in the sun when he can pretend for a time that life is wonderful and worthwhile. Well I'm a Liverpool fan so I have that 'great to be alive' feeling everyday. So let's be having you Mr Garner – bring me your Chariot of Fire. Out of the darkness a Delta taxi appears and the 'Minister of Fun', Senor David Buckley appears with a grin the size of a Cheshire cat, and a voice like a Mersey foghorn. He greets me like a New York Latino mobster greets his Sicilian cousin. There's a good vibe in the air. I can smell victory. By 7.15am we're on the road and it's all systems go.

It's a real laddish coach we're on today. Not a female or kid in sight. John Garner, who's running the bus, is in his absolute element. If ever there was a man who was born to run trips like this, it's him. He's like the ringmaster, the

MC and the variety act all rolled into one. This is his stage. He's got a microphone and he's gonna use it. With a different announcement every couple of miles, he leaves us in no doubt as to who's boss.

It's an hour into the journey and Bucko emerges from the loo and sheepishly tries to sneak back to his seat unnoticed. It's obvious to anyone sitting near the toilet that he has dropped his full pay load. As soon as he opens the door, it was like POW!! There's people coughing, spluttering and gasping for air as Bucko gives it his most innocent 'who me?' type of look – all he needs now is to whistle silently and drum his fingers on the back of the nearest seat. It's a cut and dried case though – Buckley's been caught 'bang to rights' and he knows it. Garner is back on the mic and he's buzzing.

"Could Mr David Buckley come to the front of the coach please?"

Bucko's playing. He shuffles to the front of the coach with a big mad grin on his kite, waving to the gallery. Garner gives him a stern look.

"You know the rules, Bucko lad. As you are well aware, it is an offence to drop anchor on the coach bog on the way to an away game. There's no extenuating circumstances here, lad – we're a Socialist coach and we treat one another with respect. I have no hesitation in giving you an on-the-spot £5 fine (to be given towards the drivers kitty) – and I'm sorry to have to say this cos you're a cracking lad, but it's a statutory two match ban an' all. Bucko, getting into the spirit of things, lodges an immediate appeal against his ban, citing over zealous policing and a knee-jerk reaction from Judge Garner.

The coach is in uproar. Bucko laps it up, then produces his Trump card. He offers up a £10 note as his fine, just in case he fancies a poo on the way back. The lads are roaring with laughter. Garner cuffs him and sends him on his way.

Up the A1 we have to do the usual palaver of pulling over before the police check, getting rid of the empties and stashing the full ones before the infamous Geordie plod get on for their usual pantomime. We get past 'Checkpoint Charlie' and park up near the ground. I'm the only one on the coach with no ticket and there's none to be had. It's a bad sign when we get off and there's loads of Scousers milling around looking for spares. That's the problem when you support the mighty Reds. Even for a ludicrous mid-day kick-off in the middle of the Crimbo break on the coldest day of the year, loads more fans want a piece of the action than there are tickets to go round. The clock is ticking and I'm hustling and harrying, but to no avail. Disillusioned lads accept the fact that they're not going to get in and stream off in search of a boozer.

I'm hanging on in there when a spiv says he's got one but it'll cost me 50 rips. I tell him to swivel. The match has just kicked off and I'm not paying over the odds. End of story. The tout reappears and gives me the ticket at face price. He knew I wasn't happy but he sees sense in the end. I know it was only a tenner difference but you've gotta have standards.

The climb up the steps to the away end at St James' Park is legendary. You almost feel like you should plant a Norwegian flag at the top and pose for photos, it's that steep. There's people gasping for air at the bottom of the last flight, while others egg them on going "come on mate, only one more flight to go." No wonder the singing is subdued for the first ten minutes. Everybody's wheezing and trying to bum a quick suck on the inhaler from the asthmatic bloke in the row behind.

It has to be said that the 'boys in Red' are absolutely fantastic. We are playing football like I haven't seen since the days of Barnes, Beardsley and Aldo. We were good against Bolton on Boxing Day but this is seriously looking like Championship winning form. Usually we just look solid and hard to beat but today there is flair and fluidity, and much of that free-flowing footy comes through the youthful exuberance of Emiliano Insua, a young left-back who just loves to get forward. He's one of our many "youngsters with promise," most of whom are signed from well-respected youth academies in Spain, Hungary and in Insua's case, Argentina, never to be seen or heard of ever again. But with injuries to Aurelio and Dossena hardly pulling up trees himself, Insua has seized his chance – and how. We absolutely marmalise Newcastle from first minute to last, and the scoreline doesn't even begin to reflect our superiority.

To win 5-1 away from home in the Prem is an amazing achievement at any ground but the scoreline actually flattered Newcastle. We absolutely battered them and I'm not exaggerating when I say it could've easily been ten or twelve. If it had not been for the brilliance of Shay Given in the Geordie's goal and some awful finishing, we would've been four or five up within the first twenty minutes. Sami, Stevie and even Lucas could've had hat-tricks in the most one-sided match I've seen in years. Michael Owen must be wondering to himself "what on earth have I done?" He must look up to the travelling hordes of Liverpool fans who are bouncing in their seats and then turn to the shambles that is Newcastle United and think "I really have fucked up here." A lot of Reds don't like him because he walked out on us but we all make mistakes in life. I've made a few myself and so have you, but I'll be honest, I'd have him back tomorrow. If he was in our starting line up here today at Newcastle, I guarantee you he'd have scored a double hat-trick.

My biggest concern in the first half was that with Torres out injured and Keane on the bench, we wouldn't be able to capitalise on the shed full of chances. Gerrard broke the deadlock and Sami powered in a header to make it 2-0 but unbelievably the home side pulled one back right on the stroke of half time. To go in at only 2-1 up was head wrecking. Downstairs at the break everyone was just scratching their chins going "we have just had about a million chances and we're only one goal up." We needn't have worried though because we just tore them apart in the second half, too. The enigmatic Babel, who I'm really not sure about, prodded the third one home. The fourth was a peach of a chip from Gerrard after a decent through ball from the much maligned Lucas. Alonso came on and slotted a fifth from the penalty spot after Ngog was tripped. It was just a mad, mad game. The chances kept coming and the sitters kept getting missed. And yet here we are at the end of 2008 and guess who's top of the Prem?

The coach journey back was a joy to behold. The music was cranked up, the stocks were replenished and John Garner's toothy grin lit up the bus. We even had an hours stop off in Wetherby, which is an ideal place in which to stretch your legs and frighten the locals. The only downside is that the bus is from Halewood so it doesn't drop off in town, which means you have to get off at Broadgreen or Childwall Fiveways and get a cab back to base camp. But after a day like today that is only a minor inconvenience. If we'd have been snotted 5-1 that extra journey into town would only have added to the pain. We hit Ned's about 9pm and although we're still singing, I'm beginning to stifle the odd yawn during the chorus. I get the last train home and fall into the arms of Hot Lips at just gone midnight. They say 'all you need is love' and they're probably right but all I need now is cheese on toast and a peck on the cheek. It's been a long, long day and all my senses are beginning to pack in. Touch, taste, hearing, vision, the lot. I think my body is trying to send a message to my brain that it's all over for today. End of the year, top of the league. Get in there. A very Happy New Year to you, dear readers, one and all.

JD

Preston North End (a)   2-0

FA Cup 3rd Round   Sat 3rd Jan

Ah, the magic of the FA Cup! It's still there you know. They can bugger around with kick-of times (You can play FA Cup games on Friday evening, Saturday morning, Saturday afternoon, Saturday tea time, Saturday evening, Sunday lunchtime, Sunday afternoon, even Monday evening these days), play semis at Wembley, sponsor the competition ("The FA Cup sponsored by Al Quaida, anyone?"), replace replays with shootouts …. you could even bring back Cup Final 'Its a Knockout' on the telly (ask yer dad), but come that first weekend in January, well, there are not many better days in the footy calendar.

It's a cold – no, it's sodding freezing – winter Saturday morning. I'm wrapped up in a big coat, collar up and with my warmest scarf (an olive-coloured "Scouse Not English" effort. *Note from Jegs – sure it wasn't olive-*branch* coloured, Juan?). The sun is shining, yet is f-f-f-freezing cold, and every step I take is into a cloud of my own breath. As the saying goes – it's good to be alive on a day like this. It's like the season starting all over again – the slate of the first 5 months has been wiped clean and everyone's dreams are still alive at this one moment in time (except whoever Spurs beat last night). Why, even Evertonians can delude themselves and dream about a trip to Wembley; the mad, scruffy, educationally sub-normal fools.

Limey. Early. Me, Jegs and Sammo are all schoolboy enthusiasm and New Year cheer. Its quiet, not too many supporters around, but that's because we're on one of the earlier trains out of Liverpool. I say quiet, Bucko soon booms into view (and earshot) bellowing across the concourse "Aye aye! Dodd! Mackin! You on it?" pointing in several different directions and shaking half a dozen hands all at once. Oh good, so he's on our train, then. Bucko's with his usual cohorts, Big Ian Mac, Mercer, Richie Tierney and co… there's also

Si Morris, Peter Hewie, Ian Roughley, Paul Stewart... quite a nice little crew of, shall we say *mature* drinkers on the early train.

It's a late kick-off today and we expect most people will take trains at 2 or 3pm, staying in Liverpool right until the last moment, out of the way of an over exuberant Lancashire constabulary who will no-doubt be hell-bent on disrupting any serious New Year's bevvying. We plump for the 11:57, which is busy, but not as mental as we reckon the later trains might be. We're taking 6,000 fans today, and so its no stretch of the imagination to expect that the early afternoon trains will resemble Mumbai rush hour commuter services, on the Friday evening before the Hindi Christmas Eve, 2 months into a taxi drivers strike and with a monsoon forecast within the hour. Talking busy there, no?

Bucko, Me, Kevin and Jegs find some seats, and Jegs is already looking around frantically for one last smoking opportunity before the doors slide shut. With Bucko and Stewey both in the same carriage I'm concerned it won't be long before shoppers and civilians start to wince at the word 'Fuck' being issued in excess of the 100 decibels, every fifth word. It's with great relief that Bucko spots an old pal up the other end of the train – not that we don't absolutely love the lad but Jeez he isn't easy on your ear drums. He's in the next carriage now, but we still hear every word he has to say during the hour it takes to get to Preston.

Scar and Paul Jones, two of Liverpool's top wools, get on at Wigan. They try their best to be Scousers: no colours, clobber conscious and exceptional trainers only – yet still manage to look like two sacks of swaddling. Nah, they're among our very finest, these two, and they step on board laden with cans and hip-flasks. We're all sociable types and so we've no problems taking a nip of single malt or sharing a cold Carlsberg – just to usher in the New Year, mind you. Sammo's a bit slow handing the flask back, and I catch Paul giving Scar a worried glance. He should be more worried at the effects the mid-day grog might have on our Senior Citizen – two more slurps and Sampson'll be snoozing gently, all the way to Glasgow. Sammo spots the anxious look too, raises a can and says: "Happy New Year, Redmen!"

The New Year, shite, is it really 2009? Jesus! 19 years since we won the league. 20 years since Hillsborough. Scarce believe it. Mind you those 19 years have not been the trophy desert that some football pundits and opposition fans would have you believe. In the period between last lifting the title and this season, we've won: 3 FA Cups, a European Cup (and reached another final),

2 League Cups (and another final); 2 European Super Cups, the UEFA Cup, been runners up (robbed really) in the World Club Championship in Tokyo... so it hasn't all been mediocrity with us treading water in the doldrums. If the last 19 years have seen HMS Liverpool adrift in the horse latitudes then I know that almost every other club that would have loved to have been in such distress, including one alleged 'big' club, not too far away, that's now gone 15 years without a Cup of any sort. Clubs like Everton or Newcastle or Villa or Spurs, clubs with delusions of grandeur would give their eye teeth for just a fraction – just a taste – of our post 1990 record.

About 50 or 60 or so 'lads' (ages ranging from 15 to 50) disembark at Preston Station, greeted by a dozen or so coppers with dogs on short leashes. A chopper whirrs around over head – what are they expecting here? A drink-off? Heads down, hands in pockets, everyone shuffles towards the exit, but some of our elder statesmen know a sneaky way out, and soon there's just the 6 of us loping towards Preston town centre. It's even colder than Lime Street, here – no balmy Gulf Stream wafting in from Liverpool Bay here; the weather here comes straight down the Pennines from Orkney.

"Where is it then?" Jegs asks me, looking around.

"Where's what? The ground? Miles away."

"No the plaque"

"What plaque?"

"The one about Preston being twinned with Nimes. Thought you said it was at the station?"

"I did. It is. Nimes station."

"Oh..."

There are bouncers on the doors of the pubs round here, so we walk on, avoiding the milling throng that 50 years ago thronged the mills round these parts. These days, however, the mills are all closed or turned into wholesale shoe warehouses, and the locals are more likely to be thronging Millets. The Prestonians trudging through these winter streets look like they're in an LS Lowry painting. Liverpool street scenes, on the other hand, especially those round our port-of-entry, Lime St Station and its adjacent hostelries (the Punch and Judy, The Penny Farthing and The Yankee Bar), resemble somewhere altogether more chaotic and colourful; an Hieronymus Bosch townscape perhaps. Is it something to do with being a port? Something in our sea air? Or is it something here... some bone-soaking gloom that seeps down from the Lancashire hills?

The early afternoon, pre-match local trade will soon pack these pubs in the town centre, the situation being made worse with the many hundreds of Reds following behind us on later trains, so we amble off down what I presume is the 'High Street' in search of a less obvious watering hole. Scar and Paul phone to see where we've got to, and we wait for them to catch up. There's about 10 of us now walking through town looking for The Sun Inn, owned by a Celtic fan who runs the local Preston Emerald CSC. You'll always be guaranteed a good swallee at any pub that's home to a Celtic Supporters Club. But it's not long before we've come to police attention – up ahead we can see a couple of young greenhorns muttering into their walkie-talkies.

"About 12 of 'em... aye... looking for our lot."

I'm sorry to curse, officer, but *are we fuck* looking for "your lot." We're looking for a pub – and when we find it we'll sit there and drink, pint after pint, requesting these pints respectfully after waiting our turn and tipping the pint-puller for his or her services, and at no point will we engage "your lot" in any kind of shenanigans... And I'm sorry to ignore your false-friendly "alright boys" greeting, but I haven't got time to answer your daft questions, and there's no law says I have to, either. We walk on feigning deafness, leaving the coppers flailing like desperate double-glazing salesmen on commission. 2, 4, 6, 8 of us just walk on by without so much as slowing down, as the two flatfoots resort to jumping out in front of Jegs and Scar, as though they're about to offer free installation and a 10 year guarantee. Jegs and The Scar, for crying out loud – and Preston's finest think these two gentlemen pose a threat! I mean I could take them by the hand, walk them down to any pub and immediately be able to point out half a dozen cases more deserving of their time and efforts, just by throwing a cursory glance around the bar. This crack unit of Lancashire Constabulary's finest, however, have supposedly been poring over 'intelligence' all week and posting provocative threads on internet forums trying to trace ' Liverpool's top boys'. The one who's nabbed Jegs is so surprised he's actually stopped that he genuinely doesn't know what to do next:

"Er... where you going, mate?"

Jegs glumly looks the young copper up and down – his face lapsing into pure Sid James:

"I honestly don't know. No idea where we're going."

"Right. Not going looking for trouble then?"

Jegs raises his eyebrows and sighs out loud in pure despair. In that sigh, and in Jegsy's voice, we could learn much about the pains of Modern Life...

"Look mate... I'm 51. Okay? I'm a man of 51, and I'm going for a drink. I bid you farewell."

When we eventually find the pub it's on the quiet end of Friargate and although it's only a few hundred yards from the station it's taken us about 25 minutes to find as we've walked almost in a circle, allowing us to view Preston 's many shoe shops and branches of Greenhalgh's the Bakers. There's plenty of Celtic memorabilia strewn about the pub: framed photos, posters and scarves. Stewey's salivating, eyeing up all manner of goodies to be purloined, or begged from the staff. He gets even more excited on learning that the toilets are upstairs as, in his feverish imagination, that's where the mine host will have stashed boxes of Celtic programmes and sundry memorabilia. I still have painful (from the laughter) recollections of him walking stiff-legged from a bar in Porto, having spent an awful long time on the upstairs toilet. Turned out the store room was up there two, and Stewey stashed two bottles of vintage port down each trouser leg, then had to walk like a robot to stop them falling out...

The curtains are being drawn in the pub to keep out the harsh low sunlight that's preventing anyone from being able to see the 'Live Satellite Football' on the big screen. Celtic are playing and we'd stay to watch it but the pub's just finished doing food for some mad typically-British reason like it's the staff's lunch break or something. Jegs is hungry, and he also doesn't want a Celtic game inflicted on him, so we have to split up from the others and find another pub. We leave Stewey who, for reasons only he can ever know, has his hand down the back of the juke box.

We strike off in the general direction of Deepdale and after a few hundred yards find a much quieter pub showing the Macclesfield/Everton game. Again, there's no food so we have to settle for Guinness and Salt & Vinegar crisps. The barman's a Scouser and the place is just a nondescript pub that probably comes alive with students during term time. We settle down and cheer when the team in white score against the run of play against the team in blue... only to realise much, much later that Macclesfield, the home team, play in blue, too. One of those balmy but sometimes dangerous hours slips by where you drift from sobriety into semi-drunkenness, and all seems great in this big old world of ours. And in that hour or so, the pub goes from being empty, to suddenly being packed with Preston's young lads. I don't remember *anyone* coming in. The Yoof seem okay – they're a bit nosey, one or two of them make stupidly obvious attempts to suss out our accents – but they don't seem that threatening. To them, we're three old men in their boozer. They've marked our cards, but do anything else would be... well in that world, under any code, it'd just be wrong.

Still, it's best to keep your wits about you and your eyes peeled though. You're always likely to get a harder time from these backwater yokels than you would, say, at Spurs or Villa. They're keen to prove that they're not simple, small-town dolts and can hold their own against the big city 'firms'. As a 'firm', however, we three leave a lot to be desired; least of all the desire to belong to anything known as a 'firm'. More of them come in – and these are all drunk, lively, and clearly "up for it." Sammo's looking over at them:

"Right lads – three old men like us aren't going to get done in unless we're very, very unlucky... but do we want to have to just sit here when they start all their anti-Scouse shite?"

"These? They seem alright..."

"I give it ten minutes..."

It doesn't even take that long, though. Kev and Jegs go outside for a smoke and almost immediately a little song goes up.

"Steve Gerrard, Gerrard.
He runs over kids in cars
He batters DJs in bars
Steve Gerrard, Gerrard!"

The boy Sampson might be right, this show is probably for our benefit. I still don't feel at all threatened though. They're not pointing at us, they're not even looking at us. All three of us have been up to the bar – Kevin's there now waiting to get served, stood right between two of the main Preston "boys," and if I know him he'll thicken his cultured Greater Merseyside accent to make sure they know he's not arsed about them. Jegs is sporting an inch high silver Liverbird on the lapel of his Barbour jacket (a Barbour, I might add, that's seen better days). We've made no secret of the fact we're Redmen, yet there's been no direct menace at all. Sammo returns with the pints – he's definitely on edge, here. A joker and tall-storyteller by nature, he's gone very quiet, starting to look all around the pub to see what we might be up against. The anti-Scouse songs go up in number and volume. Our esteemed captain has been involved in a bar fight on the night of the Newcastle game, and is alleged to have thumped the DJ over his choice in music. Nice one, Captain! But it's all fodder to the dim-witted Ingerlund types here in Preston. Sampson's eyeing this one fella going round the bar whispering to tough Preston eggs about visitors in their midst.

"It's always the divvy, isn't it?" says Kev, jerking his head at the miscreant – a gel-head of about 25, wearing really bad shell-toes and an Adidas tracksuit top.

"He's been here all day him, hanging round just behind us, listening in and he hasn't said fuck-all. Then the boys come bouncing in, and…"

"Ignore him. He's a tit."

Sammo chuckles.

"Oh aye… you can't get hopped on by a lad in shell-toes. But you know what I'm saying…"

The singing gets louder still. To the tune of The Torres Bounce, the Preston Gel-Heads chant:

"We bought the lad from Liverpool

And now he fucking hates Blackpool …

Neil Mellor, Preston's No. 10."

They are immensely amused at themselves (and we laughed when we heard the "fucking hate Blackpool" bit too), but after the 10th repetition of their Gerrard ditty it's getting a bit tiresome in here and we decide we'll be on our way.

It's dark now, and we can see the ground lit up, glowing like a weird blue spacecraft about half a mile away. We quicken our step. I can hear my stomach rumbling as the beer gasses and fizzes inside me. Crossing the main road we meet up with some of the Young 'Uns, Chris Murphy and Danny Nicholson among them. They're still half-recoiling from an incident with the police, half doubled-up with laughter, too. About 20 of them were walking through a park towards Deepdale. Chris found an abandoned, broken kid's bike and started riding it towards the park exit. The Preston plod, as we've said, are out in force and probably a bit disappointed there was no major incident to deal with. They've found that most Liverpool fans have zero interest in engaging the local warriors in fisticuffs, and all that preparation (I draw a line at calling it "intelligence") has come to nothing. The police are filming everything and radio-ing each other with self-important updates:

"Roger, Charlie Tango. 7 of 'em just walked past. One claims he's 51….looks a bit like Sid James."

Anyway, Danny, Chris and the lads get to the other side of the park and find there's a wall of coppers waiting for them. They won't let them out the park until someone admits to moving the bike. They threaten to arrest, detain and possibly charge all 20 of them unless someone confesses to the heinous Lancashire crime of "tekkin baak." Chris Murphy – in true Spartacus fashion – offers himself up and then has to go back, find the bush where he's dumped "baak," and return it to where he found it before the rest are allowed to proceed. As an exercise in futility this takes some beating. It served no purpose other than for the police to flex their muscles and probably get a little hard-on when they think about it, later.

"They're twats, and they're getting worse," seems to be the consensus.

Indeed. Deepdale is unrecognisable from my last visit in the 1980s. They still had the plastic pitch back then and, paradoxically, a beautiful traditional old stand – The West Stand – with bench seating, and an old barrel roof held up by elegant iron poles, like a Victorian bandstand. Both are long gone now. The New Deepdale is bright and modern, but with 4 distinct, uniform stands and 4 floodlight pylons that cast a dazzling glow in the evening air. Such a traditional scene only adds to the atmosphere and accentuates the 'romance of t'cup'. Steam is rising from the burger vans, as fans of both teams hurry to the turnstiles wrapped up as if for a snowball fight. At the Bill Shankly Stand end of Deepdale, where the thousands of Liverpool fans are gathering, stands the Tom Finney 'Splash' statue and fountain. It's a glorious tribute to a great player. The statue was inspired by a photo of Finney sliding to the ground with the ball during a Chelsea v Preston game in 1956. Large areas of the pitch were under water after a heavy downpour just before kick off. A photographer captured the moment, and Finney's sliding action has sprayed water behind him in an arc. The photo has now been recreated here in bronze, but with the fountain mimicking the water spray. Today Finney's figure is festooned in icicles, hanging like crystal Christmas decorations from his limbs, and glowing like neon.

Despite a relatively large allocation today, there are still plenty of familiar faces stuck outside without tickets, a testimony not only to the level of support Liverpool have but to the overall special-ness of FA Cup 3rd round day. All credit to Preston for not trying to exploit the thousands of visiting supporters – tickets are a mere (*mere*!) £20 a pop, less than half we'd pay to visit a much richer club from the Premier League. After scoffing (I nearly said 'enjoying') a quick burger to try and soak up some of the beer, we pass quickly inside the ground and up to our seats about half way up the stand, directly behind the goal. Inside, Deepdale is as trim and modern as its exterior. The unfinished 'Invincibles Stand' is to our left ... 'The Invincibles' – such a name might seem a tad excessive today, but this club won the double 100 years before we did, in a season in which they remained unbeaten. At the opposite end of the ground from where we are the stand is a bobbing mass of the hard-core Preston support. They're making a lot of noise.

"Are they banging their clogs together?" some bloke in front of us asks, in a wacky "I'm-from-the-city-they're-all-yokels" way. This elicits some forced laughter from the assembled Scouse scallies around him. There's a cracking atmosphere as the kick off approaches, and I expect the BBC will be waxing lyrical on air about the magic of this kind of cup tie with John Motson eulogising over close ups of small children in Preston bobble hats, cheeks all rosy red and waving excitedly at the camera. Meanwhile, back down at our end, the camera's might focus on whoever it is smoking those drugs we can smell... Jegsy's nose twitches like a rabbit and he cranes his neck to see who it is. A row or two behind us are 3 foreign looking fellas. There's a smell of skunk wafting from their direction but I can't see if its them exhaling it. Jeg's decides to say hello, just in case they do have some drugs and they can let him have a quick bang. It turns out they're from Argentina and are mates of Mascherano's. They're staying with him over Crimbo and New Year.

"This Insua looks good," we say.

They exchange glances as if to say, "If you only knew how good." They tell us that everyone in Argentina raves about him and how lucky Liverpool are to have him, and how much they're all looking forward to the Youth World Cup this month. Just as he's broken into the team, Emiliano is going to be on international duty in South America for the next month.

"You're going to miss him!" says the most talkative of the Argies.

"Yeah, and you're probably his agents," Jegsy winks.

We start strongly and once again waste several golden opportunities to take the lead (Keane, again, proving to be intensely frustrating. I think back to Baker's erectile analogy and muse that Keane could do with a huge dose of Viagra). When we do score it's a cracker from Riera (not Viagra) – a ferocious shot across the keeper from 15 yards. Once again Xabi Alonso takes a terrible, scything challenge from one of Preston's donkeys. He gets up and hobbles around, but it's obvious Xabi's wincing in pain out there. He might as well wear a target instead of a number, the amount of no-marks who go right through him from behind.

We should really have doubled or trebled the lead before the break, but our malaise of not burying sides when we're on top has reared its head again. To compound it all, poor Robbie Keane manages to 'convert' an unmissable chance from a few yards out... if only he were playing rugby! He skies it over the bar and, rather than hold his head in hands, just stands there looking at where the ball *should* have gone – Preston's net – as though, if he concentrates on the goal for long enough the ball will, after all, end up there. It's a terrible, terrible miss and not even I can defend him.

At half time we hear tales of the rail chaos and wonder how 2-3000 Reds will make it onto the first two trains home – so we make a pact that, so long as there's nothing at stake, we'll give it toes five minutes before the end. Jegsy can now disappear to the toilets for a secret smoke, only to return shortly afterwards coughing and spluttering:

"It's like a Grateful Dead concert in there. You can't see your hand in front of your face. It's boss."

Alonso doesn't reappear for the 2nd half and with our spurning of so many good chances in the first half I'm fearing a potential banana skin here. I mean Keane and Babel may as well not be on the pitch and I suspect that Rafa doesn't want to risk Torres so soon after coming back from injury. At this point I'm more than happy with 1-0. Let's just avoid the replay and let's hope that Alonso's injury isn't a bad one. And so it transpires: Preston battle, their keeper plays a blinder, and as the game's creeping inevitably towards a narrow win for the Reds, we decide it's safe to do a runner.

Heads down, we stick at it, even though we're among the first to leave the ground. 3,000 Reds into one locomotive just doesn't compute, and we're all too old for the "police holding you back" routine. We're jogging past the Tom Finney statue, now completely covered with ice, when a big cheer goes up. Shit! Was that Us, or Them? We're out now, anyway, and up ahead oh joy of joys is a waiting row of black cabs. Hallelujah! Sammo's almost crying with laughter, for some reason going:

"Are we not men? We are Devo!"

That's nothing compared to his almost superhuman joy when we roll out at Preston station, only one bemused dog handler there to hassle us, and find out there's a train to Wigan leaving in a minute's time. We just about make it, Bucko's on the phone to see where we are and Sammo's grabbed it, saying:

"Captain my captain! We'll be in Neds before you even get the station, slack Harry. You snooze, you lose, Buckwheats!!"

It's a busy train, the mainline service between Scotland and London. We find seats but we're not all together. Jegsy and Kev sit with a well groomed woman and have to talk over the back of the seat to me. After a few minutes it seems she's uncomfortable with this arrangement and she excuses herself and crosses across the aisle to a spare seat with her friends. This lets me in to join Jegs and Sammo around a table covered with the Daily Telegraph and the detritus of her journey: empty coffee cup, napkins etc. Amongst the papers we find an eyeball. Honest to God – it's an eyeball, just lying there, on the Glasgow to London train. Jegsy quite seriously checks both his eye sockets, and I'm watching him do this so I know it's not one of mine. It's plastic, but filled with a slimy jelly and it oozes and drips – quite why the fuck anyone would buy it is beyond me. I won't even touch it with my black leather strangler's gloves on. Across the aisle the posh woman and her friends are staking an audible claim as the Alpha+ Social Class on the train. They've come from London to Edinburgh for an exhibition and are returning home. Whereas we are from Liverpool, we've been to an FA Cup tie and we have had a few ales. Jegs and Kev are eating her last remaining sandwich whilst she looks away, pretending not to notice and loudly discusses tube trains and other 'London ' things with her friends. I imagine she's trying to mark her intellectual and social superiority and make us feel like country bumpkins. I laugh to myself and hope she's got a banking job in the city that's not going to be there when she gets in on Monday morning. Now try paying that million quid mortgage, love.

Sammo's insisting that Agger is the best defender in Europe and that we must tie up his contract extension as soon as possible. Indeed news reports that weekend are linking him with £12m move to Milan. We agree that it must be his agent's doings; stalling for a better deal from the club, fattening his own 10%.

"All footballer's agents are twats!" Exclaims Dodd loudly. "And footballers who have an agent are also twats. Are they too stupid to agree their own deals?"

We look at each other and silently agree that, Yes, they are.

"Agger should tell his agent to fuck off and just sign the deal."

"They won't do that will they? In fact I bet it's his agent leaking all this to the press so that Milan come sniffing and Rafa ups the offer. The player's not going to refuse more money is he, so he gives the agent free reign and feigns ignorance of it all."

"If he really wanted to play for us – and that's what matters – then he'd just sign the contract. He's still minted and the agent's still making a fortune for doing fuck all. The problem is that most players are thick or lazy, probably both. They let their agents do everything for them; open bank accounts, buy houses for them, do the books, I'm not kidding, Liverpool employ a fella to take their cars in for their service …"

"Wigan !!" Sammo shouts, as a platform comes into view. And up we get and leave, much to the relief of the rest of the carriage.

We now have a 25 minute wait for our connection and so we go for a pint. Across the road from the station is a very, very strange pub. There's no-one around, the pub is basically empty, yet there's blood all over the floor, outside and in the doorway. From inside, that weird, supercharged, psycho-house music that's only popular in places like Hetton-le-Hole is pumping out to an empty room, yet as soon as we step in there, it stops. I know it's a bad cliché, the inhospitable Locals pub that tries to hound you out by staring at you from the moment you walk in, but this is that pub! At the end of the bar are 3 girls with no teeth. Maybe that's why there's blood everywhere? Maybe we've just missed the fight of the century between these 3 witches and the entire male population of Wigan? Some tetchy argument over the merits of a local pie shop perhaps? Or maybe they've all just pulled their own teeth out for the fun of it. Who knows, but they look a bit scary – I feel much more ill at ease here than in the pub with the Preston 'yoof'. As we try and keep ourselves to ourselves they keep flashing gummy smiles down the bar. I look behind me, hoping there's someone else there, some randy local youth who'll take his life in his hands for a jump – any jump – on a Saturday night maybe. But no, there's just us. Drat!

Sky News is on behind the bar and we pretend to be deeply engrossed in soundless reports from Iraq and outside Downing Street so as to avoid meeting their eyes. All it would take would be one fatal slip in concentration from us, one schoolboy error, and we'd be done for. By returning their gaze we could possibly end up unconscious on the pavement outside. But then Sky Sports News comes on: "It was 2 nil. Torres scored at the end!" I say as the result flashes up.

"You been the match?" the witch in charge asks, her mouth all pink and fleshy as if she's chewing a marshmallow.

"Errrrr…"

Even the barman's looking at us now. He's stopped stocking the fridge with Blue WKD and stands arms folded. We must be doomed.

"The train!" Jegsy shrieks in pantomime mock horror. "Quick, men!"

On the train back to civilisation we mull over the day's events and what lies ahead. The subject of the next round comes up and we each propose a 4th round draw we'd prefer. All 3 of us plump for Man U away. Top of the League, eh? Getting cocky? Seriously, we've turned the corner psychologically and in the New Year I'm convinced that the performances will improve, they always do. No matter who the draw throws up, we'll take them.

JM

Stoke (a)   0-0

League   Sat 10th Jan

Yesterday Rafa pulled a stunt that might, in the tender candle light of a 19th League title, be seen as a masterstroke, beating the broccoli-nosed king of the head wreck himself at what's become known as Mind Games. Maybe Rafa, along with all his other bountiful qualities, is a part-time shrink an' all – but I didn't like it. I didn't like it because it was staged, so weird and so unworthy of a Liverpool manager. What happened is that after Rafa had finished his regular Friday press conference he cleared his throat, uttered the immortal words:

"About Forgoose-sonn…"

and unleashed a pre-prepared statement about how refs are letting Alex F write his own rules. It was all true, of course – and it's intended to rattle Man.U (and whoever is reffing their 6-pointer against Chelsea on Sunday). But it'll only work if we do the business ourselves – capitalise on any slip-ups and sudden, irrational penalties against United. But I still didn't like it. I thought Rafa was cut from better cloth.

I know I've been banging on about how cold it's been at some of the aways this season and I promise this is the last time I'm gonna mention the weather but fuck me, Stoke was cold. I can't for the life of me ever remember watching a game and feeling so frozen. In fact one of the strangest things happened to me at half time in the Britannia Stadium toilets. I had waddled down there like an Emperor penguin to relieve myself when I got the shock of my life. I opened my zip with shivering fingers to discover that my penis had completely disappeared. I'm looking from side to side with eyes like Jimmy Floyd Hasselbaink after he's had a penalty turned down. A full minute passes before I manage to produce something that resembles an Arctic prawn. Actually Arctic prawn is stretching it a bit – which I did, but still it stayed 'inside', if you get me I do eventually manage to piss, but most of it just turns to steam so I end up standing there like I'm on stage with Echo & The Bunnymen, all dry ice and low visibility. It was *that* cold.

I used to love going to Stoke when I was a teenybopper tearaway. Only 70 minutes away and we always took loads of fans. Back then it was only the two unmentionables that were 'all ticket'. So, to take 10,000 away in the league was just par for the course. Sometimes you'd go in their end if ours was full. The Boothen End was one of the great old standing terraces of English football, and to 'take' it was no mean feat, but we did it every year – easy. Stoke was one of those places where you knew Liverpool fans would take over. There was always the odd chance of a bit of a 'tear-up' but it's safe to say that the Scousers usually had the place boxed off.

The Victoria Ground was a great place to go, right in the heart of the community. Loads of character and almost smelling of working class spirit. Imagine if you could bottle that retro whiff. Call it 'Eau de 70's terraces'. Ingredients: Pies, piss, B.O, smoke, Bovril and stale ale. Ooooh yes missus! I don't know about you but it's got me going. And where do Stoke play today? The Britannia fuckin' Stadium. A non-descript antiseptic piece of characterless concrete plonked in the middle of another out of town, out of sight retail park. Pass me the fuckin' popcorn and tell me when to cheer. Like your Derby County's, your Middlesbrough's and your Bolton's, all upping sticks from classic old footy grounds – The Baseball Ground, Scaresome Park and Burnden were all *brilliant* spit and sawdust aways – and moving to plastic identikit stadiums in areas where nobody lives or has any love for, devoid of pubs, cafés and betting shops. Nowhere to meet for a pre-match drink unless it's in a ten-pin bastard bowling alley or at the 60-screen multiplex. If I was an Evertonian I would look at these places and have sleepless nights; because if they do finally pack their bags and run away with the circus, this is what it'll be like. Derby matches will never be the same and as much as I dislike the whinging blue quarter of the city, I sympathise.

We travelled on John Garner's coach again and stopped off in the picturesque town of Stone for a pre-match half dozen. Instead of following the majority into Wetherspoons or Yates', we found a great little independent place called Granville's. Initially the owners looked at us with a degree of suspicion. Within minutes though, our wit, wisdom and riveting conversation had won them over. We even had a sit down meal in there. Now how civilised is that on a match day? Three hours later and we're back on the coach for the final push to Stoke-on-Trent, and our 5.15 appointment with "live soccer."

Every game now is a 'must win', with United sneaking up behind us ready to pounce on any mistakes. Alonso is out injured and Lucas fills in for him. But Lucas is never going to change a game for you and what we need now are players who are ready to take responsibility. We've already dropped two precious points at home to a very poor Stoke side, so we really need to go for it today. But the sad reality is, we don't. We are awful. A pale imitation of the team that destroyed Newcastle a fortnight before. You hardly expect someone like Lucas to pull the strings but even Mascherano is looking a shadow of the player he was last season. Even though we're top of the league, people are starting to whisper in the away end that Rafa is being over cautious. He's got Robbie Keane warming up nearly all the second half but doesn't feel the need to bring him on. He's scored over a hundred goals in the Prem and yet Rafa won't use him when we are desperate for a breakthrough. Weird.

Let's face it, Stoke are limited. Their only real threat comes from their now infamous long throw ins and yet they've stopped us scoring in both games. Two points out of a possible six against Stoke City. Sorry, that's just not good enough. Stevie hits the woodwork twice in the last ten minutes but overall we were crap. It's not a happy coach that leaves the soulless Britannia Stadium. "Why, why, why Delilah?" sing the Stoke fans. Why, indeed.

We stop off for an hour in a town that I'm convinced is called Middlewich. But then again it could be Nantwich or could it even be Northwich? I'm beginning to think I've got a great play on words here. So like a smart arse I get back on the coach and say "Was that Middlewich, Nantwich or Northwich, because I'm not sure which wich is which?" Mercer stretches, blinks, and goes:

"It was Sandbach you knobhead."

Gutted. It's the most animated he's been all day and my 'joke of the day' bites the dust.

I slump in my seat and ponder whether we'll ever win that 19th title. Garner tries to rally the troops with his newly purchased 100 Great Ska Hits (£3 on offer from Keele services). But you'll need more than Desmond Decker to keep my pecker up as the lads depressingly debate the dismal display. Ritchie Tierney whose catchphrase is "Would you kiss your mother with that mouth?" is not happy with Rafa's tactics. It seems that some of the rank and file are beginning to question the great man's style of management. Me? I'm a bit split on him as I've always been. I've never been one to sit on the fence but I can't really make my mind up on him because he does make some bizarre decisions. But footy is a results business and if we're champions in May the fans will love him and if we fail again, questions will be asked over all these 0-0 draws.

We get off at Childwall Fiveways and get back to HQ for a sing song and to meet up with the lads who watched it on the box. Onlookers wince as a tuneless Bucko takes to the karaoke to murder a couple of classics. He sounds like someone's put electrodes on his scrotum while he gargles the lottery balls. A true entertainer. When he relinquishes the mic it's as if the storm has stopped and the sun has appeared. Traumatised customers pop their heads up from under the tables as 'The Voice' leaves the stage. We last till 1.30am and then head off in our separate directions. There can be no slip ups next week when our loveable neighbours cross the park for the annual culture clash. Bitterness, bile and bullshit aside, we have to get the three points. Otherwise the Mancs will appear from the shadows like the old-fashioned baddies, hell-bent on stealing our dreams and we'll only have ourselves to blame.

Two days after the Stoke match I received a number of messages to say that one of Liverpool's greatest fans Bobby Wilcox had died. Bob was a legend following the Reds, always organising coaches and offering words of wisdom. He'll be a massive loss and things will never quite be the same again.

R.I.P Bobby lad.

JD

Bobby Wilcox – A Tribute

Shortly after the incredibly news of Bobby's passing, the websites and local radio waves were jammed with messages of love, respect and loss. This was John Mackin's reaction.

The greatest Liverpool fan I ever knew, died this week. I'll correct that: probably the greatest Liverpool fan anyone ever knew died this week. As one of his friends put it on hearing the sad news:

"If Bill Shankly was Liverpool 's greatest manager, and Kenny Dalglish Liverpool's greatest player, then Bobby Wilcox was surely the club's greatest supporter."

It was always a great source of amusement to Bobby and his ilk – the likes of Lenny Woods, Sully, et al – when this accolade was suggested. It wasn't important to them, and they'd dismiss it with a "We're all Reds together." Well some Reds are more equal than others; some are writ through large with the name 'Liverpool Football Club'; some are quite, simply, legendary. Step up to the plate, Bobby Wilcox.

This isn't an obituary for Bobby Wilcox, the man. I'm not qualified to write that. I only knew Bobby as a Liverpool supporter. It is clear, however, from the tributes being paid from all quarters that he was loved and respected throughout the city of Liverpool. He was truly one of the city's greatest characters.

Bobby was a giant on the local Liverpool amateur football scene, with over 25 years service as secretary of the hugely successful Britannia FC in the Liverpool and District Sunday League. However, amongst the family of Liverpool supporters his star shone even brighter. He was larger than life, recognised by Reds the world over, and held in great respect by every fan he ever came into contact with. Wherever Liverpool played – Wilcox was there. And he wasn't there alone. Bobby organised travel, tickets and accommodation for countless fans over the years, hauling them to all four corners of Europe and beyond. Without Bobby's tireless energy, humour and plain silliness many Reds would never have made it. Without Bobby's famous 'Wilcox Tours' (Never Knowingly Underdrunk) many younger Reds may never have caught the Liverpool bug. Bobby and his famous plastic carrier bag were a common sight, a permanent fixture, almost, at airports, train stations and the football grounds of Europe. In fact, I believe his carrier bag had been to so many European away games it has more appearances than Ian Callaghan and Phil Neal combined. Those youngsters that caught the bug whilst under Wilcox's wing benefited from the experience of his 50 years of following his beloved Reds the length and breadth of the land. A good pal of his wrote this week:

"What Liverpool Football Club has lost with his passing is a true anchor to the days where lads from our city, local supporters, were given the opportunity to follow their team all over the world, and without that Liverpool loses its soul."

Bobby Wilcox was as good an example of the soul of this football club – of this city – as I have ever seen. And that's what's so important. Bobby's legacy is not the fact that he supported Liverpool everywhere they played; but rather the manner in which he supported Liverpool, and the example he was. This is his legacy, not the stamps on his passport. Above it all there was his utter devotion to the team he loved – the team he supported with all the glee of a little kid and all the experience of one of Shankly's original Kopites. He was a magnificent ambassador abroad for our club and our city. On a personal level he was similarly charismatic. Bobby would argue with you 'til the cows came home, then buy you a pint; he would burst suddenly into song without warning, sometimes whilst in mid-conversation with you, and sometimes singing total gibberish. He would mercilessly take the mickey out of you then give you a little wink; it was never serious with Bobby. I've heard a rumour that he was quiet once, but I don't believe it. If Bobby wasn't gabbling fifteen to the dozen, he was singing; if he was doing neither he was more than likely downing a pint. His singing – alongside his buddy Lenny Woods (The Mulligan and O'Hare of The Albert) – is legendary and he entertained the lads and lasses on many a long train journey, or during many a post-Derby game victory singsong in the pub. Yes, his singing... Bobby will be fondly remembered as one of Liverpool's great football crooners, and I will never hear the line "His name was Johnny Barn-es..." again without seeing his face all crinkled up and his eyes glinting behind his glasses, knowing that this was

Bobby Wilcox in his element: his mates, a pint and a song about the team he loved.

Bobby Wilcox passed away this week in the Royal Hospital in Liverpool. He had only very recently been diagnosed with cancer, and his family were with him at the bedside. He was sixty years old.

JM

Everton (h)   1-1

League   Mon 19th Jan

Derby day and I'm off the swallee. In an attempt to give my liver a rest, save a bit of money, and lose a few Crimbo pounds I've decided to lay off the ale for the rest of January. It's been 2 weeks since Preston and I'm already feeling the benefits, but tonight will be a big test of my resolve. When was the last time I went to a derby game sober? Well, I'll tell you... I think it was on April 3rd, 1976 when we won at Anfield with a late, late winner from Davey Fairclough. Remember that fabulous leggy dribble from the half way line, beating about 6 players – Mike Lyons twice? We won the title that year too, so the omens are looking good. I was 16 or so and quite a few years away from being an enthusiastic matchday drinker. The pubs around Anfield back then were full of big, burly grown up men and I was a skinny teenager in platform shoes. It was impossible to get near the bar to get served ahead of these huge fellas, all smelling of brown bitter and farts, and I didn't have the nerve to try and barge in and force my way to the front.

So I'd be in Anfield a couple of hours before kick off, sitting in the open air on the concrete steps at Flagpole Corner, reading my 10p 'Anfield Review' and waiting for my mates to come through the turnstiles down below me. But now, in 2009, I'm sitting in Aldo's bar on Victoria Street, a few doors away from Neds, and waiting for Jegsy, Bucko and the lads to turn up. Before me is a large coffee from Cafe Nero down the road. This doesn't feel right, at all.

The more I think about it, the more I curse the fixture list for giving us a derby game in January. In fact, the sodding FA Cup draw means there'll be 2 derby games in January. The only good news is that 4th round FA Cup game will also be on a Monday night, rather than a Saturday afternoon when I suspect I'd wilt and be on the swallee at 10am. So, well done Sky TV and the FA for moving the game and helping me keep to my Detox programme. Nah, who am I kidding? Well done Sky, my arse! This is just wrong, wrong, wrong... a derby game and no drinking? There are certain things that grown men should never attempt without a good swallee in them: going to a Pogues' gig, perhaps, or shagging a fat bird. It's too late now though for regrets as I've driven to the game. And here I am in a cold, empty pub trying to read the Liverpool Echo but failing miserably to find anything – Tony Barrett's LFC stuff apart – that's remotely interesting.

When the lads arrive and cram round the tiny table, all laughing and joking and slurping their beers, it only makes me feel more isolated and depressed. The bastards. After explaining again why I'm off the beer, I tell them the last derby game I can recall being sober at was over 30 years ago.

"Was that when Cormack scored?" asks Richie Tierney, "The diving header at the road end?"

"No that was earlier. This was Davey Fairclough," I tell him. "1976 I think."

"Is right J, is right... big dribble... 2 minutes to go...," says Bucko, pointing at me, then turning to Ritchie. "Remember? That Welsh gimp in goal, Dai Davies should have had it at the near post. But he was shite."

"That's the one. I went straight home on the bus, had me tea, then went to me bedroom and played records until Match of the Day came on. Couldn't even video it to watch it again."

"Is right again, J," Bucko concurs. "Never seen that goal again until the video come out years later. And it was only when I watched it I realised we missed a penalty as well in the last minute."

There then ensues a lively debate about being sober at a derby game, which concludes with the suggestion that Danny Giles has never, ever been sober at a derby game. Even when he was a kid. Now I may mock sobriety but it does get you into the ground early. Which is a pity tonight as the atmosphere is poor. Considering it's a derby game there's a distinct lack of 'edge' for this one. Back in 1976 this was our biggest game of the season, by a mile. Not any more. Playing the Mancs has now become THE biggy – El Classico! Standing up in 306 there are scores of empty seats 20 minutes before kick off as the lads prefer a last-minute pint to getting in early and taunting the 'mongs'. There's little in the way of real excitement in the air and I have a sense of dread as we approach kick-off. Perhaps the Stoke result has put the dampeners on expectations. Was Newcastle just a blip, a day when everything went right? I'm beginning to suspect so. Instead of kicking on and going for it, we've reverted to that pre-Christmas cautiousness. Sensing that all might not be well, the Evertonians are singing "Rafa's cracking up," a reference to Benitez's strange press conference last week. It staggers me how little pride these tramps have – end of the day they're Scousers, or so they like to tell us – yet they'll pick up on any Manc drivel and sing it like they've found gold. "Rafa's cracking up" is the Mancs response to Benitez' attack on Ferguson, while Ferguson himself has been playing the startled old man, acting all hurt at the "bile" and "vitriol." It could come back to haunt Rafa, this one. At the start of December we were top of the League with games coming up against West Ham, Bolton, Fulham, Hull, Newcastle, Bolton and Wigan – we could have put ourselves out of sight while Man.U were otherwise engaged at the World Club Championship farce. Since their return though, the Mancs have been quietly winning their games in hand and have snuck back to the top. Well we can put all that right tonight then, can't we? Turn these horrible bluenoses over and leapfrog back to the top of the table.

It's the least we can do for Bobby Wilcox anyway. It would be a fitting tribute to the man if we can beat the old enemy tonight and go 2 points clear. Prior to meeting the lads in Aldo's this evening I popped into Bobby's HQ, The Globe, to see a memorial banner his mates had made for him. It reads, simply: BOBBY WILCOX – LIVERPUDLIAN. 1948-2009

During 'You'll Never Walk Alone' the banner is held aloft behind The Kop goalmouth to warm and sustained applause. It's been a bad winter for losing great old Reds: Alan Kelly (father of Steve, editor of 'Through The Wind & Rain') died just before Christmas. Alan was a fanatical Red as well as a stalwart of Bootle Cricket Club. He was a great source of entertainment to the likes of me who'd go round to Steve's, and end up sitting on the couch, drinking tea for hours, and listening to him dispensing wisdom, wit and cynicism when talking about modern football in general, and The Reds in particular. It was obvious where Steve got his sardonic 'voice' from.

Jegsy arrives in Row 59 as the games kicks off and reaches his seat as Everton almost snatch a 1st minute lead. I tell him the good news is that Torres is starting for the first time in over a month. We've got Keane, Riera and Kuyt playing too – a much more attacking line-up than the one put out at Stoke. Jegsy strains his eyes checking who's out on the pitch.

"No Lucas?" he asks.

"No."

"Good."

Lucas had a stinker at Stoke and looks more and more, with every game, like he'll never make it at this level. Everton are clearly up for this. I suspect the egg-eyed opportunist Moyes can smell, if not fear, then a definite lack of confidence from The Reds, and he's hoping to snatch something whilst we're stumbling and fumbling our way round the game. We are NOT playing well and Everton are giving as good as they get aided by an uncertain Liverpool defence with Jamie Carragher looking as uncomfortable at full back as I had felt earlier in Aldo's. Even though Torres clips the post early on when clean through in the box and Riera also forces a fine save from Howard it's no surprise that the half ends all square.

The half time debate revolves around the uncertainty surrounding Keane, and Rafa's puzzling approach to the Stoke game. Do we want to win this league? If we do, then we have to look and play like potential champions and that means going to places like Stoke and attacking them. It's no good 'controlling the game' (One of Rafa's favourite phrases) you need to be creating chances and scoring goals – and having forwards on the pitch usually helps with that. A point from this game tonight will see us joint top, but no-one's even thinking about settling for just one point. Drawing at home to Everton is bad enough, but we can't allow them to be the team that's derails a title push. We need to win this.

"Let's gerrin ter these bastards!"

And for a while in the second half we do 'gerrin ter them'. A Gerrard shot is palmed across the goal by Tim Howard into the path of Sami Hyypia. Sami's geriatric legs however can't get to the ball in time and a last-ditch block prevents what should have been a simple tap-in. But its the type of incident that rouses the crowd and The Kop are roaring The Reds on now. Upping the pace eventually pays off when Riera plays a ball inside to Gerrard, for once left in acres of space 35 yards out. The defence don't close him down quickly enough and...

"Go on... go on!" screams Lou Lou

"Twat it!" Sammo adds, finishing her sentence.

And twat it he does. Not his cleanest of strikes, but the ball flies into the bottom corner across the sodden turf. Cue complete and utter bedlam on The Kop. Jegsy jumps on top of me, knocking me off balance and down onto the ground, with him screaming and laughing in my ear. He's doing this after every goal now and its getting on my tits, its like a mosh pit in here at times. I'm not 18 anymore and I'm beginning to creak. As I get to my feet there's a sharp pain in my thigh. Something's twanged or pulled – ouch! I'm not the only one. Mags is grimacing and rubbing at his leg. He lifts his jeans to show a deep crimson scrape down his shin caused by the back of the seat in front.

"Seat scars," nods Sammo. "They're the new silk scarves."

It's worth it though isn't it – to score against this shower? Gerrard is enjoying his celebrations almost as much as we are. Always the butt of Evertonian venom he's had to endure taunts all night about his children. Funny how this never makes it into the local paper whilst our entirely valid observations about Joleon Lescotts strangely-shaped head are picked up on as a prime example of how the derby has "gone sour." Everton fans are 'allowed' to taunt us about Hillsborough and Heysel because we mock them about moving to Kirkby and having a defender with a head like a Klingon. Never quite understood that; how the – admittedly cruel – jibe at Lescott is on a par with them singing: "... it could have been worse, you could have been a Red. Knocking down walls and pissing on the dead."

We have the opportunity now to really rub their noses in it as well as boosting our confidence for the Cup game next week. But we don't take it. Infuriatingly we invite them on, thinking we can keep them at bay and just play on the break. We are walking a tightrope, as one slip will cost us dear. It's doing Jegsy's head in.

"Finish them off! Go for the jugular!" he screams.

Then he suddenly drops to his knees. Ah! A quick prayer no doubt. I turn and look down to see him swigging from a bottle of Carlsberg and smoking a roll-up. He's doing this just to tempt me isn't he? He looks up at me and explains, "Its for me nerves."

As the clock ticks ever more slowly to 90 minutes I could do with something for my nerves too, Phenobarbital perhaps. I settle for chewing my fingernails. I don't like this, I don't like this at all. Rafa takes Keane off, replacing him with Benayoun, but he's finding it hard to get into the game. We have, plain and simply, stopped going for it – and a beaten team are beginning to sense that there may be something in this for them yet. And now – oh no, please please let this not happen, Lord... Lucas is warming up. Surely Rafa wouldn't, he isn't... but he is. Lucas is stripping off and, with 5 minutes of the game left, Torres is heading for the dugout. We have no strikers on the pitch. We have two players on who'll need a quarter of an hour to acclimatise to the blood and guts of the game. In short, we're handing Everton a huge psychological advantage for the remaining few minutes here, and it's critical we hold out.

They push. We panic. Lucas is trying too hard to show that he's up for it, clattering into Cahill towards the Kop side of the halfway line. He's about 30 seconds late, but fortunately the free kick is in their half and they can only lump it forward to no avail. But we haven't learnt our lesson. Carra blazes the ball into touch when he could have carried it out of defence. From the ensuing throw-in, there's another clumsy challenge and they get a free kick wide on the left, not far from the corner flag. The nerves are shredded from us lot. Sammo's almost hopping on the spot as Arteta lines the ball up.

"He's gonna shoot – look at how he's shaping up. Can't they see it? He's gonna fuckin' shoot!"

He whips the ball in with a bit of pace and Cahill throws himself at it, getting there before Pepe Reina or any of our static defenders to nod the ball into an empty net. The blue contingent in the Anfield Road are delirious. They celebrate the point like they've won the League, and I don't believe I've seen them so joyful since a 0-0 draw in 1975 when they bounced up and down underneath a huge Welsh flag singing: "Ee aye addio, we're not going home!"

So that's another two home points just pissed down the pan. The final whistle is greeted not with boos or anguish, just a silent resignation that perhaps we're not good enough. What's annoying is that this League title is there for the taking; with a bit more ambition and belief we could be 10 points clear. But we seem to be happier with the idea of "controlling the game" and hoping that we might just score one more than the other team.

JM

Everton (h)   1-1

FA Cup 4th Round   Sun 25th January

Oh no! Not you lot again. Two derby matches in a year is usually bad enough for your mental condition but two in six days is pure lunacy. I still haven't recovered from Monday night's confrontation where it seems Everton became the first team in the history of world football to actually win 1-1. The smiles on the Blues' faces in the last few days and the number of text messages I've received seem to suggest that Everton fans have secured a monumental victory; which of course in their small uneventful world they have. They have prevented us from taking a crucial three points on our championship crusade and that in their eyes is their whole reason for living. They will never win anything of value so their only pleasure in life is to try and thwart us. It is their everything. If the point they gained at Anfield was a physical, solid, visible thing like, say a gold ingot, it would've been placed in a glass case and displayed in the threadbare EFC trophy room every day and night since Monday.

Today though is a different kettle of fish. It is the FA Cup 4th Round and I'll be hoping for a bit of revenge. Anything less and life could border on the unbearable. If I'm honest and I had a choice I'd have taken the three league points and given them the FA Cup match although that would've also been unbearable. The thought of 6,000 muppets in the Anfield Rd End losing control of all their bodily functions – no thank you.

It's an early start. We meet in town at midday. Everybody's still talking about Bobby's funeral on Friday which was a unique experience. It's safe to say I will never in my life attend a bigger or madder send off than that of Scotland Road's finest. Just to put it into perspective, think of Liverpool FC's most famous Godlike figure, Bill Shankly. Well, Bobby Wilcox's funeral was bigger than our own Uncle Bill's. Amazing.

Anyway, back to today's match, we're in The Renshaw Grill opposite Lewis's statue exceedingly bare and so far there's Sammo, Johnny Mac, Chris Franks and Joe 'look into my eyes, look into my eyes' Corrigan. Phil Thompson was also in there standing by the bar. (Doesn't he ever sit down? Do you get me?) Had a couple of liveners in there and down to HQ to meet the rank and file. Ned's is busy. There's people coming and going. Steve Hitchmough pops his head in. Paul Randalls and the Cavo's and the rest of the Birkenhead Brigade sit talking in the corner. Parso appears as does Danny Giles, who looks like he's just woke up after a 12 hour bender, which he confirms is exactly what he's just done. Bucko's battalion march in. Even Colonel Hogan makes a rare appearance. Yes, this could be a great day.

Preparations have not only been going on at Melwood but also at Dodd Towers too. The Lucky Undies ceremony took place just after breakfast. Similar to when the Chancellor of the Exchequer holds up his battered briefcase before the Budget, I hold up my ruby red bills to no-one in particular and take a bow. I'd worn them in the league match on Monday so there was a bit of a last minute panic the night before when I couldn't find them. But I needn't have worried as Hot Lips had washed and dried them and put them in a safe place ready for the big day's action. The lucky undies have done me proud so far this season; Man U at home (won 2-1), Everton away (won 2-0), Chelsea away (won 1-0), Arsenal away (1-1) and Everton at home (1-1). So they're on an unbeaten run of five games at the mo.

The atmosphere is electric today, and the Kop doesn't just want revenge – it demands it. Liverpool dominate possession as expected but it is the bluenoses who break the deadlock from a corner just before the half hour mark. Cahill again finds space to power a header goalwards which is touched on by Joleon Lescott into the Kop net. Fuckin' hell! Why do we do it? We're self-harming again. Cahill's about five feet nothing and he's got free to damage us again for the second time this week. Don't we ever learn? I look to my left and the whole Anfield Rd End is going doolally with excitement. (By the way, the word 'doolally' comes from a place in India called Deolali where the British troops all went off their heads with boredom. See, this is not just a rant about the boys in Red. It's a journey of discovery with little nuggets of information which you can share with your mates when you are pleasantly pissed in the pub.) Doolally, yes Doo fuckin' lally those bluenosed bastards are going and I'm not happy. Defeat today is not an option. Half time comes and the fans are ranting and raving. Why pay £20m for Keane and he's not even on the bench?

Why is Babel playing when he's shite? It's all ifs and buts but we have to get back into this game.

The second half kicks off and Gerrard is inspirational as always. He is a beast of a player and it is he who pulls us back on level terms. Torres creates it with an audacious piece of skill. A kind of mid-air back heel which sends Stevie free. Captain Marvel twats it past Tim Howard and we're back in it. From then on in, it's just one-way traffic as the Reds lay siege to the Everton goal. Torres and Kuyt both miss really easy chances and the final whistle is greeted as expected as a victory by the Evertonians. Let's be honest. Who can blame them? They've been on the rack all game and managed to nullify their more illustrious neighbours for the second time this week. I'm pissed off and frustrated. And the worst thing of all is we've got to do it all again in just over a week's time. At least our record at Castle Doom is solid. We've won seven out of the last nine meetings, which is good, but nothing is going to console me today.

I meet Bucko, Ritchie, Mercer and the others outside the Hillsborough shop. There's a bad atmosphere. All anyone is talking about is trouble. There's all kinds of rumours and counter rumours of skirmishes amongst the two sets of fans. Benitez is also starting to get a fair bit of stick. People are airing their views in loud and aggressive tones. I just feel numb as I always do when things don't go our way. We head off and stop for a gargle in the Crown on Scottie where we can let the dust settle, get our breath back and just basically calm down. The phone rings. It's one of the lads to say it's gone off in the Thomas Frost on County Rd. Apparently there's been windows smashed and a bit of argy-bargy. Friendly derby? What friendly derby? We get a couple of cabs into town and sit off for a while in the Excelsior which is a good old traditional pub away from the impending madness. A small firm of Liverpool Urchins walk in looking like they mean business. You know that 'rogues gallery' that they have at the end of every Crimewatch programme? Where they have mug shots of Britain's most wanted. Well this tidy little firm make them look like the cast of Bugsy Malone. They don't stay long which is just as well because about five Evertonian mates walk in just after they leave. Town after a Derby these days is more edgy than it's ever been. People still have a laugh but everyone's more aware than they used to be. My bluenose mates are certainly not scallies but they're still switched on to the city's volatile nature after a Derby match. Which is why I nearly keel over with shock when Allmo, who is as blue as they come, insists he wants to go to Ned Kelly's. He reckons it's been his ambition for years to go behind enemy lines and see how the other half live. He's not a spotter or anything like that, he just thinks it's a mad idea. They should be alright with us as long as they don't start gobbing off. A quick check that they've removed metal badges etc and we're down the road and into the mix. It's wall to wall 'head the balls', all singing and bouncing like the last days of the Roman Empire – and right in the middle of them stand TC, Allmo and Coggi. What they hope to get out of this experience is anybody's guess. If the boot was on the other foot I would rather eat my own flesh than stand surrounded by baying blues singing anti-Liverpool songs from their very limited song sheet. But in some perverse way they seem to be enjoying the moment, taking it on the chin and smiling inanely. After more than an hour of listening to non-stop battle songs they decide that their mission is complete. They've met Ally, Gilly, Degsy, Danny and everybody else. They disappear into the cold night air, educated, illuminated and intoxicated. Maybe they'll go back to their brethren and tell them of this strange far off land, away from County Rd, where football fans who know more than five songs sing and dance until the early hours. Somehow I manage to get home in one piece. It's been another frustrating result but life goes on and we live to fight another day.

JD

Wigan Athletic (a)   1-1

League   Wed 28th Jan

It's still January (just!) and I'm still officially *"offit"* so I drive over to The Rocket, at the end of the M62, and pick up the Spirit of Shankly bus that's leaving for Wigan at 5:30. I'd drive all the way to Wigan myself but my car has difficulty going that far back in time, and I fear that the vibrations from driving over cobbles would ruin the suspension. The coach is only half full, which is no great surprise as Wigan's only up the road and there are plenty of other options for getting there. The first face I see on the bus is a Norwegian one. Olaf is sitting up front with a can of lager for company. They're having a nice talk about the weather. I haven't seen Olaf since the baking heat of Valencia when he was recovering from a battering administered by Berlin nightclub bouncers. I remind him of this and he lets me look for the stitches on his head... oooh! He's healing well for a ginger.

It is an extremely dull and cold evening with patches of freezing fog that only adds to the miserable foreboding I have. It all seems to be going "tits up." A 9 point lead over the Mancs (yes, I know they had games in hand!) has evaporated and we've been held in the Cup by you-know-who and face a replay I'm not looking forward to. There's only the upcoming European Cup game in Spain that provides any solace at the moment – and even the most Red-friendly of the pundits expect us to get knocked out in this round by a resurgent Madrid. Then there's the little matter of Chelsea on Sunday who will, no doubt, be bursting to avenge our win in London back in October. So, given our current form I expect we'll probably draw – at best – on Sunday. As such, nothing short of a win tonight will suffice: It's 3 points or forget it. Mind you, I said that about Everton didn't I?

That said, we never learn do we, us fans? I've already booked on John Garner's LBU bus for the 6 hour journey to Portsmouth, and I have to pick up my ticket for the Cup replay later this week. Madrid was booked within hours of the draw back in December, although we left the arrangements to Sammo and he's booked us out via Barcelona on the morning of the game, just to make the day a little more tense and interesting. It does give us an evening in Barcelona on the way back, however, so its not a total cock up by the boy Sampson.

I stare out of the window for the funereal drive up a strangely deserted East Lancs Road, deeper and deeper into inbred country. The heating on the bus is on the blink and my feet feel damp and cold. I bet Olaf feels right at home in this, though, and I check to see if he's wearing flip-flops. He's far from the stereotypical tourist Red, it must be said. To speak to him you'd think he was from Netherley, not Norway. Along with fellow Norgies Bard Thoreson, Tage Herstad and others, Olaf has become so Scouse that he makes *me* sound like Stephen Fry. So, yeah, Evertonians are right: we do have loads of Norwegians following us, but they love us so much that loads of them move here. Unlike their own Out-of-Town support that with unseemly haste beats a retreat after home games back to spinning waltzers in Rhyl or crayoning on the walls in Broadmoor. We attract support from all over the World not because they're glory hunters but because Liverpool FC is one of the truly famous names in World football. We are legendary and have a cultural resonance and importance that clubs like Chelsea and Arsenal will never have. In any case, would you call this, Wigan away on a cold winter's night with the Reds struggling for results, 'Glory Hunting'?

I should have worn a jumper under my coat; maybe two. My teeth are chattering and I can't feel my toes. And I'm in Wigan. By my reckoning this is just the perfect stage for Lucas Leiva to shine. Okay, so I'm being sarcastic – sorry. But Lucas has become the focus for everything that the supporters think is wrong at the moment. He repeatedly fails to come up with the 'promise' we're always being told he has, yet when he gets the ball he plays the safe, short option every time, instead of beating a man and making something happen. He's Brazilian, isn't he? So why can't he be magic? Why? The charitable voices say that Lucas has skill and just needs experience. The uncharitable voices – the realists (?) – are saying that vital league games cannot be being surrendered just to give Lucas a run out. I'm wavering between the two. I want him to succeed, like Keane, but my eyes are telling me it's just not happening – like Keane.

Outside the JJB Stadium, heads are shaking at the team news: no Kuyt,

Keane, Riera or Alonso. They're all on the bench. Babel's supporting Torres, and Lucas is replacing Alonso in the middle of the park. If Gerrard's going to augment the attack, that leaves Benayoun, Lucas and Mascherano in the middle. Where's the width or the pace or the threat there? Because, as sure as hell, Babel isn't going to provide any. Yossi is the only one with any idea of getting forward but his form of late... well, it stinks. It looks like it's all down to Gerrard and Torres again to provide the inspiration, even if Torres is still feeling his way back from injury. The pair of them combined brilliantly on Sunday for the equaliser against Everton, let's hope for a repeat tonight.

"Does he really want to win this game? Or is he just hoping we do?" asks Andy Knott, shivering as he sells copies of the fanzine. I shrug.

"Football's a simple game. Why complicate it?" I shudder. "It's alright playing chess in Europe but... Wigan? We should just put the best XI out and....batter them!"

We need to win tonight. We need to score goals. You need strikers out there. So why's Keane out again? Fucked if I can work this situation out. Is it the 'R' word? Has 'Rotation' reared its ugly head again. I suspect Rafa has one eye on Sunday and Chelsea at home. But I'd rather win here, as 2 draws (at best?) will leave us worse off. And it seems like the message might have got through out there on the pitch as we start brightly and, as usual, dominate possession. Torres clips the post with a great glancing header following good work from Gerrard and Babel on the wing... did I just say that? *Babel on the wing*? Well that's what we bought him for in theory, and tonight the young Dutchman's getting plenty of room and he's running at Wigan like a player reborn. Maybe this is the night we get to see what he can do.

It's pretty obvious that we have this game by the scruff of the neck. All we need are goals – plural. Wigan seem to realise this and decide that if they nick one, we'll struggle to get two. Steve Bruce can then rush off and phone Mr Ferguson for his under-the-chin tickles and saucer of milk. Actually, we are lucky we don't give Bruce the excuse to semaphore his "Look Alex! Look what I did for you!" from the touchline during this first half. We are more than lucky to escape when a free header from Emmerson Boyce drops into Pepe's thankful arms, and shortly afterwards when Skrtel appears to give away a penalty. The frustration in the away end is intensified by these scrapes with disaster and the air is filled with curses aimed at the usual suspects. Then – just when it is looking like the half is petering out – a burst of pace from Yossi Benayoun, on the right-hand side of the penalty area, down at the far end, sees him collect a short pass from Mascherano and round the keeper. It looks like he's knocked it too far but he manages to pull it back. I half-expect to see it hit the side-netting and prepare to let out an "AwwFerFucksSake!!!" Instead he drills it expertly into the narrowest of gaps inside the far post. GOOOOAAAAAAALLLL! Oh, the relief! The sheer ecstatic release of all that negative pressure. For the last 5 minutes of the half, we can at least sing and support the team; the shackles of fear and frustration having been shed by the packed away end.

I go down into the concourse during the break to see if I can get warm by holding someone's coffee for a few minutes. In fact, tonight you'd get warm by holding someone's lager.

"Alonso's had a knock. That's why he's on the bench." says a nose-tapper. Probably getting his inside information from a £2.50 per SMS message service direct to his mobile ("Just send 'IM A DICK' to 66089") that he saw advertised during Sky's Super Sunday.

"Look, he's either fit or he's not." I tell him, "And if he's fit he should be playing from the start. And even if his leg's hanging off I'd give him an hour before putting Lucas on."

He looks at me in disgust for daring to question his SMS source and holds out his hand, "Can I have my coffee back?"

"I'll take this now," I tell him.

"What? Get yer own!"

"Not the coffee. 3 points. I'll take 1-0 now. I'll take a scruffy, jammy, ugly 3 points tonight."

He wanders off with his drink to find someone who'll be impressed by his Insider knowledge.

"We're lucky to be ahead," I shout after him – then mumble to myself. "Let's just not fuck it up!"

Guess what? Yep – we followed the recent script again. With Wigan improving and causing us problems Torres is sacrificed and replaced by Riera with 20 minutes to go. This leaves Babel alone up front to worry and harass a Wigan defence growing in confidence and stature. Then Yossi goes off for Kuyt, who reverts to holding the right flank. But we need support for Babel, we need that 2nd goal, we need that cushion as I don't think we can hold out for an ugly 1-0. The substitutions baffle the away end and our dissent is audible. We've done exactly what we did against Everton the in the league and gone into the later stages just hoping we can hang on. The equaliser is as ridiculous and completely avoidable as it is expected. From our own throw in midway inside our own half we manage to lose possession within 5 seconds. Lucas – LUCAS!! – is on the edge of our box, faced with 2, then 3 Wigan attackers running at him. Jason Koumas – a devout Red, by the way, drops a shoulder and feints to go past Lucas.

"Just stand him up. Jockey! Jockey!" I shout as the rest of our team pour back to try and support him. Koumas knocks the ball past Lucas; Lucas hangs a leg out – and down Koumas goes. He's played for it. But he's played for it knowing Lucas would stick out a leg. Almost immediately Gerrard is replaced by Robbie Keane who's given a paltry 5 minutes to try and rescue the game. Too little too late.

Walking back to the coaches there is silence. A gloom to match the winter fog has descended and people are clenching and unclenching their fists; frustrated, angry yet resigned to the fact that we've blown it. It feels like a defeat. It feels like a defeat that has finally scuppered any lingering hopes if winning number 19. A negativity – a lack of belief – has killed the title challenge.

"Stop trying to be clever Rafa. Just play to our strengths. Play your best team and if you need to rest your best payers then take them off when the game's well and truly won," moans Alan Diamond who I meet in the car park. "His dithering and tinkering has put the fear of God into the fans and the players. He worries too much about the opposition. And they get a boost knowing he's worried about them."

It's true. Is that what comes from a manager who's not used to leading from the front? Is he happier when he's the underdog, when he's chipping away at a lead rather than trying to create one? His critics say that his finest 'hour' in Istanbul didn't begin until we were 3 nil down and ended after we equalised. Once we were level we seemed to stop playing, regroup and, well, just hung on for the penalties. Just go for it, Rafa! If we are to make anything at all of this season we need to lose the shackles and just attack teams. As the old Kop chant used to go:

GERRINTERTHEM!

JM

Chelsea (h)   2-0

League   Sun 1st Feb

After another disappointing draw at Wigan midweek in which we threw it away in the last few minutes again, we really need to get back on track today. We're not quite in the last chance saloon yet but let's just say the barman is polishing the glasses awaiting our arrival. Rafa's view of matches, tactics and substitutions at the moment seem to be at odds with most of the fans, which is quite worrying. The post match comments are also getting more bizarre with each game. He said the second half at Wigan was a crazy game which he had no control over. Hate to disagree but when he takes his best player off with just eight minutes left before the game is safe and then Lucas gives a ridiculous penalty away, what does he expect? The only crazy thing was the safety first tactics. That's seven out of the last ten games we have drawn, which is simply not good enough. The slump has nothing to do with Stevie's impending court case or Rafa's rant at Ferguson or even the American owners. It's down to playing your best eleven players at all times and being positive. Fortune has always favoured the brave and starting with Chelsea today we must be absolutely up for it. Lose this and next week's derby replay and we're fucked. It's a big week so let's have it.

I have a quick livener in town with Steve Hitchmough and then go up to Shenanigans to meet all the boys. Everyone is on a high because there's been a union meeting followed by a demo at the Crowne Plaza Hotel where some of the lads got past reception and actually confronted George Gillett who's been staying there. It's all rather exciting knowing that the lads have been involved in some direct action against one of our two loathsome landlords. Seeing as I didn't get to bed until 5am, all this early activity has kind of passed me by. What it has done though is given the pre-match bevvy a bit more oomph. Everybody seems a lot more animated. Johnny Mackin and John

Buchanan have both returned to the drinking club after simultaneously staying off the ale for the whole of January. I don't know how they did it but they did it – though it could get messy as the day progresses.

Sammo's in there, Mags, Danny Nico, Danny Giles, Paul from Static, bloke from The Troubadours and the list goes on. Dave Hewitson, who does the 80's Casuals t-shirts, fires the ale in. He's also got a book called 'The Liverpool Boys Are In Town – The Birth of Terrace Culture'. God, they're all at it. If they're not writing books or fanzines or singing in bands, they're making films, writing plays or designing t-shirts. Who said Scousers are lazy bastards? Thank the Lord for Danny Giles to put us in our place when we get a bit, you know, thingio. Paul from the Static Gallery mentions Marcel Marceau and that's it, you know what's coming when Gilesy twitches his nose, puffs out his chest and goes: "Marcel Marceau? *Mar-sell Mar-so* lad??!!! I'll tell you abar Marcel Marceau…"

He starts by asking if he's the latest "new Zidane" then has the bar in stitches by doing a series of silly walks followed by a Harry Worth "half in, half out" by the pub door. If ever you start thinking you know the score, Danny will remind you of the rules of life and that is why we love him.

Anyway, game on. Cabs to the ground and let's go for it. The Kop's in full voice. It's as if we all know that today could be a defining moment in the title race. Lose this and the Mancs beat Everton and we might as well wave goodbye to any dreams we might have.

Johnny Mackin appears five minutes after kick off stumbling over the seats. He's obviously making the most of his first day back on it. It's a tight game as you would expect but we're edging it. Midway through the first half and John Mackin inexplicably produces a sachet of Viagra gel and a tablet which he proceeds to digest to the disbelief of his fellow spectators. Now call me old-fashioned but why on earth would anyone want to neck Viagra at the match, in a predominantly male environment? The mind boggles. John is having a whale of a time though, completely off his tits in a world of his own. He keeps shouting things like: "Be men, Liverpool! Be a winger, Ryan!"

Maybe that's why he's done his little blue pill – to show the lads how to be men. He's stood up on his seat, head and shoulders above everybody else, shouting, well basically shouting anything that comes into his head, football related or not.

"John Collier, John Collier the window to watch!" is followed by: "ELS gives you bigger choice yes; nah-nah-nah-nah….. YES-YES!!!"

Everybody is in bulk at John's ridiculous comedy routine, everybody that is except for Roy Boulter, who proceeds to tell everybody off for being childish.

"Just watch the fuckin' match, will yer. It's Liverpool versus Chelsea if you didn't know."

Obviously no-one takes a blind bit of notice of him, egging Mackin on as he revels in his role as the new Doctor Fun. John Maguire reckons that if the Mackin Worm hits full erection by half time, he may need to do a handstand in the toilets, so he's pointing the right way.

Half time comes and goes and it seems to be yet another stalemate. Lampard gets his marching orders for a foul on Alonso on 60 minutes. It looks a bit harsh but then the same player broke Alonso's ankle here four years ago, in front of the same referee, and got away with it. So it's a case of what goes around, comes around. Liverpool are playing well but it's only when Benayoun comes on for Riera that we really start to give it a good go. The ten man Chelsea are hanging on when we get a free kick on the left in the last minute. Aurelio crosses it to the near post and Fernando Torres beats three defenders to the ball as he stoops to nod it into the Kop goal. All hell breaks loose. We haven't won a league game all January and now we've just done a hateful Chelsea team in the last minute. Get in there! A full minute after the ball's hit the back of the neck, the mangled wreckage of 306 are trying to disentangle themselves and get their heads (and limbs) together for the final minute of a now-joyous occasion. But hang on a mo…. Benayoun's got it, jinks in and out, makes space for the shot…has he overrun it? No – he slips it to Torres. He slots it! 2-0. YESSSSSSS!!! Cue more madness. Referee blows and we're back in it. YABBA FUCKIN' DABBA FUCKIN' DOO. Let's hit the bars of Walton Breck Rd and toast the boys in Red.

I'm in Bar Rouge or whatever it's called gabbing to Muffa and Paul Dava when all the ones who've been demonstrating outside the main stand come in. Hooto, Potter, Mono, Paul Rice, Danny Nicko and loads of others have braved the weather to let our American owners know what the supporters think. I wish I could be more active but just dressing myself in the morning and getting to the match on time are classed as achievements. Maybe it's an age thing or all those spliffs over the years but my get up and go has got up and gone. They're all good lads and I support what they're trying to do but lethargy crept into my game years ago. I'm not the tricky midfielder of my youth anymore. Don't get me wrong, if Hicks or Gillett wanted to come to a nice warm boozer for a heated debate, I'm in. But standing in a car park in mid winter shouting me bollocks off to someone who's not listening is a non-starter.

Me and the singing Brickie (Danny) get a cab into town and the night starts to get a little bit fuzzy from there on in. People seem to pass through the evening like a haze. I remember James Tylo coming in and saying he was a proud father of a baby boy and Ally appearing in the company of his good lady. I have vague memories of discussing the meaning of life with Nicky Alt but in all truth I was probably talking a load of old bollocks and he was probably looking for an escape route. All in all, a thoroughly enjoyable day out. Even Rafa left his best two players on the field until the game was well and truly won. Whatever next?

JD

Everton (h) 0-1

FA Cup 4th Round Replay 4th Feb

I'm really glad that this is definitely the final derby of the season. Because to be honest, I am sick of the sight of them. I'm sick of their fans with their crap songs. I'm sick of Tim (bloody) Cahill, the dashing Brad Pitt look-alike Phil Neville and I'm sick of paying good wedge to come to a shit hole of a ground where you can't see the whole pitch. I'm on the way to town when I pick up an Echo to read on the train. I don't believe what I'm seeing. It says there are still some tickets on sale at the Everton box office. What? The People's Club can't sell out for their biggest match of the season. Oh dear, dear, dear. It goes without saying that we've sold our 6,000 allocation which only leaves 34,000 spaces to fill and the self-proclaimed "Greatest fans in the world" are struggling to put bums on seats. Shame on them.

Me and Danny Giles (the Charles Darwin of his era) march up to Shenanigans where a fair few of the lads have made camp. It seems to have become a bit of an 'in' place for some of our more deep thinking fans. Almost like an old-fashioned debating society for the discerning Liverpool fan. I suppose it makes a change from Ned's where most of the clientele discuss how to behead Man United fans for much of the time. I like to think I can move between both camps without too much adjustment. John Buchanan gives me, Danny and John Mackin a lift up to the Albert where the Red masses are congregating. Johnny Mac is complaining of a sore wrist. He says something about repetitive strain injury and some bollocks about how using his computer keyboard is to blame. He gives us that innocent raised eyebrows look as if to say "What? What have I done?" His face fills with dread when he is reminded of his Viagra fuelled bender against Chelsea the other day. The comical connotations are there for all to see. He tries to ride the verbal blows like a boxer on the ropes in the final round. But the juvenile sexual innuendos come raining in from all sides. Blokes, no matter what age, all love a good old snigger whenever it comes to stuff from below the waist. Like a room full of Sid James sound-a-likes they try to outfunny each other until the well is dry. Not for nothing is Johnny Mackin known as Herr Flick…

I'm not really into marching up to the ground in a big mob, which seems to have become the norm over recent seasons. So about four or five of us just slope off from the Rouge place and around the park until Castle Doom comes into view. There doesn't seem to be as much venom in the air as the three previous meetings. Maybe we're both just sick of the sight of each other and just want to get it over with. The acoustics in the ground aren't perfect for a decent vocal backing but the away section is in fine voice. I suppose that's all down to us having the biggest official following here since the 4-4 draw back in 1991.

In an 11th-hour raid by 'Arry the Dog Redknapp, Robbie Keane has been sold back to Spurs with hours of the transfer window remaining. But Rafa, unbelievably, has declined the opportunity of replacing him. Before settling on an £18million straight cash fee for Keane, Spurs tried to weigh players like Modric, Pavlyuchenko and Aaron Lenno into the deal – any of whom I'd have taken happily. But Rafa reckons that he has adequate striking cover in the shape of Ngog, Babel and Kuyt. Methinks he's taking a massive gamble because if Torres gets crocked we'll be well and truly up 'Shit Creek'.

The teams come out and the fans swap the usual barrage of insults. In one of the most bizarre pranks of recent years, Liverpool fans shower the pitch with pairs of socks. A couple of seasons ago we released 2,000 balloon-inflated Tesco bags to celebrate their impending new home; tonight's is supposed to be another dig at the blues proposed move to Kirkby, where for some mad reason the residents of that Knowsley parish have been labelled 'sock robbers'. No, I don't get it either, but it certainly achieves the aim in winding up the 'bitter blues' in the Stanley Park End. Even the Liverpool Echo gets in on the action by running a story the following day under the headline of 'Kopites sock it to 'em!' The article has quotes from the Reverend Tim Stratford of the Kirkby residents action group saying how great it is to live there, etc. I'm still a bit bemused by it all, as are probably 95% of tonight's attendance but hey they're hardly missiles are they? I mean a pair of socks never killed anybody (unless you were on the train back from Rome in 1977).

The game itself is an absolute stinker, too. The Liverpool fans try to alleviate the boredom by taunting the Evertonians about their failure to sell all their allocation in what is (let's face it) their biggest game of the season. Even when Manchester U-fuckin-nited swaggered into town they were 6,000 under capacity, which don't look good if you're telling everyone you're the 'People's Club' of Merseyside. A people's club with no "people"? It was 'Skeletor', the boss-eyed David Moyes who initially coined that phrase on his first day in office and David has also had a few other things to say along the way. Here's what he said in his post match analysis:

"I think we're getting better but I also think we've still got a long way to go. Everybody knows what the difference is – it's the amount of money the other clubs have spent compared to ours – but it's not something we harp on about."

Not something you harp on about? Not something you harp on about! You never *stop* harping fucking on about it! He mentioned it at the last derby and the one before that, the one before that and every other fuckin' derby and every time his team plays Chelsea he harps on about it and he harps on about it every time they play Man U or Arsenal. Everybody's sick to the back teeth of hearing it. He revels in playing the role of the underdog with no money but then nearly pisses his pants when Rafa calls Everton a small club. What does he expect? The same noises have been coming out of Goodison for 20 years. "Oh look at us, poor old us. Big bad Liverpool get invited to all the parties and we're left there all dressed up with nowhere to go." "Hey! That must mean we're the People's Club."

Here's how it works in real life. Play attractive football, which will help you fill your shit hole of a ground more than once a season. Promote yourself better with quality merchandise and advertising, act with dignity and basically learn to run your club as a business instead of constantly moaning that everything is nasty Liverpool's fault. I know our own club is a bit of a fiasco at the moment but it's certainly not Everton's fault.

Anyway back to the action – or lack of it. The first half's only major incident comes when the chief talisman Steven Gerrard limps off after just 16 minutes. You know how important he is to us when you see the wild celebrations of the Evertonians at his departure. The stalemate continues in the second half. Lucas gets red-carded for his second bookable offence, leaving us with 10 men and a further half hour of extra time and penalties looming. God, he's a popular lad at the moment, old Lucas. What, with giving a cheap penalty away at Wigan with 3 minutes left to cost us two points and now leaving us in the shit in a match where we need all hands on deck – he better start pulling them trees up soon or he'll be forever the un-Brazilian Brazilian who wasn't that brilliant.

The game plods on to extra time with barely a shot in anger from either team. Torres is as quiet as a mouse. He's clearly not back to full strength yet, and he gets increasingly more frustrated as Phil Jagielka plays him to perfection. It's looking pretty desperate as Fernando is subbed and the headless Babel comes on for his standard impression of an out of control helicopter. Oh the shame of it! Rafa's playing for penalties against a team that features Andy Van der Meyde. I've got to be honest, Everton look like they want it more than us. We look knackered. And then with two minutes of extra time left, they score. Substitute Dan Gosling, who they signed from Plymouth, takes a chance and curls one in.

Imagine Rafa signing someone from Plymouth. Absolutely no chance. If they were called Real Plymouth and they played in the Spanish second division, maybe. Jagielka from Sheffield Utd or Cahill from Millwall or Lescott from Wolves. The only way those types of players would ever come under Rafa's radar is if they had names like Timola Cahillio and they came from a South American or Spanish side called FC Real Hooliganio. It's that Houllier French thing again where he signed every Tom, Dick and Pierre there was, and you can't help feeling we're missing out on the occasional diamond.

The old ground erupts. This is their moment. It's one of those horrible times that every single football fan on the planet has to endure at sometime or other, when you just want to dig a big hole and disappear. A derby defeat with two minutes of extra time left. It doesn't get any worse than that. I know the FA Cup is not as important as the league or the European Cup but fuck me it still hurts like hell. Me, Danny and a few others walk out of the ground past the celebrating Blues and head up past the King Harry to the Albert. We get there and it's closed which is not good, so we end up in the Park for a post match moan. I get in a round with Parso and his mate Buster, and Danny and Neil Bucko. The other more vocal Bucko joins us with Ritchie and Ste Mercer in tow. There's a few in there but it's not rammed like usual. Lenny Woods and a couple of other diehards are trying to make the best of it. We treble up at last orders just to be sure but the doors are locked and we're in there for the long haul.

Once the usual dissecting of the match is complete Bucko leads us into a few foot stompers. Three hours later and we're still at it. We've done the 'Greatest Hits' package and now we're giving a run out to some of the more obscure Red anthems. That's the thing about footy fans, you've just been done by your fiercest rivals and a few hours later you're singing your bollocks off as if you've won the treble. It's half two and Hot Lips phones to ask me if I want picking up. You bet your pretty little arse I want picking up! That would be worth a meal out and the biggest hug on record. She's been brilliant to me this season. From the day we moved in together, a couple of days before Liege away, she's been more supportive than any woman I've ever known towards my obsession with this great team of ours. Yes there's been times when I've had to show her the odd Yellow card but like all new signings, they need time to bed in. If we can get back on track and actually win this league, it'll be her just as much as Bucko, Kev, Danny etc that I'll want to celebrate it with. It's been a nutty old season already and I'm sure it's gonna get nuttier still, but she deserves a medal for putting up with me and all that a football season throws at you. I drunkenly sling my lucky undies in the wash telling them that they're a load of crap and they've let me down, when the voice of reason comes from the other room.

"That was a cup game honey. They're unbeaten in the league."

She's right. Played 6. Won 4. Drawn 2. Lost 0. Old Trafford, beware!

JD

Portsmouth (a)   3-2

League   Sat 7th Feb

I'm standing in the car-park of The English Rose in Halewood. 9am. Another freezing day. There's a promise of snow that could see the game called off today, and you know what? I don't think many of us actually care. It's not that the dreadful start to 2009 has knocked the enthusiasm out of any of us, but it's a 5.15 kick-off tonight and by the time we find out the game has been postponed we'll be too far from Liverpool to all go home. Instead, the coach will divert to the nearest town (or even village) of alcoholic interest for an afternoon's leisurely swallee. So, I fancy finding out the news somewhere, say, round Oxford on the M40 as I haven't had a pint of wallop around there since... well, since we last won the league. I'd say that was another omen, wouldn't you? Or is this all getting a bit tenuous now – just another example of my living in denial?

The Leather Bottle Ultra's (LBU) bus trundles into view down Lydiate Lane and even from 300 yards away I can hear a Trojan Ska classic booming as the bus rocks from side-to-side. The bus pulls up, the door swings open and I drag my coolbox of ice and San Miguel up the steps. Up at the back are the young lads, down the front the arl arses. They might have their youth and lurid tales of recent sexual escapades (usually fully documented on their camera phones), but we've got all the musical taste and a frightening capacity for alcohol. I say 'they' and 'we', but I'm something of a floater. I'm not one to kiss and tell, but I might have a 'lurid recent sexual escapade' myself recently; or does YouPorn not count? I do actually still think of myself as one of the lads rather than a tribal elder. I might have the years in the bank, but I'm also still a big kid. You know, what I really need is an away trip with Bobby Wilcox's lot; now there's a collection of professional drinkers and old school Reds that'll definitely make me feel as young, vigorous and virile as I like to imagine I am.

Another Peter Pan on board is John 'Tiberius' Garner. It might well be my mission, but it sure as shit is Tiberius's bus. Garner is (coughs) another fortysomething going on 17 and, again much like myself, possesses a huge ego. If the truth be told, neither of us are team players. We're both of the persuasion that nothing's a good idea unless it's our idea; that our musical taste is better than everyone elses' musical taste; and that, if we were running a bus to away games it'd be the best bus in the world. As such he's come prepared. There's a rucksack full of DVDs (James Live, *Quadrophenia*, *Sexy Beast*) and CDs (Ska, Punk) and whilst most of South Liverpool is still enjoying a Saturday morning lie-in, he's got the Ska pumping like it's 2am in Kingston, Jamaica. He's also downing a gin and tonic. The guy's got style. It bodes well for an interesting trip.

We stop at the Rocket to pick up some latecomers and as we wait in the lay-by, several other Liverpool coaches pull-in, pick up the last few passengers, and head off down the M62 and all points south. The Spirit of Shankly bus looks full, most of them as young as the back of our bus. I pity whoever's the steward on that one. Then up comes Wilcox Tours, or is it a Saga day-outing to Stapeley Water Gardens? And is that – surely not! Can it be that they're watching Daniel O'Donnell on the DVD?! Our latecomers finally arrive, decanting themselves from a cab right in the middle of one of Liverpool's busiest road junctions whereupon one of them falls flat on his face. As they come aboard laughing and beaming it's obvious they're completely pissed and have been up all night. Tiberius is not amused and stares them silently to their seats as he checks his watch. After taking the microphone and delivering a headmasterly reprimand he turns to the driver.

"Set a course for lager, Mr Sulu. Warp Factor One."

As the M6 slips by, the San Miguel slips down and DJ Tiberius on-da-decks is playing The Upsetters 'Return of Django'. He's also engaged in a running argument/debate with some of louder young 'uns about his choice of music. The further south we go towards the Midlands, the more and more fields are covered with snow. It'll be dark by kick-off and only likely to get colder, so it doesn't look promising – not for a game of football anyway.

Sitting across the aisle from me is Gerry Shields from Huyton. Gerry's another one: old enough to know better but has been going the game for far too long to give a monkeys. We're going through Garner's bag looking at his DVD collection and telling him that he should only bring films that were made in Liverpool.

"You know, 'Gumshoe' or 'No Surrender'...even 'Letter to Brezhnev'."

"51st State?" a young voice from the rear of the bus pipes up.

"Crap that lad, rather watch 'The Magnet."

"The wha'?"

DJ Tiberius replaces the Ska with some post-punk and I settle down with today's Liverpool Echo. In it Tony Barrett has, basically, criticised everyone at the club – Parry, Benitez, Gillett and Hicks – for turning it into a dysfunctional mess. It's amazing that we're in the league position we are in given the utter chaos reigning behind the scenes. Magazine's 'Shot By Both Sides' is playing. How ironic, given that everyone at the club must be constantly looking over their shoulder wondering where the next act of betrayal is coming from. Can anyone there actually trust anyone else? Or is it all a series of uneasy, constantly-shifting alliances? There's no black and white there anymore. Everyone is playing a series of murky grey games and hoping they're backing the right side. It's sickening that the Football Club has become, instead, this Machiavellian mess. And then to deepen the gloom there was Wednesday night's humiliation at the Pit.

One of the young lads comes down the aisle of the bus and asks me to ask Garner to change the sounds.

"Er... can you ask Captain Bligh to put some 'Madness' on?"

He's right, this lad; sometimes you can think too much. Sod it! This combination of the music – Magazine and Joy Division – and reading about the mistrust and scheming that's replaced the traditional 'sound stewardship' of the club, is doing my head inl. We need to get 'Return Of The Las Palmas 7' on and see how much we can drink. Starting 'NOW'!

"Up the 'Pewl!"

An hour later we're somewhere south of Birmingham on the M40 and the mood is good. Club politics and FA Cup defeats have been forgotten and we're all singing along to 'Our House' and dancing up and down the aisle. The news from Hampshire is that the Southampton game is off, but Portsmouth – barely an over-hit Albert Riera cross away – is still on.

"That'll be because they've actually got a ground at Southampton – you know, stands that will keep the sunshine off the pitch. Portsmouth... well, its a collection of sheds really," explains Gerry.

Garner reaches for the microphone to quieten down the bus as we pull into the service station. We don't need to attract any attention from the police, not with the pungent fumes of whatever the youngsters at the back are puffing on anyway. Garner finishes his address as they pile off the bus with an appeal to keep a low profile. Snow is piled up by like mounds of dirty laundry all around the car-park and the pavements are icy. I walk gingerly across to the toilets trying not to slip and break a leg, but only end up looking like a man trying desperately not to poo himself. The Irregulars bus is already here and within a few minutes we're joined by Wilcox tours, and the shop at the services is soon swamped with Liverpool fans aged from 15 to 70. Amazingly some of them are queuing at the till to pay for items. I discuss the possibility of the game being called off with 'DNA' Dave Hardman off the Wilcox bus. DNA assures me that if there was a doubt over the game, they'd have called it off by now. Adding that half their bus were actually looking forward to a diversion for a drink somewhere should it be postponed, and are now somewhat miffed at the prospect of actually having to go through with this madness we call following our team.

"Lenny was looking forward to an afternoon in Newbury," Dave says with genuine sorrow in his voice.

It's an attitude that does them all great credit, and I ask Dave to make sure there's a place for me on the West Ham bus in a few weeks time. In the shop I pick up a Ginsters pasty, check out the price, and put it back. Is anybody ever *that* hungry? Back out in the car park there's a spot of tribalism brewing. The Irregulars and the LBU youngsters are taking the piss out of each other. It doesn't take too long before the first snowball explodes on a coach window. Then another. Then... chaos! Within 30 seconds it's like Agincourt, the sky darkening with missiles. There are lads ducking down, deftly preparing fresh ammo, pulling at their shirt collars, trying to get snow and ice from down their necks. Others stand spluttering and spitting out ice and grit from direct hits to the gob – and they'd only got off the bus for a smoke. Everyone is roaring with laughter. Alan Cook wanders past in some discomfort complaining of grit and salt in his eye, the eye which now looks the size of a goldfish bowl. "Ow!" he yelps. "Me retina!" Can you be a bit more specific please, Al!

Garner's not impressed with this – it's attracting attention and a coach full of ale could easily be confiscated. He starts rounding up the troops and assists a few back on board with a helpful boot up the arse. As the LBU leave the Battle of Cherwell Valley Services, the last thing we see are The Irregulars turning their broadside onto Wilcox's bus and Lenny Woods, sitting like Whistler's Mother at the front puffing away on a Woodbine with a can of Mild in his hand, as the window is peppered with snowballs.

There's over a hundred miles still to go as we leave the motorway and strike south on the A34. The chance to stretch our legs and chuck a few snowballs has livened everyone up. The upbeat mood, however, is interrupted by a beep from my phone. The text message brings us back to earth with a crash.

'TRUST ME. YOU'LL WANNA TURN ROUND AND GO HOME WHEN U HEAR THE TEAM."

This is followed by:

'NEVER SEEN A LIVERPOOL TEAM LIKE IT. IT IS EITHER VERY, VERY BRAVE OR VERY, VERY RIDICULOUS."

What the fuck is going on? Is Voronin back? Did we secretly reclaim the services of Sean Dundee in the transfer window? It's worse – there's no Torres, no Alonso, no Kuyt. This is all salt in the wound of Gerrard's absence. Our attack is to be spearheaded by Ngog and Babel, bolstered by heavyweight midfielders such as Aurelio, Arbeloa and Benayoun. I cannot see a Portsmouth defence, anchored around the towering Sol Campbell and forged in manager Tony Adam's likeness being troubled by that lot. But look on the bright side, at least there's no Lucas.

"Thats it, I'm not going in," says one youngster who's come down on the bus in the hope of picking up a ticket outside the ground.

"I'm not spending 50 or 60 rips from a tout just to watch the reserves."

His frustration is easy to see. Once again we're making an easy game look difficult. We're making 3 points less and less likely. How much of a boost must it have been to the Portsmouth team to see the 'firepower' we've left out of the team?

"There's a few without tickets who are going straight the pub," Dan Nicholson tells me.

"Yeah, I heard."

"Well, if that didn't make my mind up," he says, "I just had a call from the ticket office about my Madrid ticket – it's £88. I'm going to have to pass mine on today. I can't afford to pay this AND nearly £90 next week."

"Don't blame you mate. Where are you going?"

"Brewer's Arms. Just down the road. Watch it on the telly there."

We arrive at our pre-arranged, pre-match pub stop at 3 p.m in Havant, a couple of hours before kick-off. The bus pulls into a car-park behind Carphone Warehouse and Garner orders the bus clearing of ale. The away coaches are often searched whilst the game is in progress and it's best to remove all traces of the party so as to prevent anyone (least of all the patient and good humoured coach driver) getting into any trouble. We've got another 90 minutes before we need to leave for the last few miles to Fratton Park and we split up in search of a swallee. Most of the young 'uns head into a Wetherspoons on the main road, making a lot of noise as they do so. We decide to give them, and the attention they'll draw, a wide berth and go for a quieter drink elsewhere. Even so, the small side-street pub we choose is soon visited by the police, who wander through just letting us know they're there. Can't they tell we're just here for a couple of quiet ones? It transpires that the young uns in Wetherspoons have bounced in shouting and singing and chose to give a teenage lad in a Man Utd shirt a load of stick. Soon a couple of Police vans have turned up and surrounded 'Spoons. They've then checked out the local pubs and stumbled across us. Not only that, they've decided to search the bus and have found several bottles of Budweiser that have been inexpertly stashed at the back. Garner is fuming, and delivers a lecture cum bollocking on the journey across the causeway into Portsmouth, telling them that it is behaviour exactly like that that can ruin future trips and that there'll be no pub stop anywhere in Hampshire on the journey back, by order of the Police. We eventually park up about half an hour before kick-off on an Industrial Estate close by the ground. A good 20 from our bus head straight to 'The Brewers Arms', the rest of us walk to the ground through the narrow alleyways.

Fratton Park is old and cramped and, at least as far as Liverpool fans are concerned, devoid of alcohol. I queue at a hole in the wall snack bar staffed by old ladies, and am shocked to learn we can't get a pint.

"No beer? You're joking..."

"No, love," she says.

"What about a tot of grog for the jolly jack tars?" I ask her.

"Pardon?"

"Rum!"

"We can do you a chicken balti pie, love?"

That's all we need; a team that'll be lucky to get a shot on target this evening and not even an overpriced lager to make it easier to endure. With nowhere to gather to talk to the lads there's little to do but find my seat and wait for the game to begin. When I do find it it's obvious I won't be able to talk to any of the lads here neither as there's not a familiar face for 20 seats in any direction, and a collection of accents from all over the country. I wonder to myself who's getting the credits for these away tickets, and whether any of these people will be at Old Trafford or Madrid in a few weeks time. There's not much to do but jam my hands deep in my pockets and hope that I don't frost over between now and 7 o'clock.

As we expected Babel and Ngog were posing no threat at all to David James and despite the midfield creating a few chances the game is incredibly scrappy. I'm getting text messages from the contingent in The Brewers Arms telling me how it's nice and warm, and there's plenty of TV screens showing the game. I stamp my feet constantly by now to see if I can feel my toes and am craning my neck to see Jockey Lane who I know has a hip-flask with him. I'm then examining the floodlights, the pokiness of the old South Stand, who's on the bench... anything, in fact. Let's face it – I'm bored. Just on half-time I edge to the end of the row intending to go for a quick pee and then try and sniff out the hip-flask. Just as I reach the aisle Peter Crouch nearly scores with a shot over the bar and as two blokes trot up the stairs past me, one of them says: "Does he wanna win the league or what?"

I jog up after them and as they reach the toilets I continue past them, to the exit, and ask a steward to let me out. Sod this! Five minutes later I'm at the bar in the pub and there's loads of Scousers in here who've either come down without tickets, or who've, like me, given in to temptation and retreated to the warmth of the bar.

"Don't blame you, lad," one of them tells me. "Shite, that..."

As if to chastise me we actually start the second half brightly, Ngog looking much better in 5 minutes than he did all first half. It's a surprise, then, when he's replaced by Kuyt after 10 minutes, but no surprise that we go behind when some shocking defending allows Nugent to slide the ball under the advancing Reina. The lads are shaking their heads in the pub, the same old debates starting up again. I shrug and return to the bar to get another beer in. There then follows a mad 20-odd minutes where we draw level before going behind again; the team's inability to defend a dead ball, crossed into the 6yd box, exposed again. Torres comes on, prompting anger from the crowd of Redmen in the bar that he didn't start, followed by genuine excitement that we now actually have a team on the pitch. A slip by their full-back allows Torres in and his cross shot reaches Kuyt who hammers an unstoppable shot right through David James hands into the net at the near post. We're level and Portsmouth are rattled and it's just my sodding luck that I've bailed out before the real fun started – will this team of ours ever score in the first half? Why didn't we start the game like this, with this selection? We'd have been 3 nil up, *then* we could have made changes. We've got away with it big-time here with this draw. I know we haven't won many recently, but we're not getting beat either. We've only lost one in the league all season, and if we seem to refuse to be adventurous at least we're hanging on in there. 2-2 at one of our famous bogey grounds – I'll take that, thank you very much...

But the madness isn't over yet. We push on down the wing and Aurelio manages to evade a lunging tackle and make a bit of space for a cross. In one fleet moment he looks up, whips it in and in the last beat of these last dying seconds Torres fabulously heads home, the sheer power of his connection beating James at the near post. As the away end at Fratton Park explodes in sheer joy, so does The Brewers Arms, much to the annoyance of the Portsmouth fans drifting in. As we're hugging each other and punching the air, they're giving us daggers and contemplating aggro. Outnumbered, we quickly finish the beers before returning to the coaches.

There's a party going on on the pavement alongside the long line of buses with The Irregulars, The SOS, Wilcox Tours, and The LBU contingents whooping and celebrating amongst the buses from the rest of the country. Steve Wright is grinning, ruddy cheeked, outside the Irregulars coach and asks me: "Can you defend that team selection? Cos I can't?" He bursts out laughing. "How the *fuck* did we get away with that?"

"Thing is," adds Garner, "if he'd put a full strength team out we'd have won 6-0. Cos they were crap!"

"It's like he's got a death wish. It's madness...," I tell him. " I mean, try and explain it – 'cos I can't."

These sentiments are repeated all around us. A dramatic last-minute victory is being celebrated and simultaneously derided, as the drama was all so unnecessary. We're a better team than that. I pause for breath, almost ashamed to be complaining after another victory but I can't shake off the nagging doubt that we're paying sides too much respect and not playing to our own strengths. Please Rafa, *please* – give us some performances where all we'll have to complain about is the bloody referee! At this moment in time we're top of the league and yet again its been tainted by the scrappy manner in which we've done it.

On the road home we soon forget about the first hour of the game and the victory is being rightly celebrated. The whole bus is chanting and singing; all that's missing is a few beers. This is put right when we pull off the A34 and into a Tesco's car park. The other coaches have similar ideas and suddenly a quiet

Saturday night's grocery run for anti-social shoppers is interrupted by 200 or so of us swarming over the beer and spirits aisles. There's then an ant-like trail of lads carrying cases of Becks and Budweiser across the car-park and back aboard their transport. If I'd have brought my Tesco Club Card and swiped it at everyone's purchase, I'd probably have enough points for a Ginsters Pasty now.

With the beers now flowing the remaining 200 miles fly by. It's time to turn the music up again and pretty soon Gerry, Garner and myself are energetically (that's the polite way of describing it) grooving to Carlos Malcolm's 'Bonanza Ska' much to the amusement of the young uns at the back, who deride our geriatric efforts and challenge us to a dance-off. The lights go on in Gerry's eyes and he moves to the back of the bus and hurls himself into a dazzling exhibition of acrobatic shapes, straight out of Wigan Casino, that leave those of us watching him with twisted blood. He finishes with a crazy-legs cum dying fly back-spin in a pool of spilt beer in the aisle. Sheer magnificence! The young 'uns concede defeat and vow to put this right of future LBU trips. They never do, of course.

I nod off, only to wake to the sound of the entire bus roaring out the LBU anthem, The Specials' 'Message to You Rudy'. I leap to my feet and join in, much to Gerry's delight as he now has his drinking buddy back. As we're dancing it's approaching midnight and it's been another brilliant trip – the kind of day that makes you realise just why you get up at 6am and not get home again until 2 or 3 the next day, and STILL look forward to the next one. But if we're going to go anywhere on this long trip of a season then we need to get the message through to Rafa:

> Stop your messing around
> Better think of your future
> Time you straighten right out
> Creating problems in town...

> Rafa! A message to you, Rafa!

JM

Man City (h)   1-1

League   Sun 22nd Feb

If the last minute victory at 'Eastlands' back in October was the game I thought 'it' might actually be on this season, then this result made me believe it was definitely all over. Not 'think' it was all over, but 'believe'. We were, quite frankly, shambolic and devoid of creativity. From being 7 points clear of the Mancs after Newcastle on the last day of 2008, we went into this game 8 behind them a mere 7 weeks later. Since being hailed as Champions elect after the 5-1 rout, almost everything that could go wrong, has gone wrong. And we haven't helped ourselves. We've contributed to our own collapse. From Gerrard being in the cells within hours of the game, to Rafa's strange attack on Ferguson; from the Mancs' subsequently and inexorably chipping away at our lead with lucky, fluky results because *they actually believe* they can win, to our stumbling, bumbling parade of draws writ large with a lack of self-belief; from the failure and eventual abandonment of Keane to the persistence with Lucas. Since January 10 we've picked up 10 points (including today's) whilst the forces of darkness have collected 24. It's all going horribly wrong.

After the SOS Union AGM at the Olympia, a venue that was so cold it made Fratton Park seem like Waikiki Beach, we retreat into the warmth of a nearby pub. In fact, after the Olympia, outside in the street is warmer. Me, Nico and Paul Rice meet one of Paul's mates, a City fan. He seems a level headed sort, the kind not to crow about their new found riches (I remember them singing 'We're going to buy your club, and burn your ground' back in October). That said, he is confident that they'll get something out of the game today. I laugh, but it niggles. I think he might be right but I'm not letting him know that. When he leaves I tell the others that the mood feels like it did before Wigan, everyone seems nervous.

No Gerrard – he's either still injured or being saved for Madrid; who can tell these days? No Alonso – he's suspended, although Windows' opinion is that he can't tackle and so gives away so many fouls that he's always going to get booked more than he should. And, well, you can guess what else can't you? Yes, Lucas is playing at the expense of Aurelio who did so well at Portsmouth in midfield.

The nervousness I could sense is all around the ground and The Kop is quiet. I just hope it doesn't transfer itself to the team. Then again they themselves probably have their eyes on Madrid in 3 days and their only realistic chance of silverware this season; so I'm not expecting much.

And I'm not disappointed. We miss a few chances, Shay Given plays well, but we never look like we really want it today. Predictably, too, Craig Bellamy of all people spawns a deflected goal then makes a big deal of not wanting to "disrespect" the Anfield faithful by over-celebrating. He's a sulky tit at the best of times, Bellamy, so it's hard to know the difference as he skulks back to the centre circle with a big dramatic gob on him like he's scored at the wrong end – which he has, of course. Kuyt's toe-poked equaliser 12 minutes from time brings a half-hearted expectation that we can snatch a late winner, but Rafa's already played too many Get Out Of Jail cards this year and the game drifts away to a draw. Another 90 Anfield minutes of underachievement. Will a good result in Madrid be enough to paper over the cracks?

Jegsy, Parso, Danny Giles and myself retire to The Valley pub after the game to have a moan and point the finger of blame, but when we get there we can't be arsed. We all know what's wrong. Instead we sit in an embarrassing pub full of foreign Liverpool fans praying there are no Evertonians in here feasting on this comedy gold. There are Norwegians, Dutch, Germans, Irish in green wigs and a smattering of Urdu tribes people in Torres shirts sacrificing a goat by the pool table. When we win, of course, I revel in all this diversity, buzzing off the far-flung appeal of the greatest name in world football – Liverpool F.C. But when we lose – and make no mistake, today feels like a bad, bad defeat, I wish they'd all just leave us in peace to grieve among kindred spirits. Tomorrow's another day, but today feels heavy with finality – a new dawn fades.

Bollocks.

JM

Real Madrid (a)   1-0

Champions League   Wed 25th Feb

We pull up outside his palatial apartment overlooking the mouth of The Mersey, in the cold and dark of a winter morning. The sign reads 'Crinkle Towers: The House of Dodd'. There, framed by a handsome stone Georgian window – the only one ablaze with light in the road – stands Dodd with a mug of tea. He spots the headlights as we draw to a halt and simultaneously salutes, downs his tea and puts on his coat. Two minutes later he's tumbling into the car apparently unencumbered by luggage. He holds up a small pouch, the size of a toaster:

"Spare socks, spare bills and a t-shirt … oh and a new shirt for the match."

This "new shirt" passes by without any comment from Sampson and myself as we are still half asleep. It's an easy journey at this ungodly hour of 5 am, through the tunnel and the empty streets of south Liverpool, down to JLA for our 7am flight to Barcelona. We had rather foolishly let Sammo make the arrangements for this one and as such we're travelling out on the Wednesday (the morning of the game), but not returning home until Friday, spending Thursday night back in Barcelona. Logistically it's a bit arse about face, but it is cheap. Let's just hope there's no delays. All things being equal, we'll have an hour's wait in Barcelona and get to Madrid just after midday.

At the airport we go straight through security with our hand luggage and, with just under an hour to spare, indulge ourselves in a quick pint and a sandwich for breakfast. Bucko and co come barging down towards the Wetherspoons in Departures, swigging from bottles of Becks. He's on our flight, he quietly informs us, along with about another 50 or so other Liverpool fans. We're all catching different connecting flights to Madrid from Barcelona and all arriving within an hour or so of each other. He makes arrangements to meet us in a bar in central Madrid. It's a date which I know we'll never keep.

I spy 'slippage', and know we won't be seeing him again until Boro.

Also in the Departures area are those fans on the 'School Trip'; this being the organised day-trip by the club's 'Travel Partner', Thomas Cook. We seasoned independent travellers like to look down our noses at these 'Day Trippers' as they pay over-the-odds to be led round by stewards, and bussed in and out of stadiums like Japanese tourists doing London and Oxford in the one day. As we sit outside stadiums after games, sipping iced Campari and Soda, they're herded on to coaches and delivered like veal calves in crates back to the airport. As we're dancing on the tables in knocking shops, or being chased by policemen down alleyways, they're suffering buttock cramps in seat 23b somewhere over Holland. If only life was that simple. Truth is, sometimes you have no choice but to use these day-trip services if you can't get by without seeing the Redmen abroad. If time off work is an issue – then its impossible to get to and from most European cities in the same calendar day; and though over-priced, sterile and devoid of interesting diversions, these trips are often the only option for some supporters.

One such beleaguered, time-poor soul is Peter Ford. Peter used to do the mad 3 or 4, even 5, day trips all over Europe with us... and then his kids grew up and family priorities became, well, priorities. And now here he is, a stir-crazy veteran of the war-zone of Vladikavkaz, the Herestrau in Bucharest and the top-floor striptease lounge of the Hotel Sport in Kiev, trudging along with the Euro-virgins and the shirt-wearing tourists towards their charter flight. Like a thoroughbred racehorse reduced to pulling a scrap-cart, with memories of drunken tomfoolery plaguing his ears like flies, he plods towards the gate. I see the hurt, the confusion in his eyes and I know exactly what he's thinking:

"Please God, don't let me have to sit next to Dave Murphy."

* * * *

We arrive in Barcelona and take a leisurely stroll to another terminal for our internal flight. There's an hour to wait and it's Match Day – Real blinking Madrid at that – so we go for a beer. As we sit eating strange Spanish sandwiches, one of the most terrifying moments I've encountered during a life of Euro-trips unfolds. Jegsy delves inside his Man Pouch and produces the item he referred to as he hopped in the car this morning – his new shirt. For a second I'm just gob smacked – so smitten with shock and awe that I'm literally stunned. It's only the gradual convulsions from little Sammo next to me that snap me out of it. Sampson is – and there's no other way of saying this – in complete hysterics. He only laughs like this two or three times a season but when it comes it's historic. The tears are literally cascading down his face as he points at the shirt and tries to speak. He can't say a word – each time he tries to say something it gives way to another demented torrent of giggling. And he's only right, by the way. The shirt is a disgrace. I can't quite believe it's not some surreal joke by the arch-japester Dodd, but it's all coming back to me, now. There was a sheepish phonecall at some piint when he was unnaturally jaunty and kept throwing in these innocent remarks:

"I don't usually go for official club merchandise.... me bird said it was dead cool.... Every single Liverpool fan wears black this, black that.... I just want to wear something a little bit different for Madrid..."

So this is it. It's come to this. Jegsy Dodd plans to wear this monstrosity to the game. The offending article is a navy blue polo shirt bedecked in little pink fluorescent Liverbirds. It's vile. It's hideous. The shirt Jegs now holds aloft for our approval is truly, truly awful yet he seems genuinely astonished, if not also a little hurt, at our guffaws. Sampson still can't speak.

"What do you mean you wore it on LFCTV?" I ask incredulously. "I wouldn't wear that on Crimewatch!"

Sammo pops his head up for breath.

"That'd be the crime..."

"Has it gone out yet? The LFCTV show?"

I don't know if I want to be guilty by association, here.

Jegs looks sheepish.

"Last night..."

"Ha Ha," Sammo slaps his hand on his thigh. "So *that's* what Mono meant! I got a text from him that just said: *Senor Dodd. Que?*"

Jegs solemnly folds it up and carefully places it back in the Liverpool Club Shop plastic bag, vowing to return it for a refund. For once, our rib-tickling pal is not for chortling. He's proper upset at the folly of it all.

"Last we'll see of that, then. I *knew* it was shite..."

"But you've worn it," I remind him.

"S'alright... it doesn't smell," he says checking the receipt is in the bag.

"But you were live on Liverpool's official club channel..."

"So. All the more reason they should give me the dough back – I've modelled it for them for nothing..."

Its gone lunchtime when we land in Madrid and from the text messages

I'm getting the party is well under way. It is mild and sunny day, almost warm, and ideal for sitting outside bars enjoying a few cervezas. In the cab into the city centre Dodd's regretting bringing his coat. He'd watched the Atletico Madrid v Porto game on the telly the night before and had seen the crowd wearing overcoats.

"I thought it must be chilly out here," he tells us winding down the window to get some air in. "Thought I was one step ahead of the game..."

He's half right, too. In the streets around us people are wearing coats and big jumpers, one woman walking her dog is even wearing a full-length fur coat. Meanwhile, sweat is running down my back. I should berate him for advising me to wear a jumper, but he was only trying to help.

Our hotel is slap bang on Puerta Del Sol, the Piccadilly Circus of Madrid. The area is a bit noisy, bustling and crowded, but it's ideally placed for the bars of the Plaza Major and Santa Ana. The one thing that is far from ideal, however, is that it was full. No room at the inn, despite my brandishing the booking confirmation. The guy on reception blames the website, though I suspect they'd double-booked when they realised there was a game on and that we'd got it far too cheaply. He draws a map on a piece of paper, directing us to a sister establishment, and we trudge across Sol and up towards the Gran Via to the High Tech Gran Avenida Hotel. We arrive 20 minutes later bathed in sweat and gasping for a beer. After a 10 minute discussion at reception where they claim to know nothing about the mix-up, the receptionist suddenly taps at her PC and quickly checks us in. And we're in luck: it's been recently refurbished and has that boutique hotel feel that we are becoming used to these days, and at 35 Euro a night each, it's a bargain. After a quick wash and brush-up, I fill my pockets with the essential wet wipes, phone, 60 Euro match-ticket and credit cards and off we set.

On our way back down the sloping shopping street towards Sol we meet The Echo's Tony Barrett who can neither confirm nor deny that Rafa is one bad result away from the sack.

"Nothing would surprise me," he says. "If we get thumped tonight he could be on his way... I don't know."

"Well he's thrown the league away and been beaten by Everton, so if we lose this tie... well, its 3 months left of... well, what? They might just use a bad result here to get rid of him," I say.

Tony just shrugs. He's either being professional and diplomatic, or he is just as much in the dark as the rest of us. We then go straight back to what has become H.Q. for trips to Madrid these last few months: the twin watering holes of the Museo Del Jamon and the Xabriero. The Xabriero is rammed and Corrigan has the 'Gentleman's Dining Club' banner up again calling us on to a belated lunch. After a familiar parade of seafood and wine we move over the road to the Museo where Brian Reade is there with his lad Phil. They'd just been to see Picasso's famous Civil War painting, Guernica, in the Reina Sofia Museum and they're keen to delay the drunken onslaught until as late as possible. I tell Brian of Jegsy and I spending the 3 days before the Atletico game playing out the same conversation each morning:

"Okay, after breakfast we'll walk down towards Atocha and go and see Guernica."

"Righty Ho...little coffee on the way?"

"Sounds like a plan."

Enter the dreaded 'Slippage'. A nip of brandy would find its way into the coffee and a couple of hours later we'd be propping up a bar having a quick cerveza to quench our sightseeing thirst. I've been to Madrid 7 times now and still never seen Guernica. Next time.. next time...

Hooto and Roy turn up, as do Johns Maguire and Buchanan, and Danny Nicholson. Jegsy's chatting with Abbo from Moreton, when Sammo comes in with furrowed brow.

"Everyone you speak to say's Rafa's gone. It's all over the news back home..."

He goes to an unoccupied table with his San Miguel and crouches over his phone, tapping away. A few minutes later he's back, smiling. He shows me a text from Tony Barrett. Tony has just been with Rafa at the team hotel and, far from being on the brink, Rafa has assured Tony that he's in talks to negotiate a new long-term contract.

"Says there'll be big news tomorrow..."

Across the bar from us are two old blokes dressed in the traditional Castizo costume. A Castizo is a kind of Madrileno Pearly King – although a lot less comical. They're wearing stylish black trousers and waistcoats, white shirts and black and white check flat caps. One in particular is shouting something about Real Madrid, and gesticulating madly. He's a bit too proud in his posturing for my liking, and I can think of one or two Reds who might now be face to face with him, finger-jabbing his chest and reminding him of his civic duty to be a bit more welcoming to visitors; shortly to be followed by a flurry of punches with teeth, snot and glasses flying everywhere. When he starts making what look like fascist salutes to us, someone tells him to 'Fuck Off' and we move on up the road whistling 'No Pasaran'.

In a tiny bar at the top of Calle Victoria we reconvene to discuss the frugal ticket situation. I've got one, as does Sampson. Joe Corrigan has one but he's with Paul The Papers and his missus, Gwen. Jegsy doesn't have one and of the 4 others with us they've got one ticket between them. Unlike the Atletico game there seem to be no spares floating round. A planned sortie to relieve Madrid midfielder and pal of the Dutch branch, Wesley Sneijder, of his guest tickets has gone tits up. Disastrously, Mick Kennedy has been left in charge of said tickets and was last seen laughing maniacally and unbuttoning his trousers as he directed a taxi to a whorehouse on the outskirts of the city. We won't see him again this trip. This leaves Joe, Paul and Gwen with a third of a ticket each. Paul says he's going back to the hotel to charge his phone for 20 minutes, and when he's gone Joe quite gallantly gives Gwen his ticket then disappears so she can't argue with him. Gwen is stunned. She sits there open-mouthed and then splutters, "I can't go the game on my own." When Paul returns she tries to give him the ticket and they end up arguing, as neither will go to the game without the other. Paul then gets angry at Joe for putting them both in this position. I try and raise Joe on the phone but he's gone into hiding somewhere with a bottle of Rioja. Shortly before he and Gwen come to punches and file for divorce, Paul decides to sell the ticket at face value to one of ticketless lads in the bar. Sammo meanwhile, prompted by Joe's altruism, passes his ticket on to Glen Mono whose lifetime dream it is to watch The Reds in The Bernabeu. I tell Sammo to watch it on the telly with Joe and let me know where to meet them after the game. Jegsy has disappeared, wandered off to find Bucko and the possibility of a ticket.

Around 7pm, still several hours before kick-off, there's a flurry of text-messages and I call DNA Dave about the planned 'bevvy' in Bobby Wilcox's honour. Several dozen of us congregate in a large bar at top of Calle Victoria, the scene of Bobby's last swallee on European soil. It was the bar where he appeared wearing Day-Glo green sunglasses with flashing lights the night Azzie was pickpocketed. Paul Rice assumes statesman-like control of proceedings and after a short eulogy we raise our glasses in the great Redman's honour.

I leave just over an hour before kick-off and get a taxi up to the stadium, feeling incredibly guilty about being the only one of us with a ticket. I call Joe – he eventually answers and tells me he'll find a suitably well-appointed bodega to watch the match in and he'll wait there until I return after the game. After a brief journey north along the Paseo De La Castellana out of central Madrid, I can sense the traffic beginning to thicken and slow, and then the driver pulls over a few hundred yards short of the stadium. I've about an hour to 'waste' so I head to the nearest bar I can find outside the Bernabeu, right opposite the home-end. There are plenty of Scousers around looking for tickets and warning me to look out for the Ultras Sur who are out looking to pick off Liverpool fans – preferably those on their own.

Promising myself, after my Atletico farce, to get in early I drain my beer and go for a mooch around the stadium. It's an impressive sight, far grander than the Nou Camp, and a much more traditional football icon than, say, The San Siro in Milan (which is equally magnificent but looks space-age with its huge roof of massive steel girders). I pick my way through the car park crammed with thousands of bikes and scooters and go round to the back of the away 'end' to buy a scarf – my aim being to get something that looks like it was actually bought here, at the game. After a bit of haggling – during which I twice offered more than the guy was asking – I settle on a gloriously tacky half-Real, half-Spain 'Raul' scarf with a picture of his face on it. I thought it looked okay at the time. But like surfing on Ebay at 2am, it's best not to go shopping when pissed. Ask Mick Kennedy.

The bars round here have shut up and I turn to see what is obviously our section. There are dozens of flashing blue lights and the street is closed off with yellow barriers. There's a massed huddle between me and the entrance, composed of lads looking for a 'bunk' and policemen checking tickets. Behind this melee stand Liverpool club stewards and Bryce Morrison, the club secretary, looking exasperated. He looks like he has no control over events (which, as a guest, he doesn't) and I remember thinking 'he looks like he's about to have a heart attack'. He catches my eye and calls over.

"John, if you've got a ticket **get in now!**"

He sounds like he means it, so I squeeze through and ease my ticket out of my pocket, keeping a firm grip on it as I bring the holy billet up to show to the first copper, aware that the shameful practice of ticket snatching is becoming more and more a problem as tickets for these games become more and more scarce. I feel a nudge in my back and a Scouse voice says: "Can I double-click in with you lad?" I nod, though looking ahead of me it appears to be mission impossible. The copper looks at my folded ticket and I nod at the lad behind me, as if I have two tickets. Amazingly, the copper stands aside and lets us both through. "Yiss!" grins the lad. It's a short lived victory as it now becomes clear there is a second ticket check at some turnstiles and the bar-codes on the tickets are being scanned. "Sorry lad," I tell him and go in, leaving him in no-man's land contemplating an unlikely hurdle over the 4ft high barrier.

It's a long walk up to the top tier where our 'seats' are, longer than the hike at either Barcelona or Valencia, and comparable in the UK only to the lung-busting climb into the stratosphere at St James Park which leaves even 20-year olds gasping and crimson-faced at the top. Well, think double that and you get an idea of the ascent of Mount Bernabeu. Apparently there are escalators, but they weren't working and I have to stop several times on the way up to recover, like a diver wary of 'the bends'. When I eventually surface, the view is fantastic. It would have been breathtaking, if I'd had any breath left to take. We're on the top tier and our tickets are £20 cheaper than the 88 Euro seats in the tier below and yet the view is virtually identical. The Champions League Musical Extravaganza is still being played out by dozens of children on the pitch as that ghastly anthem is played at full volume; just in case anyone's forgotten why we're here. I stand at the front of the tier and look up at thousands of faces searching for someone I know. Then I hear:

"CAIRO !"

Peter Ford's impressively hooked nose heralds his presence, as does this exclamation in his best Fast Show, Rowley Birkin voice. I climb the very steep steps up towards where he's standing holding onto the barrier for dear life, and edge down the row to greet him with a bear hug, at which he loses his balance. Holding on to each other, our footing now as tenuous as Rafa's job prospects, we pirouette momentarily – then topple sideways, but are caught in mid-air by 3 nearby strangers who push us, begrudgingly, back into the upright position. They are not amused. As we stand there, still locked in a bear hug, I whisper the immortal words we'd said to each other on countless occasions over the years.

"Mate, I'm absolutely bladdered.."

"Me too," he replies. We begin giggling uncontrollably but all around us there are tuts of disapproval from what I can only describe as uptight day-trippers upset that drunken football fans have turned up to ruin their nice comfy spec. It's not like we've come barging in pissing everywhere, knocking over small children and and swearing like dockers is it? I mean what the fuck is happening to our following in Europe? Where were this lot in Kosice? In

Strasbourg? In Moscow? In Bucharest? Istanbul has a lot to answer for.

Peter and I hold onto each other throughout the opening 20 minutes of the game, fearful of toppling to our doom over the balcony. We are amongst hundreds of fans who only open their mouths to sing the 'Torres bounce' song, and who're ridiculously pleased with themselves when they do so. To be fair there's not a great deal on the pitch for us to sing about and at least they're enthusiastic about something, even if that's just being here. Once again, it's not an attacking Liverpool side out there. We are defending in depth and playing on the break, relying on long balls ahead of Torres and hoping to stretch their defence. Real have all the possession but they're just not hurting us. Rafa's plan is probably working exactly as he's hoped: keep it tight and hope to snatch something if an opportunity presents itself. It's something I suspect the players have become used to from our many cautious, drawn home games so far this season, and practice makes perfect – no?

Both sides have one decent chance, but Raul and then Torres hurry to get their shots off and fire straight at the keeper. At least Torres' fierce cross-shot forces Casillas to parry for a corner. Despite Real's territorial dominance the highlight of the half is Alonso's fabulous shot from 10 yards inside his own half which is tipped over the bar for a corner. He wins the ball brilliantly and shoots immediately; the save causing Peter to say to me:

"Thank fuck for that! If that one'd gone in we'd have ended up down there...." He points straight down to the near touchline several hundred feet below us. Shortly afterwards the whistle blows for half-time to great applause from our section and I ask Peter if he fancies a pint.

"Can't mate – straight back the airport after the game."

"I can't handle this lot...," I tell him, casting my gaze upon the fans around me. "I should be with the lads." I recount the ticket issues and the fact that everyone I travelled with, or have been drinking with today, isn't actually in the ground. Truth is, I miss them all. These trips aren't just about watching The Reds play, they're about watching The Reds play in the company of your friends. And tonight, though it's the Bernabeu blah, blah, blah... there's little in the way of camaraderie, laughs or general silliness. What's worse, I feel like a fish out of water with these day-trippers surrounding me. That's it! I decide:

"I'm off...." Peter grins. He understands. As I'm escorted out into the street by a Liverpool FC travel steward, who's guiding me past the Spanish stewards and coppers, I feel a real guilt that my ticket could have gone to one of the lads still outside on the street looking for a way in. I've become blasé about all this and they're obviously desperate. I need to sort all this nonsense out and get a grip. But not tonight. In a taxi back to Sol I text Joe to find out where he is. He's in a bar on Plaza de Tirso de Molina with Sammo, Gwen and Papers. There's no sign of Jegsy. Sammo says the last he heard Jegs was watching the game with Bucko in a pub up near the ground. When I arrive two things immediately strike me: (1) There's no telly (2) Sampson is puddled. I suggest we move somewhere with the game on, but before we can do so we need to finish off the wine which I do by glugging down a large glass, and Sammo achieves by knocking his all over the table. Five minutes later, down a dark, narrow street a hundred yards into the barrio, we chance upon a scruffy, neighbourhood pub, El Cervezeria Marbella, with the game being played loudly on a large telly, and packed with locals. This'll do – excellent! I get the first round in of four beers, plus an espresso and bottle of water for Sampson. As I turn to put the coffee down in front of him he's already sprawled across the table, out for the count and sleeping like a baby. Aw bless!

The second half is as unexciting as the first and played out in a similar vein: Real have the ball, we defend and hold them back easily. There's just one shot over the bar from Robben to worry about. We're shouting at the telly and cheering The Reds and the locals seem to be graciously tolerating us in their midst. There are half a dozen or so 'lads' in their 20s across the bar who aren't smiling, and I keep half an eye on them as we lay into the plate of chicken thighs that the owner has plonked down in front of us. When we get a free kick wide out on the right about 10 minutes from the end I have a sudden premonition.

"Joe, what'll you do if we score from this?" He looks at me grinning like the idiot he is. And I glance over at the Spanish 'lads' who are looking at us.

Seconds later, our little corner of the bar explodes. Papers is whooping and punching the air, Joe grabs me and kisses me, Gwen beams and applauds like Paris Hilton in a new handbag shop, and Sammo grumbles and shifts about in his seat. As the dust settles the Spanish 'lads' file out of the bar, the last one or two looking at us. I immediately think we're going to get jumped when we leave and can almost hear them sharpening stiletto knives in the street. Joe meanwhile is ordering beers for everyone in the bar, including the barmen who respond by giving us more food. I spend the last five minutes beaming and slapping Joe on the back – utterly euphoric. I almost regret leaving the stadium, but not quite. I'm with my pals, and I know that all over Madrid there'll be pockets of Liverpool fans in bars running out in the street

The authors in the Museo de Jamon, Madrid

and jumping on top of taxis, dancing with policemen and kissing old ladies, and all in company of their mates.

After giving Sampson a fireman's lift to a taxi and then realising I don't know the name of the hotel, I resort to breathing on the window of the cab and drawing a map of Sol and the streets around it, then pointing and telling the driver: "Aqui!" He deposits us a hundred yards short as the street is pedestrianised and I haul the inebriated and sleeping Sampson up the hill, through reception past a laughing night porter, and up to bed. Pausing only to acknowledge the Deja Vu of the moment I turn and head for the Xabriero.

Back in Calle Victoria the lads who never made the game are celebrating. Joe's made a beeline for here from the Marbella and has the flag up on the wall again. I settle down with a pint and, in memory of Bobby Wilcox, buy a pair of green Day-Glo sunglasses from a wizened old bloke who haggles me up from 2 to 5 Euros. I switch on the flashing lights, don the glasses, and thinking I must look like a complete tool but not giving a toss, I settle back to await the night's entertainment beginning in earnest. Nico and the Belgians arrive after about an hour, having dodged the Ultra Sur near the Metro station near the ground, and put their 'Rioja Gran Reserva' flag up alongside the 'Dining Club' one. Nico's marvellously drunk and stands in the middle of the pub leading us in a sing-song. After one or two glasses (maybe bottles) of wine he falls asleep standing up and is manoeuvred against a wall to prevent any unpleasant awkwardness as the place is filling up rapidly. It's soon as packed as The Albert on derby day, and getting very, very hot, and I have to get up and go outside for a breather. I stand there in the street chatting with some of the lads when I see a familiar figure toddling down towards me, however something doesn't look quite right...

It's Giles, Danny Giles. But not as we know him. What is it? As he approaches I suddenly see the dark brown stains on his red and white bar scarf. Then I realise his head is bandaged. It's blood!

"Danny? What happened?"

"Got jumped like. Yer know. No drama."

"Where? How?"

"Outside the ground. Got me from behind. Sneaky. Like the Ities," he babbles, apparently completely unfazed by it all.

"Now you really do look like Rab C Nesbitt, Danny" I tell him, knowing this is a lifetime's ambition of his. "So what happened...?"

He tells me of standing outside a bar near the Bernabau a few hours before kick-off, when an Ultra approached him from behind and coshed him before legging it.

"That's a twat's trick that Dan. I mean why you? There's plenty of boys here who'd have been up for it."

"Sneaky, you see.," he explains. He was then taken to hospital and kept in for 4 hours under observation. I think one of the nurses did it through a gap in the curtains.

"So you missed the game?" I ask.

"Oh aye. 60 quid down the swanny."

"Oh well," I tell him, placing my sunglasses on him, "...at least you weren't alone. Come and have a bevvy."

We return to the Xabriero where the sing song is again in full swing. This is what it's all about: a bar full of great Reds celebrating a win on foreign soil. A bar full of your mates who's company – whether asleep or concussed – you enjoy. No, not 'enjoy' – LOVE!

"Bring on your Internazionale

Bring on the Romans by the score!
Barcelona – Real Madrid
Who the fuck you trying to kid -
'Cos LIVERPOOL are the team that we adore!"

JM

Real Madrid   The morning after   Thurs 26th Feb

Oooh, where am I? There's rustling in the room as I tentatively open one eye to survey the carnage. Johnny Mackin is standing there fully naked about to enter the shower. Jesus. If you asked me what vision I would most like to wake up to after an epic night on the lash, the sight of Johnny Mac staggering round with his cock out would definitely not be it. I'm trying to think back to see if there's any little snippets I can recall. I remember getting lost and circumnavigating the whole of central Madrid looking for the hotel; which obviously I must have found otherwise I wouldn't be here. Oh yes and there was an attempted mugging which I avoided by just acting mad. Top tip for you here: wherever you are in the world it doesn't matter what country, hustlers, dippers, brasses and anyone else who wants to relieve you off your money, they all have one thing in common. They don't like nutters. So if you think you're going to get hassled, don't get all defensive and sheepish. Run over to them with your arms aloft shouting "I am the son of Satan, Sam Allardyce is Lord, now give us a taste of your Marmite you tight bastards. If you haven't got Marmite, just give us some fuckin' marzipan." Just watch them go. They may not print stuff like that in your 'Rough Guide' books but it's always worth remembering that hustlers don't like nutters. So what else happened? Oh yeah, I have vague memories of a waif-like Yossi Benayoun leaping like a salmon to power a header into the Madrid net. Surely that must've been a dream. I also remember coming in and being confronted with the sight of Kev Sammo's bare arse at three in the morning. He seems to have had trouble getting over that tricky final hurdle of just getting under the covers. What is it with blokes when they're pissed at European Aways? Is there a secret charter that says that you must expose yourself and bare flesh to your room mates for no reason whatsoever. Well I'm gonna put forward a motion to have it banned. We're not in the army barracks, we're not gay and I don't think it's fair on the less outgoing people like myself to go to sleep with a bare bum exposed on the next bed and then having to wake up to see John Mac's pink dangly bits being paraded in front of my hangover. No Thank You. I blame Rick Parry – not for any reason except that it is standard Liverpool procedure to blame Rick Parry for everything. Starting from next season, these is the rules; no more nudity, use towels, sort yourself out in the bathroom and regain your modesty. Understood? Good. I'll move on.

When I turn my phone on, there's loads of texts saying Danny Giles had been attacked outside the ground. Apparently he'd been having a bevvy with half a dozen Reds in a bar up the road when a big mob of Madrid Ultras burst in and coshed them all. Danny was taken to hospital, missed the match and had five stitches in a head wound. One of the other lads also had his head split open. As it happens, it turns out we were in the next street when all this was going off. Which begs the question, if these Ultras are all so big and tough, then why didn't they come to our street for a bit of a tear up if they're so desperate for a scrap. Because where we were there were about 300 Liverpool all singing, chanting and being boisterous so it's not like they couldn't hear us cos the place was absolutely bouncing. Anyway Danny Giles survived and got his name in the Echo and best of all, got to wear a bandage around his head – just like his hero, Rab C Nesbitt. I can't wait to see him. I just wish LFC TV or someone could've interviewed him with his turban on. That would have been priceless.

Anyway we're up and running. We've done the three S's, shit, shower and shave. Fresh clobber on and we're off to the airport to catch a flight to Barcelona where we'll be spending the Thursday night. Kev and John have a gab with the Skem lads from 306 – Ian Lewis, and the famous gargling twins Chris and Andy Hudson – but I'm not the most sociable person when I've got a head that's been in a blender, so I just pretend to read a Spanish newspaper and keep schtum. We reach Barca after an uneventful flight and a ridiculously over-priced taxi ride. I've driven taxis long enough now so I know when we're being had off and this slimy little twat, with his fake shades on the top of his greasy fuckin' grinning head took us to the cleaners. I absolutely hate getting ripped off but if you complain too much it starts the day off on the wrong note, so you're snookered really. Put it this way, the cab on the way back to the airport from the same place was less than half of the one coming which really pissed me off. The hotel's fine, a bit how you say, compact. I've seen bigger bird boxes but it's clean and it's central so that'll do for me.

We're still a little bit dazed after the whole 'mad Madrid malarkey' but like true ageing hedonists we soldier on manfully. John leads us to his favourite tapas bar in the city which is a Basque place called Bilbao-Berria. Wow, imagine having a favourite eating place in a foreign city? How cool is that? I want one. I want to be able to say to my mates in the centre of Prague or Paris one winter's evening "Hey, why don't I take you guys down to Dino's place, it's my favourite restaurant in the whole of town. God, it almost makes you want to take up cigarettes just so you can blow smoke in their faces after you've said it. Anyway this Bilbao place was sound. I'm still a bit of a novice on the old tapas scene but I enjoyed it. Haven't got a clue how it all works though. How they work out what you've had, when you don't even know yourself. All these tiny little meals like a square inch of toast with a blob of cheese, an olive, a prawn, a shirt button and an earlobe stacked on top. You almost feel like you're stealing the Borrowers' dinner or something, or lifting the Lilliputian's lunch. Hang on a mo. Stealing from the Borrowers. I like the sound of that. "Stealing from the Borrowers." That's the next album title sorted then.

We go from bar to bar at a leisurely pace. None of the hyperactive eagerness of yesterday. John's got another bar he wants to show us. He talks it up a bit, saying what a laugh it was when he was last in there. After a ten minute walk we finally locate it and walk through the doors of the much lauded 'El Cid'. It's crap. There's just us three and three old biddies in there and the old girls are going at it hammer and tong. In the hour we were there, I don't think they stopped for breath once. Mad isn't it? Women the world over do love to just go on and on and on – even in a crummy side street bar in Barca that smells of boiled socks. Anyway Mackin is reprimanded on his poor choice of bar and admits the last time he was in there he was twisted beyond any rhyme or reason with about twenty other Redmen, so we'll let him off this time. As the night unfolds we discuss the frustrations of supporting a schizophrenic team like ours. After yesterdays win, we read in an English paper that we are now rated as the top team in Europe – yet we can't beat Stoke City home or away. We've just played a trilogy of matches against our bitter, twisted city rivals and failed to beat them on each occasion. The last few years we've beaten all the small sides but failed against the big boys. Now it's the other way round. Does your head in but I suppose that's what it's all about. We all agree on one thing though and that is this: that we've blown the league for yet another year. The draw at home against City was a killer and I think players, fans, manager and media all know it. It's crazy to think that we've just beaten the most famous club side in the world in their own backyard and yet we're still pulling faces and moaning about where it all went wrong. Footy eh? Fuckin' mad.

We slope up the road to a decent looking gaff by the name of Schillings which sounds a bit German if you ask me, but you didn't, so I won't mention it. We get the shock of our lives when we walk in to find none other than Michael Potter of Ole Scotty Road sitting there on the arm of an attractive brunette by the name of Dawn. Mick's as old school as they come. He's seen it, done it and got the stains to prove it. I'm amazed he wasn't at the game but the hassle of getting tickets just puts you off sometimes and he's thought "sod it, I'll have a couple of nights in Barca with me bird instead." Obviously he didn't bank on me, Sammo and Mackin showing up, but the two of them seem genuinely pleased to see us. Still, we don't want to cramp their style, so after a bottle of middling plonk we do the right thing and leave the love birds alone.

We head off in search of food and are immediately surrounded by a gaggle of eager prostitutes. We keep walking but they're all over us. I'm trying to tell this one who's got her arm around me in the politest possible terms to fuck off but she's having none of it. She's about 4ft tall and looks like Shaun Wright-Phillips with a boob job and she wants ME to pay her for a shag! She must be having a laugh – I'd rather shag Jimmy Krankie! Our pace quickens until it's almost like the chase around the tree on the Benny Hill show, when they used to speed it up at the end. We manage to shake them off but god it wasn't easy. I never knew us three were so attractive to the opposite sex. We finish the night off in a restaurant that funnily enough John discovered on one of his many gastro-tours. He reckons Keith Floyd, the chef, has done a programme from here. The place has an enormous, furnace-hot outdoor grill with literally a hundred chickens grilling slowly on the barbecue as people queue outside and in. It's great but my bed is calling and we've got to do all that getting up early business to catch flights, etc, so we just order, eat and do one.

We wake up to a text from our 'man in the know' Tony Barrett, who informs us that Rick Parry has announced he's gonna 'walk the plank' at the end of the season. Well I suppose something had to give but I don't think him going is gonna solve all the problems with a wave of a wand. Still, even if we had Ken Dodd as Chief Exec, we'd still be there following the boys in Red. I get home about 2pm and am just about to go to get some provisions for Boro tomorrow when I notice my tyre's flat. So here I am within 15 minutes of getting home, jacking my car up, covered in shite trying change a wheel so I can get some ale for tomorrow. Never ending isn't it?

JD

Middlesbrough (a)   0-2

League   Sat 28th Feb

It's an early start and if I'm honest, I could've done with swerving this one. The recovery period from getting back yesterday and getting up at 7 this morning is way too short. In an ideal world I'd have surfaced about midday and we'd have been playing at home but life ain't always that easy. So I put the jump leads on my nipples and 'hey presto', let's go. I'm up and running. Today we're travelling on the famous Bobby Wilcox coach. Even though Bobby's gone, it's still Wilcox tours, and it carries his famous motto: 'Never knowingly under drunk' – which definitely sounds like our type of coach. The pick-up is outside the Throstle's Nest on Scotland Road at 8.15am, so we can get some miles under our belt before we stop for light refreshments. Our MC for today is big Phil McKewan who has taken over the unenviable task of filling Bobby's shoes. The job description varies between ringmaster, tour guide, organiser, secretary and unsung hero. I'm sitting next to Parso, with Bucko and Mercer sat behind. I know most of the faces on the bus but I don't know them all by name. There's Dava Hardman, Macca from Kirkby, Jimmy Blundell from Vauxy, even the legendary Lenny Woods is onboard – still, I'm pleased to say, sporting his early 70's Glam Rock barnet. Is right Lenny lad – keep the faith. "Some girls will, some girls won't, some girls need a little loving and some girls don't." That's right, that's right, that's right, that's right, I really love those Tiger feet, that's neat, that's neat, that's neat, that's neat, I really love those Tiger feet." Get in there!! There's no stopping me now. "You better look out, you better beware, you better watch out if you've got long black hair." Fuckin' hell, where was I? Oh yeah, on the coach going to God forsaken Middlesbloodyboro. We stop off for a livener in a quaint little town called Barnard Castle. We have a quick 'Full English', and then dive into the Turks Head for a couple of gargles. The swinging pub sign outside features an evil looking man with a white turban on looking remarkably like a certain Danny Giles aka, for one week only, the Sultan of Birkenhead. Maybe they're related in some way. Who knows? We get the call to 'sup up' from big Phil, who's also in the Turks Head. The coach is leaving in ten minutes so we all pile out together and walk through the quaint little back streets past the twitching curtains and back to the bus. You can just imagine the phone calls that are going back and forth between the residents of this sleepy little market town. "Dorothy, it's me, Fiona. There's a big menacing gang of men just walked past our front gate all dressed in dark clothing. Must have been nigh on fifty of them talking ten to the dozen in that uncouth Liverpool accent. It looks like they're heading your way dear, so you'd better get your washing in quickly. And tell Reg to lock his lawn mover away in the shed. You know what they're like." "Ooh, I know. I don't know what the world's coming to."

We head off to the bleak, joyless place that is Middlesbrough. It's actually sunny when we get there which is totally out of character for such a grim town. Because it's a fairly new ground there are no decent pubs to visit where you can meet your mates and study the locals. So we are reduced to just standing around the outside looking bored. There's always people you know like Kev Daigle and his mates, Matt and Gary Allt. Luke from Cork's there as well. And there's Chris from Brighton's lad, Big Gilly who lives up in Newcastle these days, though he's originally from Kirkby. It's a great turnout and it's Boro's first sell out of the season, which is mad when you think they've had derbies against Sunderland and Newcastle here and played most of the big boys. It must be the irresistible pulling power of LFC. As usual the team sheet raises a few eyebrows. Martin Skrtel is at right back. Now there's a new one. He's probably never played right back before in his life but for some reason he is today – and El Zhar's in as a right winger.

The bare facts of the game; Boro scored a spawny one through an Alonso own goal to go in at 1-0 up at half time. You always felt Liverpool could get back into it. The harsh truth is that although we dominated possession (72% to 28%) we never looked like scoring. El Zhar missed a good chance early on in the second half. Babel did his usual impression of MC Hammer dancing on hot coals with a blindfold on. Like a hyperactive kid playing tick on his dinner break, banging into people, falling over and then getting up and doing it all again. One day it all might just click and he'll become a top footballer but not if that day has a 'y' in it. Dirk Kuyt had a bad day at the office as well. Played as a lone striker. His first touch let him down time and time again. The away end got more and more restless and although we support our team through thick and thin, there were some fans who were, to put it mildly, totally pissed off with the performance. Tuncay slotted Boro's second to make it 2-0 and that basically was it. Gerrard and Carragher were taken off as an indication of our surrender, so there was to be no great barnstorming comeback. The young Ngog came on to try and salvage something from the miserable afternoon but it wasn't to be. We trudged out of the ground for the long journey home knowing that our rivals from the 'darkside' have already got one hand on that Premiership title which would equal our record of 18 wins.

We get to the coach and are escorted all the way back to Leeds. Every slip road off the main route home is blocked off by 'plod'. I don't know what the police are expecting us to do as barely anybody on this coach has the energy to open a bag of crisps, never mind ransack the county of Yorkshire. I slump back in my seat, close my eyes and mull over the last seven days, trying to pick the bones out of it and attempting to make some kind of sense of it all.

As weeks go, it's been a long old topsy-turvy kind of one in a rollercoaster kind of season and to be perfectly honest I am absolutely done in. Three matches in six days where I've drank enough beer to sink a ship, had every emotion that this ridiculous game can throw at you. I haven't had a decent sleep for ages and the dark and mysterious Hot Lips barely recognises me. The bags under my eyes are growing by the day as is the swollen stomach that is beginning to protrude forever outwards. The hair is thinning and greying at an unstoppable rate and my headaches over Rafa's selections and substitutes are getting so frequent that I live in a permanent state of neuralgia.

In short, Liverpool Football Club is slowly sucking away my sanity, my health and my life. Cast your eyes around the weather beaten faces on this coach going home and you can see that our title chances have just disappeared over the horizon in a cloud of dust. Deep down we knew last week, when we failed to deal with a mediocre City team, that the white flag was about to be hoisted. Yes we've had a great week in Madrid with all the Champions League razzamatazz. All that glitter, fanfare and showbiz bollocks that goes with it but what's the point when you come back to the brutal reality of the Prem and get stuffed by a shite Boro team that haven't won a match in three fuckin' months? It's like working in a mindless, soul destroying job and then going to Las Vegas for a couple of days for a blow out – and the reality is that you've got to come back to that head wrecking job. People might say "You're lucky. Imagine supporting Leeds or Leicester or Luton. They won't get the chance to go to the Bernabéu Stadium." Well so fuckin' what. I really couldn't give a shit. I am a Liverpool fan and we had that league within our grasp and we blew it. The trophy was there looking at us saying: "Come on Rafa! Come 'ed, Stevie. I'm all yours if you want me."

Like stumbling into the sexiest woman's bedroom in the world, and she's beckoning you over, licking her lips. This is your moment. You unzip your kecks and hop around with one leg in and one leg out. You fumble around in a panic as you realise you can't get an erection. It's all there for the taking but you just can't get over the stage fright. The big chance has come and gone before your very eyes as she says "don't worry it's not your fault, I probably just need someone who's got a bit more experience – someone who knows what they're doing." And that's it. It's all over. That's exactly what our team have just done. The chance was there for all to see. And what did we do? We bottled it. We drew, and we drew, and we drew, when we should've just gone for it. Let's face facts, Chelsea and Arsenal won't ever be this poor again. They've both underachieved massively and will strengthen in the summer. If our signings from last summer are repeated we may as well forget it. Robbie Keane; sold within six months at a four million quid loss and with no replacement. Albert Riera; bright start, ran out of ideas. Philipp Degen; his performance away at Tottenham in the League Cup had the poise, agility and awareness of one of Anthony Gormley's statues on Crosby beach. And last but not least Dossena. Ah good ol' Dossena; the man who Rafa spent three years tracking and then spent seven million rips to sign. Dear oh dear, and to think Stephen Warnock was offloaded to Blackburn for buttons because he wasn't seen as good enough. Well if Dossena is better than Warnock, I know nothing whatsoever about football. In all my years watching, and following and adoring this team of ours, I've picked up nothing about the game. If Dossena is a footballer, I simply throw the towel in. To me, his is the signing that most baffles me. We spent 7 or 8 million quid on this lad. If Rafa had turned round and gone – "I've got no choice but to throw Insua in. I haven't got the dough to buy everyone I need" then the fans would've been right behind that. We'd know that the kid is raw, but we'd indulge him and support him, because we understood that Rafa was blooding him a year or so ahead of the plan. But what does he do? He wastes millions on a lad who he drops after a couple of games… and puts Insua in, instead! Between Dossena and Keane, that's £25 million on unwanted talent that might have gone towards, I dunno… Ribery, or Silva or Arshavin. Some little wizard who can actually change a game. I just don't get it, sometimes. Is it really that difficult being a Top European Coach? Probably is, you know. What do we poor fools who just turn up, know?

So there you are, another crazy week in the soap opera that is LFC. We might well win the Sooper Dooper, all singing, all dancing, Champions League (again) and yes Man U might lose all their remaining games and by some strange twist of football fate we could make the comeback of all comebacks and bring home Number 19 – but don't hold your breath. My biggest concern now, is that we don't just drop like a stone. Collapse like the middle order of an England cricket team. We must keep our dignity and battle on. It's not just the players who'll need motivating but the fans as well. We've got Sunderland on Tuesday and it's gonna be hard to summon up the spirit for *that* – but we have to stick at it. For now the main thing is sleep. I'm skint, I'm knackered and I'm disillusioned but the show must go on, as they say – or in our case, the pantomime must proceed. 'Rafa's a genius!'. 'Oh no he isn't', 'Oh yes he is', 'Oh no he isn't', 'They're behind yooooou', 'Aston Villa are behind yooooou'. Fuck it. I'm going to bed. It's been a long, long, long, long day.

JD

Sunderland (h) 2-0

League Tue 3rd Mar

A cold, windy and wet evening and I wonder why I'm even bothering. I'm also wondering why I'm here so early. Shenans is empty – there's usually Stewey here at least, ranting about something or other, and I'd have thought he wouldn't pass up this opportunity to tell us all how right he was about Rafa, about Lucas, Keane, Babel, Alonso, Ngog and so on and so on. But there's no-one. It seems we've all given up and we're licking our wounds in private. So I take a walk around town eventually finding myself down at the riverfront in front of the Liver Buildings. At least the view down here is some kind of solace, some kind of soul food. I've been avoiding thinking about Saturday's fiasco, but deep down we all know that it's put a top hat on a disastrous 2009. We've been pants. Crap. Shite. The Madrid result apart, this year has been a complete disaster and don't let anyone tell you otherwise. Far worse writers than me will be well paid to fill tomes with statistical fluff showing how we've controlled games, had more shots, conceded less goals, had longer throw-ins etc, but those of us who've been there and actually seen the games, felt the anguish and despaired at the ineptitude, know that we are not 0.36% shot-accuracy away from being better than the Mancs.

I suspect Rafa knows it as well, no matter how brave a face he puts on in public. With nothing to play for domestically I expect he'll be concentrating all his eggs in the European Cup basket. So I'm not expecting much from tonight. And I'm not disappointed.

It's the familiar story we've come to know and loathe: plenty of possession, lots of passing, and very little penetration. Yawn. Up in Block 306 however, the acceptance of our parlous situation manifests itself as a strange, carefree abandonment. The pressure is off and there's a kind of gallows humour about the place. Jegsy in particular is messing around like a 12 year old and shouting random silliness like "Knickers Knackers Knockers – We Support The Dockers" as well as cheering hugely when Lucas Leiva gets the ball, which thankfully wasn't very often. To be fair, at least there's been some progress this year. When Lucas' name was read out before kick-off it drew a smattering of derision and a fair bit of booing. This in turn, saw a large section of the crowd turn on the booers, though they fell short of taking the response to its natural conclusion and chanting Lucas' name. Is it because the shame of the West Ham game has touched a raw nerve on The Kop, or is it that when the result isn't vital we are prepared to be more patient with players?

A dull game limps goalless to half-time, although it could have been much worse had Kenwyne Jones ("Sounds like a firm of solicitors," says Jegs) not fluffed an absolute sitter after skinning Skrtel. Down on the concourse the reaction to be first half is understandably muted. Joynty is asking if anyone can remember the last time we scored in the first half.

"I know everyone's making a big deal out of the late winners, but in most of those games we should have been 2 or 3 up before we eventually scrambled a winner." he says, "We shouldn't need to be doing that.... aw, fuckin' hell, that's all we need...." His voice trails off as he spots Windows coming over, brandishing his latest anti-Rafa tome: a good 20 pages of neatly hand-written biro. Accompanied by an "I told you so, I told you so!" that we've become all too familiar with, he hands out the evidence for the prosecution. Thankfully there are only 4 copies so I manage to avoid having to take one and then feign interest in actually reading it. I have this image of him late at night, quietly beavering away like a Lindisfarne Scribe, bent over a desk, quill in hand, transcribing the gospels by candlelight. You have to admire his dedication if not his opinions.

The 2nd half is slightly better – and I'm taking credit for our opening goal! After three cries of "be a winger, Albert!" shouted more in hope than expectation, Riera does indeed skin his man down the left and gets a deep cross in towards the onrushing Ngog who gratefully nods home for a very welcome 1-0.

Jegs again on his knees smoking. It can't be nerves, this time!

"I can't smoke in me cab these days, can I? I only come the game for a ciggie..."

Benayoun adds a second after A-L-B (clap-clap!) E-R-T (clap! Clap!) once again beats his man and whips in the sort of cross that is generally described as "wicked" – so much so that the keeper can only parry the ball into the path of Yossi who prods home, and the relief all round takes the form of Monty Python humour.

"This is goal crazy madness!" says Brian Reade in a silly voice.

"Another Stromsgodset, surely..." says LouLou.

"Come on, Rafa – less of the gung-ho stuff. Let's stick with what we've got," shouts Roy Boulter.

Sammo leans into me and whispers.

"Know what, though. Beat them at theirs, put a birra pressure on.... They'll wobble, Man.U. Telling you, John – this isn't over yet."

And just as I was resigned to another year's wait in vain, I'm starting to think we might just do it. By God but it's a thankless life, this supporters chalice from which we willingly sip!

JM

Real Madrid (h)   4-0

Champions League   Tue 10th Mar

A lot rests on tonight, even if that's only keeping the season alive for a few more weeks. Though we might just keep Real Madrid at bay tonight, we'll probably struggle in the next round. I mean Sunderland never presented us any problems at all a week ago, but we still struggled to impose ourselves on the scoreline. My mind keeps drifting back to Middlesbrough though, and how an unnecessarily chopped and changed team capitulated just 3 days after winning in Madrid. That was Boro's first win in 15 games, for Chrissake! They hadn't scored a league goal in 6 weeks! They are, in short, complete and utter shite! Yet they beat us – and easily, too. For other teams (Bolton, Everton … I ask you, Everton!) a visit to the Riverside is a guaranteed 3 points. We couldn't even get the draw. The game seemed to be a distillation of our league form, having another expletive-laden first half where we should have gone in 2 or 3 goals in front. Yet again we've turned up with banjo-swinging strikers absolutely guaranteed to leave the many herds of local cows' hind quarters completely unmolested. I can't help feeling that even an out of sorts, half-fit, Robbie Keane would actually be of more use to us now than the £15 million we (allegedly) have sitting in the bank, idly awaiting the grand ceremonial opening of the new transfer window. With Torres now seemingly made of glass, and the likes of Kuyt and Babel both pathologically unable to actually run at, let alone past, defenders it's looking likely we'll continue to struggle to score again tonight, and also this coming weekend when we visit The Theatre of Delusions. Best we can hope for is to keep it tight, get through tonight, and save some face by getting a point at the weekend. To lose in Manchester, leaving them 10 points clear and sprinting over the horizon towards No. 18, would be unbearable. No, we need to salvage some pride in that game, and just be sensible tonight. I'll settle for a score draw against Real. But if we draw the

Mancs, or even a Hiddink-inspired resurgent Chelsea, in Europe in the quarter-finals then the season could come to a juddering halt.

So I find hard it to argue with Sampson's request that we "make a day of it," and I get into town for noon. In an attempt to avoid the usual ill-starred watering holes that have accompanied poor results in Europe (we can never go to La Tasca, Ma Boyles or The Excelsior again), we've headed down to the river for something in keeping with this evening's proceedings. And what a river this is. The Mersey is dancing in the brisk wind, with seagulls swooping and riding the eddies only feet above the foam-flecked waves. It looks majestic today. Madrid might have a palace and some of Europe's grandest avenues and plazas but its river is little more than a drain. The Manzanares in Real's home town dribbles past the Royal Palace like an octogenarian's ejaculation. It makes Huyton's River Alt, from where I fished mis-kicked footballs in my youth, look like The Rhine. In those days – the late 60s – Real Madrid were talked about in hushed and reverential tones. The European Cup was just over a decade old back then and they'd won the first five, including the game considered by many to be the pinnacle of club football, their 7-3 demolition of Eintracht Frankfurt in the final in Glasgow. And now, 40 years later, they're once again a giant of football having added a further 4 titles in the modern era, to once again lead the pack with 9 European Cups. There's no doubting their aura of glamour and their pedigree, even if their current form is less than imperious.

Yes, this duel between two true aristocrats of European football deserves something appropriate to the occasion, rather than just a gallon of lager in Wetherspoons. La Vinea is a new place in The Albert Dock, a wine bar and vintners with fabulous views across the dock to the Three Graces. There's not a cloud in sight, the air is crystal clear, and a fabulous blue sky frames the vista through the glass frontage. We're sitting on squishy leather sofas with ice-cold beers, examining the wine list and the menu, pondering our imminent lunch. Joe Corrigan and his lad Jack are with us, Joe having decided to swerve the nutcase Mick Kennedy for a few short hours. This is not only to enable the Dining Club to convene, but also – more importantly – to help preserve Joe's sanity. Kennedy is, at this precise moment, on the other end of Joe's mobile phone and we can hear him cackling with laughter and loudly haggling with hookers in a stretch Limo, trying to provide the pre-match 'entertainment' for visiting foreign supporters of both of tonight's teams.

There's half a dozen or so Madrid fans in the bar. They've got replica shirts on – some wearing them over their jumpers – one over his jacket!! – and are all sporting scarves and sunglasses. If they were Liverpool fans they'd be berated for being clueless whoppers, gaudily dressed idiots who get their ideas for match-day attire from any TV sitcom that requires a visual shorthand for 'football fan'. I'm not against wearing colours, I've even got my own 'Supporters All Over The World' red scarf on, but seeing grown men dressed up like children at the match just seems wrong – it's a real dignity stripper. It'd also see you labelled as a 'beaut', particularly by some of our younger support. For the Young Uns, wearing anything other than a Barbour jacket to the game is a fashion atrocity on a par with whatever the most outlandish, bleached-denim waist coated FC Hamburg fan might conjure up (imagine a Status Quo roadie in a Viking helmet). Speaking of which, I wonder where their 'lads' are, the 'Ultra Sur', the bastards who jumped Danny Giles? I wonder if they'll show their faces up on Walton Breck Road tonight? I very much doubt it.

These Madrid tourists are all very pleasant however and I can't see any of these sneaking up behind Joe to garrotte him with piano wire. One of them, a woman in her early twenties very politely asks me to take a photo of them. They group together, holding up glasses of cloudy Belgian wheat beer, silently grinning at me in a pose of still-paused bonhomie.

"Say 'Manchego'," I ask them.

"Que?" the girl asks.

"Manchego! Queso!... Cheese!"

No, she looks lost, and decides it's best just to ignore me. Click! They cheer and settle down again to their beers as do we. I'm only glad Jegs isn't here to berate me for trying to swap scarves (something I haven't done in donkey's years, honest!) or arrange a friendly kick-about in the car-park and then see who wants to be pen-pals.

After a pub crawl that takes in The Baltic Fleet, Peter Kavanaghs, The Belvedere and The Phil we are all a little tipsy around tea-time. If anything tickets for tonight are even harder to come by than for the first leg. My phone never stops ringing with pleas for any leads for tickets. It's the Last Chance Saloon, the whole season's riding on it and lads are desperate to be in there, doing their bit. It's a bit of a change from last Wednesday when I was wandering round a ghost town, like Sir William of No Mates, looking for people to have a pre-match gargle with. Part-timers! That said, you can't really blame people for more being excited about tonight. It feels special, it feels vital, and at the risk of repeating myself, it'd the sort of game this club of ours was meant for. Liverpool versus Real Madrid – oh yiss! It matters more when it matters more.

We get up to Anfield about an hour before kick-off and the air is thick with an electric expectation. There are already queues at turnstiles that are normally empty up until about 20 minutes before the game. There are a lot more flags about than usual – which is only to be expected. We've long since stopped having to cajole or encourage people to be part of the support on nights like this. The Flag Days of the 90s really made a difference on this issue. When most of the 'great' terraces disappeared in the mid 90s, nearly all of them (The Holte End, The Stretford End included) went with barely a whimper. The Kop on the other hand passed into history – into mythology – with a day that will live in the memory of everyone who witnessed it. The Kop never looked better, never more colourful than she did that sad afternoon. Whilst other fans saw off their spiritual homes with a diffidence bordering on embarrassment, The Kopites grabbed the occasion by the balls and made it their own. Witness Anfield on a big European night and compare it to similar nights at Old Trafford or Stamford Bridge or (sniggers) The Emirates... need I say more?

A good 40 minutes before kick-off I'm standing on my seat waving my arms about, like one of those annoying birds on their boyfriend's shoulders at Glastonbury, encouraging those already packed into Block 306 to ramp up the atmosphere. I'm sure Roy Boulter thinks I'm a complete tit, but I've got Jegsy and Sammo holding me up, so he's outnumbered. The Kop looks magnificent and right down at the front is a reminder for Real, a huge flag made by the Skem lads with a red European Cup on it that reads simply 'PARIS 1981'.

Right from the off we tear into Madrid. If Arrigo's Saachi's Milan side of the 90s perfected the 'pressing game', then tonight we perfected something akin to the 'steamroller game'. Real didn't know what hit them. By the time they could draw breath after half an hour they were two goals down, and it could have been 4 or 5. Without the brilliance of Casillas they could have been humiliated. Torres was quite simply unplayable – a revelation from the guy who's looked so hampered by injury in recent weeks. With Gerrard in similar glorious form Madrid don't stand a chance. Rafa's pulled a fast one, too – everyone, from Juande Ramos down to my mum expected Liverpool to do what we've been doing best (or at least, most of) this season and keep our shape, keep the ball, don't over-extend and hope for an opening. Watching Gerrard, Mascherano, Torres and Alonso in particular flying into tackles to win the ball back you'd have thought the lives of their children depended on it. We haven't played this well in years, yet at 2-0 I'm still convinced that Real can score and find a way back into this game. If this season's taught me anything it's that this Liverpool team might be just about to let you down, just when you think its safe to believe.

At half time the concourse is packed, even though it's a 'dry' UEFA night. Gary Shaw and Joynty are more concerned in showing each other their scraped, skin-less shins than celebrating. My knee's also playing up, as after the opening goal I had both Sampson and Dodd jump on top of me.

"What *was* that? That was just.... magnificent!" asks John Garner, grinning his trademark goofy smile as he rubs his shoulder. He too went arse over tit after the first goal. Indeed I'm surprised Lou-Lou still has her underwear on after those celebrations. She's looking slightly dizzy, her hair all over the place, like she's just been belted with a cricket bat.

"That was amazing." she says. "Why can't we do that all the time?"

"Why didn't we do that against fucking Everton?" growls Jegsy. This man harbours grudges like you wouldn't believe. That FA Cup defeat will rankle until next season until exorcised by a 3-0 drubbing of the small, peoples' club at The Pit, when after a bizarre touchline collision David Moyes is rushed to hospital to have Mikel Arteta's head surgically removed from his arse. That would be a good day in Dodd's books.

It's only when, 2 minutes into the 2nd half, Babel skips down the left wing and places a cross right onto Steven Gerrard's right foot for our 3rd goal that I relax and believe we'll come through tonight unscathed. In fact we can all relax and enjoy the football, stare at Louise's thong peeping up out of the back of her jeans, and sing. We've not really had a night like this this season so let's enjoy it.

"Bring on yer Internazionale..."

Even when Alonso is replaced by Lucas, there is a huge cheer (maybe tongue in cheek, but a cheer nevertheless and a great improvement from the groans of just a week ago). Lucas responds with a sound performance possibly born out of the supreme confidence now flowing through the side.

"Is that who I think it is?" asks Sammo wiping his specs, barely able to believe the evidence of his pink and thoroughly-worn-out eyes. One of the loudest cheers of the night is for the introduction of local lad Jay Spearing, who replaces Gerrard and doesn't look out place amongst such illustrious company. I check my match programme – Christ, he was born in late

November 1988, just after our 2nd replay against Arsenal in the League Cup at Villa Park (that bit isn't in the programme, I look it up later). I remember it like it was last week – Villa Park more than half empty, going a goal down, then Aldo scoring late on to cap a fabulous second half from The Reds. God, I feel old. I was as euphoric that night as I am tonight – it never dims, does it, this enduring love of Liverpool FC? It feels as good at 50 as it did at 15.

A magnificent evening is capped by a fourth goal from Dossena who's played a blinder, particularly in this second half. Sampson is again holding his glasses up, examining the lenses, with a look of utter confusion on his face.

"Dossena? Surely not…"

After the match we retire down the hill to The Valley for a pint or two and to congratulate ourselves for another storming night on The Kop. Dodd, Parso, Giles and myself slump into seats and sit beaming at each other, Parso rubbing his hands together in glee. Our beers remain untouched as we watch the goals being replayed on the telly, Gerrard's 2nd – the magnificent half-volley – drawing an "Ooooooh!" from everyone in the bar. I suddenly become aware that Dodd's eyes are not focussed on the screen and turn around to see what's caught his attention. There are 4 Madrid fans standing quite happily in the middle of the bar, supping pints. I turn back to see Jegsy snarling at them.

"They're not exactly their 'boys' are they, Jegs? Not 'Ultras'," I say in the hope of calming him down.

"Bastards," he mutters.

"What have they done?"

"Him…" he says nodding at Danny, "… in Madrid." There's not much I can say to that. Okay, it wasn't these blokes who attacked Danny but I get the gist of what he means.

"We give opposition fans far too easy a time at Anfield.," he complains in the way that only an old Road End skin can. "And you and your mates, swapping scarves…." I burst out laughing.

"What he's saying Jegs," interrupts Parso, "is that you can't hold these lads here responsible for what happened to Danny. That'd be like some Spaniards laying into Lenny Woods or Tommy O'Hagan because, say, some of The Urchins jumped them. It's not 'like for like'.." Such reason is lost on Dodd who continues to sneer and scowl. The Spaniards remain oblivious of course, which is just as well as all it would take would be one wrong glance and Ambassador Dodd would be up on his feet. Thankfully, they only stay for the one beer, and in their absence we discuss the possibility of getting the Mancs in the next round, a prospect that has Dodd's eyes lighting up. He then excitedly blabbers on, imagining thousands of lads getting the train to Piccadilly around mid-day and generally causing mayhem all day in Manchester.

"And they thought Rangers were bad?" he says with a far-away, wistful look in his eye.

However, after a brief discussion, we conclude that it would be better to knock the Mancs out in the semi's. The preferred draw would be Bayern Munich and then The Mancs, with Barcelona in the final in Rome. What we don't want is Arsenal or Chelsea – a prospect that has us all declaring that we might give that game a miss and save our money for the semi final or final. The Final? A couple of hours ago we were thinking our season was as good as over, and here we are now contemplating a trip to Rome – again. We can dream tonight but I suspect we'll be brought back to earth with a bump on Saturday. I take the last train home hoping that we just avoid defeat at Old Trafford. The sight of Bacon Face on the touchline as his horrible, horrible team take another giant step towards equalling our record would be unbearable. I text Jegs giving him my permission, and my blessing, to chin as many Mancs as he likes on Saturday.

JM

Manchester United (a)   4-1

League   Sat 14th Mar

It's the night before we play United away and I can't sleep. It's always like this. I'm like a wide-eyed kid on Christmas Eve waiting for Santa to sneak in and empty his sack all over the bedroom floor. Hot Lips is well away but I've got one eye on the clock and my mind is racing. All the different scenarios are running through my mixed-up head. One minute I can picture myself on the concourse outside the ground stripped to the waist taking on all comers, the next I'm scoring the winning goal in the Stretford End with a diving header before baring my cute little Liverpool arse to the United hordes. I know it shouldn't be like this at my age, it's not like I've never been there before. I've probably visited this corporate Disneyland of a ground more than 30 times and endured more pain and disappointment here than anywhere else in the world, but I still get dead excited at the thought of it. Maybe it's masochism? Maybe I've got a bit of a kink? But the strange truth of the matter is that I actually quite enjoy 70,000 retards abusing us non-stop for 90 minutes. It's a back-handed compliment that they're giving us really, because if they weren't arsed about us, they wouldn't get so uptight and angry. I take minor satisfaction from the fact that, while United have been by far the most successful team in the country for the past decade, they haven't really been able to savour it – and it's all because of us. Every little success, each new Premier League title was still just another step towards Liverpool's record. When they won their second European Cup in one of the more dramatic comebacks of recent years, their supporters celebrated by singing "are you watching Liverpool?" You're in Barcelona, you've been battered by a vastly superior Bayern Munich team and you're a minute away from a humiliating defeat then, not only do you rescue the game against the run of play – you go back down the other end with your next attack and you win the thing! You're ecstatic! Nothing can compare with the elation that is now coursing through your veins, and how do you respond? What's the first thing you think? Yup – it's those pesky old Scousers again! What's wrong with these Mancunian folk? Are they obsessed or something?

Even Rooney's got in on the act earlier in the week saying that he hates Liverpool. Well so fuckin' what. That's the way we want it. We don't want monkeyboy saying nice things about us. As much as the media feign shock and surprise at his statement, I quite like it. We know where we stand. It's a mutual dislike and anyone who doesn't understand it has no place at a United-Liverpool match. If you're an ex-Evertonian who now plays for the Devils team and you've endured countless songs about your sex life along the lines of "You're just a fat granny shagger," you're hardly gonna show us respect. The songs are hardly Lennon & McCartney standard but I'm sure they hit the target. Anyway I'm still fidgeting away under the quilt. Kicking every ball and saving every penalty.

Earlier on, me and the Dark Mysterious One had been to Paul Stewart's 50th birthday party at Oxton Cricket Club. Hot Lips had driven so I could have a few sedatives before the big day. As the lights came on at the end I had a brainwave. "Stewy, what's happening with the rest of the buffet?" He says it'll probably get lashed but if I want to take some I'm welcome. I remind him we're on a coach tomorrow going to the Darkside for the footy. "Shit, yeah, of course! I'll get it sorted." So me and Hot Lips stagger to the car with enough food for a month. You know the saying: "Fail to prepare. Prepare to fail." An army marches on its stomach and the troops from the Spion Kop will be well fed as we conquer Old Trafford tomorrow.

I must've fallen asleep about 6am and woke up around 9am all of a doodah. I dive into the bath in a bit of a panic. Put the phone on and text messages are coming thick and fast. It seems I'm not the only one who is mentally unbalanced when it comes to following the Mighty Reds. Hot Lips pops her delightfully dusky head around the bathroom door and says "Honey, aren't you forgetting something?"

"Err…let's see. Ticket, money, ciggies, lighter, keys, phone, axe, shotgun, crossbow, RPG. No, I'm sure I've got everything sorted."

Then between finger and thumb she dangles the ruby red lucky undies around the door. Schoolboy mistake on my behalf there. Jesus, that was close. Imagine what might've happened if I wasn't wearing the L.U's. It doesn't bear thinking about. While I'm here I might as well put on my lucky jumper as well.

Although I've only ever worn it to the match twice and we won both, so it might just be the difference between the two teams. Seeing as I've gone all Mystic Meg I may as well get the lucky charm that some Indian Yogi gave me many years ago in Thailand. Wow, he was spooky. Even knew me mum's name and that I'd had a crash four days before in England, but that's another tale for another day.

Parso's daughter Minnie drops us off at the coach pickup point and it's full steam ahead to the ground formerly known as Old Trafford. On the match ticket it actually has, emblazoned on the top, 'Theatre of Dreams'. Hahahahahahahah! I'm not kidding, they really do think they are the Disneyland of football, where sick children can come for the 'Soccer Experience' and all their hair will grow back as Riley or Wiley or whichever referee's is on the payroll today, gives outrageous decisions to the home side and everybody goes away happy. "Gee mum, I really love Man U. They're so cool. Can we come again next year?" Little memo to the owners of our club, whoever you are, and I'm being serious here – don't ever use Man U as a blueprint for our success. United may well be massive and generate far more revenue than us but just stop and look what they've become – a fat, bloated Hollywood film set full of starstruck daytrippers and tourists, who wouldn't know Denis Law from Jude Law. If this is the future which all clubs strive for then the final whistle is not as far away as you think. The idea of fans going to the match to be entertained as in going to the cinema or cricket or snooker, where their influence is nil, is upon us. Liverpool Football Club have something absolutely unique in their relationship with their fans which is envied all over Europe. The merest mention of LFC to any foreign journalist will always be followed by a knowing nod of approval and the two words synonymous with Anfield – The Kop. The two go hand-in-hand together. Without one, the other is nothing. It is a sad fact that marketing is such an important part of the modern game but it would also be a very dangerous gamble if the powers that be ignored the voices of the local fanbase in their relentless pursuit of the dirty dollar. The northern soul of our dear friends from Old Trafford, oops I mean Theatre of Dreams, has been slowly sanitised. The Stretford End, which in its heyday was second only to the Kop, is a pale imitation of what it once was, these days filled with popcorn eating non-Mancunians, who act as if they've come to watch a West End show. Liverpool Football Club, beware. If you shamelessly prostitute yourself, like United have done, you will end up the same. A magnificent stadium filled with dickheads.

Words fail me

I'm outside the ground as kick off approaches and a leprechaun walks past singing anti-Liverpool songs. Parso looks at me, I look at him. We don't get angry but we're not laughing either, we're just like "What the fuck is going on?" It's like we've walked into some LSD induced parallel universe. He's about 4ft tall with a big green hat on and a long ginger beard. Welcome to the Theatre of Dreams, the football theme park of the future. To Gillett and Hicks, this must be heaven, but to the 3,000 travelling fans this is without doubt hell. If you call yourself the Red Devils it is almost inevitable that one day you will reap what you sow. As they say folks, "be careful what you wish for because one day it might just come true." As we walk towards the turnstiles there's a fat baldy bloke singing "Murderers, murderers" at the queuing Redmen. This was originally an Everton slur about the Heysel Stadium disaster in 1985, but United and Everton have recently found a new bond which is cemented by their mutual jealousy and hatred of LFC, so if one set of fans think of something insulting to say, the other set copy. Let's face it – they can have each other.

Anyway, this bloke is over 20 stone and wearing a pair of what can only be described as 'circus trousers'. You know, the type you see in the Echo when someone has shed half their body weight and they're standing there side on in these huge pair of kecks, grinning inanely at the camera as if to say "Look at me, I used to be a fat fucker and now I'm not." And there's always an accompanying photo of him on holiday in Spain drinking a cocktail with a big bloated head and cheeks like a trumpet player with no trumpet. Well this bloke had those kecks on and they fitted him a treat.

Now I'm no hardcase by any stretch of the imagination but I just couldn't resist sneaking up behind him and whispering down his ear "I'll fuckin' murder you in a minute!!" Well the big fat divvy nearly jumped out of his substantial skin. Absolutely cacked himself he did, and waddled off into the crowd at an amazing pace, for a fat fella – he was like a pot-bellied pig on *Pets Win Prizes* We absolutely fell about the place laughing as he wobbled off into the distance.

We get into the ground and as much as I hate the bastards, you've got to admit, it is a boss stadium. The atmosphere is building and as usual you feel that rush of expectancy as the teams walk out. But when you've been here as many times as I have, you know that there's a good chance that it'll all end in tears like it has so many times before. This is not a happy hunting ground for my beloved Redmen. I look around and the whole crowd seem to be looking in our direction, pointing and shouting. It's a good job I'm not paranoid because I seem to get the impression that these wide eyed, mentally challenged half-wits don't like us very much. Our pre-match plans are thrown into chaos when Arbeloa pulls up lame in the warm up, and Sami Hyypia is given just sixty seconds notice that he's playing. From now on, this next ninety minutes are basically the last throw of the dice. For us, lose and it's all over. Win and there's a glimmer of hope.

We start okay and everything is going to plan when suddenly Park Ji Sung is felled by Reina in the area and the Mancs get their inevitable penalty in the 23rd minute. Up steps the effete ladyboy with the dancing feet, that sad conniving, bad driving, forever diving, oily twat of a spoiled brat, Ronaldo. One nil to the Mancs. BASTARDS!! Born from the devil's spawn, the ghouls of Old Trafford awake from their slumber and begin to celebrate what will be their 18th league title. It's not looking good as we've all read the script a million times before. Man U haven't lost at home for over a year and they certainly don't get beaten after they've scored first. I'm just starting to get that 'Here we go again' feeling when Skrtel plays a long ball forward and Vidic, fatally, lets it bounce. Torres is in there like a flash. He leaves the defender for dead, waits for the perfect moment and slots it past Van Der Saar and into the net. FUCKIN' GERRIN DER!! Pure bedlam ensues. Our boy Torres even gives it the big five finger salute to the home fans to let them know how many European Cups we've won as he runs over to the chaotic scenes in the away end.

We're back in it now, and the Mancs are not looking so smug as we push on with a new lease of life. A minute before the break and all hell breaks loose. Torres puts Gerrard through, Evra slides in and brings him down in the area and even though it's a nailed on peno I am still shocked that the ref gives it. Normally at Old Trafford, even if it's an attempted murder in the United 18 yard box, the referee will look to old whisky face instead of his linesman to see if he's allowed to give it – but give it he has. Jesus. We wait with baited breath for the most reliable player of the modern era to dispatch it with precision, and Steven Gerrard does not let us down. It's the perfect spot kick and the Redmen are in front. Stevie runs towards the travelling Kop and plants a kiss on the TV camera for all the Sky guys back home in the boozers. If you thought it went mad after the first goal, that was nothing compared to this. Picture yourself on the Titanic, as it's about to go down. Bodies appearing out of nowhere and disappearing again upside down. Delirious faces looking up at you from the floor under the seats screaming inaudible joyous obscenities.

People disappearing past your earlobes with demented, elated kites on them, only to re-appear in a jumbled mess, jackets ripped, hair (if they've got any) all over the place but still wearing those stupid, ecstatic, delirious grins.

The half time whistle goes and I feel like I've just spent forty five minutes in a tumble dryer. We go downstairs to catch our breath and see who's on board the good ship Liverpool today. It's all a bit manic. Everyone's talking too fast, like it's half time at a cokeheads convention. Where else can you get this rush of excitement and expectancy other than against your most hated rivals at the footy? Football is the drug and we, the football junkies, are as high as kites as we try and fail to remain composed. Downstairs I see all kinds of excited faces. There's Mark from Runcorn, John MacDonald, Tage from Norway with a grin like a Cheshire cat; there's Dave and Paul from the Timberland shop in town; Colin Jones from the Road End War Veterans committee. There's all kinds of head the balls gathered in one happy knot- all the Breck Road lads and the Kenny crew, and of course, the ever present Urchins, whose names I cannot reveal due to Health & Safety reasons. We go back up into the ground with hope in our hearts but knowing deep down that things could go horribly wrong if we don't remain composed. We're looking good and my middle aged Torres bounce is coming on a treat. It's a kind of 'knee bend' thing with my feet never actually leaving the ground. I've got it off to perfection. I know it's cheating but at my age you don't wanna be jumping up and down like a loon for too long, otherwise you'll end up in casualty with other Redmen who've over-bounced.

Oh, and just to wind John Garner up one last time, did I ever mention that it was myself, John Mackin, Sammo and Wayno who launched the inaugural Torres Bounce? Thought not.

Anyway the Mancs are getting frustrated as they try to get back into the game. Liverpool are just soaking it up and hitting them on the counter at every opportunity. Fergie plays his joker – and it's hysterical. He brings on Giggs, Berbatov and Scholes all at once in the 72nd minute. In all fairness, you think to yourself, not a bad trio of subs to bring on when you're in trouble. And it's trouble they most sincerely are in, as Vidic hauls down Stevie boy on the edge of the box on 76 minutes. It's a cast-iron red card, as well and with Vidic talking the long, lonely walk I find myself actually believing we're gonna win this one. Oh, happy days! Everybody's waiting for Gerrard to twat it over the wall, when up steps Fabio Aurelio to coolly bend a left-footer past the static Van der Saar and into the back of the net. Well that's it. My head has gone. I have this tremendous urge to strip off and run the length of the pitch waving my lucky undies above my head! This is our moment. We know they're not gonna come back from this now, and I want to do something to celebrate the moment, but I don't know what it is I want to do. Seeing as I'm on the back row I turn to the window of the hospitality box behind me and give the infidels inside my full Jack Nicholson in The Shining manic grin. Empty seats begin to appear all over the ground as the fly-by-night United fans scurry to the exits for that early dart to motorways north and south.

But we haven't finished yet. Pepe, who has clearly been instructed to bombard Man U's dodgy centre backs with aerial missiles, launches another humdinger into their half. And who's this sprinting after it like a greyhound.... Can that be Andrea Dossena, who's outstripping the camel-gobbed Rio Ferdinand? It is! He bides his time then chips a beauty over Van Der Saar's head for number four. This is unreal. Parso is gutted. He did Liverpool to win 3-1 which by anyone's standards is optimistic, seeing as Man U have only conceded four goals in their previous seventeen games. Danny Giles did us to beat Madrid 3-0 in midweek with Torres first goal and again it was our mate Andrea who ruined that bet with a goal at the death. Who'd have thought it eh? Dossena to score the killer goals against two of the world's biggest teams in the same week. As I've said before, it's a crazy old game, this football lark. One minute you're squirming in your seat as your team surrender to a side as utterly shite as Middlesbrough, the next you're absolutely twatting the most successful club in European history and then steamrolling the current English, World and European champions into the ground.

It makes you wanna grab Rafa by his lapels and shout: "Rafa! Look! This is what you can do when the shackles are off. This is what happens when we are positive. All this arsing around with safety first tactics against second rate teams, when this is what we are capable of!"

Anyway, this is a time for celebration. We get kept in the ground for hours while the irate Mancs are allowed to drift home in agony. No-one is complaining this time – we just sing and, just in case the numb, bewildered inbreds outside haven't heard enough just yet, we sing some more, tormenting them with an epic, a thunderous Torres Bounce that has the stadium shaking to its foundations. There's text messages coming in thick and fast, all basically saying the same thing. Every neutral in the country will be buzzing off this. It doesn't matter if you're Arsenal or West Ham, or Leeds or Newcastle, *everybody* hates these bastards! There's probably only Everton in the whole country who won't see this as a moral victory for football. But they're not bitter.

We are released from the ground like prisoners of war and ushered towards our transport. Although our war of attrition with United is ongoing, this battle has been well and truly won. Anyone who has ever travelled by coach, to watch their team play away from home, knows how different the contrasting moods on the journey back are dictated by the result. Well, you can imagine what our bus was like on the way home after inflicting Manchester United their heaviest defeat at O.T for seventeen years, and our biggest win there since 1936 – it was a very happy coach indeed. This has been a long time coming and me and my fellow Redmen are going to milk every last drop out of it. Like a rabbit out of the hat I produce the trays of sarnies and pies, which I had cunningly hidden in the luggage rack, to great howls of hungry approval. You just get the feeling that nobody is going home until the Redmen have been well and truly toasted like only Liverpool fans know how. It's gonna be a long and messy night.

When we get back to town, there's also been an Anny Road End old boys reunion day in the Yankee Bar for all the arlarses who couldn't get tickets. With Commander in Chief Tuddy leading them through the complete back catalogue of the Road End's greatest hits, you can almost hear their drunken celebrations as we pull up in London Road. We dive off, and head for HQ. We knew it would be busy but not this busy! We open the door and people fall out into the streets singing. It is absolutely bursting at the seams with euphoria. We try and fight our way to the bar but it's just bedlam. So myself, Bucko, Parso, Ritchie, Mercer and the Timberland Two head off to the Richmond where at least we can get served and hear ourselves think. Mick Duffy and Ged Thomas appear, followed by Maddo, then Hooton and son arrive. The whole city seems to be alive with little pockets of pissed Reds staggering around singing at the tops of their voices. And from out of the thick of the hullaballoo, the unmistakeable face of Sconch appears. As is always the case when Sconch enters the fray, you can wave goodbye to any thoughts of quiet sensible conversation. He was made for nights like these. There are no rules or boundaries in Sconchworld. Anything can happen and most of the time it does, which is why I would love to see him installed as Lord Mayor of Liverpool with immediate effect.

It's up to the Excelsior next to prepare ourselves for the big push on to Ned Kelly's. Normally it's all beards, real ale and chin-strokers at this award

winning traditional boozer but not today folks, not on your nelly. It's packed full of wide-eyed believers who have all witnessed today's miracle. Some of Shankly's greatest and most loyal disciples are present including Patto, Fitzy, Barry & Denise, Philly Mac and the Kaye brothers; Mick, Andy and Peter. Even Lloydy is home from his Canadian outpost. Right out of the blue we get a call to come to the Sir Thomas Hotel where Lord Carragher of Bootle is out celebrating with his friends and family. We throw the bouncers a dummy and employ a Christmas tree formation as we negotiate getting to the bar; it's me up front, with Bucko and Mercer tucking in behind and a very narrow midfield. Sully and Tony Hall orchestrate play from the sidelines, guiding us to where Carra's clan have made their den. Let's be honest, it must do your head in if you're a famous footballer and every time you go out, you get pissed middle-aged men in your face, wanting to shake your hand and talk bollocks about flat back fours or fat black whores but let's face facts, we've just twatted the Mancs and we want to share it with one of our city's favourite sons.

And do you know what? Carragher is genuinely made up to see us. He's as happy as we are, in fact he's glowing from head to toe with that unmistakable aura that only victory can bring. We don't overstay our welcome though and after yet more hugs and handshakes it's back to the more familiar anarchy of Ned Kelly's, which is showing no signs of calming down. Bucko has now decided that everyone on planet earth has changed their name to 'Babycakes'. He's started calling me by this dubious moniker as well, which is quite worrying. I suppose we're all allowed an extra bit of nuttiness on occasions like this but I never thought the day would dawn when I'd be referred to as 'Babycakes' by one of my match mates. This is what winning at Old Trafford does to you.

By now I am goz-eyed and beginning to repeat myself so it's time I somehow got back to Dodd Towers. I have no recollection of any form of transport being used to get me home. Was it a taxi? Was it a train or a bus? Or did I just float home on a cloud of happiness? I wake up in the midst of a mild and yet pleasant hangover and decide to buy every single English speaking Sunday newspaper in the world, obviously with the exception of any S** related publications. The headlines warm the cockles of my heart and confirm it wasn't all a dream. That lovable rascal David Buckley is already on the phone trying to get me to go to town for more celebratory drinks but I can see the smouldering look in the Dark Mysterious One's eyes. She needs a little loving and who am I to resist. I'm afraid Bucko and the boys are gonna have to enjoy the remainder of the weekend without me as Hot Lips and me indulge in our own little private Torres bounce. So I'm afraid it's back to you in the studio Brian, from a very happy house on the banks of the River Mersey.

JD

Aston Villa (h)   5-0

League   Sun 22nd Mar

We're in Shenans and all the usual suspects are already going strong. Billy Harrup's in his regular spot with fellow Irregulars Wrighty and Lou Lou. Louise is all dressed up and looking, I must say, lovely. She says her kids told her to put on a dress for a change, but we know it's because Mothers Day is THE big diary date for MILFs to get dressed up, get hammered and get... into town on the pull. Nico's here with his mum and dad – he's his mummys boy I'll tell you that, she looks like him in a dress. There's the hilarious sight of Sammo trying to chat to her, clearly unaware that neither Mr and Mrs Van Dyck speak more than a few words of English. They all get along just fine by nodding and gurning, and Sammo ends up ordering a bowl of Scouse for Mrs Nico after catching her licking her lips at his once too often. They all bowl off early to catch the 27 to the ground – the bus stop is literally right outside the pub's front door.

I get a cab with Jegs and Kev as far as The Stanley, all three of us jabbering excitedly about Man.U's defeat at Fulham yesterday and how, suddenly, miraculously, "it's on" again. The lads go in for a bevy, but I walk to HJC to drop my flag with Andy Knott – who's delivering it to an Irish pal who's taking it to a wedding! It says something when your flag gets invited to weddings and you don't...

The game is sensational in that we score early, and go on to attack, attack and thrice attack our way to a 3-0 half time lead. Kuyt knocks in a rebound from a Steven Gerrard header, Gerrard himself slots a pen and in between, Albert Riera goes absolutely potty after drilling in a beauty with his left, straight from yet another Pepe Reina long range pass. Divvies can shout "hoof" as much as they want, but Pepe's assists are providing the chances that lead to the goals that are suddenly winning us games.

Gerrard places a beautifully precise free-kick inside Brad Friedel's near post that we see perfectly from the moment it leaves his foot, and completes his hat-trick as we absolutely rout supposed Euro challengers Aston Villa 5-0. We just can't stop scoring these days, so it makes absolute sense that Paul Stewart is angry as we walk back to town in glorious late Spring sunshine.

Stewy just can't have it that we've only starting playing this brand of cavalier football now there's almost nothing to lose – and he still thinks it's all too little, too late. But if the Fulham win (with 2 Man U players sent off, to boot!) isn't enough to give the players the belief that they can do this, they should have a look in the history books.

March 22nd 1986
Luton 2 Everton 1
Liverpool 6 Oxford 0
The results that brought us level after the eight point gap at the start of March 1986

March 22nd 2009
Fulham 2 Manchester United 0
Liverpool 5 Aston Villa 0

The results that brought us within one point after the seven (momentarily 10) point gap at the start of March 2009. If that isn't uncanny – I don't know what is... anyway, even the most hardened sceptic can surely see some interesting parallels? Despite such a thrashing Oxford would end up taking 3 points from our nearest rivals, which turned the tide irrevocably in our direction. Next up for United – Villa.

I'm just saying, like.

JM

Fulham (a)   1-0

League   Sat 4th Apr

The day before the game we all assemble in the Big House on Lime Street to celebrate Nico's 40th birthday. The Belgians – Nico, Stefan, Jan, Dirk, Daffy, Wakke, Dozy, Beaky, Mick and Titch – are already on the Rioja at 10am. This could get very messy indeed. We're all off to Aintree Races for Ladies Day. The phrase 'Ladies Day' is something of a misnomer in this instance, however, as more unfeminine examples of the fairer sex you'll probably never, ever see. Sure, at 10am they all look lovely, scrubbed up with lips shining with gloss, and smelling like angels. But sometime around 3pm they morph into guttural, shoeless beasts, pissing behind Portaloos and falling over drunk. Now, whilst that's certainly acceptable behaviour for us blokes (after all God gave us willies, thus enabling more discreet public urination; and let's face it, there's nothing more manly than the sight of a chap indulging in a casual vomit whilst holding a kebab: it's what made this country great after all). But to see that doe-eyed beauty in the Cecil Beaton 'My Fair Lady' hat – that you'd previously drooled over when she was putting on a bet – squatting by a fence in a cloud of steam, holding her shoes in one hand, and squawking to her mates on her mobile.. well, let's say that not even a glimpse of her spray-tanned arse-cheeks can make that sight alluring.

Tommy Keiner's obviously turned up thinking this is a social event to rival the Henley Regatta. His choice of brown shirt and tie, brown suit and bright green overcoat makes him look like a perspiring chocolate lime, and reduces the rest of us to fits of laughter. I'm even laughing as I pick up my second lot of winnings: a fabulous 14-1 shot that now puts me £270 up for the day. I quickly seek out APB at the bar and pay my debts for the following day's trip to London: £67 for the train ticket and £47 for my match ticket. Now, that's a dear day out. Fortunately the 'Sport of Kings' has seen fit to bankroll me and we decide to splash out when we get to London.

The following morning, we're both aboard a 9 a.m. train from Chester to London and as we're both still a little drunk from yesterday Baker is, once again, talking complete bollocks. This time it's the banking system that's gnawing at him. I suspect that this is because our train is on time, it's clean and virtually empty – so nothing to complain about here then.

"I'm telling yer, Chief, banking systems can't be allowed to price their own risk... blah, blah... macro-prudential regulation is no more... the pariah status of Keynesian economists over the last 30 years...blah, blah...."

All I can think of, as he lectures me on the macro-level, top-down approach to banking regulation, is "Strongbow. Strongbow. Go the buffet and buy us some breakfast cider, you tit." Eventually he realises that he's bored me, the half-dozen fellow passengers in the carriage, the ticket collector, the woman in the buffet and those cows in that field out there, and he shuts up.

At Euston we waste no time and sprint across the station concourse, down the escalator and take the tube to London Bridge. It's almost in precisely the opposite direction that we need to go to get to Craven Cottage, but we are on a mission. On the tube we discuss our tactics for after the game as the last train leaves at 8 p.m. and with the game due to finish around 7, we're going to have to get away sharpish.

"We're going to have to leg it about 10 minutes before the end." I tell him. "It's not simple getting back to Euston by tube."

"No worries, kidda. We'll do one early and beat the rush. I know that gaff like the back of my hand. It's my manor... Sorted!" he proclaims, as if he was Mad Frankie Fraser rather than a PhD in Political Economy.

At London Bridge he jogs through Borough Market, weaving between the tourists and the market stalls, with me lagging behind blaming 'my bad knee'. Even when he stops to check where he is, he jogs on the spot and reminds me again about how he's training for some sort of marathon or other. I ask him if he fancies a few sit-ups before we have a bevvy, or maybe some arm-wrestling; you know, if we're being competitive like. He ignores me and instead we head into Tapas Brindisa for a lengthy lunch and several bottles of wine. Tony Teasdale saunters in with his tennis racket under his arm and a jumper slung round his shoulders like a gay nephew wandering in 'orf the patio' in a Noel Coward country house play. After lunch we have a mooch down Southwark High Road and find a pub that we decide will do for the rest of the afternoon. Loz Gray, fresh from his paper round, arrives shortly afterwards, as does Tony Evans, Scouser and a football editor at The Times. Tony wrote one of the best books about being a Liverpool fan, 'Far Foreign Land' charting his bizarre journey to Istanbul in 2005 and reflecting on his life as a Red, so he should know what he's talking about.

"We are going to win the league," he says. I get butterflies at hearing him say this. These last few weeks have been bizarre; we've gone from that pathetic display at Middlesbrough that seemed to finally kill off any last lingering fantasies any of us may have had of winning number 19, to contemplating actually winning the bloody thing. A win today will put us 2 points clear. And whilst a draw would not be a catastrophe, the win would be a fabulous psychological filip seeing as the Mancs crashed to a hilarious defeat here, complete with a Rooney and Scholes dual sending off, only just a few weeks ago.

"They've got Villa tomorrow. Not easy. They drop points in that one and we stay top," adds Tony.

We all nod keenly. It sounds more than feasible. We've managed to drag ourselves back on track, and by shaking off the shackles and attacking whoever stands in front of us, we've stormed back into a position where even I think we can do it. Of course, the manner of the football we're playing helps. We're now going out knowing we can win, rather than hoping we might. I put it to APB that in his erectile analogy, we have finally got our Mojo back – confidence, as well as blood, is flowing through our veins.

"Vein," he says with a knowing smile.

We spend a couple of hours discussing the dramatic turnaround in our fortunes. There's even praise for Lucas Leiva who suddenly looks a completely different player. Dossena's playing well, Benayoun likewise. Dirk Kuyt's industry has finally found it's place, and is bearing fruit. I'm tempted to use the word 'Stakhanovite'* to describe him, only I won't, because Brian Glanville uses it. The draught Becks is flowing and when we finally leave around 4 p.m. our hopes are as bright as the spring sunshine. Teasdale doesn't have a ticket, and in any case he'd be beaten to a pulp if he turned up in our end looking like Sebastian's teddy bear from Brideshead Revisited. He heads off home and APB, Tony Evans, Loz and I take a cab across south London, then over The Thames at Wandsworth and through the side streets of Hammersmith and Fulham, to a street full of handsome Victorian terraces within sight of the

---

* "Stakhanovite: An extremely productive or hard-working worker. One whose tireless labour increases overall productivity."

famous cottage that gives Fulham's ground its name. We pour out of the cab and with a few stumbles, we split up – Tony to the Press Box, the rest of us to the away end.

A 5.15 kick-off in London means that most of the Reds travelling from Merseyside will have... well, they'll have had a few ales. The usual coaches were leaving around 9 a.m. ensuring that they'd be in London a good 4 hours before kick-off. In fact most of the travelling support has come by bus as the trains back are non-existent. The train we're aiming to get isn't a Liverpool train at all, but will get us to Crewe. From there we can get a local train to Chester, from where other Reds can join Merseyrail and get back to stations on The Wirral, or even back to Liverpool. But I don't think there'll be many of us risking that, judging by the near empty train we came down on.

APB and I are wandering about up and down the aisles deciding where we'll stand, ignoring stewards pointing at spare seats, when I hear:

"Mackin! Baker!"

It's Lou Lou waving at me and beckoning us both to stand with her and some of the Irregulars whose bus she's travelled down on. Robbie Jones and Stevie Wright are in the row behind, and – along with Lou – look like they've had a good afternoon. As we expect, the away following is raucous, well-oiled, and up-for-it. We've been given a second chance and the nay-sayers are swallowing their doubts and everyone is concentrating on supporting the team – and supporting them LOUDLY! Whether or not this is transmitted to the team I don't know, but we absolutely batter Fulham in the first half. We hit the woodwork 4 times and we get the feeling that should 1 go in then 3 or 4 will follow. Torres rolls one effort agonisingly close, following a Gerrard through ball, and as the ball creeps towards the line the massed ranks of away fans seem to stand on their toes, screaming and willing the ball in. Instead it hits the post and rolls away. At half-time there are none of the doubts of weeks previous. All talk is of us winning this and, as if to rally the troops, Baker is running around like Henry V at Agincourt, fists clenched, shouting "C'mon REDMEN! C'mon!!!! We can have these! C'MON!!!!"

In the second half we come just as close on several occasions and the away support gets even more manic. As time ticks away though, I'm getting more and more nervous, grinding my teeth and letting out low, animal noises of frustration. At one point I crouch on my haunches, head in my hands with Baker standing over me, berating me for being a poof. But time is running out and we NEED to score. With 8 minutes remaining, Yossi Benayoun comes on and almost immediately has a chance. Gerrard fires one hard low shot across the face of the goal that Benayoun flicks at, sending the ball inches past the far post; then Yossi twists and turns, creating his own opening… this is it! He's GOT to score! But he goes for elegant precision and clips the ball just wide of the near post. My heart sinks. That was our last chance there, and Yossi really should've buried it. The clock moves inexorably towards the final minute of time added on. The tension is nigh on unbearable and I am rocking back and forwards, hands pressed against my face like a wailing mourner at some fundamentalist funeral. Which, I suppose, is what this could turn out to be. All thought of leaving early for the train is cast aside as all our concentration is focused on the goalmouth at the far end of the pitch. We're into the final desperate few seconds now and we pour forward for what will inevitably be the last time. Ngog cuts inside 25 yards out, thinks about shooting but instead plays a pass into Gerrard's feet on the edge of the box. He mis-controls it and the ball somehow squirms through to the feet of Yossi Benayoun. He collects it, knocks it past a defender and then lets fly a ferocious shot across the keeper, and…..

YEEEEEESSSSSSSSSSS ! YES!!! YES!!! FUCKING….FUCKING…. **YES!**

Pandemonium. Bedlam. Sheer fucking mayhem! I haven't seen celebrations like this since Michael Owen's winner in the Cup Final in 2001. I scream so loud that my temples feel like they're about to burst and I see stars. People are grabbing at other people squeezing and hugging them indiscriminately. The air is punched, people are howling, others almost bent double in relief, hands on knees. This is absolute, unbridled joy.

And we're still there 20 minutes after the final whistle. I haven't seen an exultant Liverpool away end like this in years. The support all day has been immense but this is something else. There's a non-stop fifteen minute bellowing of "We're gonna win the league" and I'm bellowing better than most. Standing on a barrier arms spread wide, I feel like its 1986 again. We eventually tear ourselves away and even as we head out of the ground we can hear several thousand Reds remaining behind to continue the chorus. It is a glorious sound.

We are laughing and whooping as we trot out and head across the park towards the Putney Bridge tube station. Fulham fans are streaming in the same direction and we're jogging past them like a pair of loons. Baker is singing at the top of his voice:

"It's 1986 – it's 1986! And now you're gonna believe uuuuuuuuus...Its 1986!"

He's running like a prancing circus pony in a high-stepping, comedic, Dick

Van Dyke jog, tousling the hair of small boys and waving at strangers whilst grinning like a maniac. All he needs is to place his thumbs behind lapels and start singing " Me ol' bam-boo, me ol' bam-boo – You'd better never bother with me ol' bam-boo...." At the far side of Bishop's Park there's an orderly 200 yard queue for the tube, but Baker jogs, with his knees as high as his chin, right to the front where we shouts "Scousers! Scousers! Must get to Euston!" before disappearing down the stairs. I follow down to the platform, struggling to keep up. He must be on glue or something. After a tense, multi-train dash across London, we make it back to Euston with 5 minutes to spare.

"A couple of cans for the journey and we're sorted then!" he declares.

"Good. I'm gasping." I wheeze.

Wisely we decide to choose an off-licence next to our platform and before we can waste our money we see Transport Police confiscating cans and bottles from passengers.

"What's going on?" I ask one of the Virgin Rail guards.

"Dry train mate. Nothing to do with us. Police orders."

"The bastards!"

Once aboard we decide to chance our arm and check out the buffet car. The steward is apologetic but the police have made him padlock the booze away and tells us it's because it's a Manchester train and Man City fans are on board, as well us couple of dozen Liverpool fans. I look around at equally thirsty City fans, who are looking at us, and we all look at the guard and say, "Do you think we can be arsed causing trouble? It's late and we NEED a bevvy!" He's adamant – though he thinks it's stupid, it's more than his job's worth to sell us any booze.

Fellow Kopite, Matty Mwanje boards the train and sits with us. He's equally distraught at the boozeless journey ahead of us. As the train lurches out of Euston he's already on his mobile searching the internet and as we're passing through north London he makes his first call to an off-licence in Milton Keynes offering the guy a £20 tip to meet us on the platform with a case of Becks.

"Just stick it in a cab then... there's 20 for you in it... and a fiver for the driver..."

But no. The guy's not having it – he ums and ahs and makes excuses. So Matty repeats the exercise for every stop back as far as Stafford when he gives up. The Man City fans in the carriage – including 3 lads no older than 13 who've been to Arsenal on their own – are impressed at Matty's ingenuity as well as our determination to get a bevvy.

At Crewe we say 'Ta-ra' to Matty who's going to Manchester and hoping to catch the last train back to Liverpool from there. Baker and I sprint up the stairs from the platform (I've run more today than Dirk Kuyt – I deserve a pint!) and across the road and into a hotel lounge bar and order a couple of bottles of Becks each. Match of The Day is on the telly and the first bottle is drained in 10 seconds flat.

"Has the Liverpool game been on yet?" I ask the barman.

"Yeah – first game."

That's rich. No matter how well we play we are never – ever – first on M.O.T.D. We're usually 4th or 5th match on, just after West Brom vs. Middlesbrough or Sunderland's absorbing nil-nil draw at Bolton. That's just bloody typical of the B.B.C. – they've done this deliberately. However, the dry train and M.O.T.D. can't dampen our spirits. We're both still buzzing from a truly brilliant day, which gets better when we arrive back at mine around midnight, there's cold beers in the fridge, several bottles of Rioja in the rack and a pizza just coming out of the oven. My girlfriend wishes us both goodnight and disappears to bed with the words, "Oh and I've recorded Match of the Day for you." Baker's impressed: "You should marry this exceptional woman!"

Like the match, the day is rescued from disappointment by a late winner.

JM

Chelsea (h)   1-3

Champions League Quarter Final   Wed 8th Apr

Ouch, I really didn't expect that. Getting beaten 3-1 at home by those West London fops. It's like walking into a room and some prankster has balanced a bucket of water over the door. One minute you're thinking everything is going so well, then next it's THUD and it's bang back down to earth with a bump. I wouldn't mind but the day started off so well. Everyone was in town before the game brimming with confidence after what's been a decent few weeks for the boys in Red. People were even talking about taking a chance and booking early for Rome, to save being fleeced like the Athens and Istanbul debacles. But after the tonking we've just suffered it'll be a miracle if we play any further part in this year's competition. Yes I know what happened in 2005 but events like that only happen once in a lifetime and for some teams they never occur at all.

Let me take you back to the pub before the game. There we were all getting a little bit smug thinking we're invincible because we've already beaten the Chelsea Globetrotters home and away and look what happens. They do to us, what we did to United and Real. Personally I don't think we're comfortable with being treated as favourites. I think we're more at ease when we've got something to fight against. When the chips are down we respond with a spirit that is indicative of the city itself and not just the football. The amount of times we've battled back from almost certain defeat in the last few years has been amazing but put us on top of the Prem and install us as favourites and we shit our pants and go to pieces.

It's 5pm in the Ship & Mitre at the top of Dale Street and Kev Sampson is with Mick Potter and Jussi from Finland. Everybody's in high spirits. Danny appears with Paul and the legendary almost seventy year old veteran Tommy O'Hagan and then Johnny Mac bursts in puffing and panting like a frustrated rapist. Not that he's ever raped anyone, he just looks a bit hot and sweaty and a little wide-eyed. Poor lad needs a drink. The man who is definitely not a magician or hypnotist, but I think he looks like one, Joe (pick a card, pick a card) Corrigan appears out of nowhere. He's a great bloke Joe and he also knows where the bar is, which is always a great sign of a man's character. We all discuss the impending match but none of us can imagine what horrors are about to unfold. We get up to the ground fairly handy and the Kop (as always) is a sight to behold. Old Trafford, Stamford Bridge and The Emirates can only dream of an atmosphere like this on a European night. Anfield has always been in a class of its own for the big occasions. Copied and admired all over the world, this partisan arena has been at the forefront of fan participation since the day Uncle Bill walked through what are now his own gates.

We get off to a great start with Torres slotting home, after a great back heel from Kuyt sets up an Arbeloa cross which is drilled past Cech. The whole stadium is rocking and the songs are coming thick and fast but so are Chelsea. Drogba goes close straight after the restart but Pepe saves a 'one on one' which really should've put the Flash London Mercenaries back in it. Again Drogba misses a sitter by twatting an easy chance high over the Kop goal and into a thankful crowd. Then in the 39th minute the inevitable happens. A corner from the right is delivered into the middle and Ivanovic rises unmarked to power a header past Reina. Fuckin' hell, it's another set piece goal and an away one at that. Kuyt has a chance straight after but misses – not for the first time this season. We've got to be more clinical when we're given an opening. The second half is all Chelsea and there's only one team in it. I hate to admit it but sometimes you've just got to hold your hands up and say we were second best. I know Evertonians have never been able to understand the concept of their team being beaten fairly and squarely, and have to resort to blaming the world and his wife for any defeat, but here at Anfield we know when we've been out manoeuvred. Don't get me wrong, it still hurts like hell when you've taken a bit of a pasting but the secret is to bounce back even stronger.

Chelsea go ahead on 62 minutes. Another header from Ivanovic from another set piece and it doesn't look good. The crowd try their best to rouse the troops. We need a goal and we need one quick but within five minutes the fuckers have scored again. It's a killer. Heads drop and the shellshocked fans look around for some kind of inspiration but there is none. There will be no pilgrimage to the Eternal City this year, unless a miracle happens. They've come here five times in the last five years of the Champions League and been rattled by the passion of the crowd on the previous four but tonight they played the perfect match. Essien had the game of his life, not only man marking Stevie Gerrard but, say it quietly, dominating him completely and running the show from midfield. We trudge out of the ground feeling down but still fairly positive. A lot has happened since that dark day up at Middlesbrough. We must dust ourselves down and be ready for Blackburn on Saturday. We've still got a lot to play for and even the greatest teams of all time have an off day every so often. It's how they respond that defines them from the rest. I want us to be like a wounded animal and savage Sam Allardyce's team on Saturday as a statement of intent. I want those Mancs looking over their shoulders with their arses twitching. I have a pint in the Valley with Kev, John Mac and Danny and then a couple in the Liverpool Arms by James Street station but tonight is not a night for a mad one, so it's the last train home to lick the wounds.

JD

Blackburn (h)   4-0

League   Sat 11th Apr

Today is not a day for arsing around. I'm feeling positive. I'm off the ale and gonna drive to the ground early to sort out my missing Chelsea away ticket and then try and hook up with the Union lads on the Michael Shields march. It's an important few days coming up and I need to clear my head. We've got a massive game today, Stamford Bridge on Tuesday then the Hillsborough service on Wednesday, so it's all hands on deck for a big, big week in the life of this football club. There must be no passengers. Everyone has got to pull together for the cause; the players, the fans, the lot. Every single person connected with LFC has a duty to remain focused and together because the unity we have here has always been our strength. And whisper it very quietly, but I actually think we might cause a bit of a shock down in London on Tuesday, now that I've had time to sleep on the defeat – but as I say 'keep it under your hat'.

Anyway let's get Blackburn out of the way first. I queue at the ticket office window behind the day trippers and wide eyed tourists, with not a familiar face in sight. After about 20 minutes I am granted an audience with the young sprout behind the glass. I hand him my season ticket as ID then ask him about the whereabouts of my Chelsea away ticket. He looks at some hidden computer screen for a minute or so and straight away I know there's going to be some sort of problem. He tries his best to explain the situation but basically the bottom line is, they've fucked up again. Remember the Standard Liege game back in August when they'd mislaid my application when I handed it in personally, for the solitary reason of stopping it being mislaid? Well, today's load of bollocks is as follows: "Yes Mr Dodd, you've qualified but you didn't show any proof of travel to Madrid for the Real game, so we've allocated it to someone else." "Pardon?" "We didn't receive any proof." "Nobody asked me for proof. I hand delivered my application. Why didn't somebody say something?" "I don't know Sir." I even produced my phone and began to show the disinterested young window-licker photographs of me gurning outside the Bernabéu stadium, with other beer-soaked gargoyles. "It's not really proof of travel," he says, in a quiet measured voice. "Proof of travel!" I say. "Proof of fuckin' travel? Well if that ain't me outside Real Madrid's ground, who is it then? The man from fuckin' Del Monte? Emperor Hiro-fuckin'-hito? The Dalai Lama? No, it's me outside the ground."

The lad is not impressed and I am ushered away by a steward.

Well, that's me sorted then. No ticket for Chelsea away and my ongoing battle with the incompetent ticket office shows no sign of abating. I wouldn't mind but before the home game against Chelsea the Dutch LFC fans were in the Ship & Mitre with three spare tickets. How is it that fans that don't even live in the UK can have more than enough to go around and still have extra ones to sell, while the local Reds can barely hope of gaining access? The whole system needs an overhaul.

Anyway, it's a lovely day so I wander up to the green by the supporters club to meet up with Kev and the lads who've been on the Michael Shields march. Carra has given a rallying cry in the local press saying this could be one of our most important games for years. He needn't worry, the fans are aware of the task today. The team needs full vocal backing and in return we need full commitment and three precious points from the boys in Red. The Kop is awash with banners begging for justice for the 96 who died twenty years ago. Stephen Warnock, a former Liverpool player and now of Blackburn, lays a wreath in front of the Kop to rapturous applause. It's a nice touch and is massively appreciated by the packed Anfield faithful. All the TV stations show this and the minute's silence on the news bulletins, but somehow manage to avoid showing any of the huge 'Justice for the 96' banners which line the front of the Kop. A very clever bit of editing and censorship, seeing as you couldn't miss them. Someone somewhere didn't want our national audience to have their evening's viewing tainted by having to look at Scousers asking for nothing more outrageous than the truth.

On the pitch the team play as if their lives depended on it. They know how badly we want this league and they go for it right from the first whistle. Torres' first goal after five minutes is an absolute beauty. There didn't seem to be much on when he collected a high bouncing ball on the right with his back to goal, but he swivelled and twatted it on the volley past Robinson for a

Young Reds continue the protest against the Sun newspaper

cracker. He added another with his head, from a set piece on 33 minutes to put the game to bed. There was no way Blackburn, under the bison-headed Sam Allardyce, were gonna come back from that and Rafa says as much with a cheeky "game over" gesture to the lads in Red.

Mascherano is like a terrier in midfield in Gerrard's absence, snapping, tackling and running around like a man possessed. Jamie Carragher is also buzzing in his role of captain, which many think he should have on a permanent basis. No disrespect to Stevie, who is undoubtedly the greatest player on planet earth bar none, but Carra is the soul, the warrior and the heartbeat, while Stevie is the engine, the spark and the genius. Personally I don't care who's skipper as long as it's one of the two Scouse talisman. I go downstairs at half-time and I can feel myself about to blow again when John Mackin asks me if I've got my Chelsea ticket yet. I explain the whole pre-match fiasco and he looks at me in disbelief. He then informs me that he got a phone call a few days ago to pick his up whenever. No proof of travel to Madrid, no DNA, no finger prints, no nothing. Considering I stayed in the same hotel as him and was on the same flight as him, I feel my blood pressure rising past the 'anything can happen' point. The second half starts and I'm still pissed off about Chelsea away. They don't half make it hard to follow this club around. I wouldn't mind but I'm paying a fortune for the pleasure of doing so, or at least, trying to do so.

We're starting to miss loads of chances again and the atmosphere is going a bit flat, when up steps Daniel Agger to hit an absolute thunderbolt into the Kop goal. That's more like it. We need to get that goal average sorted, because you never know when you're gonna need it. Ngog, who comes on as a late sub, scores in the last minute to make the result a bit more reflective of the day. We're back on top of the league for a few hours at least, until the unmentionables win 2-1 away at Sunderland in a scrappy game. Their curio of a manager refers to Rafa's "game over" gesture as being "beyond the pale." Although no-one has mentioned this – not even his most puppy-dog worshippers like Daniel Taylor on The Guardian – Ferguson throws himself back in his press-conference seat all mock despair and goes:

"Did you see that? Inexcusable. Beyond the pale."

Yeah well you went well beyond the brightest shade of pale you day you turned purple you bitter, deranged old gobshite. The main thing is that us Redmen are back on track and there's also the small matter of going to Stamford Bridge and winning by two clear goals on Tuesday. Should be a piece of piss. Tickets please?

JD

Chelsea (a)   4-4

Champion League Quarter Final   Tue 14th Apr

Familiarity does indeed breed contempt. In fact, it's more than contempt – I can't stand Chelsea. This must be the 19th time we've crossed swords with them since the first leg of the 2005 semi final. European Cup quarter final or not, this is far from being a mouth watering prospect, despite what the fawning English press might tell you. In fact it's a pain in the arse, if the truth be told. Several lads have already jibbed it. There's the cost for a start, then there is the 4 or 5 hour motorway journey back from central London depositing you home creased, tired and irritable at 4:30am. In fact it all seems a bit of a chore and although European away games like this might save you some considerable money I know I'll wake up tomorrow wishing I'd spent the extra £300 on a night or two in Prague or Paris instead. It's a game like tonight's that underlines the ridiculousness of the Champions League as a concept. And even though many regulars have decided to forego the pleasure, tickets will still be as rare as Dirk Kuyt controlling a pass or Frank Lampard keeping his shirt on. The fans' contempt will instead be reserved for their visiting fat-cats from UEFA and for the way they have prostituted the purity of the 'Coupe de Clubs Champions Europeen', giving us instead the bloated marketing opportunity that is the 'UEFA Champions League'. This new guise, this rebranding, is geared towards ensuring that the big sides continue to dominate the competition; and that everybody – the clubs, UEFA, the sponsors – continue to make lots and lots of money. UEFA have created a monopoly – and only the big boys can play. We'll probably never see parochial outfits like Steau Bucharest and Red Star Belgrade in the final again, let alone actually winning it.

'The Champions League' is the biggest misnomer since Hitler thought he could throw a 'Nazi Party'; half the competition isn't a league (significantly, the half that attracts the greatest audience) and most of the teams in it aren't

Champions. All this is designed to ensure that the latter stages are dominated by clubs with the largest fan base and a global reach (i.e.) the greatest TV audience, and that means teams from England, Spain and Italy. But there's a price to pay for this – and that's the integrity of the tournament. Only one of the three English winners since the 1992 re-branding were national champions. Hypocritically, of course, I hope we'll see a third in Rome.

The old, purely knock-out format was incredibly tense; one slip and you were out. Big sides often fell by the wayside when having an off-night in some badly floodlit stadium behind the Iron Curtain. It was true cup football. It was glorious. An in-form team could often make it all the way to the final, basking briefly in the limelight of the greatest club game in the world. Alas, where now St Etienne? And then there was the adventure of being drawn against the unknown: Liverpool playing in Reykjavik, Lodz, Tbilisi and Trabzonspor. These minnows are now routinely weeded out in the seeded turkey-shoot that is the qualifying rounds. And apart from the odd jaunt to places like Bordeaux, a European campaign is now just a repetitive procession of the familiar. Since the UEFA Cup win in 2001 we've been to Rome, Eindhoven and Barcelona twice, Istanbul three times, and now London for the fifth... even in this one season we've been to Madrid twice; the fun is going out of the competition.

That said, even if we'd never played Chelsea before in this competition – ever – I'd still be contemptuous of them. They just deserve it. They are horrible. They represent all that is wrong with 'modern football'. They are, in fact, the club that most personifies the values of 'The UEFA Champions League' (cue' pseudo-classical musical fanfare, trying to give the concept some gravitas and sense of history. And I mean both Chelsea and the competition). Their attitude is: throw money at it, sign arrogant millionaire footballers and cultivate a fanbase of clueless middle class whoppers willing to spend thousands to be part of the experience. From their gormless billionaire benefactor to their Meccano-like stadium, shoe-horned into a development complex mainly given over to million pound apartments, restaurants and expensive entertaining facilities, the spirit – the glory – of the game is secondary. Fame, glamour and money rule.

* * *

The chicken's entrails lay before me – and the day ahead didn't look too good at all. I'm standing in the road looking at the scratches and the dents all down the driver's side of my car, courtesy of a teenage girl's failure to look in her mirror before turning. As she's going on about how she'd been indicating to turn, and I'm just stood there looking at the remains of my Polo, and all I'm thinking is not:

"I couldn't give a toss how long you say you were indicating for, love." Instead I'm thinking:

"Ah fuck, this'll make me late and Danny Giles will go off on one about how he's going to miss half a pint's drinking time."

We swap details and I drive back to the house before hot-footing it back up the main road to where we'd agreed the mini-bus would pick me up. The instructions seemed watertight. Foolproof even. But not Dodd-proof. After standing round for 20 minutes I get the call.

"Where are you? We're lost."

"Lost? You've only come 10 miles from Birkenhead. It's one straight road?"

"We're heading for the A41 and …," as Jegsy speaks I see the minibus coming in entirely the wrong direction, then as it passes it takes the wrong turning off the roundabout towards Shrewsbury and away from Chester. I wave furiously and they wave back, then I hear Jegsy chuckling in my ear.

"We're going this way, the M6 is goosed. Hurry up!"

I sprint across the dual-carriageway and catch them 50 yards down the road. The A41 will take us down through rural Cheshire, south into Shropshire where we'll join theM54 at Telford and on to the M6 and that there London. This minibus was rented in Woodchurch, but it's probably never seen trees. I wonder how it will react the rolling green pastures of the Cheshire Plain.

"Is that a coppice?" asks Parso, nodding in the direction of a clump of trees in a field.

"Think so," says Jegs. "No, no … I think that's a copse."

"They're the same"

"Are they?" Dodd looks at Parso. He's alarmed because he's usually the only fountain of useless facts on trips like this when boredom necessitates such random outbursts. We cut our teeth in our teens on coach journeys like this; six hours to Norwich or Southampton for a midweek game. 50 lads on a coach without iPods or DVD players. If you were lucky the radio worked. So to alleviate the numbing boredom it was either talking shite or using hard drugs. Jegs coughs and looks out the window pretending to examine the clump of trees in question. He's on the defensive here, Parso just might be right.

"I thought a copse was just a big thicket." Jegs suggests. But he's riffing now, trying to bluff his way out of this exchange with his integrity intact.

"Might be," Parso says, then thinking on adds. "Maybe a big thicket – or several thickets that grow together – to form a copse ... also known as a coppice."

"Maybe."

"I wonder what the tipping point is when it can call itself a wood?" says Parso in that laconic voice of his that's never that far from a chuckle. They both stare straight ahead through the windscreen into the middle distance trying to decide just how, and when, a coppice might become a wood. Jegsy lights up and winds the window down. He's just about to make a statement defining exactly the watershed between wood and coppice when he's interrupted.

A voice from the back of the bus: "Slow down we've got the bizzies on our tail."

Parso checks the rear-view mirror. "No, we haven't."

"It's the Keystone Copse!" This is followed by a self-satisfied chortle. It's Danny Giles, none of whose cultural references hail from the last 35 years. He then goes off on one, mumbling random names ..."Ben Turpin ... Harold Lloyd ... Fatty Arbuckle".The younger lads – and even some grown men in their 30s and 40s – are forever baffled by his inclusion of names like Jimmy Clitheroe and Norman Vaughn in normal everyday conversations. For Daniel Giles the world still exists very much in black and white and popular culture ceased to exist when the last episode of 'Rising Damp' was aired in 1976.

"Delamere Forest ... that's near here," Parso offers, hoping to head Giles off at the pass. "Now that's a *bona fide* forest..."

Parso's now our resident woodland expert. Jegsy is uneasy about Delamere's claims to forestry royalty, however.

"Now, I'd call that a wood not a forest," he proclaims, "forests are big. Like The New Forest or Sherwood Forest."

"Nottingham Forest," Giles babbles. "Larry Lloyd."

Parso reaches for the radio 'On' button. Soon Ken Bruce on Radio 2 is Alan Partridging away and Giles falls silent before he gets to Emily Pankhurst. If Parso is never far from a fruity guffaw, Danny Giles is always within quipping range of a deft "Emily Pankhurst."

As we're cruising down the M40 my phone beeps. It's a text message from a mate, Simon Glinn, who's the manager of The Phil (the concert hall, not the pub) in Liverpool. He's forwarding me a text from Vasily Petrenko, the conductor, who is in Portugal with the Royal Liverpool Philharmonic Orchestra. Porto to be precise. The very Porto where the Mancs are playing in their quarter-final. Vasily's from St Petersburg, but under Simon's tutelage, has become a regular at Anfield so it's no surprise when I read the message.

"The Mancs staying in our hotel. I shall get the brass to practice outside Rooney's room."

I reply: "I'd have thought the brass would be found inside Rooney's room!" I feel pretty smug with my wit, only to be deflated when Simon texts me back saying: "You and about 10 other people said exactly the same thing...."

The introduction of the congestion charge has meant a road trip to Stamford Bridge now has an extra complexity. Or so we thought. In fact, its relatively easy to get to and from Chelsea and avoid the charge. And even if it wasn't, for a minibus of 12 of us, its about 75 pence each. But we've decided to ditch the car on the outskirts and take the tube into the city. Parking is bad in London at best, and at worst – as West London on match night is – it's nigh-on impossible. Danny isn't happy. He wants us to try and park a bit closer. After a brief discussion it seems that he'd like us to park across the street from the away end.

"We could get jumped on the tube," he offers by way of persuasion.

"Jumped? Its not 1982 anymore, Danny."

"Never easy, Chelsea!" Danny continues. "Never easy. Remember when Rushy scored that one ...?"

"Agreed. 20 years ago maybe. But they're all Home Counties poofs these days. Middle class. All the arl Chelsea heads must be disgusted with the way it's gone down there...."

"They were a disgrace last season" I chip in. "I was in the upper tier, right by the divide. There was some middle aged fella, in a suit and overcoat. A complete dick ... taunting me with "Murderers!" I mean he looked like my bank manager. He was standing there, arms in the air, going 'You killed your own fans!'" I couldn't take him seriously, I just laughed straight back at him."

Danny's not laughing though. Its going to take 45 minutes and two changes of train to get to Earl's Court. 45 minutes wasted drinking time. His ire is compounded by the cost of the zone card for the Underground. £6.30!!! That's at least another two pints gone. We may as well be waving lager at him, whilst he's tied to a chair, then pouring it all over the floor, laughing.

We park up out in the sticks, just off the A40, near Perivale. Giles grumbles all the way into town on the tube and eventually Jegsy uses the excuse that he still has to collect his ticket to abandon Giles and the others. Jegsy and I then head off to Earl's Court where he has arranged to collect his ticket in a pub. When we get there, there's a full-scale diplomatic incident involving John Garner's LBU bus and the coaches from the S.O.S. A spot of recreational shop-lifting at a motorway service station (the usual high-end, lucrative haul of boiled sweets, gonks and a Daniel O'Donnell CD) saw both sets of coaches stopped by the police, and held until all the stolen goods were returned. The S.O.S. bus are blaming Garner's lot for tarnishing the reputation of the Union, and Tiberius Garner is adamant that his underlings were "not acting in isolation" and were "directly contravening his dictat that they were to keep their sticky mitts to themselves." It's a sticky situation but not one that Dodd is at all arsed about, He just wants to get his ticket and some lager down his neck.

One face-price ticket later Jegsy begins hoovering up the beer and I'm more than willing to accompany him on this perilous journey. I'm starving, having eaten nothing since breakfast, and float the suggestion that after we've had a few beers we should find somewhere to eat. He looks less than excited about the prospect of wasting money on anything solid. He had brought cream-filled, choux buns on the mini-bus whereas I'd only packed bottles of lager. Despite the fact that this part of London is chocker with places to eat – there's even an upmarket Kebab place directly across the road – he fobs me off with a "Yeah, okay. Later." He's managing to live on ciggies and lager, and I feel it would be unsupportive if I abandoned him, so I forego any notion of food for the time being and carry on drinking this over-priced, fizzy, tasteless muck.

The pub crawl is taking us south down Earl's Court Rd and around 6pm Jegs gets a text message that Giles, Parso and the others want us to meet up for a few beers before kick-off. We eventually happen upon a large boozer 'The Pembroke Pub and Dining Rooms'. At first Jegsy is put off by the '... And Dining Rooms' bit, but I convince him that it's a big enough place and it's also on the route most of the lads in Earl's Court will take to the ground. He texts Parso and Bucko and pretty soon a right Chimpanzee's tea party is assembled and the bar is packed. I'm still trying to get him to agree to eat something and I read the menu out loud.

"Beer battered Haddock, Chips and Garden Peas. Tartar Sauce."
"How much?"

"£11"

"Eleven quid? Eleven quid for fish and chips?"

He looks at me like I'm mental. The only thing I can think by way of justification is: "It's London. Keeps the riff-raff out."

"Well it hasn't worked tonight, has it?" he says as Bucko comes marching up the stairs from the toilets declaring loudly, "Jegsy. Jegsy – this pub is arse!" Jegsy doesn't say anything but looks to Bucko to explain. "Says so on the wall downstairs... one of West London's landmark gay pubs."

"Figures," says Jegs.

"Why so Captain my Captain?" asks Bucko, intrigued.

"Only a hom would pay £11 for fish and chips." Well, that's put me in my place hasn't it, so I put the menu back on the bar and order another round of lagers.

It's getting late and we need to get into the ground. Bucko goes round the pub whipping the party into shape and we leave the pub en masse, much to the relief of the regulars enjoying their £15 egg on toast. To get to Stamford Bridge we take a brisk walk through the cemetery, during which the old Anny Road loons regale the younger lads with hair-raising tales of skirmishes amongst the gravestones back during "the good old days." Tonight, however, it's just a pleasant Springtime amble amongst the statuary. Yet another example of what Jegs would say is "how football is going to the dogs."

****

They're up on their feet again in the paddock below, doing the Harry Enfield 'Calm down, calm down' thing, waving their horrible, club-sponsored, plastic flags, all singing up at us.

"Too Nee-oo! And you facked it ap."

I want to punch someone, and that 15 year old in the bleached denim and the gelled hair is looking the best candidate. I'm considering hiding behind a gravestone later and just hoping he has to walk that way home. Bastards! We came down here not expecting anything and just hoping that the team would give us something to be proud of. Well in the first half they did just that – and more – and as half-time approached, Stamford Bridge saw the bright red, raucous away section rocking amidst a sea of silent still blueness. However, something niggled with me. I couldn't just live that moment and join in the delirious abandonment all around me. I was convinced we'd scored too early.

At half-time with us winning 2-0 I wandered around not knowing whether to laugh or cry. Had it been just the 1-0, then Chelsea might still have sat back and preserved what they had. But it was now too close for comfort and I was certain that they'd come out guns blazing and try and dent our confidence. An early goal for them in the second half would knock the wind out of our sails – that's what Hiddink would be telling them. But we didn't have to gift it to them did we? When Reina made a complete hash of Anelka's low cross that's what we did. We gave Chelsea a lifeline they hadn't really earned and they took full advantage. Within minutes it was 2-2, Alex hitting a rocket of a free-kick that Reina probably did well just to see as it shot past him. And we were back where we started an hour ago, needing to score twice without reply. When that horrible fat twat, Frank Lampard, made it 3-2 I just stood there feeling hollow.

"Come 'ead, Jegs. I can't take this – let's go."

"Give it five minutes."

"No. Come on."

"Why? There's about 15 minutes to go with injury time."

"Cos I can't stand these twats crowing like this. It's really doing my head in."

He just stays still, looking at the pitch.

"And remember last year?"

"What about it?"

"We left early and Babel scored right near the end."

" Well, okay then… let's *make* it happen! Yeah – if we go now we might score. … remember Preston?" I add pathetically. He looks at me, though, like I might actually be making sense.

"And Real Madrid?" I add.

"We weren't losing in Madrid."

"No, but we did score … and I left in Athens too, and Kuyt scored…."

I'm dredging up any memory I have of us scoring with me not in the ground.

He nods 'Okay' and we turn up the aisle and make our way out. As we're trotting out onto the road surrounded by hundreds of police he looks at me and says: "Athens? What if we'd equalised?

"I was prepared to miss it, just so long as we didn't get beat. Me nerves had gone completely. Totally."

He thinks.

"So, when you leave, we score. Right?" He's busy rolling a ciggie as we jog towards the station. "Have you ever thought of just fucking off going the match altogether?"

At the new Fulham Broadway tube station, we get down onto the platform quickly and straight onto a waiting train. Two lads come on just behind us, talking about the game.

"Its 3-3," says Jegs.

"Wha?"

"That lad's just said so…"

My stomach churns. This 'doing one' really fucking works. There must be – what? – with stoppage time, about ten minutes left. I bury my face in my hands, "C'mon Redmen, C'mon!" I say quietly to myself. Or at least I thought I did. The two lads overhear me, however, and a few minutes later one of them checks his phone messages and says. "4-3 to Liverpool." My arse has gone now. Totally. And Jegs pats his pockets as if looking for another ciggie even though he's only just put one out.

"Did you leave at half-time in Istanbul?" he says, looking hopefully into my eyes. Shit! He's testing me now.

"Er, no … but I was thinking about it." I confess. But all I can think about now is how much I'd love it, really love it, if we could amaze the watching world once again and win this one 5-3… And how I'd LOVE to have been able to lean over to the teenage gel-head and sing:

"Free-too! And you facked it ap!"

Soon the train is moving and within a minute or so it goes underground and we lose all phone signals, leaving us stranded in a limbo of not knowing whether or not we'd just walked out on a comeback greater than Istanbul. Long before we get back to Perivale we learn the score and to console ourselves we trudge through the pouring rain to what ranks as the most dismal public house on the face of the planet. If anything I'm feeling worse now. So much for a consolation pint. The pub's a dank, nicotine coloured cavern of a room, lit like a mortuary and devoid of customers. The only other (and I hesitate to use the word) humans in here are the staff, who are simply itching to kick us out and shut up shop. And I'm wet through. And Fat Frank Fucking Lampard scored twice. Here we watch 'highlights' of the game and wait for the others to eventually catch up with us. A short feature on Newsnight about tomorrow's 20th anniversary of Hillsborough strangely cheers us up. It puts things into perspective. Fuck it! We've been here before and we'll be here again because we are Liverpool F.C. No-one gave us a chance tonight and we went there and did that! Before long I'm intensely proud of The Reds – my team – for producing what will rank as one of the European Cup's greatest ever games.

Later that night as we cruise up the M6 at 2 a.m. with most of occupants of the bus dozing, and with Danny Giles and Tommy O'Hagan squabbling about where Tommy is going to sleep tonight (the choices seem to be Danny's couch or Keele Services), Parso leans over to Jegs and I and says without a trace of embarrassment.

"You know what though? I think I fell in love with my team again tonight."

And on that one, the Forestry Commission are in full-blooded agreement.

JM

Arsenal (h)   4-4

League   Tue 21st Apr

The day before the game about 20 or so of us spent several hours laying out 15,000 coloured cards on the seats of The Kop, and in the away seats at the Anfield Road end. As the culmination of a season's fund-raising by the Ray of Hope Appeal for the great Ray Kennedy, who served both clubs with such distinction, we – the supporters – are paying him a tribute with 2 mosaics. On the Kop will be a huge white number 5 on a red background. In the Arsenal end will be a blue number 10 on a yellow background. These were Ray's shirt numbers in his time here, and at Arsenal previously.

Just before 10pm however there are 2 other numbers that are concerning me more – the 4-4 on the scoreboard. Who the hell was it complaining about Liverpool playing restrained, cautious football? Oh, it was me. How the hell can the season be turned on its head like this? We go from having the meanest defence in the league to conceding 8 goals in a week. We go from struggling to score against the likes of Wigan and Stoke to scoring 4 against the Mancs, 4 against Chelsea, 4 against Real Madrid and now 4 against Arsenal. Some of our attacking play tonight was simply breathtaking, some of our defending was farcical. Much like the Real Madrid game, at times we steam-roller Arsenal, particularly at the start of the second half when we equalise, then go 2-1 ahead. We then gift them goals on a silver platter when Arbeloa falls asleep and allows Arshavin to take the ball off his toes for their 2nd goal, and then when Aurelio passes to the Russian inside the box for his third. Schoolboy errors. Dodd would be tearing his hair out if he had any.

That said, to concede what looked like a winner in added time and then storm back to the other end and equalise again showed tremendous character and spirit. At 4-3 I was devastated, not for me but for my lad, Sean, who was using Sammo's season ticket. Sean has had his emotions pulled and twisted all evening by Arshavin's (let's face it) brilliant finishing and looks utterly crestfallen as we stare defeat in the eye. We're battling for the title – a title he's never seen us win. He must feel awful tonight and all I want to do is to lessen the pain. So when Yossi tucks home our fourth I celebrate it hugely and wax lyrical about what a great game of football it was. Essentially I'm trying to play it all down. After all, I tell him, we've just gone top of the league again and we've witnessed what will probably be the game of the season.

"That could be the point that wins us the league!" I tell him, but he's far from convinced. Dodd is even less inclined to be cheerful, but this Liverpool team is now playing the free-flowing, attacking football we've been crying out for, for months. We should be proud of the team, I tell him. We don't know when we're beaten; that can only stand us in good stead, if not at the end of this season, then next year when the experiences and the pain of this campaign will only make us stronger, better.

On the walk down to The Valley after the game, a guy walking alongside us comments:

"What a game that was. It was worth the money I paid for my ticket." He's from Cork and has flown over today after paying through the nose for a match ticket. He's straight off back to the airport now for an early flight in the morning. He speaks with a genuine love for the team and the city, and despite the result he's just delighted that he was here, at Anfield (his eyes light up when he says the word 'Anfield'), to witness it. He knows the team and the form of the players inside out, and rattles off an encyclopaedic rundown of our results since the turn of the year. He is a genuine supporter. And if he can take this set back on the chin, then so can we.

Sampson texts me:

"So come 'ead. No texts, no nothing. 0-0, I take it?"

"Sit down," I reply. "You're not going to believe this one."

JM

Hull City (a)   3-1

League   Sat 25th Apr

And so to Hull. They finally made it to the big league after all those years of being the favourite pub quiz question of 'What's the biggest town in England never to have had a top flight football team?' Well here they are in a nice new ground full of the joys of spring after a rollercoaster first season with the big boys. It was all going so well for them after shock wins at Arsenal and Spurs and a few other notables. 27 points from their first 17 games was UEFA Cup form but with only 7 points from their last 17 games the Tigers are well and truly on the endangered species list. I've seen us play up in this neck of the woods before, a cup game in which we won 3-2 at the old Boothferry Park after being 2-1 down at half time. Aldo scored twice in the second half to put us through after Johnny Barnes had put us one up early on. My abiding memory of that day was the drive into Hull smelling like a gynaecologists waiting room due to all the fish processing factories on the route in – poo, what a fucking pong!

I did a couple of gigs here in the late eighties in a place called the Adelphi, which was quite good. And also came here once for a stag night (no, seriously), and what there was of clubland made Birkenhead look like Las Vegas. In fact when I lived in London I once shagged a bird from Hull who I mistakenly thought was Scandinavian as she had a face like a Norse (these are the jokes folks!).

Anyway it's a lovely day as Hot Lips drops me and Parso off at the petrol station on Scottie. But again it's far too early. We're only going to Hull up the M62 for a 3pm kick off and yet here we are, bleary eyed, on the coach at eight thirty in the morning. It's not like we're playing Inverness Caledonian Thistle or Plymouth Argyle away but I can understand the thinking behind it. Get some miles under our belt and set up camp in a nice little market town about twenty miles from our destination. Today's lucky town is called Howden, with its own minster (bombed out church to me and you) and its own cheese shop and a local butcher and baker. It's only a small place with about six streets but it's sound. It's got about five pubs and a solitary chippy. This is what England must've looked like before it was completely Tesco-ised. Not one shop is boarded up or empty and everybody looks happy with their lot. Local councils take note. Give planning permission to the huge all consuming supermarkets and you can wave goodbye to the high street. We like Howden – the local working men's club has been expecting us and over a hundred thirsty Kopites give them the sort of business that this sleepy town can only dream of. Our little group slopes off for a brekkie and a few scoops in the White Horse by the village square. There's a pool table which we commandeer for a game of killer which is always a good laugh and gets everyone involved. The reason why I'm mentioning this is because I won. Oh yes, there's life in the old Dodd yet. The young pretenders were sent packing with the minimum of fuss. Back in the day my old mate Charlie Galloway used to think I had a passing resemblance to 'Hurricane Higgins', so he always used to call me 'Slight Breeze Dodd'. And on the odd occasion I've even been called 'The Draft'. Not exactly 'Whirlwind White' but good enough for me. Smigger and Mark from Kirby walk in unexpectedly. Seeing as they're in a motor they must've had a tip off that we were here. I mean you don't just stumble into towns like this and bump into your mates but then again I suppose you do sometimes. Gary Allt and Matty are also in here having a quiet one.

We get back to the coach for 1.45pm and Big Phil tries his best to keep order and announce the itinerary for the rest of the day. It's a hopeless task as by now half the coach is bladdered and either not listening or chanting obscenities at him. It's all good humoured but it must be so frustrating trying to talk sense amongst the chaos. The bottom line is, if the police get on the coach and find ale, it's a big problem. Not that 75% of the people on this coach would even notice. The coach firm will get fined and then will probably refuse to take us in the future. I don't know what they put in the beer at that working men's social club but there's people here who are absolutely wrecked to a European away game degree, and it's still not even 2pm.

The bus is in full voice as we set sail for the final twenty mile voyage to the KC Stadium. Bucko is out of his seat leading them on with his rendition of the AC/DC classic "I'm on a highway to Hull" followed by Meatloaf's "Like a bat out of Hull, I'll be gone when the morning comes." As we get closer to the ground, there's groups of locals outside pubs in their gold and black striped shirts giving us the finger whilst displaying an array of dodgy haircuts that only a Yorkshireman would dare ask for in a barbers. The sun is beating down and it's an almost carnival atmosphere. They're desperate to stay up and we're desperately trying to hang on in there at the top. So it's quite noisy inside the ground. After being involved in two absolute classic matches in our last couple of games, this was back down to earth with a bump. Whichever way you look at it, this was a poor performance. The Redmen never really got to grips with a Hull side that battled as if their lives depended on it. But at this point of the season it's all about results and we got there in the end. There was none of the free flowing footy of the previous 4-4 exhibitions and there were scares aplenty before we finally put Hull to bed. Although we've been thrilling the neutrals recently, our defence has been nothing like its old dependable self. If Hull would have possessed a decent striker like the Arsenals and Chelseas of this world there's no way we would have escaped with the three points today. Even Pepe in goal, who is normally as solid as a rock, had the heebiejeebies all afternoon, as did Skrtel and Arbeloa.

We score the opener a minute before half time. Alonso takes a free kick and hits it straight into the wall but when it rebounds to him he wallops it straight into the back of the Hull net. It's a relief to go in at the break 1-0 up because it was getting a bit scrappy out there and I had visions of 'Middlesbrough revisited', the sequel. But when Dirk Kuyt puts us 2-0 up early in the second half I thought "Ok boys this is it. No mercy. Let's go for the jugular." But no. They had the audacity to keep battling and force us into all kinds of uncharacteristic mistakes. Even when they went down to ten men after Forlan aimed a kick at Skrtel they still had the cheek to pull a goal back from Giovanni. Torres, who had been quite quiet, nodded one onto the bar before Kuyt scored his second to wrap the three points up right on the end. This was no walk in the park though. In fact I was just glad to hear the final whistle.

Full marks to Hull for making a fist of it even though their fans are the most unoriginal around. Their version of the Torres bounce was pitiful. It was like a Smarties advert or a school disco where no-one knows what to do next. Then they murdered the Sunderland song "Falling in love with you" before trying to goad us with all that tiresome anti-Liverpool guff. Well, let me tell you, yer little fuckin' Tigers, if our team had waited nearly a hundred years to get promoted I think the world famous Spion Kop would have had more than a few original songs and surprises up its collective Scouse sleeve not poor rip offs of other teams' witty ditties. And as far as singing to us "your support is fuckin' shit," I say this unto thee; you Hull City fans are not fit to lace the

Adidas training shoe of any man, woman or child who worships at the Church of Anfield. We have been chosen and blessed by a higher being while you, the supporters of Hull City are no-one. You are the people in fancy dress at the London Marathon having your five minutes of fame. Then you will fade back into obscurity again playing in front of half empty stadiums. "Your support is fuckin' shit?" How dare you, you cheeky, cheeky bastards.

We leave the kingdom of Hull and head back to Howden for the second half of the Man U v Spurs match. Darren Bent scores for Tottenham early on and our coach bursts into song. We are just about to park up and get off when Spurs make it 2-0. I'm thinking to myself "Hello, the Mancs 2-0 down at home to the North London underachievers? No, surely not." When the driver opens the door everyone is off running up the road, like demented school kids on the first trip to Alton Towers, looking for a telly showing the match.

The White Horse isn't showing it but, fortunately for us and unfortunately for the six or so Man U fans in there, it is on next door in a bar called 'The Board Inn'. The sheer terror on their faces as 40 odd wild eyed Scousers burst through the door is a sight to behold. It's 2-0 half time and although the Mancs are going to turn it round with the help of an outrageous penalty decision from Howard Webb, these fresh faced United yokels are about to spend the most uncomfortable forty five minutes of their lives. Tottenham fall to pieces as the Mancs score five times in the second half but we won't let this ruin our day. After a couple of hours we stock up at the offy and head back to the Promised Land. The journey home is class. The songs get weirder and weirder and the drink flows non-stop. It's been great to see some of the old faces onboard the coach today. One of them, Vinny Garrigos, was part of our crew back in the late seventies, early eighties, when Scousers changed the face of football fashion. It brings a tear to your eye to think how cool the Anny Road End mob were back in the day. Arise Sir Vincent of Kensington, you have earned your stripes.

By the time we reach London Road to get dropped off, the bloodshot eyes of my fellow Reds tell their own story. It's been one great awayday. We're all weighed in now, but it's written in the constitution that we have to have at least one bev in town. Me, Parso, Bucko, Mercer and Paul shuffle into the Excelsior for the final fling. I'm beginning to mumble like I've got something wrong with me. It's definitely time to go. It's a group hug and then everyone goes their own way, tottering off into the distance like human Thunderbirds puppets.

JD

Newcastle (h)   3-0

League   Sun 3rd May

It was 3-0 (always my favourite Liverpool – Newcastle scoreline) but it should have been 6. It very possibly could have been 10. As such I'm slightly disappointed. And I voice my disappointment twenty minutes into the second half. I know it is 20 minutes into the half as I've just spent the first 13 minutes down on the concourse, nursing the dregs of a bottle of Carlsberg, accompanying Joynty and Gary Shaw during their 'miss a goal' exile. It's supposed to be a ritual – a superstition. They miss the beginning of the half and we score. That's the logic of it anyway. I press them on how many times it's worked.

"There's been what? Arsenal? Villa? ...that it?" I say.

"Oh no, we missed quite a few this season.." says Gary, looking at Joynty who has a bottle stuck to his lips like a trumpet, but still nods in agreement.

"Loads," Joynty adds, and rattles through a list of goals they've managed to miss whilst down here drinking beer.

It turns out that some of these were scored 7, 8 even 10 minutes into the 2nd half. Of course we're bound to score if they stay down here long enough. That's no superstition, I tell them, it's plain greediness born out of ordering 2 bottles each. Meanwhile, in row 59, I'm complaining that we've not scored enough goals, two goals against this shower is just not enough.

"We should be tonking these."

Silence from those around me, although Louise looks at me like I'm a spoilt brat complaining that my birthday cake isn't big enough.

"Goal difference," I add by way of explanation, "Remember 1989?"

"It doesn't matter," Lou Lou insists. "If it goes to goal difference, then it means that United have dropped points... conceded goals so that boosts our chances." It sounds almost plausible – even coming from a girl. But we're only 2 goals ahead of the Mancs and they've got a game in hand. I'd prefer it to be

6 or 7 goals. What's most frustrating is that Newcastle are there for the taking. They are going through the motions and offering absolutely nothing, and we're not even out of first gear and yet we're coasting to an easy win.

"Look," I tell Louise, "They need 7 points from 4 games to be sure of the title. So, say they lose to Arsenal and Man City, that's entirely possible, no? Then 2 wins will take it to goal difference if we win all ours, as would 3 draws and a win."

"Yeah but even they only lost them two games by one goal, that's another 2 goals to us, isn't?"

For some reason, although what she means I can't quite grasp the concept through my beer fug. I continue to lay out the permutations but she's long since lost interest. Whatever happens the Mancs need to start dropping points – and dropping them soon. They really have to at least draw against City tomorrow, else they'll sail over the line with a wind behind their backs.

Meanwhile this is quite possibly the worst performance by an away side at Anfield this season, and I include West Brom in that. Newcastle are woeful. They're staring relegation in the face and don't look that arsed about it. Neither do their fans. Have I missed something here? Is relegation some sort of tax-dodge or something? Contrary to popular belief Newcastle fans aren't that great. Don't fall for that old chestnut put out by a lazy press that Tyneside is a football "hotbed" and the "knowledgeable" fans are both witty and voluble. Are they shite! Okay, they're better than some, can be quite vociferous, but really – they are idiots. They sing "Toon Army," they have countless other songs that all in the wooliest phrase of all time " walking in a ****** wonderland," they're *all* overweight, they *all* wear footy shirts and they revel in some kind of blind loyalty that serves no-one except the bean counters, who see them as little more than turnstile fodder. Why aren't they out on the streets! Fight for your club, morons!

Alan Shearer is standing on the touchline bravely facing the mocking Kop chanting "Alan Shearer, Football Genius" and "You should have stayed on the telly." He grins and nods at that one – he really should have. The owner's appointment of him as manager is a joke. It's brazen grandstanding, playing to the gallery, hoping to appease the mob. The same thick mob who turn up and support and applaud idiots like Joey Barton just because he wears black and white stripes. Applauding him? They should be stringing him up.

The atmosphere is good today, but its not great, not like it was at Fulham or the midweek classic against Arsenal. You really sense that no-one here really believes we can actually win the title after that 4-4 belter, so the pressure's off in a way, and the team and the supporters are having a bit of fun. Even a possible 12 wins and a draw in the last 13 games – form that won us the title in the past – won't be good enough. We didn't lose the league with the Boro defeat or the Arsenal draw, we lost it in December and January with those draws against West Ham, Hull, Wigan, Man City and... well, you know who? That let United build up a head of steam – and a healthy lead – so that they could ride out the odd hiccup.

Afterwards the game we retire to The Valley – fast becoming our post-game hostelry of choice – to "let the traffic and the wools disperse." Sammo slopes off remarkably early even by his standards (didn't even finish his pint) and so Jegsy, Hema, Parso and settle down in the pub, to be joined by Danny Giles and a few of his mates. There's an Irish family playing pool, wearing bleached denim, with spiky gelled hair, ankle-strangling trousers and 'pumps' ... not even bad trabs, but pumps that must feel as comfy as having lino taped to the soles of your feet. It takes all sorts I suppose, but whereas bars like Le Rouge and Dodds might contain 90% local lads, this place along with, say, The Park is almost completely O.O.T. and we've been massively entertained at the range of fans we seem to be attracting these days who for some reason have chosen this scruffy pub on Everton Valley as their match-day 'local'. I suppose there's the fact that the ale in The Valley is cheap which probably accounts for it. Cheap enough to have Danny Giles insisting we stop there for a pint when it's his round. As Giles queues at the bar counting out his sixpences, florins and doubloons to pay for the ale I noticed that at least the barmaid was compos mentis this time. She understood the order, poured the drinks and managed to work the till without stopping, mouth agape, and staring at it like it had morphed into a mongoose playing the spoons.

After a few scoops Danny disappears to another local boozer that's selling cheap lager. Apparently some draught Skol from 1984 had been found in the cellar under a tarpaulin, and the landlord was selling it off for 50p a pint before the Health and Safety people got there. He's a rum old so-and-so, Danny Giles – and I can't help feeling a swoon of affection for the old nutter as he swaggers out of the pub with that almost military walk of his, honed from years of walking tall as a proud, proud Kopite. I smile and swig on my pint, and I wonder to myself whether the likes of myself and Danny The Brickie will ever walk as tall again.

JM

West Ham (a)   3-0

League   Sat 9th May

If I thought Garner was a hard task-master, he's a pussy cat compared to Phil McEwan. I'm booked on 'his' bus, Wilcox Tours, the Saturday morning chara to West Ham, and I've sped over to The Rocket like Steve McQueen in 'Bullit'. I screech into the pub car park at 10:33 a.m. I'm 3 minutes late. That's 'early' in my book – but not in Phil's. Across the road I can see him, arms folded, glaring. I grab my insulated bag of goodies and hurdle the pedestrian barriers across the busy main road. As I reach the bus-stop Phil says nothing. He glances at his watch and I suddenly feel like I'm 10 years old.

I'm the last person aboard and sit near the front with DNA Dave who gives me a 'Boy, are you in trouble' look. Alan Taylor, in the seat in front of us, is similarly agog. Punctuality, it appears, is God. I've sinned mortally – and this is my first trip with them. Will I ever be asked back?

As the bus pulls out onto the approach to the M62 I can hear a comforting 'ching – ching – ching' of glass bottles rhythmically rattling against each other like sleigh bells. It sounds like there's hundreds of bottles on board this bus and, such is the weight, the driver does not reach cruising speed until we pass Burtonwood Services, some 10 miles down the road. DNA is coughing and patting his chest sounding like he's swallowed a handful of feathers. Alan gets the hint and I hear the familiar 'fsssh!' as a bottle top is dispatched and the bottle passed over the seat. Alan and Dave like their 'ale'. Not lager or beer – ale. This is some honey flavoured, farmhouse concoction with bits of twigs and starling's beaks in it. The pair of them should be wearing smocks and leaning against some Kentish Hop House chewing grass. I've gone for my favourite coach-trip tipple – San Miguel, packed in a bag of ice-cubes. Accompanied by floury baps filled with crispy back-bacon, there is no finer breakfast on earth. However, for my first drink I've decided to take a leaf out of 'Tiberius' Garner's book and pour myself a large vodka and tonic in a tumbler filled with ice. It is, to be accurate, quite magnificent. Bobby Wilcox's widow, Mary, is sitting across the aisle and asks for some ice for her wine. We make quite a civilised scene as the bus heads down the M62, the clinking ice in our glasses providing a soothing underscore to this genteel Saturday morning. But my quiet, reflective moment of self-satisfaction is shattered when Phil comes down the aisle collecting the bus money. He doesn't say anything, he doesn't need to, he just casts a sideways glance at me and I feel utterly chastised. I know in my heart of hearts that I will never, ever, ever be late for one of his buses again.

When the bus stops at Keele Services on the M6 Phil takes the microphone and declares that we are stopping for 20 minutes. Exactly.

"You will be back here by half-past. Not 25 to. Half past." I'm nodding madly. "This gives you 20 minutes. Try not to overdo the robbing as if you get caught we're going without you."

Once off the bus I race to the toilet, unbuttoning my trousers as I cross the car-park. I'm back on board by quarter past, bladder still half-full but I'm taking no chances. When I next need a piss about half an hour later I raise my hand to ask permission. I'm telling you – this is away game travel as run by the Jesuits. That said, I very much doubt that the Jesuits would take you 10 miles past West Ham, out into the 'countryside' of Essex for an afternoon's drinking at Lennard's Pub near Rainham.

The pub is blissfully quiet until we arrive and then it is over-run for a couple of hours by the Wilcox crew, most of whom drink like someone's about to take it away from them. The pub's run by a Red; he's got photos of players past and present all over the walls of the back room (where he's laid on a huge spread of sarnies) and has – rightly – given pride of place to a full-size replica European Cup behind the bar. It's a bright but blustery day and we consider sitting outside but decide that its a bit warmer and more snug inside. Lenny Woods, however, has to go out for a ciggie and returns with a head of hair looking Lenny The Lion's mane.

"Windy out is it, Len?" someone asks, as Lenny sits supping his pint with his head doing a fair impression of a burst couch. Somehow the conversation drifts around to the first match we ever went to. Mine was mid 60s, Chelsea at home. I was in the Road End, and I was about 5 or 6 years old. I think – though I can't be certain – that it was the game when we won the league in 1966, beating Chelsea 2-0. Maybe that's why I was there, my dad blooding me with a title decider. I ask Lenny when his first game was.

"1955." he says blowing the froth from a fresh pint of Mild. "Everton away in the FA Cup. We won 4-0, and we were in the 2nd division." I am impressed. "Over 70,000 there" he adds, "30,000 of them Reds." I find it astonishing, not that we had 30,000 at an away game, but that Everton could ever attract crowds that large. "Rhyl must have been empty." I tell him.

"What about you, Mick?" I ask of Mick Roby. I know Mick's slightly older than Lenny so I expect it's a game around the same time. Without missing a beat Mick replies. "Burnley. 1947." 1947 – that was the first season after the war, the season we won the league. "F.A. Cup semi final," he goes on. "Ewood Park." My mind reels. He was watching legends like Billy Liddell, Bob Paisley, Jackie Balmer, Cyril Sidlow and Albert Stubbins. In 20 or 30 years time (when I'm the arl arse sitting at the back of the electro-magnetic hover bus taking us to an away game in Tokyo in 22 minutes) will names like Albert Riera, Ryan Babel and Andrea Dossena draw similar gasps of admiration... 'cos lets face it, they aren't getting 'em now. But then anything is possible – Lucas Leiva had another good game today and is quickly becoming a cult hero among "the lads that go." Looking back at the first Liverpool team I ever saw, were any of them whipping boys, drawing hoots of derision as their names were read out? I very much doubt it. At the merest hint of a boo I'd imagine Gerry Byrne or Tommy Smith crawling up The Kop and demanding to confront the doubters, politely hearing them out, and then chinning them. In any case, when I was a boy the players were idolised, they were just 'us' out there representing our club, our city. You wouldn't boo your family or your friends, so why would you boo The Reds? Today's multi-millionaire playboys have more in common with Elton John than they do with you or I (I'm assuming David Furnish or Liza Minnelli haven't bought this book), they live on a completely different planet. Catch any of them having a pint in a pub on Scotty Road after the game? You've more chance of catching leprosy (seriously). It was good enough, however, for Ian St John and Ron Yeats. As much as you might admire modern day footballers for their skill and their ability to pull birds above their station, they'll never have a hold on your heart like those players for whom football was just marginally better paid than being a plasterer.

An hour before kick-off, Phil announces that the bus is leaving in 3 minutes and 36 seconds. Grown men drop their pints and race for the door, elbowing women and small children out of the way. Once aboard the bus I delve into my bag of goodies and find a half bottle of Rioja. Just the thing to sober me up before kick-off, I think. Perhaps not the clearest or most sensible thought of the day. It does, however, draw a nod of admiration from DNA who's now on a purple, 7% alcohol ale, brewed by goblins in Narnia, that smells of hops and potting sheds. I imagine his farts could clear the Nou Camp and vow to sit as far away as possible from him on the return journey. When the bus arrives at Upton Park, we are directed by the police to park on Barking Road a short walk from the ground. There's a long line of coaches from Merseyside and when we decant onto the pavement and there's an impromptu get-together in the street, like a wedding reception. I sit on a concrete bollard as I finish my wine, talking to a few lads from the S.O.S. bus, who are still in shock at paying over £4 a pint in a pub up the road. The police are unobtrusive and incredibly relaxed, ignoring the cans and bottles being discarded on the pavement and the general level of drunkenness and 'joie de vivre'. Although I shudder when I see one lad pissing against the back of one of the coaches in full view of Saturday afternoon shoppers, wondering if an elite G20 snatch squad might storm the scene and stun him with a cattle prod. He gets away with it and meanders unmolested off down the road towards the ground.

Its a measure of the way football – and Barking Road – has changed that I can say that. Getting from the tube and safely into Upton Park used to be one of the hairiest little jogs of the season. But these days, there are Liverpool supporters wearing colours everywhere and not one hint of trouble. I wonder if the older West Ham skins despair (as Jegsy does) at how welcoming and friendly a trip to their ground has now become? Not that I'm complaining. There are a large group of them over to our left singing 'Justice For The 96' during the game; a gesture much appreciated by the travelling Reds who applaud them loudly. But then we can afford to be generous: for a game that had 'banana skin' written all over it, we are firmly in control and playing some cracking football. To be truthful, I'm simultaneously relieved and disappointed that West Ham haven't made a better game of this as it's a bit tedious.

We were a goal up after a minute. I believe it was a good one. It sounded good from outside anyway where I, along with several hundred others, was caught in the horrendous queue to get in. I eventually get in 5 minutes after kick off and take my spec right behind the goal, down near the front. I'm surrounded by tourists, it's like the Bernabeu all over again. The first half dozen rows are taken over in their entirety by them. The tickets obviously have been allocated en masse for travel agencies and tour operators, as the back of stand is – to a man – taken over by the usual, travelling regulars. I ask some bloke next to me who scored.

"I think it was Stevie Gerrard." he says. He 'thinks'? Doesn't he know? Gerrard gets the second too, reacting fastest to his own saved penalty. We are two up at half-time and in complete control. I expected this game to be difficult. Most people did. United fans have been paying Wigan fans top dollar for tickets for their match next week. I suspect they thought we'd drop points here today, leaving them with the target of beating Wigan to win the league. Sorry Mancs! Babel adds a late 3rd goal after West Ham make a better game of it in the second half. As it stands we're top of the league at the moment and I'm going to enjoy it – even if the consensus is it's all too little too late. We are running out of games and the Mancs are finishing just as strongly as we are. I take some solace in the fact that our win here today means they can't actually win the league on Wednesday and some fat Manc might have just paid 250 quid for a ticket. I do hope it was a Scouse tout who sold him it.

As we swarm out of the ground and back towards the coaches, the friendly Met police are calmly snapping away with cameras, taking photos of the away supporters. Our civil liberties are again being eroded but we've become that used to it that no-one challenges them. If we were Muslims leaving a Mosque or G20 protesters at a demo, The Guardian would be writing 2 page spreads on why this is being done, and I'd like some answers too. In what context are these photos being used? At what point do the police deem it necessary to take photos of supporters? How long are the photos kept for? Does my hair look nice in them?

Danny Nicholson is walking alongside me and is taking great offence at being photographed.

"Maybe it's The Plaistow Photographic Society, Dan, testing Zoom Lens of the Month?" I say. He's not amused.

"You know, it's alright for the Liberal Lefty press to make a song and dance about the eco-types and Globalisation protesters, but the biggest 'breaches' of our liberties are going on every week at football grounds." he says, very seriously.

"I know mate, but who's going to say anything to them?"

"We're all walking, talking suspects... and none of us have got a clue what for."

And with that he crosses the road back to the S.O.S bus. He's absolutely right – 20 years on from Hillsborough and we are still seen as potential criminals or hooligans first, citizens second. I head down the row of buses, back to our 'mobile pub'. Only a handful have managed to stagger back to it so far so I cross the road to the nearest kebab shop, order something that I have no idea what it actually might be and nod when asked if I wanted "everything" with that. "Everything" turns out to be pickled green chillies, chilli sauce, gunpowder and broken glass. But it has to be eaten, I need to start soaking some of this booze up as we've another lengthy session ahead of us on the trip home and I don't want Phil to be disappointed with me again.

The journey home pans out exactly as expected – excessive amounts of grog are consumed and there's a very fine sing-song led in his inimitable bedraggled style by Lenny Woods. This is followed around midnight by the Bobby Wilcox Memorial Snoring Competition. DNA Dave wins this by a mile with a low, rattling baritone effort, but then again – that might have been his arse.

JM

West Bromwich Albion (a)   2-0

League   Sun 17th May

Something terrible has happened since I last spoke to you. Following our win last Saturday at West Ham our rivals have had three matches. A 2-0 derby win over City. An extremely fortunate win over Wigan with a late goal to squeeze a 2-1 after being 1-0 down at half time. This left them needing only a point at home to Arsenal yesterday to clinch it, which they inevitably did in a drab nil-nil draw. Hardly the most exciting and entertaining finish but there you have it. The unmentionables are Premier League Champions for 2009, equalling our long standing record of eighteen wins. And yes, it hurts.

We've been expecting it deep down but when it actually happens it's still a bit of a bastard. In fact, it's more than a bit, it's a lot of a bastard. To be honest I haven't even seen them lift the trophy yet. What's the point? It'll only make me feel worse than I do now. And I'm sick of people coming up to me telling me where it all went wrong. The home draws and the early season team sheets. Yes, I know I know I know. I've already had this discussion a hundred times and they only won the bleeding thing yesterday. Whatever happens though, we're not going to let this deflect us from having a good last away game of the season.

Surprisingly everyone seems to be in really good spirits and up for it, considering the previous week's events. The Dark Mysterious One drives me to Brian 'The Truth' Parson's house. We call Parso 'The Truth' because he has great socialist values and always sees the good in people whereas I'm too cynical and judgemental to be nice to every Tom, Dick and Harry. Next stop is Kev Sampson's secret bolt-hole. Sammo needs a good blow out today as he's got his film 'Awaydays' coming out next week and he's getting it from all sides. A good old-fashioned piss up on the coach to West Brom should alleviate a bit of the stress. Although that won't stop every blagger on the bus and at the ground trying to wangle guest lists and freebies every time he stops for a breath. On we go to Hamilton Square station to pick up John 'The Olive Branch' Mackin, so-called for his endless attempts at bringing football fans together. He sees it as his life's work to bring harmony to the terraces and supporters clubs throughout the whole of the football world. What a fuckin' nutter. Surely opposing fans are there for one reason only, and that is to be abused. They're certainly not there to become friends with. Sort yourself out Mackin lad. There's no room for peace, love and harmony on our firm.

We meet the coaches on Scottie Rd and it's 'tally ho' all the way down the M6 to the Midlands. I've never seen so many Old Bill at a match since Marseille the first time. I certainly haven't seen this many for an English match in years. More than Man U away, where at least there's always the potential for World War III. But West Brom away? What's going on? Do they know something we don't? There's no real history of any argy bargy between the two sets of fans although I do remember us taking their end in the 70's and getting marched across the pitch before the game, which was a bit mad. They're probably thinking the Albion fans might lose it when we relegate them in a couple of hours. But to be fair, it's not like they're not expecting to go down. It's been nailed on for months.

The match is played just like an end of season game, with Liverpool obviously feeling a little deflated after the events at Old Trafford yesterday. West Brom went into the game without their Czech striker, Roman Bednar, who was suspended by the club pending an investigation that he bought illegal drugs after their last home game. I get the feeling that out of the 26,000 here today there may be a few others who will need mind altering substances to help ease the pain as they disappear through football's trap door. The Baggies started well and could've scored twice within the first five minutes but Reina denied Jonathan Greening with a double save. The Redmen had started slowly but on 28 minutes Stevie G caught their defender Shelton Martis in possession and before you could say "Borussia Moechengladbach" he had broken clear and dinked it over Dean Kiely and into the Albion net. He's not a bad player that Steven Gerrard. I think he shows a lot of promise. With the right guidance, he could go all the way. Another young lad who could be good, Fernando Torres, had a header tipped over before the ref blew the whistle for half time.

In the second period West Brom piled forward and had a couple of chances but Kuyt broke away in the 63rd minute, beat a couple of men and slotted it home. Game over. Another three points for the Redmen and another relegation for West Bromwich Albion. Insults are traded between the two sets of fans and the content of the chants are the usual unoriginal "Your support is blah, blah, blah" and "Shall we sing a song for you" ditties. But the most annoying one is the Albion fans chanting "United" at us. Surely that is the lowest a premier league team's fans can stoop. To chant the name of another team other than your own and even worse, the name of the unmentionables is nothing short of a criminal offence. And it is for this reason alone that I am glad to wave goodbye to teams such as West Brom. Maybe when some of their fans have learnt a bit of class, they can be accepted back to play with the big boys, but until then they can sit on the naughty step until they've learnt to behave. Cheeky bastards.

We have a decent stop off for a few hours in Stafford. Not a bad place old Stafford but a bit of a ghost town. We dive into a strangely named pub called Joxer Brady's for a quick one but it seems more than half of the hundred or so other Scousers in town have the same idea. People like Mono and Hooto etc are in there but it's a pain getting served so about a dozen of us slope off to the Bird in Hand which turns out to be a better type of boozer anyway. A couple of pool tables, a decent telly and some interesting locals. 'Slight Breeze Dodd' for the second away game running blew away all corners on the green baize. But then you probably already guessed that. What is that slogan on the banner? "Form is temporary but class is permanent." Is right lad.

We stock up with refreshments for the remainder of the journey and head back to the Promised Land. Everyone has a good old sing song as the final few miles of motorway in a long and eventful season are eaten up. It's been a journey and a half from the first league game up at Sunderland and the friendly up at Rangers. It seems ages ago since the steel girder nearly wiped me out at Liege but here we are at the end of the road. The bulk of our coach get off at the Holt in Kenny. Big Phil makes an emotional speech and thanks the lads for their support. It's all handshakes and pissed goodbyes. We get dropped in town and head for one last blast at HQ. Clink and Davie Johno bid farewell for another season. Robbie Mather who's just back from two years in Dubai is waiting at the bar for us in the company of the Kirkby legend 'Smigger'. The party's nearly over. One home game left and it'll be time to get your flip flops out. Paul Stewart's missus appears and offers me and Parso a lift home. That'll do nicely. It's been a team effort all season and the wives and girlfriends have all played their part, none moreso than my own personal Dark Mysterious One. It's just a pity we couldn't win that elusive 19th title for them but like all football fans, there's always next year, money, health and sanity permitting. Up the fuckin' Pool.

JD

Spurs (h)   3-1

League   Sun 24th May

Tonight sees the End of Season Party, the Spirit of Shankly 'do' at The Olympia. I have around 30 or so tickets to distribute (and collect money for) so I'm aiming at being in town for 10 o'clock and meeting people as early as possible, so as to free-up the rest of the day for 'festivities'. Sean and I take the train into Liverpool City Centre bright and early, but those bastard Evertonians at Merseyrail have, once again, closed the line for maintenance on a Liverpool home matchday. Aboard the Replacement Bus Service at Birkenhead Central we have to stand all the way through the tunnel. As the bus emerges into the brilliant sunshine by William Brown Street it takes a sharp left so as to get to it's first stop, Moorfields Station. As it turns we hear a loud BANG! and the back nearside of the bus collapses to the ground.

"Sounds like the tyre's burst." I say to Sean, "or maybe the suspension's collapsed." Either way this bus is knackered and is going nowhere.

"This'll do here Driver!" I shout down to the front.

Nobody moves. They just sit there in silence, obediently waiting being told what to do. Sean and I squeeze down the aisle past the other passengers and get off with the driver to inspect the damage. It's more dramatic than we thought – the wheel is missing. Gone. Disappeared. God knows where it got to as it's nowhere to be seen. The driver stands scratching his head, bewildered. This wasn't on his training course.

"You're going to need a Replacement Bus Service for the Replacement Bus Service," I tell him helpfully.

As he phones it in, I can't help but be struck by what a metaphor this has been for our season. It was all going so well – and then the wheel came off the bus. It's such a ridiculous co-incidence, such a resonant image, that I can't help laughing out loud.

Sean and I head for Matthew Street – the touristically named 'Cavern Quarter'. In The Welkin we stop for a cold beer and I send a few text messages to people who owe me money for tickets for the party. Scar comes in wearing his back-pack, which contains the 'Liverpool Originals' flag – a Liverbird wearing Adidas trainers. It cost 200 hundred quid and he was more than a bit miffed to discover someone else had a near-identical flag. Originals, my arse! Today he's looking like a bespectacled Ewok, or that 'Little Bear Up a Tree on Hampstead Heath' from Bo Selecta.

I congratulate him on his new baby, just a few weeks old. When I was in his position we'd just won the league. Sean was just a few months old when we tonked Coventry away, 6-1 on the last day of the season in blistering sunshine. Now look at him, 6ft 4 and cradling a beer bottle in his fist. In his entire lifetime we haven't managed to win the league once. When I was his age we'd just won the title away at Wolves in dramatic fashion, backed by a huge following. Upwards of 30,000 had snaked down the A41 to completely take over Molyneux, and after Wolves took the lead and hang on until 15 minutes from the end, late goals from Keegan, Toshack and Kennedy gave us a 3-1 win, relegating Wolves into the bargain. It was a mad, chaotic evening; gates were dismantled and walls scaled as we literally swarmed all over Molyneux like ants. And, guess what? Wolves are back up next season. Once again I'm scrambling round looking for omens about next season and this one hasn't finished yet.

As omens go, Spurs at home looked good back in April. The touts had certainly thought so, and hoping that we would win the league today they'd been snapping up tickets. It was seen as yet more 'evidence' that this was to be our 'year' – hadn't we clinched the title in 1988 with Beardsley's goal against them at Anfield? However, in the face of the Mancs' relentless march, as the prospect of number 19 receded, they began offloading the tickets. A few days before the game a mate of mine offered me some at face value. Knowing that the Dutch Branch would be over and would be, as usual, short of tickets I snapped them up. APB is also over from Belfast and he too needs a ticket. What with match tickets and party tickets I'm acutely aware that by 9 o'clock tonight I could have upwards of £700 in my pockets. £700 of money that isn't mine, and I'll be very, very drunk. Lurching around the Olympia with that wedge stuffed into my pockets does not seem like a good idea at this precise moment.

When APB arrives he tells me that we can't drink in Flanagan's as he has to be "near a street with cars" so that he can meet a friend and pass on a spare

Outside HQ (Ned Kellys)

ticket! As pedestrianised Mathew Street simply won't do, we go up the road to
Revolution where his mate can see us if he drives down Victoria Street. As such
we sit outside in the sunshine, have a pizza and a few beers and jolly nice it is
too. We are joined by Mairtin Kearney from Dublin and two of his pals.
Mairtin has just written a piece that's to be in the Irish Independent about
some of the more ridiculously attired Irish fans visiting Liverpool for our home
games, treating it like a stag do. He likens it to gangs of pissed up 'Brits'
invading Croke Park, waving Union Jacks and noisily getting on the tits of the
locals. It's a good point and one I'm glad came from an Irishman and not from
another Scouser who's claiming he can't get tickets for the game anymore. In
a city that's Irish to it's core, and that prides itself on welcoming strangers,
some of our support are veering towards an anti-Irishness that I find both
worrying and sad.

Our little party is bolstered by Loz Gray and then Joe Corrigan looking
flustered, no doubt trying to salvage some crumb of sanity from another
matchday turned upside down by Mick Kennedy's madness. There's a
celebratory air today; we've planned another mosaic, this time for Sami

Hyypia, thanking him for 10 years magnificent service. There's also the fact that we've had our best league season in years, astonishing considering some of the moans and groans I was writing about back in January. Back then I imagined the league campaign drifting away aimlessly and then limping into May with us holding on for a top four finish – just. Instead we've turned our form on its head and gone a run of 11 league games unbeaten since the Middlesbrough debacle, 10 of them wins. A victory today will give us 86 points – a total that would win the title most years. We're unbeaten at home and have, so far, lost only twice; and one of them was a joke of a defeat to a last minute goal at Spurs in November. Again that's Championship-winning form. Despite all the mid-season rockiness it's a season to celebrate and be proud of.

Robbie Keane is returning and I'm sure that, despite his diabolical form for the 5 months he was here, he'll get a good reception. He could have used his transfer back to Spurs as an opportunity to attack Rafa who appeared not to know what to do with him. Instead he quietly thanked the club and the supporters for the chance of playing for his boyhood heroes. The name on everybody's lips today, however, is Sami Hyypia. Gary Shaw has had a whip round and raised the couple of hundred quid necessary to get another enormous flag made as a tribute. He's been offered the opportunity of presenting it to Sami after the game, and is rapidly downing beers to calm his nerves – or is he just rapidly downing beers? Whatever – he looks banjaxed at half-time. The fame has gone to his head ever since Rafa claimed it was the support he'd got from the fans, and Gary's Rafa flag in particular, that was they key to him signing a new contract. Gary had even been invited to Melwood where Rafa signed the flag for him and reduced him to a gibbering wreck, much like the gibbering wreck he appears now.

"My flag made Rafa sign!" he slurs. "My flag. My flag."

Only someone else is waving it today as Gary's on Sami Hyypia Flag duties, though judging by his tenuous grip on that bottle of Carlsberg I can't wait to see him try and wave a 15ft flag.

It's a good, if unexciting, first half with the magnificent Fernando Torres heading home the only goal; his 50th goal in just 84 appearances. Fifty goals – none of them penalties, none of them free-kicks. God knows where we'd be without him and Gerrard. And where are we also likely to be without Xabi Alonso? Rumour is sweeping The Kop that he's on his way, that Real Madrid are sniffing and that Rafa is willing to sell.

"He's had a great season, but if the money's right, well...," says Joynty

"Wha' money? Wha'?" mumbles Gary into his dribbling chin. "My Flag! My Flag..."

"I agree" I tell Joynty. "Great player but if we get £35 million for him, I'd take it. Buy a more mobile midfielder who can get forward and chip in with some goals. In any case – he wants away. Fallen out with Rafa."

"Rafa! Rafa! My flag! My flag!"

"You must be mental," JB says. "He's one of our best players – you don't sell your best players."

"Everyone has their price. Everyone's for sale," I tell him.

"Except Torres," adds Joynty.

"Yes. Except Torres," I concede.

"And Stevie..."

"And Carra..."

Throughout the second half Sami is prowling the touchline warming up. Rafa has unsentimentally left him on the bench, and The Kop are singing his name and urging Rafa:

"Sami, Sami, Sami! On! On! On!"

I suspect Rafa wants this game in the bag, and the runners-up spot secured, before letting Sami on. When Kuyt's deflected shot makes it 2-0 we think that might be the cue:

"Oh Sami, Sami! Sami, Sami, Sami, Sami Hyypia!"

But we're kept waiting – and when Robbie Keane latches onto a through ball threaded past the last defender (admittedly the type of ball that did bring him goals at Anfield) he races clear and scores. To his great credit he refuses to celebrate, a gesture much appreciated by the 40,000 Reds inside Anfield who give him a thunderous ovation. Is this now going to prevent us seeing Sami Hyypia at all today? The answer comes with Benayoun's goal, ten minutes from the end that seals the result. A minute later Sami replaces Steven Gerrard, taking the captain's armband as Gerrard leaves the pitch. Anfield rises as one to pay their respects to the Mighty Finn who responds by almost scoring with a thumping great header which is cleared off the line by the keeper in the last minute.

At the final whistle everyone remains behind, no-one races off for a pint, not even Gary Shaw and Joynty. Sami is hoisted up on Pepe Reina's shoulders and appears in tears as Anfield sings his name. What a send off it would have been for him to have won the title at the age of 35. It's the closest we've been during his time here; a real opportunity missed because we were in the driving seat at the turn of the year. Just as our defeat in Athens saw us spurn an easy chance, against an ageing Milan side, to win another European Cup, this season saw us throw away our best chance in 20 years of claiming another League title. Those frustrating home draws against Everton, Man City, West Ham, Fulham, Stoke, Hull... just turn two of those games into victories and it would have been 19-17 rather than 18-18.

When the shackles were off in the games against Real Madrid and then the Mancs 3 days later, we were unplayable. That gave us the confidence to kick on and go for it. When we went out with the mindset that the 3 points were there for us to take, rather than trying to preserve the 1 point we started the game with, then we were unstoppable. Those home draws are 2 points lost, not a point gained. Over a series of 4 games: 2 wins and 2 defeats sees you better off than 4 draws. Sometimes you need to chance your arm, Rafa: who dares wins.

But where does that leave us for next season? Bacon Face has managed to squeeze in alongside us on our perch, waiting for the opportunity to bump us off it. It's how we react now that will define our place in the history books. If I can quote Steve Kelly here:

"What next? Ferguson 1992, or Houllier 2002? Cantona or Diouf? With a positive outlook against mid-table opposition and the transformation of bitter disappointment into ultimate motivation, anything is possible."

Are you listening Rafa?

After the players are cheered off the pitch, we meet up outside the HJC Shop. There's me and Sean, John Buchanan, Jegsy, Baker, Danny, Parso, Tommy Keiner, LouLou and Sampson. I've got £700 in my pocket.

"So then," I say. "Who fancies a bevvy?"

JM

And the missing game...

PSV Eindhoven (a)   3-1

Champions League Group Game   Tus 9th Dec

It had all started so well. There we were sitting in the sun in a secret pub garden, the day after the Cup Final. Just me, my fellow author Mr Mackin, our editor-in-chief Mr Sampson and the Dark Mysterious One taking notes. We were there to have a quick run through of what we'd written and to decide on things like the cover and title and all the other bits and pieces that you have to do when compiling a book. Initially we were going to meet in town but realised that if the impossible happens and our dear friends Everton win the Cup, town would be unbearable. Fortunately Chelsea beat them yesterday so we needn't have worried. But could you imagine trying to have a meeting about a Liverpool fans book surrounded by slobbering half-wits in Fellaini wigs singing "We don't care what the Red shite say"? No thank you. I'd rather eat my own flesh or be tied to the mast and given fifty lashes than listen to a pub full of Blues going through their full repertoire of three songs again and again and again. Sheer purgatory.

So anyway, all's going well and we're in celebratory mood – well we were, at least – that is until Kev dropped his bombshell: "So yeah, everything's sound and that, reads well, looks good but there's just one small problem... where's PSV?"

"PSV?" I say. "What do you mean PSV?"

"PSV away is missing." I look at John. He looks at me. I say "Don't be looking at me. You were supposed to be doing it. I was on holiday." He's got his arms outstretched with his palms open wide pleading innocence. "Yeah but I did Marseille." I remind him that I missed the Blackburn away and Hull at home matches because I was on me jollies and the PSV match was in the midweek between the two. So I'm hardly gonna jet back from the African wilderness on a day return to Eindhoven for the match and then be back with me fuckin' pith helmet on in time for breakfast overlooking the savannah. Kev keeps a diplomatic silence. John, unconvincingly, plays the 'not guilty' card. The Dark Mysterious One looks at me knowing full well it was John's shout because she was with me on the African adventure. I mention the Hull match and suggest that maybe if he'd looked to the seat immediately to the left of him that he would have noticed a distinct lack of me.

We're getting nowhere here so Kev adjudicates and suggests that I just write something funny about watching it in Kenya. Reluctantly I agree but deep down I want to put it to a jury of diehard Redmen. We could have John Garner as the judge. No, on second thoughts he'd have us all hanged or sent to the chair. No I'd have someone fair minded like Ricey from the fans union in charge and Brian Reade as my brief. Mackin wouldn't stand a chance. The jury would be hand picked of men who'd been to a minimum of five hundred games each. I could even put my right hand on Robbie Fowler's autobiography and swear to tell the truth, the whole truth and nothing but the truth. I reckon I'd even get compo off Mackin for defamation of character. But as it stands in the cold light of day I've got to tell you about the delights of Liverpool's away victory in the Philips Stadium in Eindhoven in early December. A match I was nowhere near.

I could lie and tell you about the previous year when we were there in the Champions League and my mate Frank, who I went with, bagged off with not one but two Swedish lovelies in Antwerp. See, I'm lying already. One was indeed lovely but I'd be stretching it a bit far to call the other one a lovely. We're in a bar by the station and he's having his usual futile attempt at wooing waifs, strays and the vulnerable. I'm taking no notice and just gabbing away to Danny and a minibus load of Birkenhead lads when this tall blonde Swedish goddess sidles over and says "Excuse me but you don't mind if me and my friend take Frank back to our room to sleep with him." "WHAT?" My mate Frank? The Gary McAllister lookalike? The same one who would struggle to attract attention even if he walked naked around the fleshpots of Pattaya with ten grand nailed to his head? *That* Frank? And off they went.

I could tell you about him coming in at about 7am a bit goz-eyed, looking like the cat who got the cream. I could tell you about me waving him and his two new friends off as their train pulled out of Antwerp station at 10am destined for a night of soft drugs and hard sex in Amsterdam. And how he left me on my own and took the car keys by mistake, so I was completely stranded. Or how I had to get the train to Eindhoven after waiting for a connection in the middle of nowhere for over an hour and then finding out that the last train leaves at half time. About having a bevvy with all the lads on that strip of bars by the ground with people like Doggo, Gilly, Ally, Tommy, Bobby, Degsy, Sconch and then having to get back to Antwerp before the match kicks off. And how I phoned Frank and ordered him, no begged him to meet me back in Antwerp. I could tell you loads of things but that wasn't this season, so it doesn't count. I'd have loved to have told you the tales Frank told me on the long drive home but the risk of your hair curling is too much.

The bottom line is that we had already qualified for the knock out stages and the match against PSV was a bit of a dead rubber but if I'd have been here, I'd have been there, if you know what I mean. But I wasn't, so I wasn't. Hope that clears everything up. By the way, if you're interested we won 3-1 with goals by Babel, Riera and Ngog. But then you probably already knew that.

JD over and out.

**"A LIFE WITHOUT FESTIVITY IS LIKE A
LONG ROAD WITHOUT AN INN."**
Democritus of Abdera (c.460 – c.360 BC)
Ancient Greek Philosopher